NGĀ MŌREHU
THE SURVIVORS

Ko te wahine he whare tāngata, he waka tāngata

NGĀ MŌREHU THE SURVIVORS

Judith Binney and Gillian Chaplin

AUCKLAND UNIVERSITY PRESS
BRIDGET WILLIAMS BOOKS

First published by Oxford University Press, Auckland, 1986
Reprinted with corrections, 1987, 1990

This edition published 1996 by Auckland University Press with Bridget Williams Books,
University of Auckland, Private Bag 92019, Auckland, New Zealand

ISBN 1 86940 147 6

Designed by Neysa Moss
Cover design for this edition by Mission Hall Design Group, Wellington
This edition printed by South Wind Production, Singapore

CONTENTS

Te Kooti at Rotorua 1887

INTRODUCTION

This book is the life history of eight Maori women. Its centre is their own accounts of their lives, told mostly in their own words. All of them grew up in communities closely connected with the faith known as Ringatu, the faith of the Upraised Hand. Founded by the visionary leader Te Kooti Arikirangi Te Turuki in the later nineteenth century, Ringatu remains today as a distinct Maori religious movement, based on the Bible but with its own leaders and traditions. Thus an intricate network connects the separate narratives, and the personal history of each woman becomes part of the larger history of those who followed Te Kooti.

This introduction is the kete, or basket, for the offerings: an outer layer of woven leaves around the heart of the matter. Not all of the women are Ringatu believers, but all have lived their lives in close association with the faith. The introduction attempts to clarify and to put into context some of the elements which are mentioned in their narratives. It is not a history of the faith nor of its founder, but it seeks to illuminate some aspects in the history of both which touch on the women's lives today.

The origin of this book lies in the history of Te Kooti. We had become increasingly aware how dominant colonialist perceptions of New Zealand's history still are. The written accounts focus almost entirely on Te Kooti as the guerrilla leader and man of war, 'the rebel'. We hoped that, by talking with some of those who followed him, we could cross such barriers. We wanted to recover the knowledge which we believed would be retained in oral accounts of Te Kooti as the prophet, the founder of the faith, and the man of peace. The last twenty years of his life after the end of the wars in 1872 were largely unrecorded save for his arrest, born of hysteria, when he attempted to return to his home in Turanga (Gisborne) in 1889. When we actually began to talk with elders, both men and women, we discovered that what had survived was not so much political narratives, although these did exist, particularly among the men, but family narratives. These are stories which link different families to the prophet. They are about the ancestors who had been with him in his years of exile, when he was living with Ngati Maniapoto in the King Country, or who had ridden to him to learn about the faith as it began to spread. For those who are Ringatu, they establish the family's particular relationship with Te Kooti. The form of the oral narratives was, as it were, fan-shaped. At the apex lies the core narrative, which establishes the family's connection with the prophet, his teachings and his particular predictive words to them. From this apex flows the personal histories of the different families, through three or four generations.

Maori history was, and still is in the telling, built around kin. Whakapapa — genealogy — is the backbone of Maori history; whānau, the extended family, and hapū, the tribe, are the essential concerns of that history. The whānau gives particular identity to the individual; the source of its mana is its ancestors. As the Maniapoto elder Henare Tuwhangai explained, 'To be a Maori is to share the world with the extended family and the tipuna, some living, some dead, and some not yet born.'[1] As we came gradually to understand this, we were led to change

opposite Portrait of Te Kooti made at the Tamatekapua meeting-house, Ohinemutu, 1887. This pencil drawing is by the Reverend Richard Laishley, a Congregational pastor. *A114/4, Alexander Turnbull Library, Wellington*

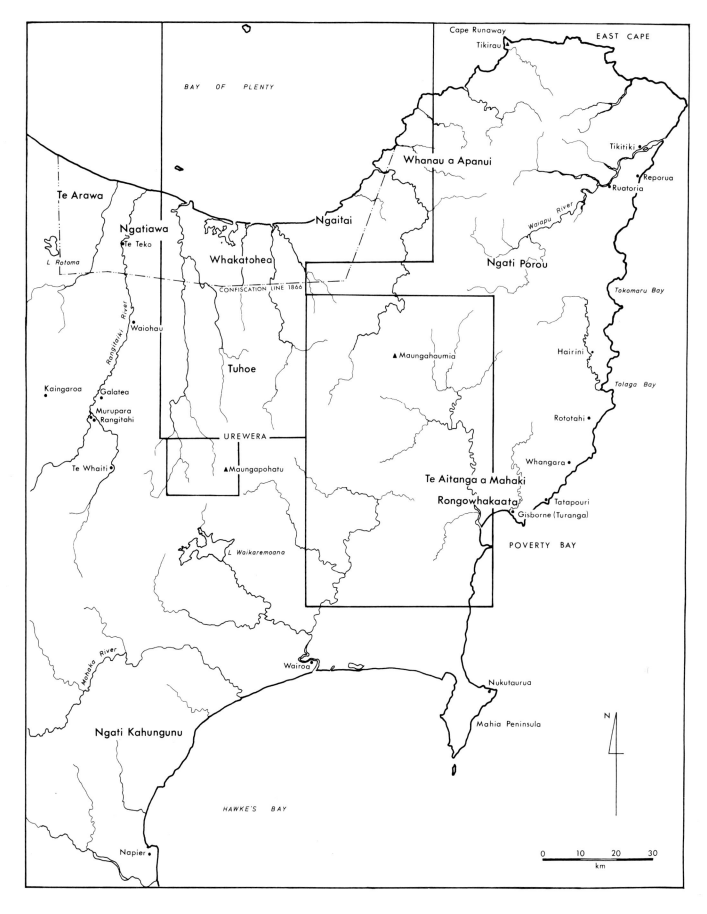

Fig 1: A map of places referred to in
the text. Insets indicate the detailed
maps, Figs III, IV, and V.

the direction of our intended narrative. Our focus shifted, and we began to talk with people about their own lives and their family histories, as they had to do with Te Kooti. This book has grown out of these conversations.

It attempts to follow, in its own structure, the nature of living oral history. At its heart are narratives which relate the individual to the prophet, or, in the case of three of the women, to Rua Kenana Hepetipa, who claimed to be Te Kooti's successor and the New Messiah, Te Mihāia Hōu. In this way the essential purposes of Maori oral history are retained: to establish the mana and authority of the individual and the family.

The book came to be about women for a number of reasons, all quite simple. Because we are women, we found it easier to talk with the women about their lives. There were fewer barriers. Nor are these as great for outsiders, like ourselves, as is sometimes assumed. Both the men and women who spoke to us saw us as recorders, not manipulators of knowledge; possibly they recognized that we would not use the knowledge for power. Most importantly, it is the women in Maori society who usually transmit the family history, and the values which it asserts, to the children. The book has taken its form in recognition of the fact that the inner strength of the families usually derives from the women. They are the bearers of whānaungatanga. As Heni Sunderland says in her story, 'Without a doubt, it is the women who have the strengths. Within the extended family and out on to the marae as a whānau as a whole, you will find it is we, the women, who are the ones who really motivate our men. They wouldn't like me saying that, but I do think that.'

History is often remarkably arrogant. It can too frequently dismiss whole groups of people as lost causes, or as merely irrelevant. Entire sections of society, usually the poor, the minorities, and the politically powerless are thereby obliterated from memory.[2] Oral history, particularly as it has recently developed, aims to recover the aspirations and visions of those who otherwise have left little record in written public sources. As Mary Chamberlain said in her history of the women of the Cambridgeshire fens, 'for much of women's history, memory is the only way of discovering the past. Other sources simply do not exist.'[3] This remark is true for any history of Maori women in this century. All the women in this book have lived through times of acute social disturbance. Their ages range, as this book is published, between ninety-three and fifty-nine. Their voices must be heard.

The individual narratives recounted here are more than personal statements. All the women grew up in small rural communities — in the Bay of Plenty, the Urewera, or Poverty Bay. These were the three areas where the Ringatu faith began to spread from the late 1870s. They were all brought up 'in the kāuta', as they put it: in other words, their families were using the kāuta, the external earth-floor shelter, for the cooking and eating of food. This is not simply a statement of their poverty but also an indication that the families were still maintaining the practices of tapu, which demanded that cooked food be kept apart from all other activities, lest the life-force be contaminated and destroyed. All their domestic arrangements, therefore, were part of the larger religious idea of their world. We can also say that what was happening to them as individuals was happening to their people collectively. Some experiences stand out as part of a larger social history: for mothers, the recurrence of death among their infants; for many husbands, becoming a part of a rural proletariat. Yet these women have remained strong and proud of their traditions and culture. All are native speakers of Maori, despite the fact that they attended schools which prohibited the use of their language in the classroom. They have retained their own tongue because their families and communities were Maori-speaking. Several of them are now conscious that they did not pass on their language adequately to their children. It did not seem then to be the matter of importance that it is now. Most of them (but not all) share the view of Maori history wherein the significance of Te Kooti lies primarily in the fact that he sought to retain the Maori identity in their own land.

The original name adopted by the followers of Te Kooti during the wars, and when they lived in sanctuary with Ngati Maniapoto during the 1870s, was 'Ngā Mōrehu', the Survivors. They were the remnants of the people, the Chosen Few.[4] When we discussed with Maaka Jones the title for this book she said, 'Yes, they are the remainders. Those who have survived. But they are also the chosen; they are the leaders. It doesn't apply to everybody.'[5] The women in this book are the Survivors in every sense of the word, then and now.

TE KOOTI ARIKIRANGI

The beginning of the Ringatu faith is dated by that Church as 12 May 1868, the day God gave the covenants to Te Kooti when he was a prisoner on the Chatham Islands. But his advent as a prophetic leader had been predicted long before. There was a matakite or seer, Te Toiroa, living at Nukutaurua on the Mahia peninsula, who, in some traditions, predicted the arrival of a strange people to the land. This prediction was made three years before James Cook came to the East Coast. These people he called Pākerewhā, and he made small figures of them out of flax and wood. Their skin, he said, would be completely white and they wore a thing 'intended for the head' – taupopoki – and they carried pipes, ngongo, and their own tobacco, tūramarama. Later, he sang another prophecy concerning the man who would come in the times of trouble, or the times of the Pākerewhā:

> Tiwha tiwha te pō.
> Ko te Pakerewhā.
> Ko Arikirangi tenei ra te haere nei.

> Dark dark is the night.
> It is the Pākerewhā.
> It is Arikirangi who is coming this day.[6]

Like all predictions, this song equivocates. It is interpreted as the prophecy for the coming of war, and also as the prophecy for the coming of Te Kooti. In one reading, it foretells that Te Kooti would take utu from his own kin for his forced exile on Wharekauri in the Chathams, and the song is sometimes interpreted as having foreseen that bloodshed. The voice of prophecy spoke through Te Toiroa again. From among Ngatimaru there would be born two children (or in some versions three). They would be cousins and come into the world at the same time. But if the first-born, Te Huiakama, child of Te Turuki, died of an illness that would strike them both, while the youngest, the child of Te Rangipatahi, lived, evil would come to the land. All these events came to pass. Furthermore, Te Toiroa named the child of ill omen Arikirangi so that all might know then that the 'new people will be an evil people', deceitful and consuming the lands for themselves.[7] He also said that this child would be taken away.[8]

Under the shadow of this prediction, the boy was born. He grew up at

Paokahu and Manutuke in Poverty Bay and he attended the Anglican mission school at Whakato, where he was baptized with the name Te Kooti. His ancestral name, Te Turuki, which he was to use after his return from exile, he took from his uncle. He had nurtured the boy after his own father rejected him and, it is told, tried to kill him by burying him alive in a kūmara pit, or, variously, a well. Te Kooti early acquired a reputation as a trouble-maker. By 1852 he was notorious for his association with a group of young men, all living at Makaraka, who took reprisal for their grievances by seizing settlers' property.[9] They were 'social bandits', those whom 'the lord and state regard as criminals' but who, in a stratified society, see themselves as fighters for justice. 'The gentry use the pen, we the gun', a nineteenth-century Italian *bandito* once put it.[10] They aroused the hostility not only of the early Pakeha residents but also of their own tribal chiefs. Raharuhi Rukupo, one of the leading figures within Ngatimaru, wrote to Sir George Grey as Governor, to tell him 'about the misdeeds at Turanga [when] the Pakeha were plundered'.[11] Young Wi Pere, who would become a leading chief within Te Aitanga a Mahaki, was involved in a taua muru party sent against Te Kooti's pā in 1853, because he 'had become a terror to the district'. Although Te Kooti himself escaped from this raid, several others were taken prisoner and handed over to their chiefs, while Te Kooti's cattle and pigs were all seized and sold off.[12] His reputation, flowing from and leading into factional quarrelling, was an underlying reason why he was sent into exile in 1866.

Civil war was brought to Poverty Bay with the coming of the preachers of a new faith, Pai Marire or Hauhau, early in 1865. Until then, Poverty Bay had remained kūpapa, or neutral, in the wars which had engulfed other parts of the North Island. The Pai Marire missionaries from Te Ua Haumene themselves said that they came to bring peace and unity, and their teachings soon spread among the two major tribes of the district, Rongowhakaata and Te Aitanga a Mahaki. Although Ngatimaru, a part of Rongowhakaata, wavered, two of its forceful chiefs, Raharuhi and Anaru Matete, became converts. So did Te Kooti's older brother Komene. Though the motives of many in joining the Pai Marire movement were undoubtedly connected with their determination, as Anaru put it, to 'save our land (te Ao) and the remnant of our people'[13] and to establish a unity across the tribes, they did not consider themselves as having turned against the settlers or the government. Anaru, in a delegation which the Pai Marire chiefs made in July to John Harris, the oldest European settler in Turanga, urged that they were being misrepresented as 'disloyal' by the Kawanatanga, or Government, faction. The erection of a flagpole for the Union Jack in May, by Te Mokena Kohere, a Ngati Porou chief from the East Coast, had been seen by most of the local tribes as being deliberately provocative. Hirini Te Kani, the paramount chief within Rongowhakaata, threatened to cut it down and even old Paratene Turangi, chief of Ngaitawhiri and another leading figure within Rongowhakaata, had only reluctantly accepted it. Hirini saw it as an open challenge to the practice of the Pai Marire of worshipping around a large niu pole, upon which they flew their own religious flags.[14] But the great masts now stood ready to confront each other as statements of alternative political and religious authorities.

The slide into civil war had become inevitable through this involvement of Ngati Porou and its powerful leaders, Mokena, and from nearby Tokomaru, Henare Potae. In June 1865, Ngati Porou became involved in a war further north, which would ultimately drag in the Poverty Bay tribes on opposing sides. When

Hirini Te Kani, chief of Rongowhakaata at the time of the wars in Poverty Bay. *Te Mana o Turanga, Manutuke.* Photographed, by permission of Heni Sunderland, by Gillian Chaplin, 1984.

Mokena's pā was besieged by the Pai Marire faction of Ngati Porou, he not only sent for European reinforcements but also for his kin at Tokomaru and Poverty Bay. Sections of Rongowhakaata then committed themselves to the Pai Marire fighters.[15] Although the northern war ended with the release by Mokena of the prisoners he had taken, Poverty Bay itself had become polarized. Moreover, a number of the Pai Marire refugees from the war now took shelter at Turanganui, many staying at the new pā which had been built at Waerenga a Hika. It was the arrival of Mokena and 260 Ngati Porou troops, together with the European reinforcements, on 9 November 1865, which brought the war to Poverty Bay.

As the fighting spread from Waiapu, the Pai Marire believers decided to reinforce a part of Te Aitanga a Mahaki pā at Waerenga a Hika to defend themselves. Mokena's involvement, and particularly the erection of the flagstaff, had been widely interpreted as a bid to claim land for himself at Turanga. His arrival in force into this world of rumour and speculation could only be seen as the realization of the fear that he intended to launch a tribal attack. Hirini Te Kani, who had consistently tried to mediate between the local factions, greatly distrusted Mokena's objectives,[16] but he had lost the confidence of the settlers, who saw in his interventions merely an ambiguous loyalty to the Crown.

Most of the European settlers and the newly arrived militia considered that war had become inevitable because they were convinced that the majority of the Maori at Poverty Bay were disloyal. They were treated as rebels without being so.[17] On 10 November Donald McLean, the Native Minister, sent an ultimatum to the Pai Marire chiefs, which demanded their 'submission' and 'surrender', on pain of losing their lands. Finally on 16 November, the government forces attacked the Pai Marire supporters and refugees sheltering at Waerenga a Hika. This assault was indeed 'the hinge of fate' for the Maori tribes on the Coast.[18] It was a war which had been forced upon them.

Te Kooti himself was, like Raharuhi, with the government forces in this conflict. His brother Komene was inside the pā. He may have been among those who fought their way in, with Anaru Matete, to help the besieged. But no loyalties

Waerenga a Hika after the siege of 17–22 November 1865. The niu pole, around which the Pai Marire believers had worshipped, lies fallen, in the foreground left. In the background can be seen Bishop William Williams' house, which was largely sacked by the assaulting troops. As John Harris wrote on 25 November 1865: 'The Pai Marire have not done us one tenth part of the damage inflicted by Morgan [Mokena Kohere] and his men.' 200 men and 200 women and children unconditionally surrendered after the six days' siege. They were told at the time that 'the worst characters' would be sent to Napier, at the government's pleasure, but that the majority would not be sent out of the district. One of the women who surrendered was Heni Brown's great-grandmother, Meri Puru, who was sent as a young woman, with her father, as a prisoner to Wharekauri. *Rhodes Album, Alexander Turnbull Library*

could, in this context, be quite absolute. Most of the Rongowhakaata among the attackers fought with great reluctance and left all the effort to Ngati Porou. Here, in the midst of the fight, Te Kooti was seized by the old Rongowhakaata chief Paora Parau: 'Ko Rikirangi! Puhia! Patua! It is Rikirangi! Shoot him! Kill him!'[19] Paora accused him of supplying ammunition to those inside, but as nothing could be proved he was later released. His rearrest and subsequent exile to Wharekauri in June 1866 was almost certainly a deliberate decision to get rid of him as a potential trouble-maker. Harris was quite explicit:

> There are several parties here, who ought to be got rid of — Koti & his brother Komene both known thieves. — broke into Bloomfield's house at Matawhira and have killed cattle &c. on several occasions and the former is known to have been a *spy* all through the opperations carried on here.[20]

Captain George Preece later said that Te Kooti had sent a message to Anaru Matete, who fled inland of Wairoa, to warn him of an assault party: 'Wednesday is the day, and Te Reinga is the place'.[21] Anaru had become the centre of continuing Pai Marire resistance. Increasingly, he came to be seen as the man destined to save the Turanga tribes from the extensive land confiscations that were now being attempted by the government in reprisal for the 'rebellion'. By February it was being said that, 'the time will en[sue] when Anaru Matete will return triumphantly to Turanga and apportion the land to the people who are to occupy it, and carry all before him'.[22]

It was in this context that both Te Kooti and Komene were included in the prisoners. Others of Ngatimaru, who had been generally denounced by a settler as 'the worst villains I have ever been amongst', were also sent away.[23] Te Kooti's opponents were, however, not only Europeans. Paratene Turangi (Pototi) became notorious for the contempt with which he kicked him onto the boat to Napier and exile. Both Te Kooti and Komene protested their innocence in letters written in Napier, just before the boat sailed for the Chathams. Te Kooti wrote:

> E hoa he ki atu naku mo te taha kia au e noho nei i roto i te hauhau me whakaatu mai taku hara kia marama ai ia au hua noa hoki au me wakawa. Heoi ano. Na Tekoti kuini maori.

> Friend. Concerning my being on this side, staying here in the midst of the Hauhau. Show me what I have done wrong that it may be clear to me and also that I can be sure, and bring me to trial. That is all. Te Koti, Queen's Maori.[24]

Archdeacon William Leonard Williams, himself an advocate of confrontation in 1865, would later admit that Te Kooti 'personally had undergone very serious provocation. Whatever other offences he may have committed he had never taken arms against the Government and yet he was deported to Chatham Island along with the prisoners who were taken at Waerengaahika and elsewhere.'[25]

It was on Wharekauri that Te Kooti experienced the visions which led to the foundation of the new faith. He recorded his illness,[26] and the manner in which God healed his soul and his body, in his diary. The first entry was on 21 February 1867:

> Ko te marama tenei i nui ai toku mate 21 o nga ra ka hemo au . . .

> This was the month in which my sickness increased, on the 21st day I became unconscious . . .

On 10 April he described himself as smitten with the same sickness,

> ano te rite kei te rakau e tuakina ana ki raro e whatia ana hoki e te hau kahore
> nei ona maharatanga kia hoki ano ki tona putake.
>
> like unto a tree that has been struck down and broken by the wind and has
> no power to raise itself again.[27]

On the 21st, he again became unconscious. This time a spirit in the form of a man, clothed in garments 'as white as snow', appeared before him. His hair, he said, was like stars; he wore a crown and a girdle 'like unto the setting sun and the rising thereof'. His fan was comparable to the rainbow and his tokotoko, or staff, was of colours he had never seen before in this world. The vision spoke in a voice as clear as crystal, saying, 'I will not forsake thee or my people either.' This figure of God, undoubtedly derived from the Book of Revelation, told him to 'write these sayings in thy heart', and said again, 'I will not forsake thee and I will teach thee.'[28] He later told him not to accept any books as they were written only by man.

Te Kooti was given two signs by this spirit. One was a lizard, or ngārara, the actual likeness of which Te Kooti had never before seen. (The ngārara in traditional Maori thought is a dualistic form, a sign of life — or specifically its conception — and of death. In carvings, it may appear as an emblem for a man who deals on the 'other' side of life, the taha wairua.) The second sign was a flame which did not burn and was, therefore, life-giving and transforming. This sign Te Kooti, according to his own account, first revealed to the other prisoners in church on 18 June 1867, and by July news of 'the new religion' had reached Poverty Bay.[29] Finally, he caught the attention of the Resident Magistrate on Wharekauri, Captain Thomas, who reported that Te Kooti had been conducting services under the auspices of the Anglican Church, but had been 'rubbing his hands with the phosphorus of matches to represent "Atua" before holding' them. He had established a profound influence over the prisoners and had led them to the belief, said Thomas, that these practices would 'tend to deliver them from their bondage'.[30]

This new faith gave the people an identity and a conviction: their escape from Pharaoh's soldiers and their return from imprisonment to their Promised Land was inevitable. As God had revealed himself to Moses in the Egyptian house of bondage, so he had revealed himself to his servant in their wharepononga, 'house of bondage', on Wharekauri. The sixth covenant given by God to Te Kooti on the island was the 'Covenant with Israel', which showed them the way. It was derived from Deuteronomy 30: 3:

> That then the Lord will turn thy captivity, and have compassion upon thee,
> and will return and gather thee from all the nations . . .[31]

The Israelite traditions of persecution and ultimate deliverance, with which they had identified, became the source of their strength. Among the lamentations which God gave to Te Kooti was the prayer, which he wrote down as 'used in the Chatham Islands':

> O God, if our hearts arise from the land in which we now dwell as slaves.... Do not Thou, O God, cause us to be wholly destroyed. Wherefore it is that we glorify Thy Holy Name.[32]

It was the faith, which gave them the 'hope so close to certainty',[33] that would be the basis of their active rebellion against their captivity, in July 1868.

The prisoners had been kept on the island longer than had been at first intended. In an attempt to ram through large-scale land confiscations at Poverty Bay, Captain Reginald Biggs, appointed the Crown Agent, had urged upon McLean that the prisoners should not be allowed to return until the issue was settled.[34] The dramatic return of the Exiles on 10 July cut across these manipulations. They — 298 men, women, and children — came ashore from the supply-ship the *Rifleman* at Whareongaonga, a stony bay south of Turanga. They had seized the vessel and its crew, with a tactical skill that foreshadowed later events, while at the island. Te Kooti then announced his intention of going inland to 'the Waikato country' and demanded that he be left unmolested. His purpose in going to the Waikato, according to one account, was 'to inaugurate a new order of things, the main feature of which is that there is to be no [Maori] king'.[35] In both these challenges to the King and the government he would be opposed.

Although Wi Pere and others wrote urging that the prisoners be left alone, the pursuit of Te Kooti was launched. As the chiefs' letter warned, 'Ko te patu ka hapainga e te kawanatanga'; 'The patu was raised by the government'.[36] This hunt for Te Kooti was initiated locally by Biggs, and Te Kooti later blamed him specifically for forcing the war. Biggs was not only the much criticized agent of the land confiscation schemes (although they were never fully realized); he expected to benefit personally from them. As military commander he lived at Matawhero, built partly on Te Kooti's ancestral land. Te Kooti's old antagonists from the Bay, Paratene and Paora Parau, were also the voices upon whom Biggs had particularly come to rely. It was, therefore, a calculated requital as well as a tactical military decision which led Te Kooti to turn upon Turanga in November 1868. It was probably influenced also by his rejection, in late October, by King Tawhiao, who warned him that he would repel him should he attempt to 'encroach upon his territory'. The King's messenger brought word that he was 'incensed with the exprisoners', because they followed Te Kooti as a prophet instead of himself.[37]

Te Kooti struck at Matawhero on the night of the 9th and the 10th. Fifty-four

A panorama of Turanga (Gisborne) in November 1868. In the centre, surrounded by the wooden fence, is the redoubt. *Brooke-Taylor collection, Alexander Turnbull Library*

people were killed, including Biggs. Twenty of these were Maori. Using Patutahi, a former Pai Marire pā, as a base, Te Kooti's organized patrols, or kōkiri, then swept the district collecting large quantities of supplies and taking about 300 local Maori as prisoners. One of these was Wi Pere who, according to Maraea Morete's account (and others), had come to believe that Te Kooti was 'one of God's Prophets & trusted him fully'.[38] Two of the women captured, Heni Kumekume and Oriwia Nihipora, would become Te Kooti's wives. They appear in this book. From Patutahi he sent a message to Paratene and it seems that here the old chief came to terms with him and returned all his arms to the government. Maraea Morete, who had herself formerly been a Pai Marire supporter, was taken prisoner at Matawhero. She witnessed the execution of her own husband there, and described the almost immediate betrayal of Paratene by Te Kooti. Paratene invited Te Kooti to Oweta pā to make peace. He was waiting for him, unarmed, when he arrived. But the old chief and six others were immediately seized and tied up.[39] Te Kooti is reported as saying, 'Greetings, my father who said, "Go on to the boat; go on the boat." Son, you go on to the axe.'[40]

The deaths at Matawhero and, above all, the executions at Oweta ensured a continuing Maori enmity towards Te Kooti. Until these events, all his actions had been marked by restraint. He had made it clear that he wished to avoid conflict. The attack on the Turanga people was a decisive change of policy.[41] Its purpose was probably to reveal the power of his God and also to intimidate those who were wavering into support for him. As Wiremu Kingi Te Paia, who went with Te Kooti, said: 'The reason I followed in his footsteps was, that I feared him on account of the death of Paratene.' He added that Te Kooti 'obtained power from his god, and was advised by him that the Kawanatanga would be by him utterly destroyed. He then proceeded to carry out his mission by overthrowing Turanga.'[42] In this strategy, he was largely successful. Many of those whom he took prisoner stayed with him, persuaded by belief in his powers. Others joined him voluntarily, like Pera Te Uetuku of Mangatu. However, Te Kooti's objective remained to get through to the Waikato and the King. But, he warned, if the King 'persisted in keeping aloof, he would be cursed by Jehovah, who would command him (Te Kooti) to march to Tokangamutu, and put Matutaera [King Tawhiao] and all his people to the sword'.[43]

It was in July 1869 that Te Kooti first penetrated the King Country. According to the Resident Magistrate posted at Alexandra, William Searancke, he was utterly ignored by Tawhiao and told simply 'to "Kati te pakiki," cease asking or bothering'.[44] When he left Tokangamutu, the 'King party fired a volley of contempt on his departure'.[45] Wiremu Kingi Te Paia, who was present, gave a somewhat different account. At Tokangamutu they were welcomed — by Rewi of Ngati Maniapoto. But Tamati Ngapora, the King's chief adviser at this time, rejected Te Kooti. His purpose in coming amongst them, he said, 'was to lower their chieftainship, and to destroy their Atua; and that they would not bow down to his Atua'.[46] Te Kooti's second attempt in December, after his decisive defeat at Te Porere, was no more successful. Again he apparently announced his intention of deposing Tawhiao, to set up the laws of his own God: that is, to overturn the Pai Marire faith which the King then followed. Tawhiao's reply to him was 'to sheath his sword and come and live in peace at Tokangamutu'. Te Kooti answered by tearing up Tawhiao's letter and throwing it in the river: 'when I go again to Tokangamutu it will be to raise the sword, not to lay it aside'.[47] In the oral traditions of Maniapoto this second encounter with both Tawhiao and Rewi is

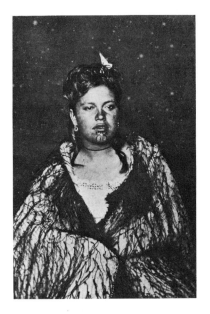

Maraea Morete, or Mere Tawharawhara. She was living at Matawhero in November 1868 and was taken prisoner there by Te Kooti. She subsequently escaped, and wrote down an account of her experiences. *National Museum, Wellington*

Wiremu Kingi Te Paia of Te Aowera hapu of Ngati Porou of Turanga. He was a convert to Pai Marire in 1865, and he went with Te Kooti in 1868, although he expressed considerable distrust both of him and his faith. He described his experiences to Lieutenant-Colonel J. H. St. John in April 1870. *Te Mana o Turanga, Manutuke.* Photographed, by permission of Heni Sunderland, by Gillian Chaplin, 1984.

still remembered. It was a clash of mana, in which Te Kooti was defeated and forced, through a lack of support, to leave the Maniapoto territory.[48]

It was there he took his final refuge, however. He crossed the border to Arowhena, with his wife Heni Kumekume and five men, on 15 May 1872. At first Tawhiao refused to see him and in December, when Te Kooti came to his camp on Rewi's invitation, he 'remained in his tent & made no sign whatever and Te Kooti went away without eating the food prepared for him'.[49] But their reconciliation took place in the following September. Tawhiao visited Te Kooti at his residence at Te Kuiti, and told him: 'Kakahuria ou, takoto ki raro ki taku takahanga waewae. Put on your raiment; lie down at my footstool.'[50] This reconciliation came at a time when Tawhiao was attempting to reassert his own leadership within Waikato and his prestige with those who had given both himself and Te Kooti sanctuary: Ngati Maniapoto. In gratitude, Te Kooti directed the carving and painting of the great house Tokanganui a Noho, which was then being built for Tawhiao at Te Kuiti.[51] For as Te Kooti said, it was from Tawhiao that he had learnt the message of peace.

Te Kooti lived under the protection of Tawhiao and Maniapoto for eleven years before he was pardoned by the government. It was during this time that he developed the distinctive rituals of his religion. Later, in 1886, the name Ringatu, which had been given to his followers because of their practice of raising their right hands at the end of their prayers in thanksgiving to God, was adopted by them. Te Kooti first instituted specific days of worship for the faith. He initiated the First

Fig. II: Te Kuiti and the King Country.

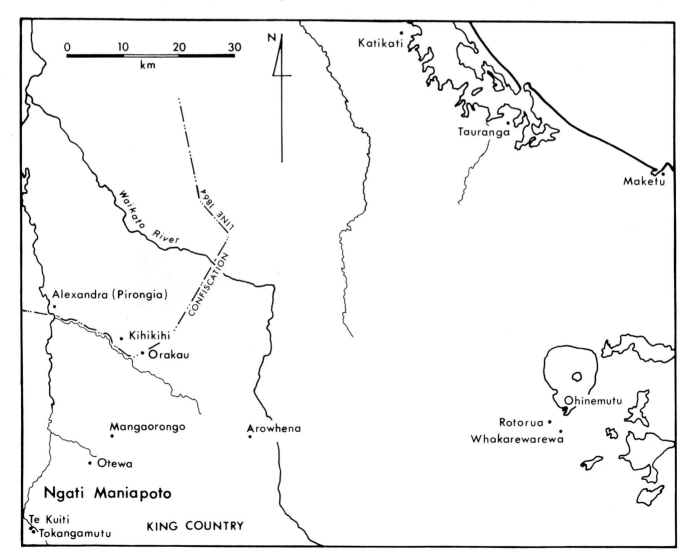

Te Kuiti in 1885. Te Kooti was then living at Otewa, about fourteen kilometres to the north-east. The koruru, or gable, of the meeting-house Tokanganui a Noho, which Te Kooti decorated in gratitude for his protection by King Tawhiao, can be seen on the right. The house was first known as Waho, or Rawaho, the Outsider, and stood in Tokangamutu, a part of Te Kuiti. It was formally reopened on 2 January 1883 with its present name (taken from a house at Aotea which had burnt down), and given to Ngati Maniapoto. It has been shifted at least twice.
Burton Bros. *National Museum, Wellington*

of January as a major celebration in 1875. It is based on Exodus 40: 2 and marks the beginning of the year.[52] The rites include a hākari, or love feast. The First of July was celebrated as the other pillar of the faith from 1876. This occasion was derived from a Ngati Porou practice, dating from 1867, when they adopted it as a day of prayer at the centre of the year. It is the beginning of the seventh month, the sabbath of the sabbath, and is based on Leviticus 23: 24.[53] The Ringatu have held these two great gatherings as the central rituals of the faith since 1876.

In 1879, Te Kooti also inaugurated the huamata, or the planting rites, which are held on 1 June (but in some areas apparently combined with the local First of July gatherings). At the commencement of the huamata, the families bring little kits of seeds to be blessed before planting. The symbolism of the buried seed, from which new life will emerge, is today also seen as the entombment and resurrection of Christ. The pure, or harvest rite, is held variously on 1 November or 1 December, and it completes the celebrations of the cycle of planting, by lifting the tapu from the growing crops. It is the celebration of the first fruits and is derived from Exodus 34: 22 and Deuteronomy 26: 2. These four days, or Rā, are the four pillars of the Ringatu year. In addition, the Saturday as Sabbath and the Twelfth day of every month were also set apart by Te Kooti as sacred days of worship. The Tekaumarua (the Twelfth) celebrates, in the teachings of the faith, the first Twelfth held – at Whareongaonga in 1868. It was in thanksgiving for the safe return of the Exiles. Te Tekaumarua also commemorates 12 May 1868, when the covenants of the faith were said to have been given to Te Kooti on Wharekauri and 12 December 1875 when, at Te Kuiti, the faith was established as a Church, with the setting up of the two Rā of the Firsts of January and July. Finally, it is the Twelfth for the twelve tribes of Israel and the twelve fruits on the Tree of Life from the Book of Revelation.

From 1877, in a series of revelations, or kupu whakaari, Te Kooti developed the rituals and texts of worship. These are the prayers or inoi, the hīmene or hymns, the modified Scriptural passages or pānui, and the songs or waiata. For the sacred gatherings, the Rā, the celebration was established as lasting for three days. It was, in a new form, the observance of the Israelites' three days of sacrifice to God. The people were expected to arrive in the morning on the eleventh of each month and not to depart until after breakfast on the thirteenth. It became a function of one of the officers of the Church, the pirihimana (a transliteration of 'policeman'), to see that these rules were obeyed. In 1892, the year before his death, Te Kooti devised a formal structure of church officers, including the pirihimana, in order to ensure that the faith would survive him. He created then the position of Poutikanga, or Main Pillar, who was to set the rules and practices of the faith, although the first one was not appointed until 1914. The tohunga were to conduct the services. The tākuta, derived from the emphasis on healing in the Epistle of James 5: 14-15, were a separate order to offer prayers and services for the sick.

At the Rā, a koha, or an offering of coins as a sacrifice, was always made by the congregation. The money was blessed and set apart. Today, in the Haahi Ringatu, this money may not be used for food, but only for nominated community projects. After the service, one of the pirihimana will announce the koha, or the amount collected, and the numbers are translated into texts from the Book of Proverbs. The passages are then read out and this is called 'te kupu o te Rā': the word of the Rā. It is seen as the interpretation of the current situation of the people and the faith. The Rā is the ritual occasion for laying burdens and troubles in front of God. As such, it is the replenishing of both the spirit and the body. In the establishment of the Rā and all its procedures, as well as in many other ways, Te Kooti laid the structure of a permanent faith. And, from the later 1870s, his teachings began to spread.

The areas where the new practices took hold were Bay of Plenty, Urewera, and to a lesser extent, Poverty Bay. The tribes who became followers were those who had given him support in the wars, Tuhoe and to some extent Whakatohea, but also those who had not: Whanau a Apanui of the East Coast and parts of Te Arawa and Ngati Porou. People from these communities started to come to Te Kooti at Te Kuiti. Ned Brown, Heni's husband, told us how his ancestor, Te Hira Uetuku, who had been a prisoner on Wharekauri, rode there in 1878 to ask Te Kooti about his land, Mangatu. 'Te Kooti had a habit of misleading people to test you at all times to see how good your faith is. So when he got there . . . Te Kooti said to him, "Well, now that you're here, I see you people are very tired. Here's a bottle of whisky." Well, his friends all got that bottle of whisky, all had a drink. But my grandfather refused. My grandfather said, "No. I came for a purpose and my mission is about Mangatu."' Because he had passed the test set for him, Te Kooti gave him a 'mauri mō te whenua' — a mauri for the land. 'Pertaining to some powers unknown to us. That he will preserve your rights to the land, whatever it is.' He told Te Hira to take back the mauri, said to be a portion of Te Kooti's diamond, which he had carried with him to light his path in the bush. (In some accounts Te Kooti is remembered as wearing the diamond in a little flax kit around his neck.) He told Te Hira to plant it on his tribal mountain, Maungahaumia: 'That is the mauri, to hold and preserve the family in the years to come.'[54]

Similarly, Te Kohi Delamere rode from Maraenui to discover the tenets of the faith, as Maaka Jones describes in her account. Moerangi Ratahi of Ngatiawa also recalled how, when a young girl, she was taken to Te Kuiti to be healed (from what was probably tuberculosis) by him. The whole family came to live with him and, she said, 'Te Kooti healed them all by the laying on of hands, as in the Bible. He then prayed and they all regained their health.'[55] Te Kooti — or Te Turuki as he often called himself from 1868 in rejection of his baptismal name and the identity

The unnamed women. On the left is 'Te Kooti's wife' and on the right, 'Topia's wife'. Topia Turoa of Ngatihau was one of the major Upper Wanganui chiefs and a leading figure within the King movement. He had, however, aided the government against Te Kooti in 1869-70 because he saw him then as a divisive force and threatening to the King. The date of this photograph is unknown, but it is probably from the time of Te Kooti's sanctuary with Ngati Maniapoto. *Brierley collection, Alexander Turnbull Library*

created by the missionaries — became well known as a healer. This tradition of spiritual healing descended from him to others, in turn, and for many became an integral part of the faith. Mana whakaora, faith-healing, is understood as a gift of God; it is said to be a power granted only for a limited time to a particular person. One of those who carried on this tradition, and to whom a number of the women in this book have turned, was Hori Gage of Omaio, who died in 1961. He acquired a large following and for a while led a separate section of the Church known as Rangimarie. But as Heta Rua warned, these are powers which are entrusted. One must not overreach oneself. 'He was all right from the start off. The same thing with Rua. Most of these people. Even George Gage, the same. He had been given the job as faith-healer and he goes and do something else. He won't live long, I can assure you of that!'[56] Heta's directness is healthy. His is a voice demanding a continual testing of all leaders and their activities.

By the early 1880s, the Ringatu faith had swept most of the communities of Tuhoe, Whakatohea, Ngatiawa and Whanau a Apanui. It also spread in parts of the East Coast among Rongowhakaata, Te Aitanga a Mahaki, Ngati Porou and Ngati Kahungunu. It would remain limited to these tribal areas. The King movement always remained separate, following the new faith of Tawhiao known as Tariao, which he also developed in the mid-1870s. The Resident Magistrate at Opotiki, commenting on the wide appeal of Ringatu in the Bay of Plenty, observed sagely that their adherence was not an act of hostility to the government but a belief that Te Kooti 'is something more than a human being. Many Natives have visited Kooti lately to consult him with respect to cases of sickness amongst them. Kooti is represented as telling them "that it was no use their coming to him,

On the painted pare, or lintel, of this meeting-house Tuwhare, built at Rangitahi near Murupara, a portrait of Te Kooti can be seen — he is the figure on the far right. This photograph was taken about 1905. *Birch collection, Alexander Turnbull Library*

Detail of the pare.

as he was no god, but only a human being the same as themselves." Even so, he enjoined them to adhere to his form of worship.'[57] This denial of any claim to be more than man is reinforced by most Ringatu tohunga today, when discussing Te Kooti's teachings and his role as the founder of the Church. It is stressed that Te Kooti himself never claimed Messianic powers.

In February 1883, he was formally pardoned by the government for all his acts of war. Thereafter, he was free to travel and live as he wished — or so it seemed. He called this agreement of the 12th, 'te maungārongo': the long abiding peace. But as he also told the Native Minister John Bryce: 'You did not make peace. I have made it myself. I ceased the strife, and will never return to it. In 1873, I ceased strife; I have not since returned to it. I came into the presence of Tawhiao, and will not withdraw myself from it.'[58] From this date, Te Kooti would take his stance upon the law, despite the legal manipulations which would be used against him. One of his best known sayings is one which he made — and not out of innocence — just before he died:

> Ko te waka hei hoehoenga mo koutou i muri i ahau, ko te Ture, ma te Ture ano te Ture e aki.

> The canoe for you to paddle after me is the Law. Only the Law can be pitched against the Law.[59]

After his pardon, Te Kooti moved to live at Otewa, about half-way between Kihikihi and Te Kuiti. It was from here that he began his journeyings to visit his followers and to make peace with his enemies. He hoped to come back to Turanga. In 1887 he planned to return to open the new meeting-house, Eriopeta or Rongopai, which had been built for him by Te Whanau a Kai people of Repongaere in response to his command to them to build the gospel upon charity and love. Rongopai means 'the Gospel', or 'Good News'. Preparations for this event had been made for over a year, and even Paora Parau had written to the government to tell them that the people of Turanga were building a house for Te Kooti's arrival to 'give the public an opportunity of seeing what sort of man he is'.[60] The house was to be opened on 1 December 1887, and then postponed until 1 January 1888. But the settlers, remembering the past, started to panic, as did some of the chiefs. Both Ngatimaru and Ngaitawhiri protested, and Te Kooti was finally dissuaded from this visit. The most famous of all his waiata, 'Pinepine Te Kura', dates from this occasion. It is an adaptation of an old oriori, or lullaby, and it was composed at Whakaarorangi, Otewa:

> Pinepine te kura, hau te kura. . . .
> Tenei te tira hou tenei haramai nei.
> No te rongo pai no te rangimarie.
> Nau [mai] ka haere taua ki roto o Turanga
> Ki whakangungua koe ki te miini
> Ki te hoari ki te pu-hurihuri
> Nga rakau kohuru a te Pakeha e takoto nei. i-e. . . .

> Whakakake e te ture i te kiinga o to waha
> No runga rawa koe
> No te mana o Kuini e tu nei
> Na Rangi-tu koe na te kotahitanga
> Na Taane rawa koe nga pure tawhiti

Te kaunati hikahika
Te kaunati a to tipuna a Rawiri
I haere ai i tere i nui ao,
Ka hika i tona ahi, kimihia e te iwi
Te ara o te tikanga i pai ai te noho i te ao nei. i.

Kei Turanganui he mata pu
He patu i te tangata kia mate.
Na te maungarongo hoki ra i haere ai i te ara . . . .

Karokaro i te tae-turi oo koutou taringa
Kia areare ai, me te whakarongo mai
Ki nga ki atu kaua ahau e patua.
Moku anake te ārai o Turanga
Te matenga o Mahaki i mau ai te rongo patipati. . . .
Whiti ke mai koe ki ra-i-nahi nei. i.

Te ai o mahara ka mate au i Waerenga-a-Hika.
Te ki mai koe me whakawa marire
Hopu ana koe i ahau kawe ana ki Wharekauri.
Ka manene mai au ki ro te wai
Ka u ana ko Whare-ongaonga.
Ka pa ko te waha o te Kawana.
E hika ma e! Ina ia te kai.
Tooia ki uta ra haehaetia ai
Tunua hai te manawa ka kainga ka pau,
Mo Koro-timutimu, mo Tauranga-koau.
Koia te riri pokanoa,
Ka kai ki te waipiro ka kai ki te whakama ki te mau-a-hara,
Me whakarere atu ena mahi kino e hika ma. e-e.

Little tiny treasure, treasure of renown. . . .
A new company of travellers is setting out.
A people of faith and peace.
Let us travel on to Turanga
Where you shall parry the Minie rifle
The sword and the revolver
The murderous weapons of the Pakeha lying everywhere. . . .

You the law, push on up as you proclaim
You are supreme
Even above the power of the Queen,
From Rangi-tu, the Sky above, from the unity,
From Taane himself, the ancient pure rites
From the fire-generating stick
The fire-stick of your ancestor David
Employed as he travelled the wide world,
Generating his fire; you the people
Seek the path of righteousness that we can live peacefully in this world.

In Turanganui are to be found bullets for guns
With which to kill man.
But it was in peace that I travelled the pathways . . . .

Clean the wax from your ears
That there might be no obstruction, then you will hear me
When I say do not destroy me.
Mine alone is banishment from Turanga
The fate of Mahaki, a deceiving peace was made . . . .
You, the recent arrivals.

You wrongly thought I would perish at Waerenga-a-Hika.
And instead of judging me fairly
You seized me and shipped me to Wharekauri.
But I slid into the water
To make my landfall at Whare-ongaonga.
Where I heard the voice of the Governor saying,
'Oh my friends! Here is food.
It has been hauled ashore and cut to pieces
The heart has been cooked, to be eaten and consumed,
For Koro-timutimu and Tauranga-koau.'
Hence this needless strife,
Which comes from the consumption of liquor, from shame, from hatred.
Therefore, I say, abandon these evil ways, my friends.[61]

In February 1889 when he tried again to return to Turanga, he was turned back at Waiotahe in the Bay of Plenty, where he was arrested. He was accused of unlawful assembly and disturbing the public peace. These charges were legal chicanery. The government had consistently assured him that his peaceable movements about the country were quite lawful. But after tortuous legal battles, the Court of Appeal in 1890 upheld the decision that he was guilty.[62]

Te Kooti sought always to end his exile. At Otewa, he was living by sufferance on land to which he had no claim. He requested from the government a place on which he and his followers could live — a hundred men, women, and children, he said, in February 1884.[63] The land which was purchased by the government for him at Orakau, however, turned out to be almost entirely swamp and

Waiting for Te Kooti at Takepu marae, Te Karaka, Sunday 24 February 1889. This house, Te Poho o Pikihoro, had been built for Te Kooti in the previous year to welcome him back to Poverty Bay. But he was arrested at Waiotahe in the Bay of Plenty on 28 February, and was never allowed to return. Photograph by William F. Crawford, Gisborne. *Gisborne Museum*

uninhabitable. Finally, in 1891, he was given a block at Wainui on the Ohiwa harbour, a part of the confiscated Tuhoe lands. He sent Rakuraku, a Tuhoe chief from Waimana, to look at it. When he returned he told him this place was ' "only fit for goats and crawly things. Not fit for human beings." So Te Kooti said, "Well, all right. That land God has given us. I'll go there. And stay with it." '64 Wainui, however, was only formally settled as a reserve, and developed as the marae for the Church, after he was dead. He remained a prophet living in exile, without a tribe: alone among his followers. Yet his legacy is that he was able to create a sense of continuity and community for the women with whom we have talked.

RUA AND THE SUCCESSION TO TE KOOTI

Almost from the moment of his return from Wharekauri, Te Kooti had looked towards a successor, a man of peace and greater than himself. He made a series of predictive utterances, beginning in December 1868, which foresee the one who will follow. At the terrible siege of Ngatapa, Te Kooti uttered these words:

> Ahakoa hui te motu nei e kore ahau e mau i a ratou e kore hoki ahau e mate kia puta mai rano te tangata mo muri i au maana ahau e hopu a ka haereere ano ahau i tona aroaro a mate iho ki raro i ona waewae.

> Although this island gathers together, I shall never be seized by them, neither shall I be killed until the man to follow me appears. He will capture me and I shall go about in his presence and die under his feet.[65]

It was on 1 January 1877 at Te Tahawai, Katikati, that he first made the prediction that this man would arise from the area of the Mataatua canoe people, who had, almost entirely, committed themselves to him:

> Anatekere
>
> No Nga Kuri a Wharei ki Tikirau, kei waenganui te tangata mo tatou. He tamaiti pai he rangimarie. Nui atu hoki tona mana ahakoa 2. 3. 4. aku waewae ka haere mai ahau ka koropiko ki raro ki ona waewae.

> Anatekere
>
> From between Nga Kuri a Wharei and Tikirau shall come a man for us all. A good and peaceful child, he shall have very great powers. Though I may have two, three, or four feet, I shall come and bow down at his feet.[66]

These boundaries run from Katikati to the East Cape. The reference to two, three, or four feet may be interpreted as walking, hobbling along on a stick, or riding on horseback, although the words echo the riddle of the Sphinx solved by Oedipus. (There, the animal which goes on four feet 'in the morning' is the child, who crawls.) Rua Kenana took this prediction concerning Te Kooti's successor for himself. In 1905 he first claimed to be the one spoken of, and undertook a series of quests to fulfil the tasks set by Te Kooti, through which the leader would be recognized.

Rua must have known Te Kooti. His father, Kenana Tumoana, was killed at Makaretu in November 1868, fighting along with him. Rua was born in the following year, and, as a small child, lived at Maungapohatu, which was one of the main centres of Tuhoe support for Te Kooti throughout the wars. He associated with the Tuhoe elders, who stayed with Te Kooti during the last year of his life when he lived at Te Horo and on the Hokianga Island in the Ohiwa harbour. Here, at Te Karaka on the shores of the harbour, Te Kooti died on 17 April 1893. The Tuhoe have always had a close relationship with Te Kooti. The arbitrary land confiscations of 1866, imposed in reprisal for Whakatohea's execution of their missionary, Carl Volkner, took in most of the low-lying territory of Tuhoe in the Bay of Plenty. Bitter at this loss, Tuhoe committed themselves to Te Kooti when he sought their support in 1868-9. Because they sheltered him, they suffered from a scorched-earth policy directed against their homes and their crops. But they had made a binding covenant with him. On 20 March 1869, at Tawhana in the Waimana (or Tauranga) valley, the Tuhoe leaders dedicated themselves and their land to him. Te Kooti said:

> 'Ka tango ahau i a koutou hei iwi mooku a, ko ahau hei Atua mo koutou, a ka mohio koutou ko Ihowa ahau.' Ko koe hoki te iwi o te kawenata.

> 'I take you as my people, and, I will be your God; you will know that I am Jehovah.' You are the people of the covenant.[67]

There remained, however, a task for the Tuhoe. He told them: 'Te Atua-tanga kei a koe, te Kawenata kei a koe' — 'The God-head is with you, the Covenant is with you'[68] — but they needed unity. These words challenged the leaders of the Tuhoe people. Their underlying purpose is characteristic of the prophetic form of leadership: it anticipates and initiates, and by foretelling seeks to direct the people into action. Its authority lies in its vatic quality; the words possess power because their source cannot be questioned.

Rua, of course, was not the only one who claimed to be Te Kooti's successor. For many within Ringatu he served only to divide the faith, for he was never accepted universally. He claimed, however, to have fulfilled many of the tasks set. He went to Turanga, 'the seat of hatred', and there he entered the sacred house of Rongopai. He was baptized with his new name Hepetipa, Hephzibah, in fulfilment of another prediction of Te Kooti's:

> Otewa Hanuere 25. 1885

> Te kupu whakaari mo te maungarongo. . . . e ki nei ka karangatia koe ko Hepetipa, to whenua ko Peura, no te mea ka hua reka a Ihoa i a koe, a ka whai tahu to whenua.

> Otewa January 25. 1885

> The prophetic saying concerning the lasting peace. . . . it says you shall be called Hephzibah, and your land Beulah, for the Lord is well pleased with you, and your land shall have a spouse.[69]

This prediction, and the Scriptural text upon which it is based, Isaiah 62: 4, Rua took as his own. The words are Isaiah's vision for the Israelites: their land would cease to be desolate and become fruitful again. The new name of the leader, Hepetipa or chosen by God, was a statement of the Lord's rejoicing over him as over Jerusalem, and the people themselves took the name Iharaira, the Israelites. Rua was baptized in 1906 by Eria Raukura, the leading Ringatu tohunga, who had fought alongside Te Kooti in the Urewera and lived with him during his exile in the King Country. Eria — Elijah — had himself been baptized by Te Kooti in

1881 as the main teacher for the faith. His acceptance and baptism of Rua, thereby re-enacting Elijah's role, were critical factors in Rua's emergence to a position of considerable influence within Tuhoe.

Rua built his new religious community at Maungapohatu. This was the city of deliverance, called Mt Zion or Hiona. Here, too, the unbroken thread leads back to Te Kooti's founding vision, for Maungapohatu was to be the city of the faithful, Ngā Mōrehu, or those 'whom the Lord shall call'. The community was modelled on Jerusalem in the time of Solomon, but many of the religious observances were also based on indigenous Maori practice. The inner sanctum, called the wāhi tapu, was strictly maintained in the early days of the settlement and no one was allowed to enter it in work-clothes, or clothes that had been worn in the kitchens. Everyone had to sprinkle themselves with water on entering or leaving, in order not to infringe the tapu of the pā. In these rules, Rua was extending traditional Ringatu practice whereby the ancestral meeting-house was considered tapu and, consequently, no food could be eaten in it. Rua kept the entire inner dwelling area under such restrictions. But he called these the rules of the new tapu and, in fact, rejected the old.

Te Kooti had revived many aspects of traditional tapu. The life principle found in every living thing (the mauri in Maori thought) was protected by the rules of tapu. One of the strictest observances was that cooked food, and any aspect of the preparation of food, being noa, must be kept apart from all other activities. Hot water, therefore, was considered a pollutant of tapu. Water from the roof of a meeting-house was considered dangerous too, because it had touched the roof (the spine) of the ancestral house. It was always considered extremely dangerous to touch either the head or the back of any person who was in a tapu state. As in many other old cultures, the house represents and contains the tribal ancestors. Its head, its backbone, its ribs, and its belly are seen as enfolding and protecting the living. Rain-water from the roof could not, therefore, be collected and used for drinking. Behind these rules lies the ancient Maori cosmology, by which the state of tapu is the expression of being under the influence and protection of spiritual forces. This fundamental concept Te Kooti retained, for his teachings included the deliberate revival of much that was part of the traditional Maori world.

Rua changed many of these teachings. In April 1906 he abolished the Twelfth, the sacred day established by Te Kooti, specifically because it belonged to him and

above Rua at the entrance gateway into the wāhi tapu enclosure at Maungapohatu, Christmas 1908. Notice the turnstile, as well as the cans for water used to sprinkle oneself on entering or leaving. The emblems on the gateway are the club, the sign that Rua was the coming King in the line of David, the comet (Halley's comet) and the morning star. These two stars were understood to be the emblems for the two sons of God, Rua and Christ. Mihaia is the statement that Rua is the Maori Messiah. Photograph by George Bourne. *Auckland Museum*

above, left Hiona, Rua's circular council-chamber, whose design was based on the ancient mosque in Jerusalem, the Dome of the Rock. It was, in intention, a reconstruction of King Solomon's Temple. This photograph was taken in April 1908. It shows Rua, his seven wives of this time, his eldest daughter Whakaataata (Meri Tukua), and Whaitiri Rewiri, his eldest son's wife, who brought up Puti Onekawa as a baby. Back: Te Akakura (Patu); Te Aue; Rua; Whaitiri; Whakaataata; Mihiroa. Middle: ? Whirimako; Pinepine. Lower: Wairimu; Pehirangi, Puti's mother. Photograph by George Bourne. *Auckland Museum* his times. He also abolished the Firsts, with the huamata and the pure ceremonies of June and November. He kept only the Saturday Sabbath. He deliberately sold off ancestral carvings, objects of mana and tapu. He visited some of the old sacred places to lift the tapu from them, for it seemed that their guardian atua had become angry and malevolent and were now the sources of sickness and trouble. He also allowed the eating of food in the ancestral meeting-houses. These were no longer treated by the Iharaira as tapu. He thus attempted to abolish all the old forms of tapu. In their place, he emphasized new forms, based on the Scriptural disciplines of the Israelites living under the laws of Moses. He set up a teaching and healing order called Levites, or Riwaiti, the order of ministers which Moses had established, to instruct the people in the new ways. The Iharaira lived under these rules, which set them apart from the old Ringatu, or Herora, Herod's people, as the Iharaira called them. It was a conscious act of separation. His followers grew their hair long like the Nazirites, a specific sign of their separation and dedication to God.

In September 1915, Rua brought to an end all these rules. One stage in their re-enactment of the Biblical story had been completed.

> Ae, kua mutu ngā tauira. Kua mutu ngā tauira i whakaritea mai ai i te wā i a Mohi ra. Kua mutu ēra whakarite ki ana tāngata makawe-roroa.

> The teachings were brought to an end. The teachings set down from the time of Moses were fulfilled. All those laws were finished with his long-haired people.[70]

The rules of tapu surrounding the Levites were lifted so that they could now, for example, enter the places where food was prepared. They all cut off their long hair. The wāhi tapu was cleared. Rua and his wives went to live at the new pā at the bottom of the valley at Maungapohatu, which he called Maai, or the place cleansed of tapu restrictions. Rua himself was free to enter the kitchens and the eating-places. They were all freed — 'kāre he tapu'.

> I te whakakorenga o te tapu i ngā Riwaiti, koia ra te mea. Kua māmā hoki. Kua pai noa iho tēna ki te haere ki tēna wāhi, ki tēna wāhi, ki ngā mahi kua māmā hoki.

> When the tapu was removed from the Riwaiti, that was the thing. They were not encumbered any more. They were free to go where they wished, and to work where they wished, there were no more ties.[71]

He had brought them into the New World and the years of the New Covenant.

In 1916 an armed party of police came to Maungapohatu and Rua was arrested on charges which were designed to remove him as a troublesome leader within Tuhoe.[72] In a way which he had not anticipated, the past was repeating itself in the present. As Paetawa Miki, kaitiaki of Maungapohatu said, 'It was Te Kooti all over again.'[73] Rua was imprisoned until 1918. When he returned, he found that a vigorous rival faith had established itself at Maungapohatu: that of the Presbyterian mission under the leadership of the Reverend John Laughton. In the end, the two men established a unique relationship, in which Rua allowed the missionary to instruct the children. The three women in this book who were brought up at Maungapohatu in the 1920s were taught by Laughton or by his successors. Perhaps the greatest testimony to Laughton's irenic vision was the dedication of the new meeting-house at Rua's community at Matahi in the

Tauranga valley, Te Huinga o Te Kura. 'The Coming Together of God's People' is one translation for its name. The house was opened on 1 January 1925 as a house of unity for the Iharaira, the Ringatu, and the Presbyterians:

> We are all in the one house, Presbyterian, Ringatu. The Twelfths is a time when every people is welcome, just to have a chat. We give you your part. You have your part. When I finish mine, well, your turn coming up. One turn, then another. That's why Rua built that house for Mr Laughton, for the Twelfths. That's why he named that house.[74]

Rua also rebuilt the Maungapohatu community. It was reconstructed in 1927 as part of a deliberate effort to regather the people in the heart of their ancestral lands. The settlement in which the three women grew up was, therefore, very different from that which Rua had originally founded in 1907. But it still maintained strict community rules. Those concerning the maintenance of hygiene in the homes were enforced by the women's committee. The families all observed the Saturday Sabbath, which was now held at Maai. The people sat in front of the veranda of Rua's house, Hiruharama Hou, from where he and the Levites, who took the religious services, used to speak. They maintained some important forms of tapu – relating specifically to the rites of passage, birth and death, the times when the wairua, the soul, enters and leaves this world. The people also anticipated the coming of the millennium, or the return of God to earth. Rua taught that the salvation of the people – the recovery of their confiscated lands and their autonomy – would be brought about by direct divine intervention. But the fulfilment of the New Covenant still remained conditional upon their faith.

Rua died on 20 February 1937. He had promised to return to them on the third day. The third day is the day of Christ's resurrection, and also the day on which it was believed that the manawa, the very breath and heart of life, finally departed the body. Among his followers today, who live mostly in the Tauranga valley or at Ruatahuna in the Urewera country, some remain certain that he will return to earth as the New Messiah. Others are less sure that the prophecy will be fulfilled.

It is of primary concern within the Maori world that the mana, or authority, of leadership is transferred from one generation to another correctly. The successor is 'chosen' and his mana is then revealed in his actions. Leaders are, therefore, tested in a multitude of ways, since there are many manifestations of leadership. But the divinity of it is an integral part of the Ringatu tradition. In that specific sense, the leaders are untouchable by the colonizers. Matiu Paeroa, for example, who was one of Te Kooti's secretaries and who wrote down his teachings, was believed by some to have inherited his mana through Te Kooti. It was a gift bestowed upon him, and he was protected by divine forces. As he transcribed the sayings, and the predictions, the psalms and the prayers in his office at Wainui, 'the rainbow always stood above it'.[75] It was his kaitiaki, or guardian. Important men traditionally had a quality of tapu placed upon them, which included their own kaitiaki as a form of protection. In Ringatu thought the rainbow is a sign from God. It was given by the Archangel Michael to Te Kooti as his particular sign and it can be an omen of good or ill. Its significance can be read by those who understand it. Matiu became a Ringatu tohunga, and later returned home to Waiapu and founded there a centre for the Ringatu faith among his own people, Ngati Porou.[76] This cloak of divinely-bestowed leadership, however, he is said by some to have transferred to Sir Apirana Ngata for Ngati Porou. In the Ringatu tradition, then, the flow of mana and tapu from God descends through the prophet to the men and women

Wainui, 1978. In the foreground is the memorial erected to Te Kooti, 'Poropiti Tianara': 'Prophet and General'. Behind is the meeting-house, Te Ohaki, opened in December 1903 and renewed in 1942. Photograph by Gillian Chaplin.

who are the leaders. They each bear a portion of the original powers of Te Kooti.

There would, of course, be problems of disunity. Te Kooti himself had anticipated the divisions which would beset the Church after his death. In his ōhāki, his dying speech, he therefore determined that Wainui should be the centre for the faith:

> Te Hanuere te Hurae kei au kei Te Wainui. . . . Ka takoto ka takoto atu ahau ki Te Wainui.

> The January and the July are with me at Te Wainui. . . . I shall lie, I shall lie on at Te Wainui.[77]

It was here that the first group of leaders, including Matiu and Rikirangi Hohepa (son of Te Kooti's younger brother, Hohepa, and Te Kooti's adopted son) built, in 1893, their Ark of the Covenant. Here, too, they constructed the meeting-house called Te Ohaki, which was opened ten years later. Those who grew up within the faith remember clearly the gatherings at Wainui — 'the eye of the island', as Te Kooti called it — and the 'spiritual way of life' in which they were instructed there.

But Wainui could not hold the Ringatu together. Rua took many away in 1906-7. There were others who also claimed prophetic powers: Wi Wereta of Tokomaru and Wi Raepuku, or Ohana, of Wanganui, were two whose claims to be the One foretold also led to separate branches of the Church being founded early this century. Thus the faith fragmented, some following their prophetic leaders, others holding to the old teachings. Yet even within the older form, changes took place, for Ringatu is not a static force, but a living faith. Paora Delamere, from 1938 the Poutikanga (Main Pillar) of the Haahi Ringatu, the registered Ringatu Church, made major changes in both ritual and interpretation. His daughter, Maaka Jones, talks about some of these in her narrative. He abolished, for example, the long-standing tradition of burning coins as an act of sacrifice. The coins were given as a 'sin offering' and, in obedience to the laws of Moses, were 'burnt in the fire'.[78] Places where the burnt coins were hidden were considered tapu and came to be seen as sources of danger and misfortune. These Old Testament practices Paora Delamere gradually came to believe were no longer appropriate, as increasingly he placed emphasis on the doctrine of Christ's atonement for sin. Where once the followers of Te Kooti in their prayers 'cut off the conclusion, when we ask all through our Lord Jesus Christ',[79] the faith came to accept the doctrine of salvation through Christ. Thus the Haahi Ringatu, under the leadership of Paora Delamere, has moved to a full adoption of Christian teachings. But it began as a theology of liberation for the Lost Children of Israel – and it has not forgotten its origins.

Today there are three major branches of the Ringatu. Te Haahi o Te Wairua Tapu evolved from the followers of Wi Wereta, and its name is the original name intended for the Church by Te Kooti. Its strength is mostly in the Poverty Bay district and its emphasis now falls on the evangelical elements in Christianity. Te Haahi o Te Kooti Rikirangi was founded in 1937 and derives from the teachings of Wi Raepuku. It is centred in the eastern Bay of Plenty, particularly amongst Ngatiawa and Tuhoe of Te Teko. Te Haahi Ringatu, which was registered in 1929, is also centred in the eastern Bay of Plenty. It administers the marae at Wainui. Its tribal support is primarily Tuhoe, Whakatohea, and Whanau a Apanui. While there have been several attempts at reconciliation, the three major branches have retained their separate identities, although all accept one another as Ringatu. The followers of Rua, the Iharaira, also consider themselves to be Ringatu.

Ringatu has consistently been the strongest faith among the Maori population of Whakatane, Opotiki, and Waikohu. In Cook County, centring on Gisborne, it is second only to the Church of England. These basic geographical boundaries of the faith were created by its historical origins. Today, there are about 6000 adherents, or two per cent of the Maori population of New Zealand. Its numbers have grown in the last two decades, though its proportional strength has shrunk. But its influence is much broader than these numbers would suggest, for it is seen as the *essentially* Maori Church, with its hymns and its waiata retaining old linguistic and compositional forms, with melodic continuity and quarter-tone singing, to convey the Scriptural messages.

Wi Wereta of Tokomaru. He is claimed to have travelled to Te Kuiti to get the 'mana whakaora', the power of faith-healing, from Te Kooti. Wi Wereta was very influential among the Ringatu in the Poverty Bay and Wairarapa districts from 1900 until the early 1920s. This portrait hangs in Te Rawheoro meeting-house at Tolaga Bay. Photographed, by permission of Sonny Kutia, by Gillian Chaplin, 1985.

WOMEN IN THE MAORI WORLD

Women in the Church, as in Maori society itself, have many roles. One of the common misconceptions in much written ethnography is that women in Maori society were simply 'noa', translated as 'ordinary' and 'without tapu'. It is clear from the narratives recounted here, and from other sources, that there were indeed women of rank who *intrinsically* possessed both mana and tapu.

> He mea ano ko nga wahine nga tohunga, a he nui te mana o te wahine tohunga. . . . he wahine rautahi ranei, he wahine kau ranei ko te ariki o aua wahine hei tohunga, a mana e mahi nga mahi tohunga katoa, i te mea ka akona ia hei tino tohunga, mana e kai nga kai tapu katoa e kai ai te tohunga ariki.

> Women were also tohunga, and great was the mana of a woman tohunga. . . . A childless woman, or any woman could from her position as first born, become tohunga and undertake all the tasks of a tohunga. Since she would be instructed as a full tohunga she would eat all the sacred food which a chief priest would eat.[80]

Women tohunga existed from pre-European times. One of the greatest of the early nineteenth-century visionaries, Papahurihia, derived his prophetic skills and much of his knowledge not only from his father but from his mother, Taimania. His wife Kikihu was also said to be an oracle.[81] There were also important women leaders in pre-European times. One was Rongomaiwahine, the fourth wife of the chief Kahungunu. It was *she* whom Ngati Kahungunu people of the Mahia peninsula chose, early this century, to portray on their marae flag, flying it above all others. In a waiata whakamanamana, song of challenge, they sang:

E wha aku mana turuturu o te ao, ko Ihowa, ko Te Karaiti e
Ko Te Wairua Tapu, ko Rongomai-wahine e e.

I have four permanent mana in the world, namely, Jehovah, Christ
The Holy Ghost, and Rongomai-wahine.[82]

There were also numerous women prophets in the nineteenth century. Remana Hii of Waihou in the Hokianga is the most well known, because she clashed with the law in 1887. Her followers all wore white robes as an emblem of peace, and she created for them a 'Holy Land', a Wāhi Tapu, wherein nothing coloured black should be seen — neither horse nor fowl — that might desecrate it.[83] Waioeka Brown of Puha, granddaughter of one of the Wharekauri prisoners Tamihana Teketeke, was sent to one of the last of the whare wānanga (houses of learning) in Poverty Bay to be taught the ancient karakia and whakapapa of Te Aitanga a Mahaki. She was considered a very knowledgeable old lady within the Ringatu faith of that region. Among Tuhoe, Putiputi Hikihiki is remembered as a Ringatu tohunga and healer. Those who went to her took small coins — a threepence or sixpence — as an offering. These were the coins which would be burnt in the fire of sacrifice. Some of the young men who went off to the Second World War went to her to seek her blessing and protection before their departure.[84]

Women of rank transferred their rank to their children. The early French explorer R. P. Lesson noted the 'wahine tohonga [sic] or wise women' as well as 'wahine ariki' on his visit to the Bay of Islands and commented, 'An oddity, however, is the fact that the higher the rank of the mother, the more illustrious is the child, because it is from her that he derives his title.'[85] In Maori society, lines of descent and the birthrights acquired within the hapū may be traced through men or women, and there have been many women whose rank has outweighed that of their husbands. From them their children will derive their elevated status. Elsdon Best, commenting on Maori descent lines, recognized that 'Uterine filiation is of undoubted importance among the Maori, *especially when conveying rank*; . . . if the mother was of higher rank than the father, then their children would prefer to trace their descent through the mother, with whom their increased rank and prestige originated.'[86] Mana whenua, mana specifically deriving from the land and thus giving the child claims to rights and shares in that land, was a birthright and was closely interwoven with rank. But in the days before the Maori Land Court had imposed its legal criteria for 'collective ownership', the traditional criteria of residence and usufruct — 'ahi kā', keeping the hearth warm — were necessary to those rights. It was considered particularly important that women of rank continue living with the hapū after their marriage. Such a woman was important because of who she was, not because of whom she married. If she lived with her husband's people, probably at least one of their children would be sent as a whāngai to be brought up by her parents. In this manner the 'hearth was kept warm' and her lineage maintained.

The rights traced from women by their children were rights derived from women of status. There was a preference for the senior male line in tracing seniority in many tribes but rank, rather than gender, was quite possibly the main determinant of roles in pre-European Maori society. Rank was no more a prerogative of males than tapu, and for female chiefs and tohunga rank transcended gender. Their seniority of lineage was traced by primogeniture, and

Puti Hikihiki, with her husband Te Maipi Te Whiu. Photographed, by permission of Rata Takao of Piripari, by Gillian Chaplin, 1977.

also through the seniority of the wives in a polygamous marriage. The acquired mana of the families was recalled – and shaped – in the oral histories. For some women at least there was always an articulation between gender and rank (as well as between rank and ability), which has been largely overlooked in the anthropological accounts.[87] Warfare and oratory may have been primarily male activities but even in those women participated. Women could instigate war by their speeches, women could take part in haka as a pōkeka, or statement of unity, and women even fought in war – certainly in the nineteenth century. Women also mediated for peace. Many of the economic activities were shared.

One of the most significant tasks in which women participated was to make noa, or free, people and objects which were under the restrictions of tapu. Tapu was intrinsic in all living things, according to their quality or kind. But there were also extensions of tapu appropriate to certain activities or states of life, and which had then to be lifted upon the proper occasions. Such would be the tapu-lifting rites performed when the child's navel cord fell off, at its first hair-cutting, at the opening of a meeting-house, and after the burial of the dead. The rituals to lift the tapu restrictions – whakanoa or whakakorenga – were often performed by women of rank, but usually by women who were past the age of child-bearing (ruahine), so that the potential life within them was not touched. They drew the dangerous, life-destroying elements of tapu into themselves and then sent them back to their point of origin, that is, to the world of the gods and the spirit forces.[88]

In traditional Maori thought, women were seen as the beginning and the end of life in this world. Not only do they bring the child into the world of light, Te Ao Marama, but as the great myth of Hine Nui Te Po constantly reminds, the vagina – 'te ara mai o te tangata', or the pathway of mankind to life – is also the place of misfortune and the source of death: 'te whare o aituā'. Women's tapu exists because they are the channel between the realm of divine forces and the human realm. Old women of religious power were perhaps not as feared as old men were, but it was still within their authority to 'relocate *tapu* or godly influence'.[89]

'He wāhine, he whenua, ka ngaro te tangata': 'by women and land, men are destroyed'. This well-known whakataukī refers to the causes of warfare. But, as in all languages, recurrent metaphors powerfully convey the concepts of the world which the speakers inherit and hold. Maori is rich in such metaphorical systems. The land, 'te whenua', and women are also the *source* of life, and 'te whenua' is the word used for the lining of the womb and the placenta which nourishes the foetus. The placenta must be buried within the land after birth and so made one with the earth again. To be in childbirth is called 'e whānau ai'; thus 'te whānau' is the extended kin group or family into which one is born. 'E hapū ana' is to be pregnant, to be conceived in the womb; so 'te hapū' is the clan, the tribe into which one is born. But it is not the flesh only which carries such a weight of meaning: the very bones – iwi – are the people, all the people, living and dead, the tribe to whom one belongs by birth. The *living* community, then, is born of woman and nourished on the land – and may be destroyed on their account.

The women in this book talk about their own lives, and about those from whom they trace their descent. They also talk about their particular knowledge and their particular roles. For all of them, the family – the whānau – and its survival are central concerns. The experience of childlessness, wharengaro – literally, the house destroyed – is the thing most feared by Maori women, because of its remorseless frequency in the recent past. Infant mortality, which is higher among Maori than Pakeha, is directly related to poverty. Most Maori infant deaths, which have been recorded since the 1920s, occur in the post-neonatal period, that is between one month and one year of age, while Pakeha infant deaths occur mostly in the neonatal period. The conspicuous cause of death in Maori infants is respiratory disease. Such diseases are attributable, on this scale, to the poor housing conditions in which many families were, and are, living. All the women in this book were born and brought up in conditions of material poverty. They and their men were often without work, and their experiences were not untypical. The Maori as a people had been stripped of many of their economic resources, and their communal autonomy was already shattered by the beginning of the twentieth century. This loss of land and authority was the direct consequence of the process of colonization. Few Europeans were aware of the causes or the realities. Writing of the early 1930s, when the women of this book were all growing up or having their families, Elsie Locke said after a visit to a Maori settlement near Port Waikato, 'Nothing in my education or experience gave any clues as to the reasons for this poverty. I did not [even] know that Maoris were discriminated against in unemployment relief. . . . The general idea around . . . was that Maoris were too easy-going by nature to do anything to better themselves.'[90] These stereotypes prevailed at every level of society, even among young and enthusiastic radicals like Locke, and no means of understanding the actual history which had created this poverty was then offered.

The education of the children was the particular concern of Maori women. Women were, in fact, repositories of knowledge, and family history was passed on by them. This book is an attempt to transmit 'family' histories to a wider audience. In the past, Maori grandmothers wrote oriori, or lullabies, for their mokopuna in order to teach them their history. It is not accidental that Te Kooti's song of betrayal by the law, 'Pinepine Te Kura', is an adaptation of an old oriori; it is indeed particularly appropriate that it should be so. The concept of whānaungatanga emphasized by Maori women today is essentially that of holding and preserving the practices which knit and strengthen the bonds of the family and the hapū. The Maori Women's Welfare League's recent report on women's health revealed that, of the women whom they surveyed, those who did not know their tribal roots, and were not involved in hui and all the other activities which create a sense of particular identity, actually faced higher health and social risks. The report re-emphasized the importance of the whānau, the kinship ties, in the creation of a sense of well-being among Maori women.[91] Every one of the women in this book has a strong awareness of both their tribal and their Maori identity; and every one of them conveys it in her narrative. They are all women whom you respect when you meet them. Their integrity, their positive energy, their totality as human beings are pre-eminent.

These women have all endured the colonial experience and, as a consequence, reveal elements of a colonization of the mind, which was imposed upon their generations. They accept as inevitable the poverty in which they grew up. They accept the proletarianization of their kin as being usual: they and their men were mostly shearers or casual labourers. They still tend to accept their inability to master or manipulate certain aspects of Pakeha society. The stripping-away of power from the Maori people created this sense of subordination in those generations which grew up in the earlier part of this century. If New Zealand is to avert the crisis of anger which it now faces, the Maori people need to share the power in this society.

'We are what we remember. Society is what we remember.'[92] The narratives of these women are part of an oral history which remembers the injustices of the colonial past. Pakeha memories have largely suppressed that element of the past, perhaps because the objectives of the colonizers were quite different from those of the colonized. The gap between the different perceptions of our common history held by the two peoples is wide, but it can be bridged. The narratives told here are part of the oral history of a faith whose central concern was the survival of its people. The visible strengths of the women derive much from the fact that they do *know* who they are. They bring the past into the present. At their centre is a confidence that they have endured – and more, an awareness of their close links not merely with past generations but with future generations as well.

THE MAKING OF AN ORAL HISTORY

Until the mid-nineteenth century, Maori society was an oral society. Oral forms do not immediately die with the introduction of literacy. The telling of tales, the singing of songs, the reciting of genealogy and proverb are still today the main forms of transmitting the people's history. New events become part of the tradition. New waiata are composed to tell history, and old ones adapted. Tradition is not static. There is a constant dialogue between the past and the present, and the patterns of thought are still primarily those of an oral culture.[93] The conversations presented here, however, belong not so much to the more formal 'domain of living oral tradition' as to the domestic 'domain of reminiscence'.[94] Nevertheless, they contain accounts which are part of the collective public knowledge shared by others in their own communities. Events of significance, which a particular individual may experience, or a tipuna may have experienced, pass into the community's history and are wrought into the traditions over a period of time. Putiputi Onekawa's narrative concerning her father's journey to Gisborne in 1906 to claim the succession to Te Kooti is one example. The verifying personal details, which she adds, help to guarantee the veracity of the story for the listeners, but the central core of the narrative will be known by others and told by them with their own embellishments. Essentially, the narrative carries a symbolic weight. Its purpose is to reveal Rua as the predicted Messiah. Events, as they pass into traditional narratives, are shaped for a purpose. The recollections in this book are primarily personal. But they are, at the same time, much more than merely 'life histories'. They contain memories which belong to other people, and they describe significant communal events. Moreover, many of the explanations for those events derive from the teachings of Te Kooti.

He bequeathed to his followers a 'testimonial' form of narrating history, in which events are seen as bearing testimony to some earlier prophecy. Unexpected episodes may be interpreted as the fulfilment of an equivocating prediction, or warning. Thus meaning becomes, as it were, an encrustation on events. The subsequent choice of *action* stems directly from one's understanding as to the *causes* of the events. How we understand the present will be determined by our understanding of the past. The myth-narratives, which record the people's history, are directional. They present a view of history which is religious and predictive; they are also primarily concerned with establishing ngā tikanga, the right ways of doing things for the future generations. In history of this kind, the stories become the proof of continuing divine guidance and intervention. This hermeneutic system of explanation Te Kooti derived both from Maori oral traditions and from his extensive and detailed knowledge of the Bible, which is itself written with similar intentions and perceptions. He joined these two traditions of explanation and meaning to create the body of interpretative thought which is Ringatu.

As far as we are aware, the only other published interviews of any length with women of the Ringatu world are 'Of Love and Death: Matarena's Story', a dialogue with Matarena Reneti of Te Teko in 1980, and an account, based on tape recordings which are now lost, of aspects of the life of the centenarian Moerangi Ratahi of Whakatane, published in 1971.[95] Matarena's story is similar in form to seven of the narratives here. As she put it, 'This little knowledge I have, this biblical knowledge in the Ringatu faith, this is giving me the courage to speak into this machine for the young people of the country to hear.'[96] All the stories here are also derived from tape-recorded dialogues. They have been edited, simply because the verbatim transcripts are far too long for anyone to want to read. Our conversations were relaxed and they ranged over many subjects. We did not consider ourselves to be conducting interviews but rather to be talking together.

One of the essays is written in quite a different form. This is the narrative of Te Akakura Rua. Akakura died in 1980. In some ways she, together with her sister Puti Onekawa, were the originators of this book, as was their sister-in-law Te Paea Rua, who had died the year before. Te Paea's tangi at Matahi began as the book *Mihaia* was brought back for the first time to the people of the valley. We came to acquire a profound respect for these women, because it was from them we learnt the meaning of integrity and survival in ways of living which had been, to our eyes, harsh in the extreme. Akakura's story is written from the tape recordings we had made with her when talking about her father for our earlier book. The other texts are all transcribed from recordings made specifically for this book.

The conversations were deliberately unstructured. We asked only the basic questions: about each person's birth, schooling, and marriage. We asked who were important to them, and who brought them up. We asked about their own children and if they had tamariki whāngai. But we left the direction and the development of thought to each woman. We tried not to interrupt too often except to clarify who 'she' might be! ('Granny, she was a wild man!' said an elder to us once, referring to Te Kooti.) Each dialogue generated its own shape and its own life. The narratives present the views of the narrator. We have not expanded into areas where other views, or more information, could have been added. The narratives are the women's stories, the subjective reality of their lives. We have no wish to 'explain them away' by adding a more conventional historical context. However, with the exception of Te Akakura, we have given brief outlines before each narrative, touching on specific matters which may have been taken for granted in the stories.

In editing from the original transcripts we have deleted all our own comments and questions. We have also made cuts in the texts, but have made no insertions of substance which are not indicated. The few that have been made (most frequently to explain a gesture) are marked by square brackets. We have brought together material which was recorded on different occasions into one continuous narrative. In that sense, the texts are constructed, but we have always preserved the original phrasing and, we hope, rhythms of speech. As indicated above, we have sometimes interchanged pronouns and names for clarity's sake. On rare occasions, the tense of a verb has been altered to avoid confusion, but never so as to affect the frequent use of the continuous present, which native Maori speakers naturally adopt in English. The only other alteration has been to standardize the use of pronouns to conform to sex. In Maori English, 'he' and 'she' are quite often used interchangeably because 'ia' is undistinguished by gender in Maori. Many personal names are similarly not sexually identifiable.

The conversations were conducted in English. Consequently, all the women are speaking in their second language. Their fluency in English varies. We consider it, however, more appropriate to record their spoken words than to have translated them from Maori, thus imposing our own words upon them. We believe that the individuals are their most eloquent translators. The English of those who speak Maori as a first language is energetic, vivid, and often highly metaphorical. Undoubtedly some will argue that the conversations should have taken place in Maori, which would have produced different emphases and also differences of substance. That is true, but then we could never have participated, and this book would never have been written. We enjoyed the many, many hours spent with the kuia, talking, laughing, growing sad, recovering and changing moods together. It is because we valued the intensity and joy of the experience of sharing in knowledge and insights, and of learning vastly different ways of seeing and doing things, which we first discovered with Te Paea, Puti and Te Akakura, that we undertook the book. It was an exhausting experience, because we were, even if only to a limited extent, participating in others' lives. We travelled thousands of kilometres to do it. There were things we didn't understand and may still not have fully grasped. We also found ourselves having to adapt to rapidly changing social situations. Neither of us is very good at singing waiata, and one of us can't carry a tune at all. But the book is about the sharing of experiences and feelings and we discovered ourselves to be creating this volume because we wanted to — for aroha.

We have included the whakapapa of each woman, with her permission. Puti Onekawa verified the correctness of her sister's. The principle which we adopted here was to include those tīpuna and close kin who are mentioned in the narratives. All the children born to the narrator are also included. The individual portrait of each woman was taken in the place which seemed to be most appropriate. Heni Brown is portrayed before the old meeting-house Te Ngawari, named by Te Kooti, in which she lived for a time as a young married woman. Reremoana Koopu stands in her sunny garden at the home where she and her family have stayed since 1915. Maaka Jones is photographed at Whitianga, her family marae and one of the strong centres of the Ringatu faith. We photographed Hei Ariki Algie in her living-room in her own home, with her sister Lena, because that was what she wanted. We returned with Heni Sunderland to Muriwai, the community by the lagoon where she grew up with her grandparents. Miria Rua was photographed at Te Ao Hou, Rua's family marae, which she and her husband still help to care for. Puti Onekawa walks along the road up the Tauranga valley as she has done a thousand times in her life. Each photograph, we hope, conveys something of the spirit of the woman whom we grew to know and love. This is our koha to them.

There are many other people to be thanked. Not least are Dave and June White of Paerata Ridge, who for many years have looked after us as we have come and gone at odd hours of day and night. Don and Margaret Sinclair of Gisborne also provided us with sustenance and much good company, while Lionel and Daphne Chaplin were always there on the wayside. We would particularly like to thank Denise Hakaraia, without whom the book would never have been completed. She knows the reason why. There are all those with whom we have talked over the years and from whom we have learnt so much. Some are no longer alive. If our conversations have ended, our thoughts about them continue: Ned Brown, Frank Davis, Te Huinga (Jack) Karauna, Harimate (Materoa) Roberts, Heta and Te Paea Rua, Horo Tatu, and Te Puhi Tatu in particular have played important parts in this book. We would also like to thank James Belich, Robert (Boy) Biddle, George Brown, Monita Delamere, Gil Hanly, Charlotte Hitaua, Iwi and Heurea (Tom) Hitaua, Witi Ihimaera, Catherine Ingram, Jane McRae, Joe Te Maipi, Hirini Melbourne, Joan Metge, Rangi Motu, Margaret Orbell, Margaret Rapana, Anne Salmond, Michael Shirres OP, Jeff Sissons, Meri Taka, Ans Westra, and Haare Williams. Each in different ways has given us help, support, and advice. Let us not forget the husbands of Puti and Miria who were there patiently in the wings: Mac Onekawa and Mau Rua. We would also particularly like to thank both the whānau of Maaka Jones for making us so welcome at their family wānanga at Whitianga and the four children of Reremoana Koopu — Toma, Taka, Iri, and Arama — who looked after us in their family home on the cliffs of Maraenui with such grace and care. We would also like to remember Tina Brown and Rutene and Tiwai Irwin of Mangatu, Elizabeth Moeau of Gisborne, and Teruaraima (Kui) Emmerson of Muriwai for their help and kindness.

Sheila Robinson of the Gisborne Museum, Anton van der Wouden of the Whakatane Museum, Roger Neich, formerly of the National Museum and now at the Auckland Museum, John Sullivan of the Alexander Turnbull Library's photographic collection, Gordon Maitland, the Auckland Museum's photographic archivist, and Heather Simpson of the Registrar General's Office, Lower Hutt, have all given much assistance. Wiremu Parker, now retired from Maori Studies at Victoria University, and Merimeri Penfold, who is also Ahorangi from Maori Studies at Auckland University, have given invaluable advice on the Maori texts and translations, and we are greatly indebted to them. Professor S. Musgrove attacked the prose of his daughter with his usual skill. Freda Christie helped with transcriptions of some of the tapes, while Caroline Phillips drew the maps for us. Rosalba Finnerty compiled the index. Anne French gave us useful editorial advice and support. Research grants from the University of Auckland covered a part of our equipment, travel, and photographic expenses, while other costs we bore ourselves. The royalties we will share with the Maori Women's Welfare League. The Lotteries Fund Board also gave us a grant which enabled us to make archival duplicates of original tape recordings. These will be preserved in the Maori and Pacific oral archives of the Anthropology Department at the University of Auckland. The John David Stout Research Fellowship gave Judith Binney the chance to turn the tape recordings into this written text, while Ruth Harley and Michael Volkerling put up with her while she lived in Wellington. Gillian Chaplin is indebted to the Auckland Museum and the Auckland City Art Gallery who gave her the time for this project.

We were both present at all the conversations. These, in turn, engendered endless conversations between us — on the road, and afterwards in Auckland — as we attempted to understand the world into which we had stepped and find the ways to describe it. This work is the distillation of all these different conversations: it was truly jointly created. Judith Binney edited the transcripts and wrote the introductions, while Gillian Chaplin took new photographs and brought old ones to life.

Judith Binney & Gillian Chaplin
Auckland, January 1986

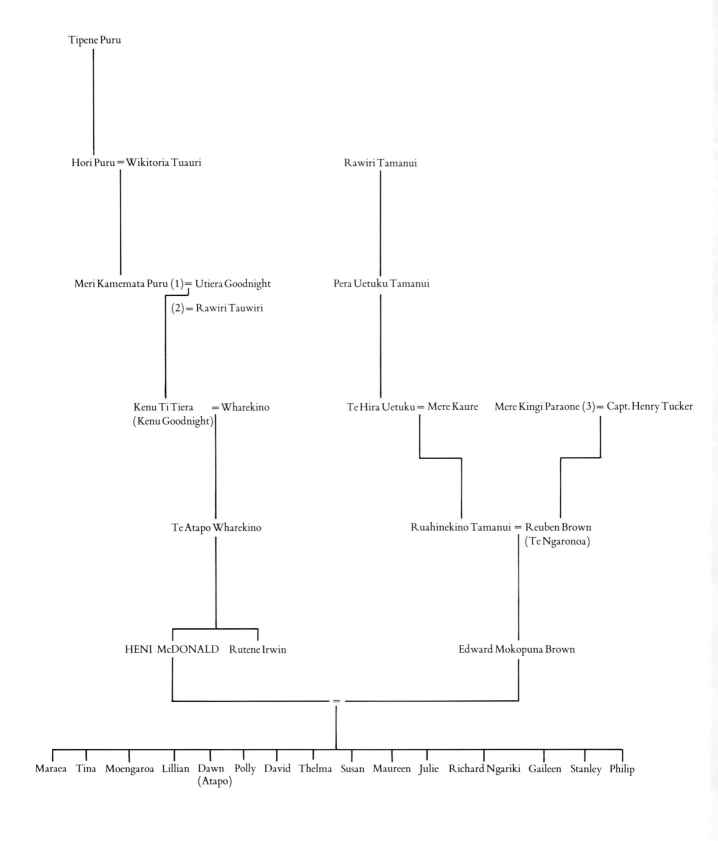

Tipene Puru

Hori Puru = Wikitoria Tuauri

Rawiri Tamanui

Meri Kamemata Puru (1) = Utiera Goodnight

(2) = Rawiri Tauwiri

Pera Uetuku Tamanui

Kenu Ti Tiera = Wharekino
(Kenu Goodnight)

Te Hira Uetuku = Mere Kaure

Mere Kingi Paraone (3) = Capt. Henry Tucker

Te Atapo Wharekino

Ruahinekino Tamanui = Reuben Brown
(Te Ngaronoa)

HENI McDONALD   Rutene Irwin

Edward Mokopuna Brown

=

Maraea   Tina   Moengaroa   Lillian   Dawn   Polly   David   Thelma   Susan   Maureen   Julie   Richard   Ngariki   Gaileen   Stanley   Philip
(Atapo)

HENI BROWN

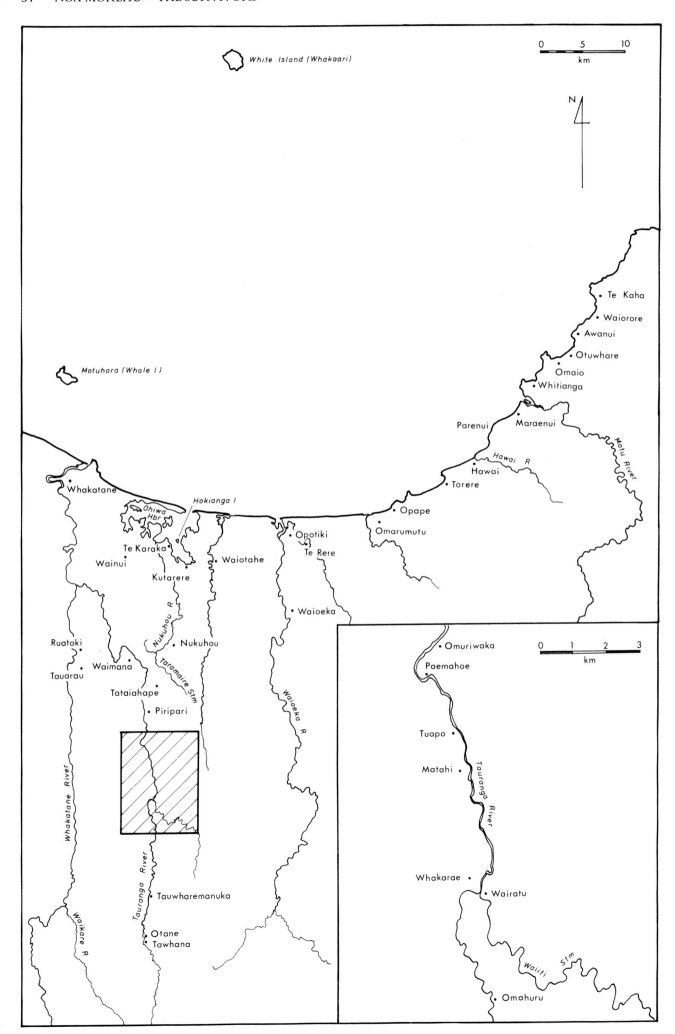

*W*e met Heni Brown as we met all the women in this book: we were told that we should go and see her. We first came to Whatatutu, where Ned and Heni Brown were living, on 14 February 1982. From the moment we entered their home they showed the warmth and generosity which became our well-spring. We talked with Heni about her own life also on three subsequent occasions: 27 and 30 November 1983 and 3 January 1985. Her narrative is from these four conversations.

Heni Brown was brought up at Torere, a small Ngaitai community in the eastern Bay of Plenty. Its leader in the time of the conflicts with Te Kooti had been Wiremu Kingi Tutahuarangi, who was an Anglican and hostile to the Ringatu teachings. He remained a strong government supporter until his death in 1888. But some of the people in the settlement were Te Aitanga a Mahaki followers of Te Kooti's from Poverty Bay, and others living there adopted his religious teachings, which spread rapidly in the Bay of Plenty during the later 1870s. In 1887, when Te Kooti came to the eastern Bay of Plenty to celebrate the First of July (described in Maaka's story) he composed a waiata especially for Wiremu Kingi, who had written to the government warning them of the forthcoming hui. He called him the croaking 'shag' of Torere — 'Te Kawau', the bird that calls for itself alone, 'Ko au'!*He reminded him that the journey he was making was 'in lasting peace' — 'te haere nei he maungarongo'. He asked dryly, 'Perhaps you have not heard of the power of the Queen', referring now to his own pardon.[1]

Torere itself was an isolated community until the present road from Opotiki was constructed in the 1920s. In the 1936 census, which for the first time included the Maori population of the particular communities, there were 273 people living at Torere, of whom 246 were Maori. Ten years before, the European population had been only fourteen. The community subsisted largely on maize and small dairy herds, the cream being taken out by bullock-dray to Opape. It was in this small settlement that Heni was born in 1919 — on her own testimony, for her birth was not registered. She started at Torere Native School in 1928 and continued there until the end of 1934. The school itself was unsure of her age, and in estimating her birth date wavered between 1919 and 1921. After leaving school, she was taken to Mangatu, the inland settlement of the people of Ngariki, in about 1937 or 1938 to marry her husband, chosen for her by her great-grandmother. Ned's first wife (whom he had married in 1936) was from Omarumutu, a nearby settlement to Torere and, as Heni indicates, there was a long history of land dispute between Ngariki and the Bay of Plenty tribes which lay behind these marriages of reconciliation. Ned and Heni were formally married, to conform with European law, after the birth of their eldest daughter Maraea, in the Registry Office in Gisborne on 22 February 1940.

Heni Brown's married life centred around the people of Mangatu. At first, she considered them to be different from herself. She contrasted them with her people at Torere, where everyone used to bring their baskets of cockles, or bread, or a chicken, to share — 'and they all cook it — the whole lot of them. We believed in sharing . . . and that's how I was brought up. When I come to Mangatu I start sharing out to everybody, and they won't share it to me! . . . I think Ned's people over here are too rich, because we are poor Hōris over there. They are different over here.' Heni may have been expressing her feelings of being an outsider at first, but she certainly became part of the community. She was an instigator of the many complex practical jokes which the young married women played upon their men — and as Ned played upon her, in his turn. On one occasion, his black horse was painted to look piebald so that he failed to recognize it; on another, when the men were all drunk,

*It is I

Fig. III: Bay of Plenty and the East Coast.

page 33 Heni Brown at Mangatu, November 1983. Photograph by Gillian Chaplin.

their wives tied their penises to their toes, so that when they sobered and tried to sit up — 'Well, I had to cut the string quick!'

The Maori community of Mangatu lived near the township of Whatatutu. In the 1930s the marae with its cluster of houses was beside the Mangatu river, about three kilometres away. Constant flooding, however, had already forced the abandonment of the old meeting-house, Te Ngawari, in which Ned and Heni first lived when they were married. It still stands today, lonely and derelict in the swamps, the mud packed half-way to its eaves. The later meeting-house Te Ngawari has also recently had to be shifted up to Whatatutu, because of recurrent flooding. Ned, who was a Ringatu tohunga, believed these problems had all been foreseen by Te Kooti: they arose because the land had been alienated from Ned's people, Ngariki Kaiputahi, the original owners, and taken over by the 'conquering' Te Aitanga a Mahaki.

Such a predictive view of history runs through all the accounts given to us. For Ned, the land had been passed 'under tapu'. As he said, 'Ka hoatungia e ngā tīpuna, e ngā pakeke, he tapu ki runga i tēnei whenua.' ('The ancestors, the old ones, put a tapu on this land to retain it.')[2] The guardian mauri whenua for the people of Mangatu is a diamond, believed to have been given to Ned's ancestor, Te Hira Uetuku, by Te Kooti. It is hidden on their sacred mountain, Maungahaumia. But Te Kooti also predicted: 'E kite ake ana au i tō koutou whenua e tere ana e tere ana ki te moana, aa, [e] kore rawa e pupuri.' ('I see your land drifting, drifting to the sea. And you will not be able to retain it.')[3] The history of the Mangatu land, as Heni's account indicates, has been, from their perspective, a history of different alienations. Her struggle has been to reclaim the land for Ned's people.

In 1936, Whatatutu and its environs had a Maori population of about 200, and there were about 340 Pakeha, many of whom were farming. The Mangatu lands had been managed by the East Coast Commissioner since 1917 and, run by leasehold, they were extensively in debt. But by 1947, when the sheep stations were returned to their Maori owners in an Incorporation, they were becoming profitable. Although Whatatutu, in 1936, was a predominantly European township, Pakeha do not play a significant part in Heni's story. Indeed, Mangatu is a community that has retained a very strong Maori cultural identity. Unlike most of the other women in this book, Heni did not mention any particularly important relationship with a Pakeha individual, be it a schoolteacher or a missionary. Her father was a Pakeha, but he had little influence in her life. It is perhaps also significant that by 1971, the last year in which the census recorded the Maori and European populations of the country's communities, Whatatutu, where Ned and Heni finally came to live, had become a largely Maori township: of its 272 people, 203 were Maori.

Heni Brown takes her Ringatu identity from her great-grandmother, Meri Puru, who dominates Heni's account of her own life. Unfortunately, we have been unable to find a photograph of Meri Puru. She and her father, Hori, were prisoners on the Chatham Islands with Te Kooti and escaped with him in 1868. As the oldest in her family, Heni is caught in a common dilemma for many Maori women — rank is determined by birth, but in matters of political leadership women may be overruled by men. Mana tāngata, authority over people, descends to the senior male in most families and in most hapū. But mana whenua, trusteeship of the land, may abide with women, and Heni talks about her understanding of this role. It would appear from her account that she spoke for her half-brothers and sisters because of her seniority of birth, though it is doubtful whether she would have had the power to exclude them from her mother's land had she tried. The point of the account she gives is, however, to stress her love for them and her wish to ensure that they were all included in the land.

For both Ned and Heni, the Ringatu view that events and time are cyclic gives the *assurance of an ultimate fulfilment of the divine promises, spoken to the people by Te Kooti. Those who came after him, the matakite or clairvoyants, are also believed to possess, at least for a time, predictive powers derived from Te Kooti. Ned and Heni have consulted them at various times, as have most of the women. Ned also talked of the 'Apostle Matiu', Matiu Paeroa, who was a Ngati Porou elder, and one of Te Kooti's three secretaries. From 1885, Matiu began to collect systematically the prayers and predictive words, te kupu whakaari, of Te Kooti. Ned specifically attributed Sir Apirana Ngata's political powers and skills to the gift of Matiu. Thus leadership is seen as being transferred as a gift, the fount of which is Te Kooti, prophet of God.*

The dialogues we had with Ned and Heni took place in their home at Whatatutu and down at the pā at Mangatu. On the last occasion when we talked with Ned, in November 1983, he took us to see the small whare kape, the tapu house where the Ringatu prayer-books and texts used to be kept, behind the old Ngawari. He talked of the way the tohunga used to be initiated in the Mangatu river and became gifted with unknown powers. And he described again the predictions from Te Kooti for the Mangatu land.

Ned died on 7 July 1984. He had foreseen his own death. As Heni put it: 'He knew. He told me. "Mamma, I've only got a few months to live." "How do you know?" "It's prophesied." The night before he died he had a pray in his room. I could hear him. Thunder and lightning that night. I knew he was praying in earnest. Then all of a sudden he came out to me. He said to me, "Kāre roa" — that means, won't be long now. I said, "What for?" "I'm going away, a long way." "How do you know?" "I saw him standing in my doorway." "Who?" "The man in white with blue, blue eyes." I knew who he was talking about. The Karaiti — Christ. "Are you sure Ned Brown?" "Yea, he's coming to get me today." ' Ned died the following morning, felling a tree. The manner of his death ('by a sharp blade') had been predicted to him by 'te wairua', the spirit who had appeared to him in an earlier vision, in February 1984. 'It was meant to be. It was predicted', as Heni said. And when we called to see Heni, after he had died, a small shower of rain fell while we were there. Heni told us, 'That's what the Maoris call "he aroha". It's a good sign. Ned must be saying, "Oh, there's Judith and Gillian, come at last." Anā ko marangai! You see, it won't be long! That's aroha. Spiritually, eh? Anā ko marangai!'†

I had better start from the beginning. I was born on 13 November 1919 at a place called Torere and I was brought up by my great-grandmother, from babyhood to womanhood. She was a staunch believer in Te Kooti. When she was a young woman, they transported her with all the other Maoris around Gisborne to the Chatham Islands — to Wharekauri. Whakarau they call them. My great-grandmother, Meri Puru, was one of the whakaraus — the captives. She was in that massacre at Waerenga a Hika. She saw her own grandfather get shot, and she never forgot it. I remember her saying to me when I was a girl, they were driven on the buggies to Poverty Bay, all the Ringatus in those days. Oh, it was sad. They were taken to the wharf, and Captain Porter was with the soldiers, the red coats she calls them: 'ngā hōia koti wherowhero — koti toto' — eh?‡ And she called, 'Captain, captain!' 'Hurry up, hurry up! Go on the boat. Go on the boat!' And Te

---

†There's the rain!

‡the soldiers with the red coats - bloody coats - eh?

Kooti called out to that fellow, Porter, 'When I come back I will slay you!' Which he did when he did come back.[4]

She came back with Te Kooti, from Wharekauri, and was with him too, for a little while, at Te Kuiti. Then when her first husband died she went back to Torere. She brought us all up; four generations she brought up.

She was a mākutu old lady, and I didn't realize it until I grew up and they told me that my great-grandmother had some mana. Some power. She could destroy, you know — some kind of prayer that she uses and it reacts on to that person. But I didn't know until when she was dying and she told my granduncle to bury her upside down — her body — put her body like that in the coffin. And her hair — pango mōtō, *black* hair — it was right down to her legs. They covered her back. They made it like that — across. They had to cross it on her back. They had to get her hair like that. All her korowais and everything went with her. They had to be buried. I wasn't allowed to touch any of her belongings. It is to do with the mana she had. So her spirit, her power, her evil, or something, won't come back. It will stop it from coming to destroy the living. Hori Gage[5] was the one who told me, because he knew I was the mokopuna. He didn't want to hurt me, and he said it in a nice way: 'Heni, I had to do that.' 'WHY?' 'It goes back into the earth. If I didn't, her mana, her power, will come back.'[6]

That power was given to her by Te Kooti. He bestowed it upon her. According to her, it was when she was a young lady of thirteen or fourteen, during the war at Waerenga a Hika. Because she was in there, with her mother. And Te Kooti gave her all those powers; she could use the mana for good or for evil. She always used to say if Te Kooti was alive, he would have done a lot of miraculous — or whatever you call it, mana, eh? — to help the people, the *Maori* people I mean.

Maori prisoners at Napier, crowded on the stony beach just below the prison-house and barracks, waiting to embark for the Chatham Islands. This photograph is said to be of the group, which included Te Kooti, that was sent in June 1866. Photograph probably by Charles Robson.
Alexander Turnbull Library

How she got to know Te Kooti was her aunty, Heni Kumekume. She was Te Kooti's second wife. She's from Whakatohea. My *real* name is Heni Kumekume; I was named after her. We were brought up over there, at Torere, but we belonged to a different tribe. My great-grandmother stopped me playing with other Maori children. It was a feud; the Pakeha call it a feud, but she told me that it was because the ancestors of those people murdered our ancestors. She told me the history, hundreds of years ago.[7] Maybe it is an interest to her, but it wasn't an interest to me because I was only a child. But I grew up like that. Of course, we were immigrants. She had come back from Mangatu to Torere, and in those days we were so very poor. We used to live in a kāuta – the same as I did when I got married! In Torere, we had a kāuta, and all the rich Maoris surrounding, they were there before we did. And these people, they never come near us, because we belong to a different tribe. You know how young girls, they like to go and play marbles with other children — I wasn't allowed. Because *your* father was not connected to *my* family, I wasn't allowed to play with you. I was forbidden. Me and my brothers and sisters. When we go to school, she makes sure that we go to school in silence, we're not allowed to talk to other children. A strange boy came there, he was from Ngapuhi, and I wasn't allowed to talk to that boy because he belonged to a different tribe. Then somebody told on me, told my grandmother and she locked me up for a whole week. And the teacher used to say to me, 'What's wrong with you, Heni?' 'Nothing.' 'Why don't you go porohiana, outside?' 'No, it's all right. I'll study in school', and all I do just read, read, read, that's all. And then go home. Pick up my few books and go straight home. I was like a prisoner — however you say it in English — but that was my life. I was not allowed to go to dances, I wasn't allowed to go visiting anybody, because they don't belong to my people.

As I told you, we were living in a mud-floor house. I know what it is like to have no money, because that is how I was brought up. I remember my great-grandfather, Rawiri Tauwiri, he used to travel for miles to go and work — just to keep us alive. Ten shillings a week — it was a big money in those days. He went fencing and shearing for these Pakeha farmers around the area. But we never starved. My great-grandmother, Meri, she used to go and dive for mussels and whatever, and fishing at night time — kahawais. My uncle had a boat and he would bring us some fish. When he had a boat full up, he'll ring the bell and everybody knows, oh, he's got the fish! They all go there and they help themselves. We had

Heni Kumekume, wife of Te Kooti, after whom Heni Brown was named. Heni Kumekume escaped with Te Kooti into the King Country in 1872 and remained with him. A drawing of her was made by J. Kerry-Nicholls when Te Kooti came to a hui held at Mangaorongo in 1883. She was also with Te Kooti in 1889 when he attempted to return to Poverty Bay. This photograph was taken by S. Carnell of Napier and it probably dates either from Heni Kumekume's own visit to Gisborne in February 1883, or more likely from Te Kooti's visit to Porangahau and Napier in December 1886-January 1887. *Alexander Turnbull Library*

Torere marae, with the fish drying on the fence for a hui early in 1935. This was the year after Heni left school. Photograph by Moore and Thompson. *Auckland Weekly News, 8 May 1935*

The portrait of Heni's mother, Atapo
– Dawn – Wharekino, which hangs
in the meeting-house Te Ngawari at
Mangatu. Photographed, by
permission of Tiwai Irwin, by Gillian
Chaplin, 1984.

cows, we had pigs, we had everything — but no money! Not a penny. The only
money we get is just what Grandad brings home. We had acres and acres of
kūmaras and spuds; we used to sell it to the Pakehas in Opotiki, just to get some
money for a bag of flour. Did you know I used to wear flour-bag bloomers? My
mother, she was clever that way, she used to dye a hundred bag of flour. They wash
it in caustic sodas — and white as anything. She used to dye them, pink, blue, yellow
and then she used to make my petticoats and put laces at the bottom, and my
bloomers, and sometimes she forgets. Remember those Snowball flour bags? She
forgot one day, but being a young girl I just put them on, and I was swinging away
on the swing, and I could hear these boys, 'Snowball! Snowball!' Oh, I howled, I
howled! I never went to school for a whole week!

Well, that's the hardships we had in those days. One pair of shoes for twelve
months! One day my great-grandfather went to work for some European people
in Opotiki, the Webbs. First thing he bought me was a pair of white boots. Oh,
you know, buckled up. Well, I got to hide those boots from the other Maori kids;
they might steal my boots! After school I used to put them on and these kids used
to say to me, 'Do you think you look neat?' And I'd say, 'Of course I do! I look
flashy!' I only wear them on special occasions. And my one and only dress, hide it
away, because we used to wear dungarees, you know, boys' clothes, all the time.

I loved those years; but I had a very, very hard life. My mother never lived with us. She was a wanderer — a gypsy — all over the place. She never lived with our great-grandmother, because our great-grandmother pushed her out! She was against my mother for marrying European husbands. But when she has these babies she doesn't know where to go; she brings them back to my great-grandmother. My mother left me as a baby; I hardly saw her until I was seventeen. That's how we were brought up. Meri Puru brought us all up, nine of us, from different fathers. Well, I'm the eldest and I've had seven Pakeha fathers! But our great-grandmother, she loved us and she brought us all up. And the love is still there. My mother's blood is in those Pakeha kids, and I couldn't hate them. Why I am telling you this, I experienced it myself, when she died.[8] You know how the judge calls you up: 'Come on Heni, you're the only one I can see should be entitled to everything, because you're the Maori one.' 'That's all right. They're still my brothers and sisters. Anyhow, we are not fighting for our fathers' rights; we are fighting for our mother's rights.' He looked at me twice. In the eyes of the law, the Maori Land Court, I should get everything, because it is my great-grandmother's land. I said, 'It makes no difference. They're still my brothers and sisters. I don't want you to separate us. As I told you, she brought us all up.' He looked at me hard. He says, 'Oh, the old kuia brought these up?' 'Yes!' I didn't want to disown them. So I put them all in Mangatu. He said to me, 'You are only one in a hundred, Mrs Brown.' I said, 'Oh well, we were all brought up together. One family. Maybe our mother was a philandress, or what you call it! Doesn't matter. That's *her* life, eh?'

... As I told you, I was brought up in the tapu, real sacredness. My great-grandmother was a kuia tapu. Te Kooti made her like that. When we have our kai, she doesn't have kai like us — she only has a little bit, just a cupful outside by herself. She was very sacred — to herself. But she can cook! Anything for us! But for her to eat like us, No! She has her own rautao. Because she was with Te Kooti all her life. You see her daughter? That's the only child was given to her. I said to her, 'Why didn't you get more kids?' She said, 'No. Nā Te Kooti i here taku wharetamariki.'* Wharetamariki — that means her womb. The baby was Kenu. She had it in the whata, you know, those houses of theirs on the ground. They put the whāriki, mat, down and then they have a church. She never had pains like I did, she said. When her baby came, when it was born, Te Kooti got hold of her wharetamariki [placenta] and he put it in a cloak, he kākahu, and they hung it up over the fireplace. Ana. Whakamaroke. The smoke, underneath, dried it up.[9] Then they took it and buried it. And he said to her, 'Kāhi koe e whai uri',† that means she will never bear another child, but from this child you will have generation after generation. It will multiply. It's true today! That's the prophecy Te Kooti told my great-grandmother. From her, it's my mother and me, and then my big family. It was the offering, ka hereia. But she always said to me, 'Engari koe, taku mokopuna. Ka nui te tamariki ki a koe',‡ and she was right. I am the one with a lot of children. It was a prophecy — ngā poropiti, nē?

I am sixty-four now,[10] and I have seen a lot of miraculous things happening in my lifetime. As I have told you, the Maoris have got some powers, some good powers, I suppose, mana pai ora tōu. I used to go visiting Hori Gage; he was a marvellous old man, and I have seen a lot of miracles happening in his Rā. This

Kenu Goodnight, the only child of Meri Puru. From Te Ngawari, Mangatu. Photographed, by permission of Tiwai Irwin, by Gillian Chaplin, 1984.

*Te Kooti bound my womb.
†You will never bear another child
‡But you, my grandchild. You will have many children

little boy couldn't walk, he had been on crutches all his life. I see the mother carrying this boy into the meeting-house; I don't know what is happening. They have a church going, everything going. Ha! About half an hour later, I see the same mother with the little boy, he was walking! Out to the car. How did that happen? I was thinking Hori Gage must have some powers unknown to us. Then my little baby was very sick. I took him to Hori Gage. And I said to him, 'Oh, Poppa. Tāku pēpi. She's going to die.' 'Oh, kai te pai. Kai te pai.'* So he took her in the room; I don't know what he did to her. And he said to me, three days of grace, for me. Not to swear. I told him I won't. There was something wrong with Julie;[11] she couldn't eat, she couldn't sleep – choking, eh? That was the baby he cured. If I had taken her to the hospital, she would have died. What you people call it, quinsy?[12] We call it puku. But the Pakeha, the doctor, said they call it quinsy; it blocks over here [in the throat], so you can't breathe. Now I have seen a Maori lady with the same baby: can't breathe, the baby's face gets listless, and this Maori lady turns around to get olive oil on her hands, and she presses it underneath, stroking its throat [downwards], four times, and then gives the baby a dose of castor oil, and the baby is well again. She presses it. It breaks. The phlegm. It goes into the puku,[13] and that castor oil brings it out. The baby is running around again. That's puku. That's how you cure it.

I'll tell you an experience of myself. Because I couldn't get another son – I had one son, David – Ned and I went to Hori Gage. And he said to Ned, 'I only want your wife.' He took me in this room, and laid me down, and all these ladies were rubbing my puku with olive oil, and they were chanting, the Maori way of chanting. I couldn't understand what they were saying. Then he said to me, 'Ka hapū koe. To pēpi he tāne.'† That means I'll get pregnant, and my baby will be a son. But I'm not allowed to swear, I'm not allowed to argue or anything. I said, 'Why?' He said, 'Because the baby that I am praying to God is going to be at your puku, it's going to be a boy.' That's my son I lost. His name was Ngariki. I was warned not to swear. But I did! I lost my son, my second son, because I swore. I didn't mean to, but the doctor was telling me, 'Go on Janie. Push!' I said, 'I can't!' 'Yes you can!' He went like this, bang, to my bum! And I just call out, 'Out you bastard. Christ is born!' That's what I did say, God is my witness. And the baby came out; it was a beautiful baby. Richard Ngariki. He's buried up there.[14] So you see, these Maori things to me are real. If you disobey what they tell you, it happens.

Ned and I, we go to clairvoyants, matakite. Ned goes to Hori Gage; and he goes to Kapi Adams.[15] What they prophesied for my husband and I, it is true today. I've seen it happen in my own time, in my own life. It's never failed, the whakamana. It seemed to come to light. See, he's fighting for his land now, through the predictions from clairvoyance people, way back in 1944. That's the greatest clairvoyance I've ever known: Hone Koopu, from the Coast. He derives from another section [of the Ringatu]. He came [to Mangatu] in 1944. And he prophesies Ned's life. He said, 'I feel sorry for this child crying for its mountain' – Maungahaumia. So he came for the following Twelfth, and they had a three-day service here, and they prayed for the three days for Mangatu. And he predicted that the land will come under the Incorporation, but to come back to its *original* owners, it will be a matter of time: 'Mā te wā, nē?'‡[16] But it's been prophesied.

Hori Te Kouarehua Keeti (George Gage), April 1956. Reproduced by permission of Katerina Maxwell, Opotiki.

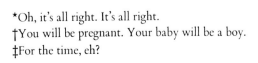

*Oh, it's all right. It's all right.

†You will be pregnant. Your baby will be a boy.

‡For the time, eh?

Ned: His powers come from the Apostle Matiu [Paeroa]. Matiu was the same disciple of Te Kooti who gave his powers to Sir A. T. Ngata. Matiu's powers are from Te Kooti. These powers we are talking about, the Ringatu know of them — all predicted by Te Kooti years ago!

Heni: Well, I believe the Lord is guiding our lives, Ned and I. 'Cause this land business was done in the church, three days of grace, and I believe the Lord will bring this land back in his time. Not in our time. No. In the Lord's time. It is revolving every year. People seem to be coming closer to us, people are responding.

See, when I am travelling on my car, when I get up in the morning I always ask him to guide me safely. I drive by myself on my car, and the day I leave here and the day I get to where I am going — my destination — nothing happens. He seems to open the way up for me. Hardly any cars on the road, and I am there. As soon as I get there, my daughter is calling out, 'I knew you were coming, Mum!' 'Why? How?' Oh, the rainbow was standing outside the house, and my little girl was saying, 'Nanny coming, Nanny coming!' And I am there! That's my life. That's how it is; my spirit seems to go ahead to my mokopunas. See, if him and I leave now, the mokopunas in Havelock North know; they tell their mother, 'Papa and Nanny coming!' 'Where?' 'On the truck.' As soon as we come round the corner, there they are. 'Cause that rainbow — te kōpere. That prophecy was given to Ned eight years ago[17] by Kapi Adams. No matter where we go, that rainbow go ahead of us. That is his guardian, that rainbow — tana kaitiaki. It was bestowed on him by Hone Koopu, the first matakite, and Hori Gage, and Kapi Adams last. The rainbow, that's a sign from Te Kooti. I'm only talking of my experience. And when I saw the rainbow, this morning, just standing over there — oh, it must be a visitor! And it was you! For a Ringatu, always, the rainbow, that's a sign. Always.

Ned: At Wainui, where Matiu deciphered the teachings, the prayers, the hymns and the psalms, every time he went into this special office, the rainbow always stood above it till the time he finish. The time he enters in to study and the time he comes out, the rainbow is always there: te kōpere.

Heni: It was very strict in our time. When I was a girl, I was only fifteen, but we used to go to the Tekaumaruas, right round the Bay of Plenty — Opape, Te Rere, Waioeka, Waimana — and Wainui. In those days we used to go along the beach, the Opape beach — we used to go by buggy. The old buggy days! At Wainui, Wi Raepuku was our tohunga. At Torere we used to go every Twelfth, and every First of July, and every Fifth of an August.[18] That was our main praying days, three days. We used to go to the Tekaumaruas at Opape, that's the other marae in Opotiki. And three days in grace. No washing clothes, no shoes allowed in the meeting-house. So strict that the mothers were forbidden to go outside to wash clothes. It was sacred. But we managed somehow. Everybody sit in the meeting-house, only the tohungas allowed to stand up and speak, no woman is allowed [to speak]. We had to sit quiet — there's always a tohunga at the door, and the bell rings, and then away they go! They take over, the men. The women just stand up and sing. No kids allowed to cry. It was a very holy thing, when I was a little girl. We were taught before we go to those Ringatu churches, and we respect it. We don't play around like other kids. No. Our great-grandmother, we just sit beside her and she talks to us; when the bell rings we all have a church. We just got used to it. But now it's different. In those days, no, they kept it to themselves. I remember my great-grandmother, if she has a karakia in the house, and somebody comes over there, she tells us to go to the door, don't let that person in. Only herself and us. When she's finished — ah, well, that's different! In the dark, she can sing all those karakia, no trouble! She stands up in the dark, away she goes!

An incident happened down the pā. Our great-grandfather was out shearing. Raining! Thunder! Lightning! And the meeting-house door flung open and she called out to us kids not to say anything. She stood up and she started in Hepi — she was praying in Hebrew. About half an hour later she called out to us, to one of my brothers, Rutene,[19] go outside and open the door, you will see the rain stop and the storm stop. My brother looked at her and he looked at us kids and he opened the door. Not a drop of rain! You see, there's the power. I don't know what it is, but maybe it is the power of her prayer. The Ringatu faith is so — to me, they were nearer to God in that way.

Te Kooti was given that gift, they say, by God. I don't know. All I know, Granny said the power was given to Te Kooti to guide his people and to look after them. She was in that massacre at Waerenga a Hika and although she was old she still had that memory. And that's why she wouldn't let me marry a European. That's why she brought me all the way from Torere to marry my husband. When I was at the age of fifteen she brought me to marry him. I was what us Maoris call he puhi; wahine tono, given wife, I suppose. She said she doesn't want me to marry any other man but the man she chose for me. I used to say to her, 'WHY? It is a free country. Everybody else gets married!' But she said to me if it wasn't for her I would have been dead, and she's right. Now, I had to respect my great-grandmother because she taught me a lot of things that other young girls today wouldn't believe. And she guarded me all the way. When men come over to our place to ask for my hand, she always said 'No!' She forbid all other men that come to ask for me when I was a girl of fifteen. She had only one mind — this man, Ned, over here. He's a different tribe; he is a Ngariki Kaiputahi — that means a tribe that consecrates themselves as one people. And they are like that! They are the originals from over here. And Meri's father, Hori Puru, was the first Ringatu at Mangatu; he was one of the whakarau.[20] But you see, another family, the Wi Pere family, got the land. They took it to the Court [in 1881], to deprive Ngariki of the land. The whole Mangatu block. *My* ancestors got into that land by Wi Pere. But the land originally belonged to my husband's tribe. It should go back to the originals. And then it is up to them to put us in, through aroha. It is not up to *those* ancestors.[21] But that's why she brought me over here to marry him. She brought me in a buggy as far as Opotiki, and on the cream-truck to Matawai, from Matawai right here. That's how I was brought to marry Ned.

I didn't know him; he didn't know me! Funny thing, when we came to meet one another, I said to my great-grandmother, 'Who is that man sitting over there?' And she said, 'Turituri tō waha!' For me to shut up! 'Turituri tō waha, Heni!'* He didn't want me, and I didn't like him either! Then she said we are not allowed to sleep with one another until she blessed us in the water. But he understood; that's the marvellous thing about him, he seemed to understand what she is saying, and then he used to say hello to me, and I said hello to him, but there was nothing in between! Then she took us down to the Mangatu river. What the Maoris call whakahono, whakahono i a koutou,† that means to unite my husband and I in the eyes of God. She blessed us in Maori, our karakia. Karakia ai ki a Te Atua,‡ for him and I never to be separated. No matter what we do in our lifetime. I remember

Hori Puru, who was captured at the siege of Waerenga a Hika and sent to the Chatham Islands in 1866. He became the first Ringatu tohunga at Mangatu. From Te Ngawari. Photographed, by permission of Tiwai Irwin, by Gillian Chaplin, 1984.

Ned Brown on the occasion of his marriage to Heni in 1940. Photographed, by permission of Heni Brown, by Gillian Chaplin, 1983.

*Hush your mouth, Heni!
†to join you both
‡Pray to God

my great-grandmother saying, 'Kāre koe e whakarerea mokopuna',* that means you will never leave your husband, no matter how bad he is or how good he is. Well, I've been with him forty-five years![22] Whakapiri, what the Maoris call whakapiri, to unite our spirits together. We blend into one. No matter what he does, or what I do, the Lord is always there to hold us. God will always knit us in spirit, and that was her prayer to God.

We are in the water, we both stand there, and we put our heads in the water; we come out and we cross our hands. 'Ko kua whakapiri māua',† none of us will part until the day we die. And that's mana. She was praying with the other tohunga, Ringatus; there was chanting, those waiatas: they were singing all those hymns. Ned and I just stood there; we didn't know what was going on. And then all of a sudden, the rainbow stood on the other side of the Mangatu river, and she blessed us then. She said our marriage will last a very long time. And it has.

But when she finished she said to us I had to stay away from my husband for three days. I am not allowed to sleep with my husband until she says so. E toru ngā rā, eh: three days of grace. So that thing will work. I stayed with her in the meeting-house for the three days in grace; all she did was just pray, just pray. And he went away to work. When he came back, she said, 'Now you can touch my mokopuna.' He wasn't allowed to touch me before then. That's how I was, you call it a virgin. After the third day then she said to him, 'Now, you have her.' But he never rushed, you know what I mean, he was not a man to — he was real gentle; he understood what she was saying, I think.

But we never got legally married until I had two children. At that time, social security was so important, that we had to get legally married![23] But we lived as man and wife for three or four years before. Then she told me she going to marry me in the Pakeha way, legal!

Oh, we have our fights and all that. We have had terrible arguments! But every time I run away from him, aha, next day I'm back again! I leave him; I come back again! Been like that for years! *She* said to me, no matter how much I run away, I'll always come home. And I have. It was that binding, spiritually — i te taha wairua.‡ I do — I do run away — and I come back home to Ned Brown! Never once in his lifetime, he's left me! *I* take off. But he says to me, 'You'll be back!' And I have, ever since! Never once has he raised his voice, or raised his fists. It's me that does the strain. He is too — how you Pakehas put it? — too honest, too sincere. But not me. I should get a lot of hidings, but no, no, because of that thing. That binding — whakapiri, nē?

I have had a happy life with him. He is a good husband; he is very faithful to me in every way. We used to live in the old meeting-house. I'm telling you the truth, we had a home in the old meeting-house, the old one in the flax. It was called Te Ngawari. That means to be kind: to let it go out freely so that others can benefit by it. Te Kooti told these people at Mangatu, 'Kia ngāwari'. Because these Ringatu people, these elders, got selfish and what knowledge they had, they didn't like to let it go out. So it is his kupu whakaari on that house. To be kind; let the faith go out. For three years we lived in there, as our home, nē? because he had to go shearing, fencing, all that. I used to cook in an old kāuta. My great-grandmother she felt sorry for me because we couldn't get a home, then. About two years later

A portrait of Wi Pere MHR from the house Eriopeta or Rongopai. His mother, Riria Te Mauaranui, from whom his mana flowed, perches on his shoulder like a watching owl. Reproduced by permission of Mahanga Horsfall. *National Museum*

---

*You will never leave, grandchild
†We have been united
‡on the spiritual side.

Heni Brown at the age of sixteen.
Photographed, by her permission, by
Gillian Chaplin, 1983.

she came back to Mangatu and she bought us a nice home, and that's the home I
brought up my fifteen children, down the pā, the Mangatu pā. But I rather liked
the meeting-house, because everybody come in and have a talk to you — have a
kōrero around. It was like a unity, everybody comes and talk to you, and make
friends with you, and I really loved that life. And in the morning I would go and
cook our breakfast in our kitchen. We used to have a kāuta with a mud floor, and
she used to call out to me, 'Heni, spray the water and get the manuka broom and
sweep it — the dust won't fly around.' It was very, very clean — spotless!

Then, when we were at the pā, we milked forty cows, and had pigs,
everything. Milked by hand. Him and I used to get up every morning to milk
them, and our children as they grew older — the six girls used to help us. Because
I never had my sons until later. She was still alive, my great-grandmother, when
I had my first son. I would have had twenty children if they had all lived — but
fifteen alive. But she saw the first son. She was 105, I think, when she died.[24] She
was one of the oldest kuias in those days.

Ned: She used to rake up the chips around the wood heap, light a fire, and she'd
cook these Maori leaven bread. She would make about eight or nine for the day,

left Te Ngawari in the swamps at
Mangatu. It was built about 1922
under the direction of Wi Wereta; all
the framework was erected before
sunrise. Hidden behind it is the small
concrete whare kape, where the texts
of the Ringatu prayers and hymns
were once kept. Te Kooti is said to
have predicted the erosion of the
lands at Mangatu with these words: 'I
see your land going into the river and
going out to sea. This is the work of
prominent men.' Photograph by
Gillian Chaplin, 1983.

above Heni and Ned before Te
Ngawari, where they lived when they
were first married. Photograph by
Gillian Chaplin, 1983.

and she would sit there all day, just stoking this fire up.

Heni: I can't make that kind of bread! She used to go down to the kūmara pit
and she'll pray. I wasn't allowed to go near that kūmara pit — only him, because
he is a man, you see. She always says, a woman goes into a kūmara pit it rots the
whole kūmara! Ko pirau ngā kūmara! She'll put all the ferns there in the pit in the
ground, because Ned always makes us a kūmara pit. She goes in there and bless it,
then she puts the mānukas down, and carts all the kūmaras on the kit. She takes
them in herself and she places them like that; every kūmara is placed on top of the
other. You never see those kūmara pirau, never. As soon as one of the girls goes in
there — oh! she knows! After that she always locked it — put the padlock on it! Only
her can go in, because she blessed it. We can't karakia; we don't know how to pray
— but she does!

It wasn't hard when we were living here, because his parents were good to us,
too. As I told you, he was a good provider, a good husband — never stay home one
day, always working. We never run short of anything. No. He goes out shearing;
I stay home and milk the cows. I never once went shearing. I don't like the smell
of that fleece! Ugh, I get sick! No, I stayed home and looked after the kids, while
he goes out shearing, fencing. He'd stay away about three weeks, four weeks.
Comes home weekends to bring us some meat. I had a good life with him, but *my
own* life, no! I had a hard life.

But he was cheeky to my great-grandmother! Very cheeky! She told me never
ever touch any of her belongings! And Hori Gage warned me, 'Don't you ever take
your tipuna's things, ngā taonga.' Because it will be upon me; I will be the same
as her. I said, 'I don't want to be like that!' So they buried all her things when she
died. But him! I didn't realize that when I was pregnant — true, I am not telling
you a lie. I was pregnant with my first child. I was three months, and he showed
me this petticoat. I didn't know that it was my great-grandmother's and I put it
on me. You remember those petticoats with the beautiful designs, handwoven,
some lace, those Indian petticoats, in flower patterns? This one was done in cotton,
red and white this petticoat; it was so beautiful. I put it on me and he said to me,
'Oh you are just like your great-grandmother!' and I said 'That's all right!' You
know, a week later, I lost my child. As God is my witness, I lost her. I don't know
what happened. I was in the meeting-house, I took the petticoat off, and the next
minute I was lying in this meeting-house and I could hear these chanting sounds
around the house, and I thought it was a lot of children, coming in, and — oh, I've

gone pōrangi! Next minute it just came out. I screamed, I yelled; nobody heard me! So I just crawled out of the meeting-house and his mother came up to my assistance, otherwise I would have been dead. She told me, 'Te panekoti o tō tipuna! You had no right to wear it!' '*Your* son gave it — and I lost my child!' A little girl. She was so beautiful. I didn't like to bury her; but we had to bury her. His father, Reuben Brown, wrapped it up neatly, and had a church over it, and they buried it at the cemetery over here. I had no right to wear her clothes. That was my first experience of my great-grandmother's belongings.

And then the second experience, when he told me that he left her false teeth underneath my pillow! He's a hard case, my husband! He plays jokes on me! I'd buried all her belongings. Not one thing was left, except her false teeth! I didn't know that Mr Brown had hidden them underneath my pillow! And I dreamt that night she was calling out to me, 'Heni! Kei hea aku niho? Aua! Kei hea aku niho?'* She kept calling out to me in my dream; and all the time Ned Brown planted them underneath my pillow! Next morning he said, 'Did you have a dream last night?' I said, 'Yes. Granny was calling out for her teeth!' 'Yes! Underneath your pillow!' I lost my temper and I banged him! I said, 'Why do you play jokes on me?' 'Ah well, to see how good she is!' He laughed and laughed. He got punished for that — he broke his leg!

I respected her; I had to because I am her mokopuna. I am the next in line. I am the eldest. But being a woman, I wasn't respected — because I am a wahine. She gave the mana to my brother — to Rutene — to the tāne. But in the whakapapa, I am the eldest. I used to think, you're the eldest, you're the rangatira. No. Not in the Maori world.[25] No. Always the man. We could go to a marae, him and I, they look at me, I'm the eldest, but they always turn to my brother, nei, ko ia te tāne!† No matter where we go! But the whakapapa always goes back in the mātāmua; mātāmua means the eldest. But never give out your whakapapa to another person. You know why is that? In years to come they can turn round and put their name there. They can use it for land. They can deprive you of your rights in any land. That's how they used to work in the olden days. That's when the Maoris call it whānaukō, they take over our leadership. So you never give your whakapapa to another person. Never. I know my genealogy. I study it, you see; but I don't study others. I don't even study my husband's. It has got nothing to do with me. It's not up to me to study his family tree. I am only his wife; I am only his mat! He whāriki noa koe,‡ that's what my great-grandmother used to say! That's the old Maori way! And I used to cry. 'What are you crying for?' 'You've called me a mat!' I was supposed to bend to him. And my brother? I may be older than him, but a man is always the head.

You see, Meri Puru's family was a wharengaro. That means a family that just died, no issue. Her brothers all died. Oh, she had a brother, Rangi, and he had a son, went to school, finish! Ka mate!* Not a one survived! The Maoris call that a wharengaro, in other words, so their generation won't live, and there is nothing. When Meri Puru died, the lineage died. The mana died, the Puru died. She always tells me that the sacredness is on her head. The mana of her tīpuna. That means

---

*Where are my teeth? I know not! Where are my teeth?
†he is the man!
‡You're just a common mat
*They died!

from generations to generations it comes down from the oldest to her. How I found out, she never used to wash in hot water; she always used to have a calabash, a gourd, and she used to cut the top and put the cold water in. She always said to Ned and I, 'taku māhunga he tapu',† the sacredness is on her head. Never touch it.[26] Well, he didn't understand that, but I did. I warned him not to put hot water in, 'cause she'd go pōrangi! And he laughed! 'That kuia whaiwhaiā!'‡ He went and put the hot water in; my great-grandmother yelled out, 'Tō tāne he kōhuru! Your husband is cruel!' And she ran from our house right to the Mangatu river! I was chasing her! And he was laughing! I wasn't! And she jumped in the river! That was the sacredness of her own body.

Every morning at six o'clock she will have church — she had her own room — and the whole house is silent, even my children. We respect her, her pakeke. She babbles on in this other language, in Heperu, karakia Heperu. When she finish she'll say, 'Haere mai', and we all run into the room! But she always tells me to tell my kids never touch 'tāku peihana' — 'my basin'. The day she died she called for her trunk. Remember, in the olden days they used to hide everything in tin trunks? With the handle? And I said to my mother, 'What's in that tin trunk?' 'Why?' 'I want to have a look!' And she said, 'Where's that old kuia?' 'Oh, she's out in the kitchen.' And I lifted the lid. Aue! She had all those greenstones — everything! And the beautiful things that were given to her from the Queen of Waikato. And when she died they buried the whole lot. That old kuia might whaiwhaiā us!

... I lost five children. I lost the first one, as I told you, before my daughter Marakea. I had six daughters, and then I lost another son. And I lost Richard. And I lost the two babies: I had them in the picture-theatre in Gisborne. It just came away. Maybe because I start swearing at my great-grandmother. I don't know. She said to me that I look for my own trouble — and I always get it. You dare not swear at her because you would get it. Well, that's my experience of my great-grandmother. She had that mana — or witchcraft, mahi Maori.

... My girls, most of them have European husbands. I never stopped my daughters. They always say to me, 'Mum, why didn't you marry a white man?' I said, 'I was forbidden. I wasn't allowed to go with any man until I was told to.' But now that they are married to European husbands, that's their business. But I go to these huis, and I listen, and I hear them say like this, 'Oh, Mrs Brown, your daughters are married to those honkies, eh?' And I say, 'What's wrong with them? They're human beings like us.' 'Yes. But they should marry Maoris like themselves.' That's prejudice. And I stand up and I say to them, 'How do I know that your great-grandfather, or your great-grandmother wasn't a European, before you stand up and say those things? When I look into your background I find your grandfather was a Pakeha, and your great-grandmother was a half-caste Maori. What right have you to throw stones at me?' As I told you, I was brought up in a kāuta, a mud floor; that was my life. But it took the Europeans to bring me out of that life into a nice home. And my father was a European, and I had about six stepfathers, all Pakeha. And Ned's father is a Pakeha,[27] so you see our children sort of grew up in that life. My girls, they go to high school and they get educated and they get good jobs. And they believe in education. I never had that opportunity when I was a girl. I don't care if I am a black Maori; I still love my

†my head is tapu
‡That bewitching old lady!

Pakeha. The Pakeha way of thinking; the Pakeha way of education. Why should I dominate the Pakeha? Why should I be prejudiced against a European? So I don't interfere when they get married to their European husbands. 'Oh, Mum I am marrying a Pakeha!' 'That's all right. That's your life!'

… We have one whāngai. That's his brother's mokopuna, Ned's brother's. She was only a little baby – three months – and the mother didn't want her, so the welfare lady came over here, 'You want a baby Mrs Brown?' 'Where?' 'Over there. They don't want the baby. No, you can have it Mrs Brown!' Away I go and get the baby. 'You want another one Mrs Brown?' 'NO!' 'Why?' 'I am getting tired! I already brought up fifteen; that's enough!' The welfare lady look at me and laugh: 'No, have another one!' 'NO.' We could have brought up a lot of welfare kids, but I couldn't take it. Not because I didn't want them – but him and I like to be on our own now and again!

But I like my Maori people. I mean the old Maoris. I loved my great-grandmother. Because she brought me up through sickness, and everything. Hardships. You know she used to burn the coins, pennies, behind our kāuta? That was their belief. Hika! We used to watch her. You know those two-and-sixpences? She used to burn them! And when she goes away, my brother and I raked it out, go and get a sandpaper to shine it up again. And she caught us! She knew! Boy, Rutene and I never go and pinch it again!

But I had a good life with her. She asked my husband and I if we could take her back to Torere, to die. She wanted to go back home to die. So we took her back. She only lived for a few weeks; she prayed for herself to God to take her spirit. That's the power of the karakia she had. If I speak too much about my great-grandmother it is because of that mana. When I was very sick in hospital,

Ned and Heni Brown in the living-room of their home at Whatatutu, November 1982. Photograph by Gillian Chaplin.

about two years ago,[28] and I thought I was going to die, I saw her standing right at my bed. I said to the nurse, 'Oh! What is that old lady doing there?' And she said, 'Why, you are pōrangi, Mrs Brown!' And I said, 'No.' She was praying. Then the next day I was all right. The nurse said to me, 'What was it, Mrs Brown?' 'Oh, my great-grandmother came to karakia me, last night!'

I am only talking about my life. But that's the power she had.

Heni Brown died on 11 December 1990.

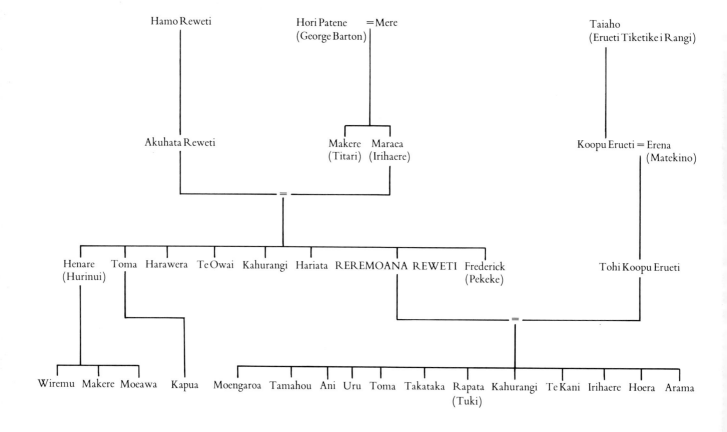

Hamo Reweti

Hori Patene   = Mere
(George Barton)

Taiaho
(Erueti Tiketike i Rangi)

Akuhata Reweti

Makere   Maraea
(Titari)   (Irihaere)

Koopu Erueti = Erena
(Matekino)

=

Henare   Toma   Harawera   Te Owai   Kahurangi   Hariata   REREMOANA REWETI   Frederick
(Hurinui)   (Pekeke)

Tohi Koopu Erueti

=

Wiremu   Makere   Moeawa   Kapua

Moengaroa   Tamahou   Ani   Uru   Toma   Takataka   Rapata   Kahurangi   Te Kani   Irihaere   Hoera   Arama
(Tuki)

REREMOANA KOOPU

Reremoana is the oldest of the women with whom we spoke. She was born at Otuwhare, in the eastern Bay of Plenty, on 7 January 1893. Otuwhare is one of the tiny Whanau a Apanui communities which are scattered along the narrow coastline of the East Cape. She went to school first at Omaio, then Auckland. In 1911 she came to live with her husband, Tohi Koopu, at Maraenui, a settlement roughly ten kilometres from her family home. She has lived there all her adult life.

In the world in which she grew up, the only means of communication with other parts of the country (apart from the rough horse-tracks of the East Coast) were the schooners and ketches, which travelled between Auckland, Opotiki and Gisborne bringing supplies. These she remembers vividly: the Kaeo, the Mahi, the Tamahae. She herself, daughter of an important Anglican family within Whanau a Apanui, was sent away in 1907, at considerable expense to her parents, to the newly established Queen Victoria Maori Girls' School in Auckland. She spent two years there and then worked for a while in Auckland as a seamstress. But, as she tells, she was summoned home, and from that time remained on the Coast.

Most of the people at Maraenui are Ringatu, and that faith has always had the largest following among the Maori population in Opotiki County. We first went to visit Reremoana knowing that her husband's whānau was one of the leading Ringatu families. Tohi's father, Koopu Erueti, was the President of the Ringatu Church until his death in 1937. Maraenui itself had become committed to Te Kooti and the Ringatu beliefs by the early 1880s. Its meeting-house, Te Poho o Apanui, erected in 1872 by Te Tatana Ngatawa,[1] who had been an opponent of Te Kooti's in the wars, was reopened as a Ringatu house of prayer in 1887. When Te Kooti visited Maraenui, for the First of July in 1887, he composed a waiata in praise of its two chiefs, Te Tatana and Paora Ngamoki:

Akuanei au ka takahi i te ara noho ana hoki au i Maraenui ra ia hei hapai kupu ma hau e Te Tatana. Tu noa hoki au i te akau ra ia nou tou pono e Paora Ngamoki e.

Soon I shall tread the path to stop at Maraenui, to bring the word to you, Te Tatana. I merely stand on that rocky shore, oh man of faith, Paora Ngamoki.[2]

Nevertheless, Te Kooti prophesied that the house, and the faith, would decay: he warned the people that the place would become Maraekōhatu – the marae of stones – because the people would forget about their God. Aware of the prediction, Paul Delamere, the Poutikanga from 1938, built a whare karakia, a house of prayer, at Maraenui, on the site of the original meeting-house. All the people of the neighbouring communities were involved. Maaka Delamere (Maaka Jones), who was then attending the Omaio primary school, remembers how her mother and the other women stayed at the marae during the construction of the house, and they undertook the cooking for the men, who were bound by the restrictions of tapu while they were working. The whare karakia still stands today on Maraenui's stony driftwood-strewn foreshore, although this house, too, has fallen into disrepair. There have been plans to demolish it and rebuild, but its future remains uncertain.

Only a handful of families live at Maraenui. When the 1936 census was taken, which distinguished Maori and European populations within communities, seventy-seven of the eighty-five people living at Maraenui were Maori. Neighbouring Omaio, where Paul Delamere and his family lived, was somewhat larger: there were 171 people, of whom 150 were Maori. By 1971, Maraenui itself had shrunk to only seventy-five people of whom seventy-four were Maori. The size of the community has remained almost unchanged over the last ten or fifteen years, though it had been one of the major centres of Maori population

previous page Irihaere and Reremoana, with their little dog, Spot, in the garden of their home on the cliffs at Maraenui, May 1984. Photograph by Gillian Chaplin.

on the Coast in Te Kooti's time. It has slowly dwindled as its resources have become exhausted. Reremoana's story reveals how the community was stripped of its wealth, largely through external exploitation: coastal whaling, a basis of a brief local wealth, was over by the 1930s, while over-extensive sheep-farming by the great runholders largely destroyed the land. Now, the last major resource of the people, the fish, is threatened. Ruthless commercial fishing of snapper in the Bay of Plenty has led to serious consideration being given to the banning of all fishing at the mouth of the Motu river during the spawning season.[3] Such a ban, coming into force at the start of summer, would also prevent the kahawai catch, on which life at Maraenui has been based for centuries. Were this to happen, Maraenui would die.

Reremoana's world has always been predominantly a Maori one, but not an isolated one. She and her husband constantly looked after visitors who passed up and down the Coast, particularly before the bridge across the Motu river was opened in 1929. Many of these travellers were Pakeha. Reremoana's grandfather was himself a Scandinavian whaler, who had come to live on the Coast. Her life has been devoted to looking after people. She has never worried about who they might be, Maori or Pakeha. She was ninety-one when we first visited her and she was much more concerned about looking after our well-being and comfort than about any questions of racial concern that we might care to discuss.

It was when we met Reremoana that we learnt that she herself had not been brought up as a Ringatu. Thus we also encountered that particular Maori skill of tolerance and adaptability within different forms of Christianity. She brought her children up as Ringatu and she attended the main Ringatu services at Maraenui. But she still considers herself an Anglican.

As she talked with us, one of her clearest memories — and undoubtedly a narrative that she has told many times in her life — was of the drowning of sixteen children from the Omaio school on 5 August 1900. It was only by chance that Reremoana was not with them. For the two communities, Maraenui and Omaio, the loss of so many of their tamariki was a tragedy of huge proportions. Because the Ringatu seek explanations in predicted destiny, some remembered the words of warning of Te Kooti concerning their neglect of the faith. Reremoana herself would have no truck with such interpretations. At the same time, the community turned its back on their schoolteacher, the Reverend Henry Young, not because they blamed him for the deaths, but because he acted after the event with such obtuseness and clumsy compassion that he forfeited their co-operation. We find that hidden within the narrative of the community's pain is another significant theme: the inability of a Pakeha schoolteacher to understand that the rhythms of mourning in a Maori community must take their own time and their own forms.

Reremoana's account of these events reveals both the strengths and weaknesses of oral history. She seemed unaware of the community's hostility to its teacher and its consequent efforts to drive him out. Her father apparently did not sign the large petition of 18 March 1902 to have Young removed, although most of the people of Omaio, Otuwhare, Waiorore, and Maraenui did. Later, Reremoana stayed with Young and his family when she lived in Auckland, another indication that her father had dissociated himself from the hostility which had developed. Nor did she comment on the enormous pressures that the disaster placed on the resources of the community and the marae. In Maori eyes, visitors must be fed. By September 1900, about seven hundred mourners had been received at Maraenui, and as Young commented directly, the 'people have been hard pushed to find food for their visitors'.[4] Many of the local families became very sick with dysentery, while the planting of the next season's food was seriously delayed. But Reremoana's account of the parties of people coming — in anger as well as sorrow — conveys the strength of the feelings about the deaths within the whole of the Bay of Plenty in a manner which no written record could describe.

Death would strike the Whanau a Apanui communities again. The 1918 influenza pandemic devastated Omaio and Maraenui: in the three weeks between 12 November and 3 December twenty people died in these two small communities.[5] The Black Flu – so named because the corpses often turned black – swept through the eastern Bay of Plenty in mid-November. There the Maori mortality was among the highest in the whole country. These deaths most notably struck the young adults. Only two years before the schoolteacher at Omaio had commented upon the low fertility among the Maori population there: 'Out of 34 married couples here 15 are childless. Four of the latter are upwards of 45 years old, the rest are under. The terms of married life range from 15 months to 40 years.'[6] Whanau a Apanui was only a small tribe – just over 700 in the 1901 tribal census – and its population losses in the early years of this century were desolating. After the death of the children, most of the people of Maraenui changed their names so as never to forget. All the hapū changed their names. In this manner, the whānau carry their history and transfer it to the next generation as well. It is not surprising that Reremoana's memories focus on these two community disasters, yet the spirit in which she talks is of one who survived. It was she who made us certain that our decision for the title of this book was the right one.

The family home, where we talked, is a kauri weather-board villa built on the high cliff overlooking the vast foreshore, the marae, with its meeting-house and its monument to the schoolchildren, and the wide, ever-shifting, treacherous mouth of the Motu. Out to sea lies White Island, its constant plume of smoke a guide to the winds and the weather for the old people. If the smoke drifts up the coast, it is a good sign, they say; towards Opotiki – watch for rain! Reremoana is at the centre of a very loving whānau. She herself had twelve children and three of them are present in our dialogues. There are her two daughters: Toma, born in 1916, and Irihaere, born in 1928. Her youngest son, Arama, who was born in 1933, is also here. Reremoana is old now, a woman who has spent most of her life caring for others. But her family are with her; it is her turn to be cared for. The conversations we recorded took place on 10 and 12 May 1984, and on 4 December of the same year. Reremoana's pragmatic nature and her optimism can be deceptive, for at times they hide the struggles of the Maraenui people. Hers is the spirit of endurance which the Maori have needed for most of this century.

Back: Whetariki – Frederick – brother of Reremoana; Kapua, daughter of Toma, Reremoana's brother; Reremoana. Front: Moeawa, daughter of Hurinui, Reremoana's brother. Moeawa was born soon after the drowning of the Omaio schoolchildren in 1900, and was named for her elder sister Makere, who had been found dead on the river-bank. Photograph by C. H. Harris, Waipukurau. *Reremoana Koopu*

I was born at Otuwhare; that's where our parents lived. It's just the next settlement. My mother is Irihaere and my father is Reweti – Akuhata Reweti. We were quite a big family, nine of us – my five brothers and my three sisters. No whāngai, that's all, just my brothers and sisters. We had quite a lot to do. Maize, plucking maize, and digging potatoes, and digging kūmara. Those are our main jobs. We had quite a big patch of maize. Each family has their own patches, and we all help. Just the family. Our father, he used go around with the sailing vessel. It comes from Auckland, and it brings stuff for all around the coast. He works on that boat, backwards and forwards to Auckland. It collects – oh, anything – maize, pigs, kūmaras, potatoes, and takes it to Auckland. Down to Gisborne, and then back from Gisborne, around the coast, and back to Auckland. I never went with him, oh no! I go to Auckland all right, but I go to Opotiki and take another boat! No, he brings the supplies, clothes, food – mostly food – bag of flour, bag of sugar, oatmeal – all those things. And of course the Maoris they sell their own fowls, and maize, and pigs when he comes. Maize and pigs are the main thing.

There's hardly anybody there at Otuwhare now. I feel so sorry for our place. No living creature. Our old homestead was so close to the main road that they shifted the house — on the hill, further up. We get all the dust, and everything! So they shifted it — right at the back there, right to the top. But it's gone now. Only our meeting-house is there, Poho o Rutaia.

We had a kāuta, then. It is a big one, though, with a big chimney we cooked in. You have your fire and you would cook all your kai there, with the pieces of iron to hold your pots. We had our kitchen things buried in the chimney — oh, it was nice. We had big pots — whaling pots — that belonged to my great-grandfather, George Barton. Hori Patene they call him. He was a whaler. He stays there, at Otuwhare, but he travels round. He has a boat, eh? And he supplies the marae with all these boilers. All these things belonged to him. When he finished he gave all those things for the marae. Big boilers. That's where they boiled their water for tea. They hooked them, put them on the chain, and you've got the big fire going! They cooked all the kai for the huihuis in the chimney, and then they would have the table outside, spread outside. We had a cloth, long pieces of calico, and you roll it up, and that's where you used it for a table-cloth. When you want your table set, you just spread it out, on the grass. And people sit on the side, on each side, on the ground. Just sit on the ground, no seat, no nothing. You were lucky if you have a rug, or a coat, or something — oh well, you put it down for you to sit on.

The men goes out fishing, and get the mussels. Yes, the fish and the mussels are the main thing. Of course, they have their own meat, they kill their own for meat — pigs or cows. The men folks have their fire outside to cook the meat. They have pots, and they have wires fixed to these pots. They have a big fire, with a post on that side, and a post on this, and another bar across. And you put your wire over that bar for your pots. Oh, I tell you! Oh well, they seemed to survive. Now, when you look back, oh — hard! Of course, later on, we got some more modern things there.

I don't know, we seemed to be quite happy then, as long as the work is finished, and done, and the kai cooked, and that's all that matters. As long as they can cook their kai for the visitors, and the men have the big fire going outside, and the women folks do the hāngi. They cook the kūmaras, potatoes, kamokamos, anything like that in the hāngi. We had our kitchen right on the main road — and everybody passing through, people going to Opotiki on horseback, going on the beach, passing our kitchen: 'Hey, come on, have something to eat!' You know what Maoris are, 'Oh, haere mai, get the kai in!' Of course, they would be *too* happy to get something to eat before going on to the beach, round the bluff, and on to Hawai.

I went to school at Omaio. It was quite a big school. That's where we learn the English. You are not allowed to talk Maori in the ground. You'd be punished. You've got to write so many times, 'I shouldn't be talking Maori', oh, about fifty, on your slate. It was quite all right. Great teachers we had, the Youngs. The father, Mr Young, and the four girls.[7] Mabel was a nice one. Jennie, she's good, but she's hard! When I went to work in Auckland, I stayed with them, and she was all right with me then! We were all at school at Omaio — I was at school then — when the children were drowned in the Motu river.[8] I was coming with them. I was coming because my brother lives just down below, at the bottom of the hill. He had two, a boy and a girl, and we were all coming. And I thought, 'I will come with them, too.' But my sister, Hariata, said, 'No. You had better go back!' It's so many for her to look after, walking, walking all the way. And to cross the river. The two

One of the ketches which regularly plied the East Coast, bringing in stores and shipping out wool-bales in the later nineteenth and early twentieth centuries. This photograph is of the *Tamahae*, anchored at Omaio beach about 1929. Notice also the whale-boat in the foreground. The *Tamahae* was owned by Billy Walker, a hotel-keeper in Opotiki. Captain John Skinner, who Reremoana remembers in this context, owned and sailed the schooners *Awanui* and *Kaeo*, between 1891 and 1918. *Whakatane Museum*

of us, me and my mate, Pohatu, and my brother's children, Wiremu and Makere. Of course, my sister has to look after them, eh? But I said to my sister, 'I want to come, too!' 'No, you'll stay!' 'But I *want* to come!' And Pohatu, she said, 'And me too!' 'No. It is so many of you, I can't look after the whole lot of you!'

No, we insist on following them. So we came along, from school, and there was a hotel there, right at the bottom, not far from the cemetery. All the children coming past. And this woman, she saw us. She's an aunty of ours. And she said, 'I think you two girls better go back.' She knew that my sister was trying to send me back. And, of course, the two of us start to cry and cry. She said, 'No use you crying. You had better go back. Your sister is right, she has got so many to look after on the way, walking.' So, oh well, she came out with a packet of lollies. 'Now, here's some lollies for you. You better go home!' They are gone, my sister and the others! So we went back. So we were the lucky ones.

The teacher was expecting them to be at school on Monday morning. And the teacher was puzzled, so many of them absent! So he started enquiring. They send a man over, and he came on his horse; he rode over here, right to Maraenui. He crossed the river, and all the time some of them are already on the river bed, but he didn't know. He was crossing at the top crossing on the Motu. He came across and enquire after them. He said, 'Where are the children? They are not at school. Why are the children not there?' You know, enquiring of the parents. 'Well', they said, 'huh, they left yesterday, early enough to get there.' That was Sunday. 'Well, none of them are at school.' Then they start to panic. They know now there's something wrong. So they all went to the river. And, ha! there were one, two, three — just washed there, just on a bank. Not drifted out. It was my niece, Makere, and another one. Her nose was bleeding and she was still warm. And then the word came through to Omaio that there is something wrong.

Oh, I remember that time. We were only small. We had to come with our parents, and the parents were crying all the way from Omaio. Oh, I can just remember, the families coming along and the children coming with them, during the night. Most of the people here lost two, the boy and a girl, some two boys. But all two, two, two — the whole lot.[9]

Schoolchildren at Omaio, about 1900. Reremoana is in the second-to-front row: she is wearing a white dress and is the third from the left. Her sister Hariata, who was drowned, is in the back row, standing second from the left. Her brother's son Wiremu, who was also drowned, is sitting third from the left in the front row. Makere, Wiremu's sister, who also died, is in the same row as Reremoana, seventh from the left, wearing a white dress and a brooch. Lilian Young stands on the left, next to her father, Revd Henry Young. Edith Young is on the right. Photograph by C. H. Harris.
Reremoana Koopu

Drawing from the *New Zealand Graphic*, 18 August 1900, of the tragedy at Omaio. Ani Delamere, who was with the children, is shown on the river-bank. Some of her clothes were found there, suggesting she had tried to swim out to rescue the children, but her body was never found. Contemporary accounts indicate that there had been a flash-flood, or a freshet in the river.

And, of course, a Maori says, oh, this and that, and that's why it happened. There was a tohunga at the river. He camps there. You know what tohungas are. He goes round and try, and people go to him. This man, Rihara, he had his tent on this side of the river, and he had, oh, a lovely fire that morning. He had his fire going, and his cooking. And these children, going back, seeing a nice fire, they kept on jumping over the fire. One after the other! You know what kids are! Well, they put it down to that. That's why those children were drowned. They blame it to him. They say it was him that got these kids drowned. It's all Maori talk.[10] It's all humbug, I think. Just a mere accident and careless. The canoe was overloaded. It's just those things that will happen. And the two adults with them, they couldn't even help them — too dark.

All the people changed their names. Everybody.[11] My brother, Henare, became Hurinui: that means the whole lot of them, all drowned, all turned over. Te Hurinui. That's the whole lot, not one but the whole lot. Not a survivor. Two adults and sixteen children. His wife, Taimana, changed her name to Whakararo. For the little boy, her baby, Wiremu, who was found on Whale Island. It means drifting, on this side, this coast, drifting downwards. And my mother's was changed. Her real name was Maraea. She got that name, Irihaere, because they had to put the body in a basket. When they found him at the island, they had to put him in a basket, a coal-basket. It was hanging from one of the masts of the ship that found him, the *Terranora*. And that's how they brought him back. Irihaere is because they hung him up. That's how they brought him back. They bore him up in a basket, hanging. And that's my daughter's name, too. That's where she got her name. Another one, the grandmother of the child, became Ketewaro. That's the basket: the coal-basket. Then there was Mere Brown — Mere Pita — she didn't go with them, though she was at the school. Her name became Matemoana, for the whole lot of them, all drowned at sea. My mother's sister, Makere, she changed her name to Titari. That's because they were cast away — all over: scattered. They were picked up from along the river, and on this side of the Parenui, where the waterfall is.

Oh, the drowning of the children was the worst thing. My sister wasn't found. Quite a few of them. So we have the names in the next generation, too. Tini, meaning many children — 'tini o ngā tamariki'. Moeawa is another. They were both born soon after, and her name means asleep — dead — by the river — for my niece that they found on the banks of the Motu. Akuhata is the name my father took. For the fifth of August, the day it happened. And my own daughter, my first: Moengaroa — that's for the long, long, deaths.[12]

Of course, all the hapū here, of Whanau a Apanui, take their names, now, from this. Ngati Horowai, they're the people of Omaio, and Ngati Horomoana from Maraenui, here. They both mean swallowed by the sea. And Ngati Paeakau, from Whitianga — that's cast along the shore.

left Unveiling the monument at Maraenui erected by Te Whanau a Apanui for the children, on 23 March 1905. James Carroll, Minister for Native Affairs, is speaking. Photograph by T. Macquarters. *Auckland Weekly News, 6 April 1905*

below 'Taane Pawhero', the temporary meeting-house built by the people of Maraenui for the unveiling of the monument to the children, in March 1905. Akuhata Reweti, Reremoana's father, stands to the extreme left, wearing a large straw hat. Taiaho, the head of the Koopu family, is seated on a box in the front, holding his bowler hat. Notice the bell to the left of the house, used to summon people to the Ringatu services. Photograph by T. Macquarters, Opotiki. *Reremoana Koopu*

Then my father, Akuhata Reweti. Oh! He never touched snapper, my father. Because he knows that the snapper eats anything. So he never touched it — although he goes out fishing. Eating that fish, never! And one of the Ngamokis,[13] he never touched the kahawai from Motu. That's a fish they get from Motu. Never, never, he touched that fish.[14]

About six months, I think, yes, people were coming and going, and people arriving. I remember those days — oh, terrible! They used to muster all the little ones, all the children, in a house there. If they know there is a big crowd coming, they know exactly what they are going to get, you see. So, they collect all the children and close them up in a house there. These people, when they come to the tangi from all over, you know, Whakatane and Whakatohea,[15] and all over the place, as soon as they come round the point they start throwing their dynamite. Just to let these people know there is something coming! They throw that dynamite in the sea, and, oh, you see the water! Just there, not very far. Then they throw another one, just below. They were angry. Because the parents were careless in not going to see the children across the river. Letting them go like that. And this man, Pani, had to ferry them.[16] That's why they were angry, because none of them went with them as far as the river. It was he taua. All these people are under taua, because they let a terrible thing like that happen. Yes. Oh, every mob that comes, they had to lock us up, put the children away, because they know there's trouble.

People from that end especially, right to Whakatane, and Tuhoe, and Ngaiterangi from Tauranga. Oh yes, from all over there. As soon as they come round the point, then they start throwing. That's a warning, you see. Warning that they are coming on the warpath. They throw their dynamites, all right, when they come round. Then right here, the last one. But the one they threw at the marae in front of the crowd, it's a dumb one! Not a live one! But they thought it was alive, and they were all scampering! The last one they throw, just here — below — and *it* explodes! But the one they throw at the marae it is a dumb one. Of course, some of them scattered, but some of them stood. They didn't move. Old Taiaho, my husband's grandfather, knew it was a dumb one. He went and get his stick and, you know, get it away, throw it away! Laugh! — when Tohi was telling me about that!

When they picked up the bodies, they bring them and put them in front of the old meeting-house, Te Poho o Apanui. It was there, where the church is now,

Inside the dining-shelter, or whata made of raupō, which was built specially for the unveiling in 1905. Photograph probably by T. Macquarters. *Reremoana Koopu*

the whare karakia. They put the bodies in front of that old house. This one in the photo, Tane Pawhero, that was just for the time being, at the unveiling of the children's stone. That was five years after the accident. It was just a temporary one, that thatched whare. Because they didn't have a house. And that dining-room they built, too. It is from the unveiling. They had everything! Knives, forks, cruets for the salts. And butter on a stand. They were pretty!

Then they built the big house, Te Iwarau: '1900'. And that's what it remembers. The year when those children were drowned.[17] And every Fifth of August they have a huihui, ka huihui ki konei.* All the parents, all the relations, they come here and have a tangi. They stay here for about three days. Oh well, they've finished with that now, coming here.

. . . I went to Queen Vic.[18] I was there for two years. I enjoy being there, but I can't really remember what. They taught us Maori, there. It was different from Omaio, oh yes, but I've forgotten it now. Before I left school, the teachers got me a job working in a dress-making shop,[19] in Kingsland, with Mrs Purdue. First I ever knew Kingsland. There were three girls and, of course, there's a senior girl to take us. We had sewing machines but all we do is just to help her, tacking, and cutting and things like that. We don't really do the sewing up. I was there about a year, oh, over a year. But then I had to come back. It would be about 1910. My mother wasn't too good; there was somebody else to look after her, but I came back just to be with our mother.

I came back on the schooner from Auckland to Omaio, with Captain Skinner.[20] He was a friend of our father. He can speak Maori, and he mixes up with the Maori very, very well. When I was at Queen Vic he is just like a father to us. He's good that old man. He comes and takes us out for the day. He takes us on his boat in Auckland, at the harbour. Of course, the teachers know him well. He really gives us a great time! One thing we saw, was the Great White Fleet – the American

*coming together for that.

Hui at the unveiling of the monument. Kneeling in the centre, with his bowler hat in his hand, is Taiaho. Akuhata Reweti stands behind to the left, wearing the straw hat and a striped tie. Titari Patene, Reremoana's mother's sister, stands second on the left, wearing a white blouse and a black skirt. The Pakeha in the centre (who also appears in the preceding photograph seated on the right) is Fred Bridger of Opotiki. In the background stands one of the new wharepapa, weather-board houses. Photograph by T. Macquarters. *Reremoana Koopu*

fleet.[21] You know, all the lights and everything! You are not allowed to go out by yourself until somebody comes for you, but this time all the girls, they were allowed. They arranged for something to take the girls out; got something to drive us in. It was exciting — especially getting out! Go right round and back to school!

Captain Skinner's is a sailing vessel. It takes about four days from Auckland. We know him very well. He brings stuff for the Coast. He brings all sorts of clothes — used clothes. And blankets, shawls — whoever wants them, he supplies. Very handy; they were good clothes. I suppose he collects second-hand things and brings them, and then he sells them very, very cheap. Good clothes and blankets — the grey blankets. And when he finally finished trading around the Coast he settled at Little Awanui. You know, that island at Awanui, between Omaio and Te Kaha? And afterwards he came to Omaio; he had the shop there. Great man, old Skinner. He is buried at our cemetery at Omaio.

Sometimes he used to come from Awanui to his shop at Omaio. He rides, of course, in those days. And when he comes along, the women they are washing in a creek. They have a big board and a stick to hammer them, you know, wash them. We never had any tub, we never had any wash-board, but we washed them in the creek. And then on a piece, oh — big blocks, and a stick, just to hammer the clothes. And he comes along on his horse, and sees these women, washing their clothes. Of course, he knows them all. And he passed some remarks! He said, 'Oh, no wonder you say (talking in Maori) that Skinner's clothes are no good! A board at the bottom and a stick at the top, hammering!'

That's one thing with him, he knows exactly the ones that can't afford — he gives them their [credit] — put them down for a certain time. Oh yes, I tell you, he is a kind man. He was well liked by the people. He never bought land here. No, he never. It's that shop he bought.

When I came back, I lived at Omaio. With my brother, Harawera, because he owns the shop right at the bottom there. It used to be the hotel. Of course, that place is ours, all that section is ours. Ohini o Makoma. That flat land was all our section. And when the hotel closed, my brother shifted down there. He put up another house from odds and ends of timber from the old hotel. He got it hardly

Reremoana on Orakei beach in Auckland, one Saturday afternoon, about 1909. She is in the centre, wearing a black dress. The girl on the left, wearing a white blouse, was her 'mate' from work. The older girl on the right lived next door to her. The others are family friends. *Reremoana Koopu*

Maraenui in 1907. In the background is the promontory Parenui, lying to the south-west of the community, and around which travellers had to ride at low tide to reach Hawai. The long low raupō building was the dining-shelter, erected two years before for the unveiling of the children's monument. In front are maize stores and kāuta, cooking-huts, for separate families. The first on the right is a kāuta for one family; the next two are maize stores for other families. The finished wharepapa, weather-board house, standing near to the meeting-house is Te Hurinui's, Reremoana's elder brother's house. *Auckland Weekly News, 14 February 1907*

for nothing. It was quite a comfortable house, and it's not far from the beach. So we stayed there. I lived with him, and my parents were at the old homestead at Otuwhare. Of course, I didn't want to come back. I had a good job in Auckland!

It was afterwards that my marriage was arranged. It wasn't our — like his and mine — I wasn't there at all! It was arranged between my parents and my husband's parents. It was their wish! You see, the families are related. The Koopu family, this is their home, Maraenui. Tohi's father, Koopu Erueti, he was the head of the Ringatu Church, and he had a house here. So we were married here. We had just a quiet wedding in their home, the old people's house, down by the meeting-house. Canon Pahewa, the Anglican minister of Te Kaha, he came down, he took the service.[22]

And then we lived with the old people in their home. We had to stay with them for quite a while. In the meantime, we got all the timber for this house. And we built this house. My brother is the main builder — Toma. He came over from Otuwhare and helped. He was the builder of the wharenui, too.[23]

My own parents are Church of England and I was brought up Church of England. But most of the families here are Ringatu. My husband is a Ringatu. So I had to! We have the Twelfths here. I go to them here. But I stay put here. You see, it goes around, the Twelfth. The next one is at Hawai, and then it goes back. The first one round, Waiorore, and then along, Otuwhare, Omaio, and here. Oh, oh, and Whitianga for the Firsts![24] My husband stays here, too, unless it's a big one, say the First of January and the First of July. Those are the big days, four days, July and January. They go round, but I never go to any of them, unless it's down here. They are in other places and it's too far. No, unless it's down at the marae there, I never go. I'm not a real Ringatu; I'm Church of England. My husband, he's more of a Ringatu than myself. I think Ringatu is all right, to the ones — you know. I admired them sometimes because they keep to their thing. Good. And although I am not a Ringatu myself, my children are.

Irihaere: I was brought up in the Ringatu faith, although I am a Catholic now. It was so nice. I can remember, we were only small, but we went to all the Easter camps, and we had our church things down at the marae. All the little kids. We had to learn those prayers. When they had their rounds, each child had to stand up and do their thing, all the prayers, the Ringatu prayers! I can still remember it. We used to have church, teachings, in the meeting-house and we learnt all these

Tohi Koopu as a young man, when he was attending St. Stephen's School in Parnell. Photographed, by permission of Reremoana Koopu, by Gillian Chaplin, 1984.

Ringatu prayers. Paul Delamere would take us, and quite a lot of his daughters. And then the older people from here.

Reremoana: And the grandfather, Tohi's father.

Irihaere: My grandfather was head of the Ringatu Church, initially, before Paul Delamere.[25] So he was head of the Church at that time. My grandparents were so dedicated; so was my father. But he didn't seem — I think he let other things . . . My grandfather's knowledge and all this dedication to Ringatuism, didn't rub off on his own children. Not like Paul Delamere's family, for instance; they are very good. It was Paul who built the whare karakia at Maraenui.[26]

The Koopu family outside their home in 1913. Back: Koopu Erueti seated, and beside him, standing, his son Tohi. Front: Tukutaura from Maraenui; Erena (Matekino) Koopu; the Bishop of Waiapu, Bishop A. W. Averill, who was visiting; Taiaho, with his little mokopuna Mahaki Koopu; Tatana Koopu, Tohi's brother; Tuakana Poihipi (Kuki), who appears in Maaka's story; Te Puke Te Kau (Tamaiti Kore), who was one of the Maraenui elders; —; —; —. *Auckland Weekly News, 10 April 1913*

The hui at the unveiling of the monument to Koopu Erueti at Maraenui, June 1939. About five hundred people attended, and Sir Apirana Ngata, as MP for Eastern Maori, officiated. The meeting-house Te Iwarau is on the right. *Auckland Weekly News, 14 June 1939*

My father was so busy, I suppose. He was so involved in all sorts, whatever was going on. He helped his grandfather, because they were intensely tied up with land — with land problems. And his father. Between them, they were like bush lawyers! They were *marvellous*. They must have been, with their scant knowledge of the European ways of conducting things, and yet they used to go from here to Wellington! It meant they had to go from place to place on horseback. You know, to settle all these tribal things about land. The lengths they went to to try and get things sorted out. My father helped him a lot, after he went away to school — to St. Stephen's.[27]

Reremoana: And Paora Ngamoki. That one!

Irihaere: They fought all these battles together.

Reremoana: But they're all gone, they are all gone! My husband, he does all sorts. He used to go bush-felling — oh, it's a hard — I don't like that at all! They go out felling at the back here, oh! Yes, and shearing. At shearing time, there's a lot of sheep from the back there. There used to be a homestead, the Saxby station, at the back.[28] During shearing time they had about ten shearers, all from here. But I didn't go with Tohi. I didn't think I can throw the fleeces! But it's not hard work, when you get used to it. You see them, it's nothing to these girls to pick up the fleece. I cooked for them. As long as you've got everything, the meat and everything, well, you're all right. Just like cooking for your own family![29]

Of course, I had to look after my children. Oh, I had quite a lot! I had twelve children! I had a big family. And after they are all grown up I got one of my mokopunas! I lost one, just a baby. He was only, oh, six months, I think. That was my first son, Tamahou. He had bronchitis. He died in 1914. But my first child was Moengaroa. She was born in 1912.[30] Auē! We got married [by the Church] after that! So then I looked after the family! I didn't work like before. I finished with all that after I got married.

They were all born at home, here. Their father helped me. Yes, he's good too. I like him because, when I am like that, I'd rather just have him.[31] Just my husband. Oh, I had one at my parents' place. Yes, that's right, one. And my mother comes, when she is needed here. Oh yes, those days! Every two years, more or less, I had my children!

Toma: At least I was born *inside*! That was in 1916. Most of the children here were born on the beach. Most of the women, they'd go down, light a fire, and boil the water. Salt water. At Te Kaha too, just below the hotel there, that's where the old kuias had their babies.

Reremoana: Oh well . . . I had to look after people. Oh, and feed them! You see, there's no road, no bridge, nothing from Te Kaha. And my husband used to ferry them across the Motu river. 'Cause he is the one that looks after the ferry. Anybody wanting to come over the Motu, they light a fire on that side. That's a sign there's somebody wanting to come over. They want the boat. Of course they can't cross the river — too high. So they just light that fire and as soon as I see the smoke, oh my goodness, there's another fire going! So Tohi just goes over and take — it's a punt — and he brings them across. First of all he brings them here and they have their kai here! Oh, my goodness me, I used to get wild! He said, 'Don't get wild. You have got to feed them.' And I said, 'I get hōhā!' 'Never mind, give them something to eat.' And then they'd leave their horses here, and they'd leave their saddle. Put them in a little shed we had at the back there. And leave the horses. Then they'd ring for a car from Opotiki to come and pick them up. Oh, it was a blessing when that bridge was open![32] No more staying here, and leaving their horses, and feeding them! I tell you! This place was the half-way house.

Irihaere: Yes, she used to have football teams. I said, 'Where were *we*?' 'You were all put in one room!'

Reremoana: When the bridge was open, it was quite a big gathering. Tohi got a lovely gold watch presented to him by the Coast people. And that chiming clock.

Irihaere: *That* was from the Pakeha people in appreciation of what he used to do for them. Because he used to put them up here, whoever! Inspectors, school inspectors, they all stayed here!

Reremoana: Mr Bird, we used to have him here.[33]

Irihaere: He used to be my nurse!

Reremoana: That's our mate! One year he came here and camped. He stayed with us for quite a while. Talks fluent Maori. It's good.

Toma: Mr Bird! I'll never forget that fellow! He became more or less part of the family. He loved his food cooked just — and she used to cook them just the way he wanted them! I thought, 'Oh, gee!'

Reremoana: It was a blessing when the bridge was open! Once, we were going for the day to some of our relatives across the river and our horse stumbled. I had Iri strapped, you know, tied in front of me, tied especially for riding. Oh, it was a clumsy horse! I tried to pull it to stand, but the current was so strong and away we went in the river, with her tied! Ani was at the back of my horse, and she was floating away, and Iri was in front, tied around me! And the bridge was nearly finished then. I looked at that bridge! My word, I nearly lost my family! I thought I was drowned!

But the Flu was one of the worst times. Oh, we had it badly. Yes, we were all sick with that Flu; we were all sick.[34] We had this house then, but this [door] used to be the back door. I used to sit on the back door, there, and call our fowls. My husband was very sick, and the children were very sick, and I was the only one that can manage to cook for them. And I used to think, 'Gee, what would I give for my patients in the line of stew? Oh, I know the best thing!' So I got a few maize, and I called my heihei. And they all come along, they know it is feeding time. I had quite a lot of fowl. I used to throw the maize in here. And the fowls come in here, and I used to close the door! And that's how I catch the fowl!

But the trouble is, when I get the fowl, I don't know how to — could I have courage enough to cut the neck? I think, 'I'll try.' Took my heihei up on to the block, and then, 'Now, what am I going to do next?' I got my axe. I turned my head around and I got my thing in the wrong — it struck the block, not the neck! 'Oh dear, what am I going to do now?' Of course, I tied the fowl. And this fowl rooster was just lying on the — so I turned round again and I put my axe — and that time I got my fowl!

But the rest of the family were very, very sick down at their house below, at the pā there, Tohi's sisters and his mother. They were *bad* and the grandfather had to look after them. When I finished cutting this fowl up, I looked back, and I saw this girl. 'That must be Kawhena!' Taiaho, her grandfather, had brought her to be with him in the meeting-house. And I saw this little girl hanging over our tank, trying to get some water. She was so dry. Our tank wasn't on a stand, just low, on blocks, and I saw this person. She had managed to come up the hill and she was bending over our tank. Of course the grandfather didn't know. So I came along and I said, 'Did your grandfather see you?' 'No.' 'I think you had better go straight to bed.' 'But Aunty, I am so dry.' 'Never mind, I will get you something to drink. Some hot drink. I will boil up some water. You shouldn't go there and drink that cold water. Get to bed. I'll get you something.'

There were so many! The whole lot of them. I had to look after that, what with my own, her, and the brothers – all sick. That girl, Kawhena, died. My sister, Kahurangi, and my brother, Te Owai, died. Oh, yes, I tell you, the Flu was bad. But the loss of the children was far worse. The others died at home. You saw them. But different with the children that were drowned. This little community lost so many.

Toma: She more or less looked after all the ones that got TB, too. I think every family had tuberculosis. Very few escaped that.[35] Most of *my* brothers and sisters. They had camps, then, right in the bush. You've got to get them away from the sea air – that's what the doctors said in those days. Moe, Taka, Uru, those three were at the camp at Matawai. Plus the cousins. And we had two relatives that died here, and she more or less looked after them, in turn. Uncle Tatana, they had to bring him back from Matawai, and Dad had a tent built out there. She looked after him till he died.[36]

Reremoana: But I tell you I had a trying and a hard time looking after my parents *and* looking after my family when we had that Flu. That was the hardest time.

But there were lots of other things, too! Just to think back! You know, before the road came, people going through to Opotiki, they had to ride their horses round to Hawai. Round the bluff, round Parenui. They have got to wait until the tide is out, because they can't get round that point, when the tide is full. 'Cos the waves bash right against the bank. And now, going on the road, they look down and they'll say, 'Oh, look, where we used to wait for the tide!'

They *survived*. With all the hard work. They survived.

Arama: Yes. Perhaps. But the men here: they didn't only have one job. They had a variety of jobs. All shifting around. There was forever a lot of things to do. If it's not bush-felling, it's fencing, and stock management, and all that sort of thing. Our father had a variety of jobs.

Reremoana: They had these farms on the flat, too. There used to be people working on the [development] scheme and Tohi looks after them. So many men working on the flat. And, you know, he was postmaster here, too?

Toma: I can remember he had a little shed over by the river, on the Haupoto station, the Saxby brothers' station. Where the stores used to be unloaded. I helped him out. But having to ride every day! So he had the office moved into the house. And after he died, in 1959,[37] my mother looked after it! I said, 'Oh, close it up!' I mean, there she was, on her own, with the mokopunas. I said to the others, 'None of *you* are willing to look after the Post Office. Oh no! All right! You all get private bags! No more coming over here to get the mail!'

Arama: And our father, he used to work, in the early days, at the Saxby station up the back. That shed had about ten stands and that's very large by modern standards. It was one of those big, old sheds. The men who would be working there would be from all these little communities. Then, later, the land here was under a Maori development scheme, as our mother mentioned. Our father was the one who looked after it. He was the foreman. That was just before the Second World War. Then, of course, they closed it up. And partitioned the farms into dairy units. So these three units were formed. Then, because of the modern trend, the units became uneconomical. Unless, of course, they were made bigger! So they absorbed one farm. Now, there's still two, under the Maori Affairs.

Originally, those farms carried stock cattle and sheep. Our father was looking after the stock. But a lot of their work was boundaries. Fencing off, scrub cutting. Ragwort cutting — I remember that one! Was one of those things that went on forever and a day! It was all slasher! And further round, at the point there, there was a landing-place where the men beached their whales. In the 1930s. My father — all his generation — they went whaling. Others more than him. But they rendered the oil down and bartered it. Particularly for timber. There's no kauri round here, and that's how it was brought in for the meeting-houses.[38]

Oh, once upon a time — going back about thirty years, it was all right. They had the numbers here. People. It was during the development of the area. *More than thirty years ago!* But we have found over the years that there's — about twenty years ago, yes — the urban drift. Everybody was asked into the towns to seek a living. Very few stayed back. I stayed. I was one of those that had to keep the home fires burning. It was all right, a few years back. But it is virtually not a living, but just a way of life. Oh, we have survived — somehow.

I am the youngest son. In fact, I was brought up in Tuhoe land. And it's only because we tended to drift around that, suddenly, they came and got me back over here.

Reremoana: Yes, he was about three, when he went to Waimana. You went to school there.

Arama: Oh, on and off ! We tended to move around where the shearing was. I actually started school regularly when I came back here. I don't think we were very long in one area. I have been to Maungapohatu, Te Whaiti, down to Wairoa, round Gisborne, and all those places. My foster parents really worked on shearing gangs. That's Tareti Moko and her second husband, that blind old fellow, Horo Tatu.[39]

Toma: And I was a whāngai, more or less. I actually lived with the Webbs at Omaio. And some of the older ones lived with our grandmother, Irihaere, and her sister, Titari.

Reremoana: You know what! When we went to get Arama — he was about seven — he hugged into the post! He wouldn't come away! I was telling his father, 'No use, look at him! He is hugging that post, we can't get him away!' We just wanted to give him a break, eh, bring him home for a while. Oh, no, not him, he wouldn't! He wouldn't part away with his parents. So we had to get another boy, his mate, and then he is satisfied. He will come! We had to bring that one with him! Oh well, I don't blame him, because they took him just as he was only small. The adoptive mother, she comes round now and again. Not forgetting him!

There's one thing round about here, you know, we never starve. The Maoris here, that's one thing they don't like, getting hungry. Going without their kai. They'd always like to plant something. And there's lots of fishing. Oh, no, no, not the women, but the men. They go out fishing. If not the river, just out there, on their boat, or on the shore, just on the sand. And the younger ones go out on their horses, round the point there. And it doesn't take them long before they're back with their mussels. We never starve here. Unless you're lazy. There's plenty of fish at the sea, plenty of kai. But when you're lazy, oh well, it's a different story altogether.[40]

Irihaere: I've heard her saying that her life was not really hard. She is telling one thing — but no, she is really playing that down! She's *worked*. She has had a hard life. Really hard.

Reremoana Koopu died on 14 July 1987.

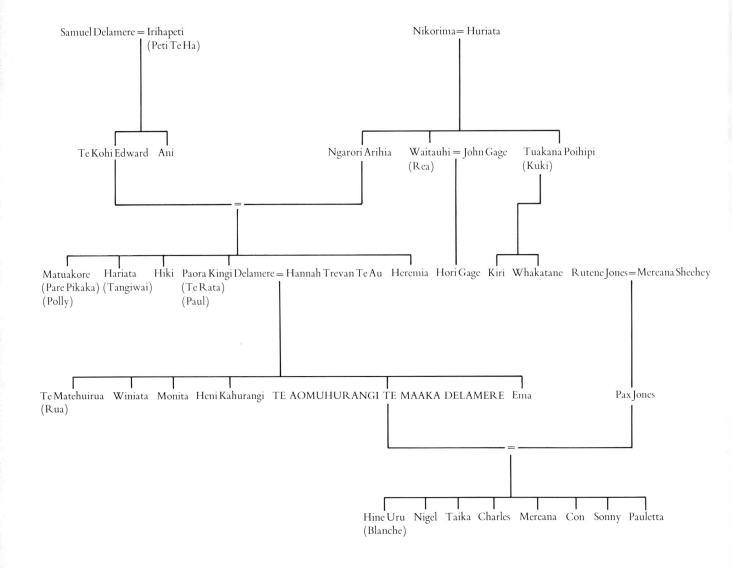

Samuel Delamere = Irihapeti
(Peti Te Ha)

Nikorima= Huriata

Te Kohi Edward   Ani

Ngarori Arihia   Waitauhi = John Gage   Tuakana Poihipi
(Rea)   (Kuki)

=

Matuakore   Hariata   Hiki   Paora Kingi Delamere = Hannah Trevan Te Au   Heremia   Hori Gage   Kiri   Whakatane   Rutene Jones=Mereana Sheehey
(Pare Pikaka) (Tangiwai)   (Te Rata)
(Polly)   (Paul)

Te Matehuirua   Winiata   Monita   Heni Kahurangi   TE AOMUHURANGI TE MAAKA DELAMERE   Ema   Pax Jones
(Rua)

=

Hine Uru   Nigel   Taika   Charles   Mereana   Con   Sonny   Pauletta
(Blanche)

MAAKA JONES

*M*aaka Jones is the daughter of Paul Delamere, the Poutikanga of the Ringatu Church. She was steeped in the Ringatu teachings from her earliest days. As she says, she knew that she had a 'commission' in life and this was fulfilled, in 1968, when she became a registered Ringatu tohunga, or minister. But there was, and is, a residual hostility towards a woman performing the sacred rites. Maaka's position within the Church derives from her family heritage — from her father, but also from the older women of rank within Te Whanau a Apanui, whose ancestry gave them their right to speak. For Maaka, her mana descends from both her paternal grandparents. Her family role also derives, most importantly, from her grandmother's younger sister, Te Waitauhi, who was a tapu woman. Waitauhi was the mother of the matakite Hori Gage, who became influential among the Ringatu.

Maaka was born on 8 November 1927. She was named Te Aomuhurangi Te Maaka, the Lifting of the Morning Mist. She grew up at Whitianga, the family home of the Delameres, which lies a little further north on the Tai Rawhiti, the East Coast, from Maraenui. The ties between the two communities were and are very strong, and it was during her childhood that her father erected the whare karakia at Maraenui, the first centre of the faith among Te Whanau a Apanui. One of the more famous of Te Kooti's waiata is that which he composed for Maaka's grandfather, Te Kohi Delamere, when Te Kohi invited him to the Rā at Maraenui on 1 July 1887. Still sung today, it is an adaptation of an earlier waiata aroha, a love song, and it is for the people of Te Whanau a Apanui.

> E pa to reo e Te Tai Rawhiti e
> Pākatokato ana te aroha i ahau
> Me tika taku rori, me tika ki Maketu ra e
> Hangai tonu atu te rae kai Kōhi
> Kai atu aku mata, kai atu ki Motu ra e
> He huihuinga mai no nga iwi katoa
> Hoki atu e te kino, hoki atu ki to nohanga e
> Kei te haere tonu mai nga ture
> He aha rawa te mea e tohe riria nei e
> He tuahae kei korerotia te rongo pai.
> Me tu ake au i te marae o te whare nei e
> Ki te whakapuaki i te kupu o te Hurae.
> He aroha ia nei ki nga morehu o te motu nei e
> Mo nga kupu whakaari e panuitia nei
> Ma koutou tatou e kawe ki te wai wehe ai e
> Kia mutu ake ai te aroha i ahau.

> Your voice calling from Tai Rawhiti touches me,
> Forlorn still the love within me.
> Straight is my road, straight to Maketu there,
> Then forward on to the headland at Kohi
> My eyes gaze on, over to Motu there,
> A gathering place of all the tribes.
> Go back evil, return to your dwelling place,
> For the laws will continue to come.
> What is this thing that causes constant quarrelling,
> It is jealousy lest the gospel be preached.
> Let me stand up at the marae of this house,
> To speak the message of July.
> My concern is for the remnants of the people of this land, and
> For the words of revelation being proclaimed here.
> May you take us to the water to sprinkle ourselves,
> So that my distress may cease.[1]

previous page Maaka Jones at Whitianga, January 1985.
Photograph by Gillian Chaplin.

Te Kohi Delamere is a central figure in the history of Te Whanau a Apanui because he bestrides two worlds, as Maaka comments. He became a convert to the Ringatu faith only after the wars of 1868-72. He visited Te Kooti at Otewa to learn the hymns, the prayers, the Scripture verses (pānui), and the songs, and it was he who brought them back to Tai Rawhiti. In their turn, Paul and Maaka created the first published text of the Ringatu faith, Te Pukapuka o Nga Kawenata e Waru a Te Atua me Nga Karakia Katoa a Te Haahi Ringatu *(The Book of the Eight Covenants of God and all the Prayers of the Ringatu Church), written for the centennial of Te Kooti's return from captivity, held at Muriwai in 1968. In this book Te Kooti's prayers and verses are presented in their original form, because (as Paul said in 1970) 'they are the Word of God. One cannot afford to make a mistake.'*[2] *But the faith has evolved over the years. Maaka's account, most clearly of all the narratives in this book, indicates the degree of change that has taken place in both ritual and belief. Originally, it was probably correct to say that Te Kooti 'does not believe in the New Testament, but is constantly quoting the Old'.*[3] *The extensive evolution of the faith towards the acceptance of Christ, particularly under Paul's leadership, is clearly shown in Maaka's narrative. The influence of Sir Norman Perry, a close friend of Paul Delamere's and a former missionary to Omaio, undoubtedly accelerated these changes. Nevertheless, the original vision of Te Kooti on Wharekauri, that God had promised to him that the confiscated land — their Canaan — would be restored, creating Maori autonomy, has not altered for many Ringatu. For Paul Delamere, Te Kooti was essentially the conservator of 'things Maori', while adapting them to a Christian ethic.*

As Maaka grew up she was taught the karakia, prayers, by her father in the traditional way, although for her the teaching took place at home. She went to the new Easter camps which Paul also started, just before the Second World War, in order to teach all the children. Both she and her younger sister, Ema, who also appears in our conversation,[4] *often travelled with their father to the Rā, the gatherings of the Ringatu, held on the ritually important days of the First of January and the First of July. Maaka was also sent away to Turakina Maori Girls' College for two years, in 1943-4. Here, she found that the Presbyterian teachings reinforced rather than contradicted her Ringatu upbringing, a comment that other women made to us.*

From Turakina, Maaka went to Gisborne, where she married Pax Jones, of the Rongowhakaata tribe, on 10 June 1948. As Maaka explains, it was the loss of their first child, at the age of five months, in 1950, which brought both Maaka and her husband again into a close involvement with the Ringatu. She went to her father and asked him to pray with her, lest her house become a wharengaro. With the conception of her eldest daughter, she went with Paul to the water, or te wai tapu, to be blessed. In so doing, she had renewed her links with ancient Maori practice.

Today, Maaka lives in Wellington. Her husband died in 1980 and she works as a teacher of Maori at the Correspondence School. She is widely consulted on many aspects of Maori knowledge. She is known for her compositions of waiata, two of which were published in the recent major anthology, Into the World of Light, *and she was one of the advisers on Maori poetry in the new edition of* The Penguin Book of New Zealand Verse.[5] *She is also frequently sought out as a tohunga by Maori people living in the city, not necessarily Ringatu. Her aim is to teach people to help themselves. She seeks to encourage them to look inside themselves to understand why their problems have arisen. She seeks also to reinforce their sense of pride in being Maori. She herself draws on many sources of strength. Not least is her belief in the importance of the family, and of its kaitiaki, guardian forces. Her understanding that there are such forces, which are transferred from one generation to the next, is a central one in Maori thought. For the Delamere family there are at least three kaitiaki: the owl, the dolphin, which is painted on the walls of the family dining-hall at Whitianga, and the rainbow. The rainbow is an omen for all Ringatu. According to where and how it appears, it is interpreted as a warning for good or for ill. The rehita, the white lunar rainbow, Maaka describes as usually an ill omen. Nevertheless, it was also Te Kooti's particular guardian sign, given to him, it is said, by the Archangel Michael when he appeared before him to tell him of the new God:*

> *Na, ko tenei ka waihotia e ahau te kopere hei tohu ki a koe mo te mate raua ko te ora. Ki te kite koe e tu porotahi ana taua kopere, a i nui te nganana, ara te whero, he tohu tena no te mate. Ki te kite ano koe i taua kopere i pai tona tu, he tohu tena no te ora.*
>
> *A ka hoatu ano e ahau he tohu mou ake, hei tiaki ano hoki i a koe, ara, he kopere ma, tona ingoa ki ahau, he Rehita.*

> *Now, this rainbow is left by me for you as a sign of misfortune and good fortune. If you see the rainbow cut short, and there is a great red glow, it is a sign of death. If you see that the form of the rainbow is complete, that is a sign of life.*
>
> *And I will give you another sign to protect you, that is, a white rainbow, which I call a Rehita.*[6]

Like the mana of the tīpuna, guardian spirits may be transmitted to the living. The interpretation of their appearances and warnings then rests with them, as do the words of the ancestors. In this manner, while there is a constant dialogue between past and present, the decisions, and the responsibility for them, belong to the living.

We first talked with Maaka in her flat in Wellington on 20 and 21 August 1984. She then, with typical generosity, invited us to her family wānanga, or school of learning, at Tutawake, their meeting-house at Whitianga, in the New Year. The purpose of the wānanga was to teach the younger members of Te Whanau a Paeakau — whose name derives from the drowning of the Omaio schoolchildren in 1900, for it means 'cast along the rocky coast' — their history and their faith. Maaka, her sister Ema Rogers, and their elder brother Monita, who is also a Ringatu tohunga, and a well-known figure on the Whakatohea Trust Board in Opotiki, were the main teachers. The wānanga became, at the end, a discussion on how to reach out to their absent young, living in the cities and particularly in Auckland. This gathering had enabled those present to 'connect up with our kaumātuas', as Riki Gage, one of the younger men, put it. 'It's no good having the knowledge without being connected', he added. 'It's the sense of affinity that comes just from being here, sleeping together, talking, arguing, eating together, that makes you feel, well, your chest goes out bigger!'[7] It is that vital sense of affinity, of belonging, which the whānau decided that they must bring to the city children. It was during the last full day of this wānanga, on 2 January 1985, that we recorded our conversation with Maaka and Ema in the meeting-house.

There were other women who were tohunga before me in the Ringatu faith. There was Te Onewhero from Kutarere, a dear old lady. And there was one other, from Tuhoe.[8] But with my father's family it was Waitauhi, and her cousin Taiheke, who were the tapu women and my grandfather made them so. My Dad trained me. 1968 I became a minister. When I say train, I just went along with him and observed, which is the kind of thing that they expect you to do. He said nothing; you did just what you were asked to do. And I got properly involved.

The most important person to me was my Dad, mainly because I think we all had built some importance around him, all our life. We were at the age round about six, seven when he took over the reins from his father. And he was learning, learning all the prayers that he could learn, and all the waiatas, the hymns, the psalms, and you name it! And to keep him company, he used us kids in the process. No lights; learning in the dark. He would be in his room, and we'd be in ours, my sisters and I, and my brothers. He'd start the prayers off and we'd get the message, we are learning tonight, what we call akoako. You know, he can pick out who is missing! And away we'd go in the dark, word for word! And he would repeat it and then he'd sing out, 'Mate, it is your turn!' 'Kahu, it is your turn!' If you make errors he would say, 'Nah! Go back again!' And you made sure not to go back, 'cos it would be a long lesson! And the first thing in the morning all we'd hear is this knock, knock, knock and that meant 'Wake up'. Whatever position you were in, you sit up! Then he'll start; he'll sing away and no one would join him. He knows we are asleep again! And then knock, knock, knock, everybody! That was discipline. Disciplining ourselves to get up and say your prayers and that was a one o'clock prayer in the morning! Sometimes I wondered, just like the other kids, gosh, you gotta go to school, milk cows in the morning! But it was disciplining us to do things for ourselves; and that was *important*.

I was born at Whitianga. The seed was planted there, from Te Kooti. It was intended for Maraenui, but my grandfather, Te Kohi, grabbed the seed, what we call te kākano, and that has remained now with Whitianga. Te Kooti used to come and visit my grandfather at Maraenui; he tested him. He appeared, and you only saw his cloak. He would catch my grandfather up at all times. Grandpa didn't know he was on the marae, but he saw a cloak, just the flashing of a cloak — someone entering and flashed out again! And he looked up; he knew it was Te Kooti. He'd done that three times, but he never caught my grandfather asleep! There was one time, the last time, the night before Te Kooti was arriving to visit him. Maoris in those days used to be able to foretell that someone was coming in: Grandpa had that gift of God. He said to his people to prepare themselves and if Te Kooti arrived on the marae, instead of receiving him, there was not to be a child nor an adult outside the house. They all had to go in and remain inside until Te Kooti had left. And everybody asked him why. He said, 'Well, he's coming here to test Te Whanau a Apanui.' And Te Kooti came outside and did a haka and things like that. And he performed; he tried to draw them out, but they didn't! And he said to my grandfather when he left, he'd never catch them shirking! His faith will live forever more. And that has remained; that's with Whitianga.

My grandparents had a home at Maraenui and they had their marae, the meeting-house and all there. Then the Motu river changed its course and scoured out the land; where the river is now there was land belonging to my family. It was called Te Kari, and they grew things there. I used to go there and get the cows, the new cows that had just calved, and catch the horses they'd let go. But because of the hazards of the river they moved to Whitianga. My grandparents had their home there, they had the wharepapa, but Grandpa had this little house that we called Grandpa's house. And then the meeting-house is utilized because his family grew and grew. Whitianga is our family marae. We were allowed on the veranda of Grandpa's house, but not inside. It was only a small place, where he could have his bed, and it had two windows. My Dad built it. But it was strictly private and we weren't allowed to enter that room at all as it was tapu. It was forbidden. It was a separate place for worship or healing — removing demons — that kind of thing.

Te Kohi Delamere. *Tutawake, Whitianga*. Photographed, by permission of Maaka Jones, by Gillian Chaplin, 1985.

But my grandmother, Ngarori, and her sister, Waitauhi, they sat at the door. In spite of the fact that women are doomed, or classified, as unclean in all aspects in Maoridom. But these women were tapu women and he bestowed that role on to them. And he also lifted the tapu in order to allow them to go out. No one was allowed in there till the ceremony was all over – maybe a week. Then he lifted the tapu to allow them to leave the tapu area.

That grandaunt of mine, Waitauhi, she held office – this is amongst her own family – her duties were the welfare of the Church, directing that things were organized, family behaviour, family structure, that kind of thing about the community, their own community. She was one of the kuias who went with her brother, Tuakana Poihipi, and Te Kohi, to see Te Kooti. They couldn't get to him, at Te Horo, with so many surrounding him. But they met him on the road, on horseback. Te Kohi gave his horse a kick and sort of signalled to him. And Te Kooti knew this fellow wants to see me. So he dropped back to where they were, way at the back, and they asked him, 'What about having a Rā, down here?' And Te Kooti sang that song, 'E pā tō reo e Te Tai Rawhiti', his feelings were so great that someone had asked him to come to bring the Rā here, and from the Tai Rawhiti. They were all there, Te Kohi and Tuakana, and Te Kooti cantered his horse alongside Grandpa and sang that song, meaning your voice struck me at that particular time; I've heard your voice, Tai Rawhiti. But I am heavily sad in my heart; I cannot come.[9] That's how that waiata goes, and it's important to us, to our

Ngarori Nikorima. *Tutawake, Whitianga*. Photographed, by permission of Maaka Jones, by Gillian Chaplin, 1985.

family. People were trying to capture Te Kooti, hold him prisoner, at that time, eh? for fear of his spreading the gospel.[10] What is this thing that is stirring: 'hoki atu e te kino' — depart evil! Let me stand on this marae — that marae was Maraenui; he would be there spiritually, even though he could not come. That waiata is a beautiful one, that particular one.

Ema: But for the tohunga role, as a woman, Granny Waitauhi was the one. I remember Aunty Kiri — that's Tuakana Poihipi's daughter — telling us, when the old lady came over to visit this kuia over here — Ngarori — when she set off, all the mokopunas got a bit hungry. They knew there was meat in the outside safe, so they got it and cooked it, and then they looked around for the pūhās. And the only place to find the pūhās was in her tapu garden. You see, the First of June was the planting of food and every Ringatu plants on that day, or before, and from June to November you don't eat any veges from where you plant. In June you plant your kai and then you harvest in November.

Maaka: There's also that special garden, it's called a māra tapu. Nobody goes into that garden. It's just a small — we had one at Whitianga and it was walled off — and that's God's garden. What grew there belonged to him, and no woman is allowed into that garden. Now — Granny Waitauhi had already planted their kai in their own garden, and you are not allowed to eat anything from your new garden, even though they're ripe, until 1 November.

Ema: But the mokopunas went and cut all the pūhās and put them in the meat.

Well, they had their tea! But there was some left over and then they heard the old lady come back! See, normally, she used to stay overnight, but this particular time she came back. She saw the left-over pūhā from the garden and the meat! She took the pot straight to the creek – it was a *long* walk – and she *threw* it in there! She left it for a whole week to get the tapu out of it! And the eldest got a hang of a thrashing, because she was the eldest and she knew they were not supposed to touch those kai. That's how they were, that generation, positive in their beliefs. Waitauhi used to sit at the door of the meeting-house every time they have karakia, and when all the little mokopunas were kicking one another, or running out, now and then she'd open her eyes, and grab one of the shoes outside there – and bang! She'd fire a shoe at you! She was the one – if anybody had a bad dream, 'Come on, everybody in the meeting-house', didn't matter what time of the night. Get them all in! They're going out, shivering, right in the middle of the creek, and she did the water, Waitauhi. They come back again, and the next day somebody else has had a bad dream! She did a lot of that, you know, to safeguard you, to make those things not happen to your children. She could conduct a service. Waitauhi is the water – when you go to wash your hands – when we come off the cemetery – we tāuhi, sprinkle, ourselves with water, and that was her name.

Maaka: Grandpa, Te Kohi, appointed her when he came back from Te Horo. Because at that time he was active. From his time, beer or anything that might cause violation here wasn't permitted on this marae. And it still isn't. You know, my grandfather was a soldier of the Queen, he fought for the soldiers, but he got interested in Te Kooti when he was taking refuge in the King Country, and he went there. He went to Te Kuiti, and his knowledge came from Te Kooti. He went there to go through basics; he wanted to know the Church from its roots, how it was formed, what it was all about. And after Paora Ngamoki (he was the chief of Te Whanau a Apanui, he held office before my grandfather) – *my* grandfather – to Koopu Erueti, and then my Dad.[11] They're all related.

Ringatuism was great in those days. They travelled miles to have their meetings. They met and they'd go to Maungapohatu, in the Urewera country, and sometimes Mum and Dad would be away a week, just travelling. It took a lot of time and they stayed there for the absolute [the full] three days, and then return.

And the other thing: Grandpa was so tapu. He never used hot water on his body. And he particularly wanted Daddypa to take no hot water, too. But Dad

The whare karakia at Maraenui, built by Paul Delamere and the families of Omaio and Maraenui. The white monument to the left is for the Omaio schoolchildren who were drowned in 1900; that in the centre is for Koopu Erueti. Notice the bell in the porch of the whare karakia. Photograph by Gillian Chaplin, 1983.

Paora Ngamoki, chief of Maraenui and a major figure within Te Whanau a Apanui. *Rangi Motu, Auckland*

said to him, 'Oh, I can't do that. You can have that; keep that to yourself. My wife is a South Islander and she is Pakeha sort-of, and my children — I don't want anything to reflect back on the kids.' So he didn't have to carry that one out; but he said the rest he'll have. My grandfather was called by us Dr Coldwater! But during the time of that great Flu epidemic, he contracted pneumonia rather seriously. Dad and Mum had not long come back from the South Island and Dad said they'd have to use hot water — he was perspiring with all that — to help him with the hot water-bottle. But Grandpa refused; and he got worse. He was in a tent out here. And Dad pleaded with his father to allow him just — just his feet! Grandpa had to lift that tapu himself, remove it on himself, and then Dad said, 'That's hopeless! Allow me to come to there [to his chest].' Well, he got by different stages to his knees! And Dad was trying to get that hot water-bottle to his chest. And he said, 'All right! To here! No more! It's tapu!' And he permitted him to do that. Dad said he didn't waste any time, using the hot water-bottle, and his fever broke. And he was pleased, because after that he put all his tapu back on himself again. He was a man of that kind, that standard. He didn't need hot water; he never used it again. He never allowed food over his head, of any sort — cooked, raw, whatever! We all grew up with that respect; there were certain things we didn't do with Grandpa. But Granny might spill a bucket of water on him and enjoy it!

So you see, it was all through my life, with my parents, my grandparents, my grandaunts, we observed, we behaved, and you learnt that way. You didn't ask too many questions. At home, since I was six, we had the Easter camps and from the moment I learnt how to speak — and Maori was my first language — I learnt to pray. You heard it so often that you could rattle things off, or join them! It was that family communion, family unity, we had. When my grandfather was ageing — because he died at ninety-six[12] — he knew he needed a member of his family to take over the reins from him. He mentioned it several times when in session with his family, but the others weren't interested at all. The older sons weren't interested. And so it was in one of those sessions that the family had got together, and my Dad rang the bell — it was his duty, being the youngest boy,[13] to ring the bell for the service. After the bell had finished ringing, he came in and it's time for service. And Grandpa sat there. And Dad told him again, 'It's time for service.' And then my grandmother started to get fidgety, and she turned round and *she* told him the bell had stopped! He ignored her. She was going mad but much as she wanted to holler, she couldn't because the order had gone, the bell had rung. Twenty minutes they waited for my grandfather to get up and conduct the service! And Dad realized he was waiting; Grandpa's thing was taken off him. He wouldn't take part. And my grandmother asked the eldest son, next one, and the next one, right round the room and they all bowed their heads. Then she looked at my father, and he was standing up. He started because it was so terrible, sitting there, and everybody holding their tempers when it is time for church. So Dad had to do it himself. He knew one hīmene, he knew a pānui had to start it, and a waiata, how to start it, couldn't finish it off himself, but he could finish the whole service. And he started! From then on, Grandpa didn't do much of that, unless my father was absolutely stuck. As I told you, Grandpa used to live in the little house there. And my grandmother used to say, 'Oh, don't go to him. He's gone all silly up there.' 'Eh?' And Dad would go and he used to tell her, 'Just leave him alone.' He would go himself and speak to his father, and he gave him what he wanted. Dad said it was just as though there was nothing wrong with him; it was all clearly stated: you have to do this; you do that. And here's the meaning. Immediately after, he'd close up again. And it forced Dad into a situation where he had to get cracking. He started to learn all the karakia, pānui, waiata, and all those things. He had to learn a lot in such a short time from his father. One of them was what going to the fire was all about: the burning of the coins. He had to go through all that. His uncle helped him a lot, Tuakana Poihipi. And it forced Dad into a situation where he realized he'd have to give up the things he always liked to do, and wanted to do, like boat-building and sports.

It was the same for me. To become a minister, you go through a formality, they assess you on your ability, in your performance. My father, as the head of the Church, took me with him and he observed me, while I was observing him! I was asked to bless a house on my own, with him there, and go in with him to heal, delivery, and things like that. He'd ask me to perform, administering on to the patient. And you went through that knowing full well — sometimes it was very, very nervy, very moving, very emotional, and very exhausting — because you are under the power of someone else. That's how you go through your ordeal. It's not a matter of two weeks; it's a matter of time. Then I was ordained by him. You go through a form of being blessed. It was in my house, at home in Gisborne. It's a test, just as he went through a lot of tests, after his father lost his memory in the service. My children are Ringatu. They in turn, as they grew up, learnt. One of my sons goes with me everywhere I go, and he observes. And there's one or two times, I have had to ask him to conduct the service when I'm not feeling well. I'd say, 'I want you to come with me and you conduct the service.' But when it comes to administering on to somebody, I'll take that role because until he's a registered minister there are certain things you do not do.

. . . At Whitianga, we didn't have Twelfths, but we had Firsts, the First of June and the First of November, that's the huamata and the pure, one for the planting and one for the harvesting, the first fruits, the taking out of the garden. It was their pattern that basically Te Kooti had set up for them. When Te Kohi went to him, to ask about the religion, he would only give him so much. He said, 'That'll do for you; the other part is too tapu.' But Grandpa said, 'Let me have that too', and that part was the huamata and the pure. The old fellow brought it back to us. The day before the First of June you take your basket, your kete, with whatever food you want to plant, they're all seed, ngā purapura; each person would bring a little kit and they'd hang them on the lemon tree that used to grow by the meeting-house. This side of the tree was tapu because it leaned onto the house; we never ate the lemons on this side. The meeting-house, to us, was tapu. You'd see all these baskets, about two dozen baskets, hanging up on that lemon tree. They were from each mother. It was lovely. That's really the common role of the women, getting things ready, and to bring the kai along, and put it up there, ready for the tohunga. Then the night before the First, the bell rings and we all take our baskets, and they are placed in front of the meeting-house, and the bell is ringing. It rings until everybody has been there. The seeds are placed into bigger baskets, and then you all queue up and you go along picking the things up and feeling them. You go from basket to basket, and then you go inside ready for the service. There were rows of people; the women would take the babies and press their hand on the basket. Whāwhā they called it: 'haere ki te whāwhā'. And the bell's ringing.

Ema: And everything about the process was tapu. If men had cigarettes in their pockets, they must put them away. You go just yourself, clean.

Maaka: You are given the blessing of touching those things. Then you go inside. The men, the tohungas, they'd pick up those baskets, to plant the seeds.

Three sisters: Kahurangi; Maaka; Ema. Photographed, by permission of Maaka Jones, by Gillian Chaplin, 1984.

Some will be allocated to the special garden. Another group will be allocated to go to the sea. They take some of those seeds down to the sea and they are thrown to the four corners of the earth. That's asking God to produce fish. Dad used to go right in waist-high in the waters, saying his prayers.

Ema: And they'd plant next to the shore there, that's for the land. They'd have their karakia down there, all to do with planting.

Maaka: And some they plant at the guarded fence, in the fenced garden, and they are taken care of by God. No one goes in there; that's God's garden. On the First of November the tohungas, the men, harvest from that garden. They bring it down and bless it, and they keep some from that garden for the following year. The river is also opened then. They'd catch kahawais for the hākari and everything is cooked for the feast on the First.

All the women go home and get the fruit that's ready from their orchards and their gardens and they'd share. Everything is put into the hāngi, even tobacco! In those days they used to dry tobacco in the kitchen over here, and they'd put all that in, kūmaras, torori! Make sure you don't get the flavour from the tobacco! And grain, apricots — they're still green! — and loquats. There used to be a big loquat, on the other side of Grandpa's house.

Ema: We'd be on that loquat tree, we'd hear them having their service, blessing everything, and as soon as we hear the 'Āmine', we're on the tree, looking around, and somebody else is in that strawberry patch out there!

Maaka: And we'd set the table outside for the hākari. They laid the tables like long white sheets, calico strips, and we'd eat from that. But not long before he died, Dad got rid of all that. He said, the generation today cannot, they're not holy enough to operate that performance. Rather than they get hit by not doing it right, he got rid of it. Because, when you do not carry things out according to God's plan, someone suffers. Rather than have degeneration after him, because of ignorance, he decided to do away with that. He felt it was too tapu for them to handle.

Ema: Aunty Kiri, she was one of the old people, women, in *his* time, who objected. She stood up in this meeting-house and said to him, 'What right have you got to change all these laws?' Somebody else stood up and said, 'Yes, you've got no right to do that; this is how it was handed down from the pakekes.' They were really hostile. And he stood up, and he said, 'Well, he's noticed even old Whakatane Poihipi, that's Aunty Kiri's brother, he's been with him for years, he's not doing things properly.' Everything, the kai, had to be planted before the three o'clock bell, before the setting of the sun, but he'll wait till after, and then go. Things like that. When you do things to God, you must be positive yourself, in tapus and all, otherwise it will reflect back on the kids or somebody. His way of thinking, today, it's better that we got rid of all that and let our children grow up in the understanding that you are with Christ. It's the only way out of things today.

Maaka: My father broke away from a lot of the old things, like the sacrificial things they used to have. We used to take offerings to any feast that we have, a Rā. They used to take the koha, and take out from the offering a percentage, and take it down the road to get burnt, as a sacrifice. It was called going to the fire. The burning of the coins was a symbolic form; an offering. Well, Dad broke away from a lot of things that were not required — because of Christ.

Ema: The other thing that Dad stressed was that there were various stages of the Bible. He taught us about Christ and that's where we are now.

Maaka: He also explained the reasons why that planting was the type of Christ

— you know, how out of the old seed you get the new plant. They had to keep last year's seed in with the new seed, as well as keep seeds from those that went out to the sea. That's God's, to reach all parts of the world. In that garden they had to make certain that there were old seeds *and* the new seeds, and the intermingling of that growth. It is symbolic of society's growth, as well as the growth of a people, and the type of Christ — that new crop. He lived again after the Crucifixion. All that is in it, in that teaching, which he was properly taught by his father.

Dad explained that Isaac and Moses were types of Christ, pre-Christ, that God had planned. He was going to sacrifice his own Son. So those things are done away with, those burnt pennies. Dad went round lifting the tapu off all the pennies lying around where people burnt offerings. There were heaps on the beach, and we all helped clean the pennies. They were black and green! He started lifting the tapu on the koha places about forty years ago. And he asked Norman [Perry] to put the pennies in the Church bank.[14] And people waited to see if Dad was going to die. He said, 'No. It's in there if they read their Bible. You're wasting time thinking that those pennies will look after you.' It was about 1968 when he stopped all that.

. . . You know, Whitianga, when my mother first went there, was still so

top Haka at the opening of Te Poho o Rutaia at Otuwhare in 1916. Otuwhare is Reremoana's and Paul Delamere's marae, where both were brought up as small children. *Whakatane Museum*

bottom A welcoming haka, or haka pōwhiri, performed by both men and women at the opening of Te Poho o Rutaia. *Whakatane Museum*

primitive. It was awfully hard for her to adapt. She was brought up an Anglican, a staunch one. But she became a Ringatu and she was my father's strength. She really was. She gave up lots of things to be beside him. She went wherever he went, always, and in a lot of things, like checking over a script when he was going to speak at an assembly meeting, she did all that. To be plumb on what the Bible said, what the reference was, because Dad wasn't educated like his other brothers.[15] And there was a lot in English. But when he got it properly and then he translated to the Maori Bible, he was accurate. But Mum helped him to get it so accurate. But when she first went there, to Whitianga, she felt no one liked her. She couldn't speak Maori and she used to cry a lot because she couldn't. And she couldn't stand the suckling pigs! Even though my grandparents had this big house, next to the marae, they suckled pigs quite handy to the house! And Mum said they didn't even know how to knit; she used to make bootees and things for my eldest sister, Matehuirua, and then she'd wash them out and then dry them outside and she said when she wasn't watching, they'd all go and peep! 'Oh, look at this! Wonder what these are for? Must be for the baby!'

. . . They all went whaling from here. Grandpa Kuki, Uncle Karauna, Hiki, and Dad. You see, my father's family, my grandfather's family, and my great-grandfather, they were all whalers and that was predominant in their characters. That's how my great-grandfather Samuel landed here, as a whaler,[16] and the whaling boat is an important element in their lives. My grandfather, he had those Maori super-powers; he was steeped in Maori mana, my grandfather. He could go whaling and he could see the whale coming up there, and the boat this way, and his son, Hiki, would rave at him that the whale's going to come up *that* way — the wrong way! But when they would get to that point, Grandpa'd order the harpooners to get ready, to stand up, because of those things that he had. They were mostly of the sea. And the dolphin is one of our kaitiaki — but it is from Samuel to us. And going back to the name Delamere, it's of the sea — or of the mother.[17]

Uncle Hiki, Baby Whale they called him, used to go out, and he always wanted to do the harpooning, and he nearly always missed it! The whale would come up at a certain distance away, and Grandpa would say, 'Row this way; it's going to come out.' And the laws there, when you are at it, you don't swear. But Uncle Hiki'd sing out, 'Why row *this* way? The bloody whale is coming up *that* way!' He violated all the rules at sea; that's Uncle Hiki! He picked up my grandfather's harpoon and used it; he had no right to touch it! He threw it away through temper at whaling! But it was returned by those seaweed people, sea-gods, atuas in the form of people. They walked the marae and they warned my grandfather. An eye for an eye. You see, he had that Maori mana, and he had become a Christian and he knew that he couldn't carry both. He had to get rid of that Maori mana, Maori mākutu. What you'd call exorcism; pāuhua is what we call it. He had to do it to himself, and his family. He had to deliver his whole family from those things that he had. Well, they didn't want to be got rid of! So they warned him! And his daughter, the eldest of the family, Polly, she nearly lost her life because of that, whilst he was in the course of doing it. She got very, very ill. And so he urged them *all* to pray. They all came together; she pulled through that; so did he. She was the last one he was doing that to. He was a great man really; greater than my Dad.

There's waiata that relate to those whaling incidents, and the women sing those waiata. There's one that relates to the loneliness of the women; they're left

Cutting up a humpback whale at Maraenui. Photograph by Canon Hakaraia Pahewa. *Auckland Weekly News, 11 December 1919*

Hannah Delamere; Matehuirua, her eldest daughter; Paul Delamere. This photograph was taken in the South Island, before the family returned to Whitianga to live. Photographed, by permission of Maaka Jones, by Gillian Chaplin, 1984.

Matuakore (Polly) Delamere, the eldest in the family of Te Kohi and Ngarori. *Tutawake, Whitianga.* Photographed, by permission of Maaka Jones, by Gillian Chaplin, 1985.

when the men go away and sometimes they'd stay out there till midnight. Chasing the unknown out there. And they'd land somewhere else with their whale; not back home here. But when they catch a whale — and they were still going out when I was at school[18] — they'd render the oil and send it away.

Ema: That's how they started to build their maraes up. The money from the oil.

Maaka: Sovereigns.

Ema: The old house here, at Whitianga, had no floor; then they managed to put a floor in.

Maaka: They'd catch a whale and the *whole* district would share in that, not just the people that caught the whale. They'll all gather to help with the rendering, cutting the meat, and they take their portions to feed their people. It was a great community effort, and that way of life brought the people together, closer than today.

Well, I grew up there. Went to school at Omaio; walked there; walked back! About three-and-a-half miles each day! Started school when I was six. It was a long walk from Whitianga, but we enjoyed it in the cold — frost-bitten feet, hitching a ride with someone who's got a horse, and then you are left behind, bawling your head off! That was life; we learnt a lot of that! When I was about ten we moved over to Omaio, so I didn't walk so much then. But we'd light the boiling coppers for my mother early in the morning, on the way to school. She'd take all her coppers down to the creek below our place and she'd go down there and wash and boil the sheets. We in turn had our own billies marked with your name on it and you took your own billy down on the way to school. We used to go right home for lunches, and get your billy dipped, and back home and leave it there. That was when the tanks ran out. And Mum would always greet you, 'DID you bring your water?' 'Yes. With my lunch.'

Omaio was a lovely school to go to, because we were mostly Maori. The people were involved with their school. My father was the chairman till I left that school and had a lot to do with the running of the school.[19] He was a great organizer, before he really gave up his time to the Church and he used to run the sporting club. Each year we had a huge sports-meeting that included all of Whanau a Apanui. He was a great footballer himself. He used to play football with Rua, and he said the only way to catch him was to let him pass and then swing onto his long hair! Because once he got that ball he was like a greyhound! At school, we were forbidden to speak Maori. You got the cane or the strap. All native schools, all around. There was no chance. Looking back, it's appalling. But Apirana [Ngata] had something there really; we *had* to learn how to speak English.[20] But we should have been allowed to speak outside, in the playground. In spite of all that we didn't lose our native tongue. At *that* time.

I won a boarding scholarship; I went to Turakina. It helped develop the things that I had learned. I grew up as a Maori child, but at Turakina I extended the things Maori that I knew about. All our classes were taught in Maori. The teachers that taught us Maori were Europeans and they spoke Maori beautifully. They were fantastic. I couldn't have been to any better school than Turakina because Miss Kinross was a superb principal.[21] Turakina reinforced all the things that are important to me today. You extended and learnt about Scripture. Mr Laughton also used to come and visit us.[22] He was a great friend of my father; they used to exchange views on Christianity. From college, it was the growth of what was instilled in us by our parents.

Maaka; Hine Uru, her eldest daughter; Pax Jones. Photographed, by permission of Maaka Jones, by Gillian Chaplin, 1984.

I was there for two years and then I went nursing, in Gisborne. I wanted to be a teacher, but my mother had decided that the only job in the world for a young girl was nursing; you clocked in at such and such a time, and you don't mix up with anybody — safest place to go! But I'd already applied to be a teacher and after I'd left, my papers for teaching arrived — but I was already nursing! So I could have been a teacher right from the beginning! And I performed! But I was a good nurse; because that was what was required of us. I often used the knowledge that I'd learnt from my Ringatu upbringing with the sick. Particularly with Maori patients that were Ringatu — they'd want a prayer, and we'd share a prayer. You'd put that into action. Unknown to me all that was building up.

A favourite portrait of Maaka's, taken with Hine Uru. Photographed, by permission of Maaka Jones, by Gillian Chaplin, 1984.

I was twenty-one when I got married. My husband, Pax, was Anglican and I got married in his church, not because I wanted to, but I had to, because we were a long way away from home. He was a railwayman and we moved back into town [Gisborne], bought our own house, brought our family up. I have eight children, all alive. But I lost the first one. Pax's uncle was an Anglican minister and he refused to come. I didn't blame him really at that time. But I went to my Dad to ask for a family. We prayed together and as soon as I was pregnant he took me to the water for blessing. Hine Uru is a person who is asked for; she's our eldest girl. And after that, every christening we took the kids back to my Dad. And that's how they all became Ringatu. And Pax was pleased really, because he was involved in the Ringatu Church and he helped with his own people in Gisborne. In Gisborne, we started the Ringatu Sunday school and then we got the parents involved, and the women, the mothers, joining and learning. Our kids also went with their Dad to the Anglican Sunday school and to church; we didn't want to create barriers.

I didn't have any whāngai, but we took in children because they couldn't get on with their own families. Sort of wards. We'd make sure that they attended school quite regularly. The Maori Welfare people, they'd go out to these families in the rural areas, and often they'd ask, 'Oh, do you know someone?' and they'd suggest us. And it used to annoy me sometimes, because I was struggling with bringing my own children up — they were all young together, they needed our fullest attention and you'd get the odd child in between, extra! A young girl, when it is not your daughter, you are inhibited a lot in the manner that you control them. One girl there, for about a month, she thought she could just take off when she wanted to, and that presented problems because we were off looking for her, up to town! But it didn't influence my daughter. It made it easier. My children were often out looking for them with us! We have managed to retain our strengths as a family from our upbringing. We have managed to impart the things we learnt from my mother and father, my grandparents, my grandaunts and uncles.

When I went to Christchurch to do my training to certificate myself as a Maori language teacher — that was in 1974 — the whole family came. I'd been teaching long before that — oh, since 1958! You see, I left nursing, I brought up my family, and then I went back to teaching. But I ended up arguing with senior teachers what Maori was all about. So I finally accepted to go to Christchurch to train. I was glad I went there because our particular group did in one year the course of three-year teachers and we got certificated fully, just like them. It was all compressed into one year. I went straight into promoting itinerant Maori teaching in Christchurch in secondary schools. I was on my own promoting Maori there for two years before I managed to get another itinerant teacher in. There were four when I left — to come to the Correspondence School here [in Wellington].

It was from Turakina, which reinforced the Christian side of things, that I

Paul Delamere at
Rongomai-Huatahi meeting-house,
Omaio, 1970. Photograph by James
Cooke. *Wilson and Horton, Auckland*

sensed that I had a later commission in life – somehow or other I was going to be
totally involved later on in life. Being a Ringatu minister – as a woman – I've had
some trying experiences. Like going into strange people and being asked to perform
a funeral ceremony, and you don't really know them. Right out to the back of
Ngatapa, and you feel strange when you arrive at the place, and you wonder
whether you are doing the right things, and you do ask God to be with you, for
Christ. The strangeness is that there are men there, and there's resentment, you feel
it. You know that someone else there – you see, there's lots of ministers that are
not registered, they cannot conduct a funeral service, and they are there, and they
know all the karakia, but they have no power to perform. And you're looking over,
and you're saying to yourself, 'Well, those people, they know. I know that they
know. But they're listening –'. It's having authority over the men, as far as Maoris
are concerned.

But my father instilled into us, each and every one of us, that you make prayers
part and parcel of your life. He and I wrote the books, the prayer-books, together.
The first one was for the centennial at Muriwai, in 1968. It was done in order to
offer the younger generation something worthwhile. And he chose Muriwai for
that centenary because those were Te Kooti's people that had branded him, sent
him to the Chathams. 'Go te poti, te poti!'[23] He stated that, to him, the most
important thing was to have the centennial there, to make amends, a form of
repentance. It is time that his people accepted, not him, but what he founded. The
revised prayer-book I finished typing the night before I left for Christchurch.

As a minister in Wellington I am called away all hours to go and tidy up some
mess that some young people have done to themselves. These children often don't
belong to the Ringatu faith, but something's happened in relation to their
Maoriness. The last lot I went to help out, sixteen youths (they aged from thirteen
to twenty-two) and they'd been working under the P.E.P. scheme.[24] These
children had been forced to go and clear the cemeteries. And they were told to have
their lunch in there. Some of them got very, very sick. And they'd looted stuff from
everywhere they'd gone, not just cemeteries. They'd taken a carved walking-stick
from a blind person, a Maori blind person. They thought it was a great joke. As
soon as I sat down, I said to them, 'There's something right behind me that's
bothering me.' No one mentioned anything. 'Well,' I said, 'there's something right

behind me, must be something you children know about.' And they said, 'Oh, it's the walking-stick.' And they said that they were seeing people demanding their stick back. They were all spooked. They said, 'There's a whole lot sitting up by you', and I said, 'Oh, well, forget about them. We will get down to what you've been up to.' And they each told their experiences and I said, 'Well, all this relates to the whole lot of you have got things that do not belong to you. You've been on cemeteries.' '*I've* brought that stone from the cemetery.' '*I* brought back something else from the cemetery.' Well, it told its own tale.

I get called out sometimes three nights a week for that kind of thing. And before I actually bless them, I give them a lecture, telling them just what it is like being sent into an urban situation and the difference being at home in a rural area. The extended family doesn't work here as it did back home. You were able to borrow and return, you could go along and pick up somebody's bike, or horse, or whatever, but here in the city it didn't work the same. And you have to explain that, and all the values that they had left behind, that they had forgotten about, and their association with drink, their association with people pushing drugs, or whatever, and it is a different kind of world. When they arrived they were too young to live in the city and not being able to cope they got into pranks. It is pretty sad. But they are Maori, and it is because of the fact that they are Maori that you do that extra bit.

Other Maori people have brushed aside their Maori side. They have gone Pakeha-wise. They get so far; they have got to stop and come all the way back. There's many cases like that. And the more they dabble with things Maori, the more they come up against a lot of problems for themselves. They are not aware of their kaitiakis; and they are not aware of their tribal affiliations and just what made them a people. For us, for my family, our kaitiaki is the rainbow. It was handed down from my grandfather, to my father, to us. Before he accepted Christ, Grandpa was given through his ancestors that mana Maori. He had to take it. He was burdened with all that. He had all those gifts — for reading signs, of the sea, of the skies, of the land. He'd be in his tent, and he'd lift the flap up, and he'd peer and he'd say, 'Oh, there's a sign up there.' Even the drowning at Motu, the schoolchildren; he had foresight that that was going to happen.[25] He had had the signs and he read them. The rainbow. Something was going to happen between Maraenui and Whitianga. So he told the people to pray. But they ignored him. My father had been told not to go with the other children. Otherwise, he would have been on that canoe. And Granny Kararaina, who was brought up with them as a whāngai, she ran after the others but my father chased her and he hit her — he gave her a hiding! So she grew up with that knowledge — how she had escaped — and became a firm believer in the laws of the Church and of obedience to them.

The rainbow is God's way of talking to you. And there's different signs that I know, good or bad. Before I leave Wellington on a journey, I say my prayers, for safe — and along that journey a rainbow is sure to appear somewhere. If it's not a very good sign, right across your pathway, you better say 'Stop!' and have prayers. It is a warning. You see them at night, too, that's the rehita, a white rainbow, a lunar rainbow. That's a bad omen, usually. The rainbow, we have been taught is a warning, mostly. It is saying, remember me. Rainbows are the gift of this particular family. Grandpa could read them, and Grandpa could tell you exactly what's going to happen. His son, his youngest son, Heremia, he begged him not to go to the war, the First World War. Grandpa told him, 'You are not going to come back', and he said, 'Oh, how do you know?' 'The reading is there.' But he went —

Hiki Delamere in his soldier's uniform of the First World War. *Tutawake, Whitianga*. Photographed, by permission of Maaka Jones, by Gillian Chaplin, 1985.

Bearing the coffin of Paul Delamere, December 1981. On the side nearest to the camera are Tamahehe Takao, a Presbyterian minister, from Te Waimana; Hamahona Rikihana, a Ringatu tohunga; Sir Norman Perry, Paul's close friend and a former United Maori missionary to Omaio. The pallbearers all represented different Christian denominations. Photographed, by permission of Maaka Jones, by Gillian Chaplin, 1984.

and it was rather nasty the way he died. He was blown up. He was instructing, and his hand-grenade went off.

At the time my grandfather was living with us, we had this morepork and it perched above the table in the old cook-house where we had meals. It was frightening and it would swing upside down there. It was about *all* the time. You'd go outside and see it; come back inside, and it's inside. We weren't allowed to hit it or anything. My Uncle Hiki, come back from the First World War, he was a real Army fellow! He was caught several times trying to kill it! He tried to throttle it with flax, but the old lady, Ngarori, intervened, 'Don't you do that! That's Te Kohi's kaitiaki!' And when my father died,[26] and he was lying for one day at the meeting-house at Otuwhare, where he was brought up as a child, three owls flew up into the house. One flew off each side into the rafters, but the third sat high above him as he lay there. And when the body was brought to Whitianga, they flew ahead of the *mate* the whole way. Those guardians are from Te Kohi to Daddypa. When I got home to Whitianga, this morepork led me into the house: that's how *I* knew he had already gone, though he was still warm. And afterwards, when Winiata, our eldest brother, went home, that owl stayed with him for a week.

From our upbringing, we have learnt what a family is all about. What the Maoris call whānaungatanga, but it is deeper than that. We learnt it from my grandparents, from my grandaunts and uncles, from my mother and my father. You ask about the women: well, *without* the women in organization, arranging things at a hui . . . that's where my mother came in, and my grandmother. Ngarori was the one with the discipline. She would speak on the marae. With Whanau a Apanui, we can get up and talk on certain maraes, certain women, when it's absolutely necessary. But only certain people, and that lot is my family. My grandmother was the eldest of her family and being the eldest she had that seniority, and she was very well respected. Her tongue was like a whip![27] And Matuakore, Aunty Polly, she was the eldest in Dad's family, and she's the boss! It was she who used to tell my father to come and tōpū with her — sit at her feet. He'd say, 'I don't want to sit with you!' And she'd say, 'You'd better. It's an order. I'm your boss!' — but very affectionate! In the Church, too, they have their roles to play. Inspection, discipline, administering to the sick. Those were the major roles of Taiheke and Waitauhi. The most important pattern for me, however, was that familyness of praying. We have adopted that from them. That family unity, that family communion, was instilled into each and every one of us, and it's proved its worth.

Taking Paul's body from Whitianga across the bay, in remembrance of his great love of the sea, to his burial. Photographed, by permission of Maaka Jones, by Gillian Chaplin, 1984.

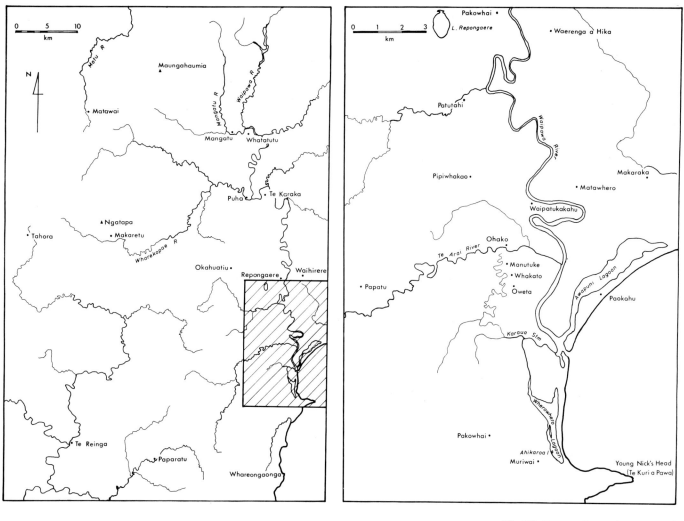

Fig. IV: Poverty Bay. The course of the Waipawa river, the Awapuni lagoon, and the Wherowhero lagoon are drawn as they were about the turn of this century.

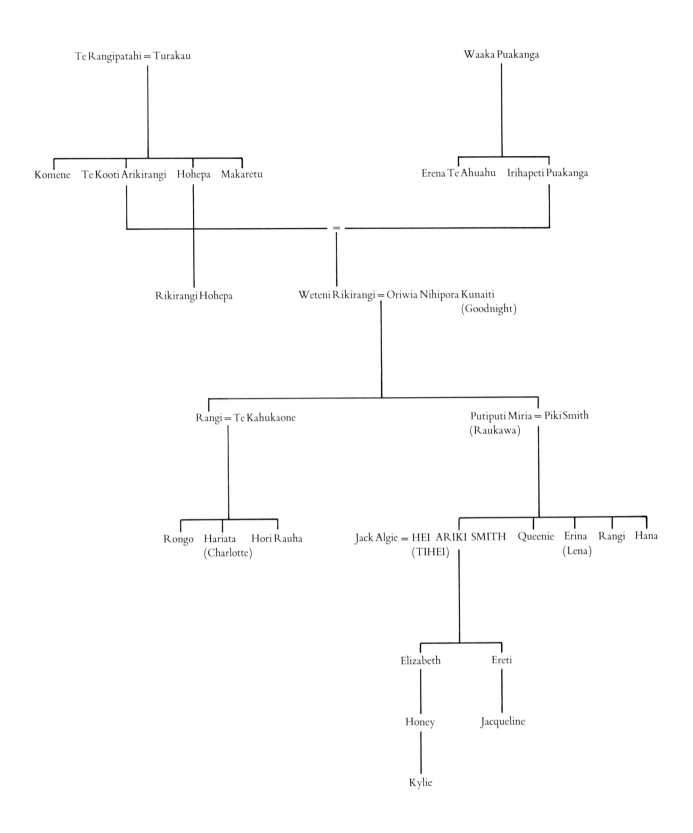

HEI ARIKI ALGIE

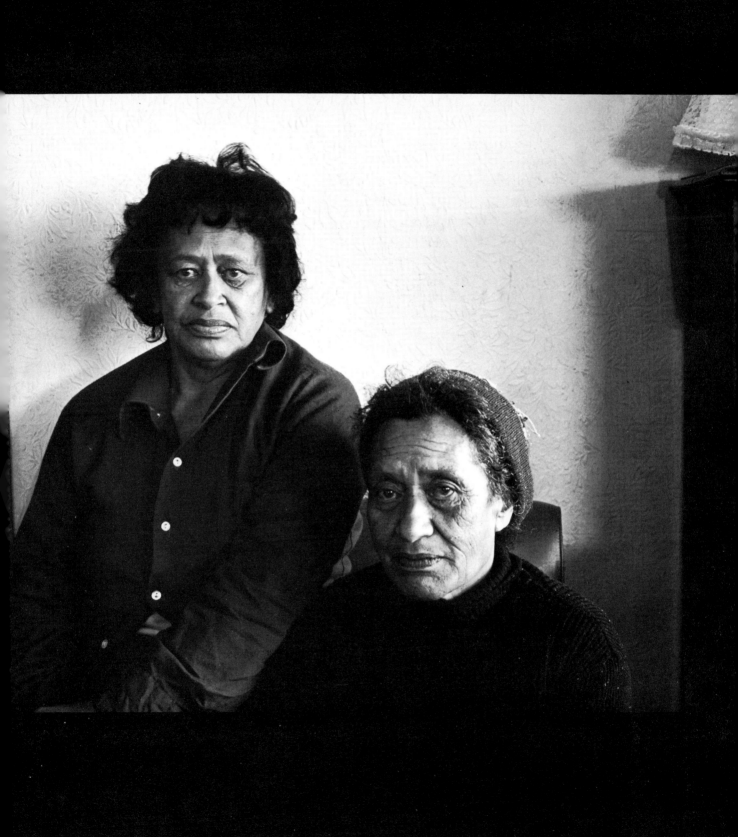

*H*ei Ariki Algie, or Tihei as she has been called since her schooldays, is the senior great-granddaughter of Te Kooti Arikirangi. She was born on 9 December 1913 and is the eldest daughter of Putiputi Miria, who was the only daughter of Te Kooti's only son. Although Tihei is not the eldest in the Rikirangi family, her cousin Charlotte being born six months earlier, she has become its head. This mana she traces from her mother and her grandmother, Oriwia Kunaiti: that is, from the women.

Tihei's story reveals how those who take for granted the triumphs and superior morality of the colonizing interests can force a family into feeling ashamed of being who they are. Te Kooti has been described as a violent 'rebel' and 'murderer' in most of the written accounts. The hostility in this caricature was also fed by the local antagonisms in Poverty Bay. Te Kooti ordered the imprisonment and the execution of some of his major opponents, both Pakeha and Maori. One of the leading Kawanatanga chiefs had been Waaka Puakanga, who was the father of Te Kooti's first wife, Irihapeti, and the grandfather of his only son, Weteni. He was taken prisoner by Te Kooti in the raid on Oweta pā on 14 November 1868. Paratene Turangi, the Rongowhakaata chief with whom Waaka had been closely associated, was also shot there with five others.[1] These executions were deliberate and selective utu, or requital, for their part in sending him into exile and for sustaining the pursuit and opposition to him. Te Kooti also took many Maori prisoners from Poverty Bay and among them was Oriwia, who became one of his wives. She was later recaptured by Ngati Porou at Te Hapua, in the Urewera country, on 1 September 1871.[2] But Oriwia herself had by then become a staunch Ringatu and she returned for a time to Te Kooti, when he was living in exile with Ngati Maniapoto, before finally leaving him. Her personal history apparently was not passed on to her grandchildren.

Many Maori families in Poverty Bay have ancestral histories which can be traced to both the opponents and the followers of Te Kooti, as civil war was forced upon them. The East Coast war was precipitated by the government view that there was no neutrality: support for the new faith, Pai Marire, which was brought there by its missionaries in 1865, was axiomatically seen as a statement of disloyalty to the Crown. From this date, families and individuals were compelled to take sides. When Te Kooti miraculously returned from exile, with all the former Pai Marire prisoners but as the leader of a new faith, Ringatu, these painful divisions were immediately reopened. Each Maori family has, therefore, had to take its own decisions about the transmitting of its history. Putiputi, Tihei's mother, recounted her own difficulties in coming to terms with her descent. In her childhood, she said, she was accustomed to hear her grandfather denounced 'as a brigand and a mass-murderer. . . . She lived to hear tributes paid to him by the highest in the land' — the Governor-General, the Prime Minister, and Church leaders — when she attended the centennial gathering for the return of the Exiles, held at Muriwai in 1968.[3]

Tihei only learnt about her descent from Te Kooti when she was about fourteen years old. Her grandfather, Weteni, was present as a little boy at Oweta pā. He was being looked after by his guardian, Natana Takurangi, who was taken prisoner by Te Kooti. One of Te Kooti's wives pleaded for Natana's life because of the child, but he was executed.[4] The little boy then remained with his father but was captured with a group of refugees from Te Kooti's camp at Patutahi on 15 December 1868. He was then sent to Waiapu to be brought up by Ngati Porou, his father's antagonists.[5] Weteni learnt to dissociate himself from his father. Consequently, Tihei's own attitudes towards Te Kooti were, and to some extent still are, ambivalent. But in her account she is very clear about the importance of family and, in stressing its centrality in her life, she is also emphasizing the responsibility that she now has, as the head of Te Kooti's family, for the Ringatu. This is a role for which she may not have been fully trained but which she sees as a vital part of her life.

previous page Tihei, with her sister Erina, May 1982. Photograph by Gillian Chaplin.

Tihei was born and grew up at Manutuke, a small and predominantly Maori community on the banks of the Te Arai river, about thirteen kilometres to the south-west of Gisborne. She attended Te Arai school (as the local Maori school was then called) between 1921 and 1928 and she has lived at Manutuke most of her life. The settlement is particularly famous for its five meeting-houses, which belong to the Rongowhakaata people. They include the elaborately carved and painted Te Mana o Turanga, completed in 1883, which was a centre for the Ringatu Twelfths, and the much plainer house, Te Kiko o Te Rangi, built about 1920, which is Tihei's marae.

Manutuke's population has not changed significantly during Tihei's lifetime, although the proportion of Maori living there has risen. In the 1936 census, of 540 people at Manutuke, 360 were Maori. By 1971, the township had grown to 672, of whom 485 were Maori. As Tihei recalls her life, it is apparent that she has undertaken the many roles which are demanded of women when they are both mothers and income earners. She worked as a fleecer on shearing gangs both before and after she married. As she said unequivocally, it was hard work. She married on 23 December 1944. Her husband, Jack Algie, was a Pakeha carpenter, and later building supervisor, for the local Maori Affairs Department. When they had earned enough money to build their own home she left her job, but she returned later to work seasonally at Wattie's canning factory, where she suffered a partial loss of eyesight from being splashed by caustic soda, used in hot water to peel tomatoes. Her husband died in January 1967 and Tihei now lives with her mokopuna, Jacqueline, whom she has brought up from birth. The most important thing to her today, she commented, is her work on the Incorporation committee of Te Whakaari, the block of land in which she is a major shareholder, her portion being inherited from her grandfather.

We visited Tihei three times in her home at Manutuke. On the first occasion, in 1982, her younger sister Erina (Lena), who lives close by, was with her. We had originally intended to ask Lena to be part of our story, but she suffered a stroke in February 1983, which left her unable to talk. On the occasion that we met, Lena was full of life and energy. She spoke vividly of the day when the Rifleman was captured on Wharekauri by the prisoners. They performed a haka for the crew and, as the men dropped back, the women came forward, singing, gyrating, and 'shaking their bums' at the seamen. The sailors started to grab at them, and were drawn by the teasing, inviting women into the centre of the group, where they were seized by the men hidden inside. It was the women who, by enticing the sailors to their captivity, initiated the escape of the Exiles. This story, more than any other, remembers the neglected women prisoners on Wharekauri.

The first conversation we had with Lena and Tihei took place on 17 May 1982 in Tihei's home. We talked in her front room, where the family photos and sporting trophies are proudly displayed, and Tihei brought in her heirlooms from Te Kooti for us to see. This occasion was not tape-recorded, at her request. We have here drawn on the notes which were written at the time. Subsequently we recorded two dialogues with Tihei in her home, on 26 November 1983 and 7 December 1984.

I didn't know anything about Te Kooti. I used to hear how he was a rebel and all that, and I didn't think I was connected with him. We weren't encouraged to talk about him and whatever he did, if he was a good man or bad man. We weren't. But then we were asked to write about Te Kooti at school. I was in Standard Six. And I didn't *know*. I didn't know anything about him. I went home and talked about it, and was told to forget it. 'Don't worry about it! It is over! Finished.' I went back and told my parents that my headmaster was threatening to strap me. Because

Identified as Weteni, son of Irihapeti Puakanga and Te Kooti; it is, however, more likely to be a portrait of Weteni's son, Rangi. Both Rangi and Weteni were said to have resembled Te Kooti closely. The flowers are a sprig of kōtukutuku. Photograph by C. P. Browne, Gisborne, 2 April 1908.
Alexander Turnbull Library

I didn't know anything about Te Kooti. And I asked them — *then*. My mother said, 'Oh well, it is too late now.'[6] And she started telling me who we were, who he was. My grandfather was there and she said, 'That is his son sitting over there.'

He never talked about Te Kooti and never told us anything about him. I must have been about fourteen then. I was frightened — I was frightened that someone might take to me because of what *he* did. Except, of course, some of the big girls and boys at Manutuke school: there was quite a few Ringatus around at that time and they knew who Te Kooti was. They were the ones that were taught. I wasn't afraid of them. But other than that I was. I must have been very timid at the time.

The first Twelfth I went to was after I left school. I was taken by old Tawhi Brown — Mrs Wi Pati[7] — and Waioeka Brown, to Takepu. I went with Charlotte. Charlotte was their favourite[8] and she was the one they used to take around. It was because she wanted someone to go with her, they took me. Those two old ladies — they knew all about Te Kooti. Tawhi was brought up by him. She used to go to those open-air services they had at Whareongaonga, in my grandfather's time. They used to go there for a Twelfth — they'd walk all the way — and Tawhi was one of the very few women who got there. They discarded the ones who hadn't got the faith. They could tell why people wanted to go. If you have faith in what you do, you'll do it! That power the Ringatu had, it is gone with those old people. Waioeka was another. She was always talking to my grandfather; she was always around to my grandfather. She would come out and have a talk with him; I don't know what it is about, but she used to make these special trips down on her gig. She was the one, she knew all about Te Kooti and she knew all those waiatas. She can tell you the history.[9]

Waioeka Brown. *Te Aroha, Tapuhikitea, Puha.* Photographed, by permission of Charlotte Hitaua, by Gillian Chaplin, 1983.

Not long after I left school I contracted this TB — I went to work, nursing in the Cook hospital, straight after I got proficiency[10] and I think that's where I must have got TB. I was in hospital for about two years. When I came out, it was Waioeka who took me to the water, to bless me. They did that on a cold morning, too! I have never forgotten the cold morning! They walk you in there and, well I remember this for myself, they just sort of dump you in and out. As long as your head is covered. Or throw you backwards, that way. Waioeka took me to Mahia; it must have been the first Twelfth after I came out. Or, it could have been a January, because there was such a lot of people there. There was quite a few who were sick. Those old people, they heard I was coming out and they just picked me up and took me! Though I think it was with Mum's consent. I don't think she would let me go, seeing I was just out of hospital; she must have been there. I remember I only had a singlet. Mother, or somebody, put a blanket on me and we went in. And that was all I had. And out! The tohunga was an old blind man, and there was a lot of people from all over — so I think it could have been a very important Ringatu meeting.

One of the places I went to was Wainui. I was about fourteen. My grandfather, Weteni, and Rikirangi [Hohepa] took me.[11] My grandfather went there for something. They wanted him, and they took me. They wanted to take me there; they thought that by taking one member of the family they'll find where they buried Te Kooti. Of course, my grandfather, he boobooed that. He didn't believe that. And he went away to Auckland to the races and left me there with these people! They took me on a canoe. I remember going — walking first and then getting on this boat. This is night-time. They were rowing me to wherever I was to guide them. Rikirangi was on that canoe. He said it has got to be one member of the family, and they had to keep me awake. Hoera [Poaka], he was a tohunga from there, up that way, went on that canoe.[12] And others from Ruatoki. But they didn't keep me awake! They just told me we were going for a ride, and get some flounders in this creek. Because we had to walk to this boat and I could feel these things, and I was slipping, and they said, 'Oh, it's flounders' I was tramping on. We got in the boat and away we went. I enjoyed all that, until — I can't remember going off to sleep! But I did. I have told that yarn to several people and they just looked and said, oh, I should have kept awake! I might have found out where they had buried Te Kooti. But when my grandfather came back to the pā, he heard about me and he laughed at them. He told them, 'No'. Perhaps that's why he took me; he knew what they were going to do and tested them out. It must have been a test for them, for those tohungas. They never ever tried it again!

Te Kooti Arikirangi Te Turuki at Rotorua, 1887. This drawing, by Revd Richard Laishley, was made at the same time as the full-face portrait, reproduced in the Introduction. *A 114/4, Alexander Turnbull Library*

We had to eat outside, at Wainui. They spread a mat or whatever they had on the ground. Frosty morning too! I couldn't get over that! We had to sit out there and eat — this is breakfast. And we never got to sit, 'cause they say it's too wet! Out

– eat – finish, and we will go back in the meeting-house. And have your prayers. They pray all day just about – or to me just about!

We went to Ruatoki. It must have been July, a First of July, because I remember this frost. And they set the table out there, on the grass. You sit down, or you kneel, and you eat. They never had a meeting-house, or a kāuta. All their little houses – you see them coming out with whatever they have cooked, for the meal. Not like us: you have one kāuta and you cook everything in that kāuta. No, they were coming from all round, their little homes, each one bringing something for the table. You might have the potatoes, and I'll have some meat, and someone else will have meat – and whatever.[13] The same thing was happening at Wainui. They had a carpet – like runners, you know?[14] They put it on the ground. This was at Wainui, and they did that at Te Reinga too, where I went with my grandmother. Sometimes they cart this carpet around. If you've got the Twelfth here, and the next Twelfth is there, they just take everything. This carpet, they just take it around. Where you are going, take your carpet! And they'd take plates, cups, everything. They send the food along first. And then they go with the cooking utensils. I might go with about half-a-dozen cups – even just four – it is plenty, because someone else is coming with cups, well, mugs. There always seemed to be plenty of everything. And they used to have rourous. The women are making their rourous.

When we went to Wainui, we went on the gig, the big one. Two horses drawing it. And you sleep on the floor, the kids, sometimes. Or you'd sleep under it, because it took two or three days to get there. I know we used to pull up, make a picnic of it. All get back – and away we go again!

Going to Te Reinga, we have to leave early to get there, too, with these old people. We would go with my grandmother. As a child I'm always up there with my family, living in their raupō huts. Because Oriwia goes to visit her two brothers, Paratene and Parangi. Her father was Waata Paratene Goodnight, or Paratene Te Rongo and they were all Ringatu. Staunch those Goodnights! *She* was brought up at Waikaremoana, but her brothers were brought up at Te Reinga, and we'd go there to see them. It was a lot of fun to go there. I rather liked the life. Just raupō huts, which I thought was very comfortable. And they had special little huts, with just the top and one side, and they have a fire in there. That's where they cook. If it's a cold night, they take the ashes in to where they sleep. That time of your life you do enjoy, when you are a child. Go diving in the river where that waterfall is – and I always looked forward to going on the hill and sliding down on the koka leaves. Go eeling with them, and of course, you fall asleep, and sleep on the bank! Just cuddle up. And you wake up and you are sliding down! I have a rod, a stick, and just a bobbin, with worms. You thread the worms, and make a bobbin of them, and put them on the end of your stick, and dangle it in the water. That's all we do. The kids say to me now, 'You gotta have a hook.' I say, 'We never had a hook.' 'How can you catch it, then?' I say, 'Eel, when they get their mouth round the worms, they never let go! So, when you flick them out, well, then they drop off. That's what we do!' My grandson, he says he's got to go and get a bait from town. I say, 'Go out there and dig up the worms!' He says, 'They are too small, those worms. You can't slit them.' I say, 'Put them in dock leaves and tie them up.' You show them how to do it. 'Oh, just like that?' 'Just like that!'

Sometimes, you get the small eels. You go and just track, track, track, and get the water dirty. Just like calves, you know; you put your hands underneath their belly and throw them. Well, that's all the little ones – and they are the sweetest eels. Ngōiros, they call them. You cook them on an open fire. Just light a fire and put them on stone, pieces of stone, hot stone. Put them on and sort of grill them. Lovely. But you are not allowed to do that when they are fishing. You have it after. When they finish the fishing, then you can have your eels. Oh no — even the bones you don't throw back in the river. You dig a hole and bury them around. They say unless you do that the kai will run away. It will never stay there. It won't be plentiful like it used to be.

It's like when you go out to the sea to get kinas. You're not supposed to eat kinas and throw them back, or even when you shell them. Some people, they go to the beach and they take jars and they take the kinas all out and put them in jars and then throw the shells back in the sea. Maoris, that know, don't do it. Some of these Maoris, they see you do it: they'll growl. You are chasing it away from their village. And they want them to come back. They say it's true. When you start doing that, you go back — there's nothing! Never take a small kina. Wherever you turn a rock over and there is a little kina, you turn it back. Turn the rock back. That's their belief. At that time, I never used to believe it. I'd turn a rock over and leave it like that. And the old people, they'd come around and see the stone turned over and put it back. Now, I like to believe it. I try and tell my children.

We were brought up by my grandparents and my mother. Four of us, Charlotte, myself, Queenie, and Mary, we were all round about the same age.[15] Mary was adopted by my grandmother. Her mother died when she was a baby, in childbirth, so my grandmother took her and brought her up. We lived in the old house very near here, at Waipatukakahu. The four of us used to sleep on the veranda; they had a bedroom for us there, with the canvas round. It was Waaka Puakanga's house and, according to our family, Te Kooti was brought up there. I don't know. Of course, it was Irihapeti's land.

The family, photographed on 9 December 1914. Back: Weteni Rikirangi; Te Kahukaone, wife of Rangi Rikirangi, holding their son Hori; Putiputi Miria, with Tihei on her knee; Oriwia Nihipora, with Meretene (Mary) Himoa. (Oriwia's moko can also just be seen.) Front: Hariata (Charlotte) Rikirangi; Rongo Rikirangi. Charlotte and Rongo are the two older children of Rangi and Kahukaone. In the foreground are fine cloaks, one of which was placed over Tihei at the family arrangement of her marriage, which, however, did not eventuate. Photograph by T. Thomas, Makaraka, Gisborne. *Tihei Algie*

My grandmother taught us a lot of things. She taught us anything to do with the Maori. She taught us to poi. In the evenings she used to make us do the poi — it might be long pois, it might be short pois, might be the double poi. She was always busy doing things like that for us. Weaving, making kits, and mats, she taught us all that, even making piupius. She used to sit and teach us. My uncle Rangi used to go and collect the kiekie. Every time she talks about it — she is going to make a hat — she tells him to go and get them. And he comes back with the kiekie. I don't think there is any round about here, now.

She also used to make us say our prayers, every night. In the morning she just taps on the wall and wake everybody up. Sometimes we go into her room and sit down on the floor, or on the bed — anywhere — as long as we're there. And take part in that morning service, or at nights. Always. Never miss. As I grew older, I started going harvesting round here and she used to get us up *early* — so we won't go without saying our morning prayers. She used to come round, 'Wake up! Wake up!' Have your morning prayer and *then* she gets your breakfast. I don't know why we didn't carry on. I think we were too busy doing other things.

She was very tall, taller than my grandfather — and older. She was about three or four years older than him. I have heard he ran away with her.[16] I always used to admire her hair — she had long, long, fine black hair. I always liked to put my fingers in her hair. One thing she was very strict about — she doesn't like us bothering her when she is cooking. Because it's wasteful — wasted food. If you are going to do it for her, you had to do it properly. Like baking bread. She'd tell you, 'It's your turn to bake a bread', and you stay there till it's done. And that's what we don't like. She is very strict with her cooking. By the time you are finished washing your hands — you've got to wash your hands — you're tired of it, you don't want to do it. 'Get out! Run away then!' She does that on purpose, so we'd leave it alone.

But she never mocked. I think she was rather remarkable. She taught herself to speak English to us. Different words she'd pick up and she'd remember. And when we started to talk about her, she knows what we are talking about! And she'd tell us too! My grandfather, I think he went to school; where or how long I can't remember. But he could write. The only thing I have seen her do is to sign her name. We'd give her papers and tell her to sign her name, and she does.

She wasn't a midwife, but if she had to, she could. There was a lot of them round here used to do it, but my grandmother didn't. But she'd go along. Different lots will come and say, 'Will you give so and so a hand? So and so is having a baby.' And she'll go there. Just to keep the fire going, boiling water, keep other kids away or whoever. Anyone around about here, Manutuke — she would consider them all her family.

Mum had us at home, or some of us, and my grandmother was there. Because I remember our grandmother taking us all in to the stable — we used to call it the stable — there was an upstairs, with stacks or whatever they are underneath, and she used to make us comfortable in there. We're on top. Get us out of the road while the doctor was in the house. Mum always had Dr Wi Repa. For the two youngest in the family, my brother and sister, anyway. He was a Maori doctor around here for years.[17] He always had my grandmother. He didn't want anyone else. Sometimes he used to pick her up and go and help other women. She was very strong.

There was a traditional way — at least what I heard — of limiting families. The mothers are made to have flax roots.[18] They boil the roots and a mother drinks the water. Every month. That's what she uses to clean her out. It's a good opening medicine. And that prevents her hapū — pregnancy. If you take too much of it when you're pregnant, they say you lose it. If you are a few weeks in the pregnancy. But I only heard that. They say, 'Ah, well, if your grandmother was alive, or if your mother was alive, you'd do this, and they do that.' I don't know.

My grandfather ruled the family. He really did. Because we all lived together. With my father he used to say, if they are going to do this, well — and Dad used to do it. Grandfather would say, they plant potatoes tomorrow! Whatever Dad's doing, he would drop tools. My grandfather wouldn't allow us to go to the pā. These other families, they go with all the children to the pā, but my grandfather didn't allow that. My grandparents used to go — quite a bit. But he didn't like to see us go over there. When the meals are set out and everybody is watching whatever the kids do, well, the grandchildren have got to go home! Have their kai at home. That's why he said, 'Stay home'. Naturally, Mum had to stay home with us, so we were never forced to go to the pā. But when my grandfather died we lived at the pā for a while. Oh, that was a big tangi — long tangi, too. Must have been there for about three months. It was at Ohako, over here. Where the Ringatu used to have their open-air services, before they had a house. When they built the house, they named it Te Kiko o Te Rangi, the Flesh of Heaven.[19] But that tangi, it started off with my cousin, Hori, he was killed on the Te Arai bridge on a horse on Christmas Eve [1927]. He was thirteen.[20] My mother and my grandmother were bringing up the four of them after my uncle Rangi's wife died. Between them and us there was ten to bring up. It was the Christmas season, so we shifted to the pā. We all went there and stayed there. Of course, we thought it was a good life, lots of people there. Then, not long after, my grandfather died.[21] So we more or less stayed on the pā. It was a long time afterwards before we went home. There were people coming from everywhere. You know, we think it is all over and then we get the message — another party is coming! Get together again, everybody! You know, round the district: 'Come'. When that is all over, they stay for two, three days, and then they go back, wherever they come from. That's all over, and then we hear someone else is coming! They don't do that nowadays. With my grandfather they come from Ruatoki, even Waikato. I just wait and see all the people coming. It was because he was Te Kooti's son. I remember they were arguing where they should bury him. These people would come and they would say, 'Oh, they are coming to take him', and then there would be a big argument. And I remember that is what they say, 'Oh, your grandfather is going to go away; they are going to take him away' and you'd just sit there and wait and see if they will. They didn't take him.

My grandfather was brought up as Church of England; but my grandmother was Ringatu. It's only when I go to these Twelfths that I start to think *that* might have been where I should be. You see, I think I am in the Pakeha world. But when I go to the Twelfths and I understand what they are talking about, and what they want us to do, I say, 'Yes, you are right.' I get drawn to them. I feel closer to them. But my mother, she was brought up more or less among missionaries. At Hukarere. She was quite young when she went to Hukarere College and she stayed there. I used to hear her talk about Miss Williams, Miss Bulstrode and Miss Emily.[22] They were like an aunt to her. Very close kin. She went back to my grandfather, but only for a little while. Most of the time she was there. Because my grandfather was going around working on the stations, shearing and that, and he didn't think it was a life for his daughter. That's why he left her at school. That's all he did, worked to pay

Putiputi Miria, when she was at Hukarere Girls' College. Photograph by Mrs Cobb, Napier & Hastings. *G. & D. Hill collection, Hawke's Bay Art Gallery & Museum, Napier*

for her board. My mother was very religious, being brought up in the Church of England with the Williams family, and Miss Bulstrode and Miss Emily. So it was her way, too, not going to a pā. Too many children to lug around to a Maori pā. And my father, Piki Smith, was the same. He was from Ngati Kahungunu, but I think he was a Pakeha Maori, too. That kind. He didn't care much about anything to do with the Maori pās and things like that. I went that way and my mother more or less encouraged it. I suppose if she didn't I would probably have been a real Maori.

I have lived all my life in Manutuke. Te Arai school — that's all my education. And I had to leave school several times because I was always sick then. Once, I must have been about eleven, there was typhoid and we weren't allowed to drink the school water. One little girl died, a Pakeha. And I was lucky to pull through. So I missed school, and had to go back later.[23] We were taught in English, but we were never told, 'Don't talk Maori at school.' The only time we got the strap it's when they hear you swearing outside, in the playground, and they would come out and find out who it was. I was never beaten or told, 'Don't talk Maori.' I don't think my teachers at the time stopped us. They were local people — and I do know they understood when you start swearing in Maori! Soon haul you inside for that!

After I left school I contracted this TB. I wasn't allowed to work, then, by our grandparents. I had to stay home and make do with what Dad brought back for us. I didn't start work till I was twenty-one. Both Charlotte and I — we just had to stay home. See all the other girls going to work! I told Mum if she didn't let me go I was going to run away! Before that, when I was a child more or less, we'd go harvesting for old John Clark.[24] Hay. Driving the sledge! He had the only farm round here; he bought a lot of land from the Maoris. He had all this hay and he

Putiputi's wedding, at Holy Trinity Church, Manutuke, in 1912. Piki Smith stands with his bride. Seated, second left, is Rangi Rikirangi, Putiputi's brother. Weteni stands second from the right. Photographed, by permission of Tihei Algie, by Gillian Chaplin, 1982.

used to have all the sledges — kōneke. My father had the shearing contract and my grandfather was a shepherd for him. But that's still home: you get up in the morning, come down here, get on your sledge, and away you go! When I *left* home to go to work, I was twenty-one! And I had to run to my *own* father's gang!

He was looking for fleece-os. He had the shearing contract with the Barkers — Percy Barker.[25] So that night Charlotte and I hopped on a car that was going there, and went. Went and got in the girls' room at Rototahi. And went to sleep. Mum and Uncle George — her cousin — arrived next day to take us home. And Dad told her to leave us. He said, 'If she can't do it — out! Seeing they're here, they can just jolly work hard.' That's my first job. Run away from home to go to Dad! I wasn't so bad as he thought! So, every year we went out with him. It was a great time. Plenty of fun in the shearing sheds. There were always six girls, the fleece-os. And six shearers, two pressmen, and a sheep-o. I suppose we got about one-and-sixpence an hour. I can't remember. I know it was a nice big cheque. Well, in those days it was big money. The Barkers had good accommodation for us, for the workers — about four rooms, two for the men, two for the girls. It's the workers themselves, after they damage their mattress — with pillow fighting and all — and then they've got to put up with lumps and that! Then they moan!

I had to do the cooking sometimes — when the cook go on strike! But that was only in an emergency. We used to have an old man and he liked his bottle of whisky. Every time they come to town, they say, 'Oh well, we're not going to see old Claude for a couple of days!' He'd turn up — but he'd still have a bottle of whisky in his swag. That's when either I do it, or Charlotte. But later, after I was married, Dad and I were running the big gang. He had two gangs going, contracted, and him and I ran that one. I used to cook for about eighteen then —

'Three generations of direct descendants from Te Kooti', Manutuke, Easter 1936. Back: Erina; Rangi, Tihei's brother; Arapera (Bella) Halbert, Tihei's cousin; Walter Whaitiri, another cousin; Tihei; Lucy Koko, a friend. Centre: Queenie, Tihei's sister. Front: Putiputi, holding Bubby Oriwia Moeau, her granddaughter, Erina's child; Rangi Rikirangi, holding his granddaughter, Te Kahukaone Ripene. Photograph by Mrs G. H. Henderson. *Alexander Turnbull Library*

all over a smoky fire! It's not like now. I was living at Papatu then and working all round Glenroy. I had to cook for them, and then I had to do Dad's books. When they needed a fleecer, I get in the shed and do the shed work. I'd be away four days and come back. My children were very young then, so I took them with me. I had a very understanding husband. He knew I was out there to get money for us. He used to call in sometimes, on his way back from the Coast, and stay and give me a hand to wash the dishes. Then he would come home. He said, as soon as I had earned enough money — *finish*. It is hard work. Especially when they are a tough lot and when they are shifting to another shed, and they had all those pubs to pass! Oh, you get there, and you cook the meal — and you sit and wait for them to arrive! But my Dad, when they are doing that and come back at that hour of night, he serves them out. And he does the dishes for me. Only right.

I got married quite old, really. I was thirty-one! Oh yes, I had that Maori one set aside for me. But I was so young I didn't know what it was all about! I think I was still at school. It was Christmas and we went to the pā at Te Reinga and it was there. They were sitting around talking — I didn't know what they were talking about, wasn't interested, and then they covered me with this mat. It is just another mat — 'Oh, thank you very much' — and that's all it was to me. Later on, when my mother saw I was starting to take an interest in boys, she told me I couldn't do these things and it was then she said, 'That's what the mat was all about'.[26] But I got out of it. He died. He died suddenly. He was from Ruatoki. They asked us to go to this tangi at Ruatoki and that's when I was told that's what it was. They chose him, I suppose, to get me back there.[27] Sometimes I used to ask Mum and she said, 'Ah, don't worry about it. He's dead.'

So I met Jack — he was a great sportsman — and I was in my prime at hockey. It's through that we started going together. My *father* liked him very much. It was my mother that couldn't stand the idea of a Pakeha. But she wouldn't come straight out and say what she thought. But she would be there when he comes to visit; then, when he goes, she says to me, 'What is *he* coming for?' I'd say, 'Well, I didn't tell him!' Later, of course, she took to him. Loved him!

After we were together for a while, and the children were around, she was the one, when I started talking Maori to her, to say 'Don't'. She said, 'You have got to respect Jack.' And I said, 'You would be surprised what he does know!' Might be all guesswork — but he picked up a lot when he started working with the Coast people, Ngati Porou. He was a building supervisor all along here, on the Coast, for Maori Affairs. But, I will admit, his children were brought up as Pakehas. That is why it is difficult for my two girls to learn to speak Maori. Because it wasn't spoken in their house. With my mother, of course, when Jack was not there it was always Maori. To me, my children should have picked it up — and they do understand. They are trying to teach themselves, now. I said, 'When I'm with my mother you're there. Why didn't you pick it up from me and Nan? That's how I learnt Maori.' 'No.' 'Now you've got to go and get taught!' Here we are — I am seventy next week[28] — and at my age we are trying to drum it in our children and grandchildren! This kōhanga reo and matua whāngai. My granddaughter says to me, 'What's matua whāngai?' I say, 'I am an adopted parent. This is what we are trying to drum into you, now, what it is all about!'

I had one whāngai. That is the only boy I have got. I had him before I was married. He was about five *then* ! When I got married I said, 'I got a baby!' 'Oh, have you!' Of course, Jack used to come home and met Tommy. I said, 'This is my baby'. Tommy was my baby. He didn't mind; he loved Tommy. I brought him up from a tiny baby. He was my cousin Mary's son. As I told you, her mother died when she was a baby and my grandmother took her. And we always thought we were sisters, till we grew up and oh, we're not! I took Tommy when she was sick and went to hospital. She had three children and her husband left her. I took two and when she settled down, she took the girl back. But I got attached to Tommy, or got used to having him around, so she wasn't going to get Tommy back! I used to cart him off to work with me. And Jack, he was good. I mean some fathers, Maoris too, couldn't take to — well, relate like Jack did. Then, later, we had foster children.

They came to us from Welfare. My girls had got married, when this lady, she came out here and asked me if I would like to take a couple of the children. Of course I didn't mind. I never had any one, then. My husband says, 'How can you look after them? You are too old.' And I said, 'Well, tell them to bring young ones!' Because, when they bring those old ones, oh, they want to run away, they want to go to the pictures, want to go to town! The little ones, when they come to you about six or seven, they are really good. So they brought these children, and they were all right. These were Maori children. Oh, I did have one Pakeha; she was only with me for a week until they found a home for her. But these Maori children — I felt sorry for Maori kids when they bring them from broken homes. I would hate to think they might be going away and I didn't know who would look after them like I would. I would give them all that love and care that I could do. And I said, 'No, leave them.' So they stayed with me until about sixteen, seventeen and they got out of Welfare, and went to work. When Jack died[29] I thought it is time I didn't have any of them. But then they said to me, that's the time I *should* have them! Something to do. Look forward to children after school instead of just staying home, moping around the house. So I had them for a little while. I have only given up not so very long ago. It was when Jackie, my mokopuna, started to grow and she was getting into their habits. Wanted to be cheeky. They never used to do that to me, but when they go to school they tell me they are pretty cheeky. Then I notice it on Jacqueline, so I thought, well, I had better stop or I would be getting mine into trouble. Jackie I brought up right from birth. I took her from her mother. I helped with the others, too.

We are a close knit family. Every time any of the family is in trouble, sick, we always are there. That sense of family, it comes through the women. Yes, it does. From my grandmother, and my mother, and of course, me. It didn't come through the Te Kooti line — wasn't very many men in that line! See, my uncle, he had one son who died and Rongo, the other, had daughters. Twins. His son died too.[30] That was the finish of Te Rikirangi's. Te Kooti, Weteni, Rangi, Rongo — finish! And of course our line — oh — girls.[31] Me being Mum's eldest girl and then to my eldest girl, Elizabeth, and hers. My grandmother tried to teach us — the girls — then my mother took that role on after Granny died.[32] I suppose it's only natural that I should try and relate to Elizabeth. It just follows on. Her daughter, Honey, is very interested in Ringatu. Her Kylie is the first one in this family to have been blessed by a Ringatu. And they tell her she is a Ringatu. She loves going to a Ringatu meeting — church — and she *listens* when they're singing psalms! And then she drops off to sleep, and when she wakes up they're finished, and she says, 'When are they going to start again!' She goes to kōhanga reo and, now, she comes home and she says I will say a *Maori* grace for you, Nanny Kuia!

I look after the greenstones, now. They came to me when my mother died. They are from Te Kooti. By rights it should be Charlotte, because she is the eldest

Rangi Rikirangi, Te Kooti's grandson, in 1906. He died on 22 July 1961 aged seventy-five. *Hawke's Bay Art Gallery & Museum*

The taonga of Te Kooti. In the top left is the portion of the greenstone 'chair of peace'; the pounamu heart belonged to Te Kooti's sister Makaretu; both the short pendant and the long ear-ring belonged to Te Kooti — the ear-ring has been mended with a silver band; the long mere is Kapiti; the shorter fighting mere is Mikaere. Photograph by Gillian Chaplin, 1982.

and her father has been the eldest of the family. But she has always asked me to go with her in anything that is to do with the family; she won't go on her own. And when my mother died, Charlotte took what she wanted and that's it, the rest she didn't care. So I had to take them because Mum left them to me and I had to look after them. They should go to my daughter; it goes down from daughter to daughter. Straight down. My granddaughter, Honey, she is very keen. She will look after them. The stone was part of Te Kooti's chair. It was a big block of greenstone for him to sit on. It was a chair of peace. Wherever he went they took it, and he sat on it. But it was never on the ground. He used it for special occasions: for peace. After he died, they cut it into four quarters. One went to Tuhoe. Tawhi had one; one went to Wharekauri, I think; and one is with us. Tawhi knew about the cutting. They cut it up with a greenstone axe. Instead of giving it to Weteni, they cut it up into quarters. Perhaps it was jealousy. But there is a tradition that a gift always comes back. When you give a cloak away, it always comes back. Maybe that is the purpose. To give it away and it will come back, and the four quarters will be joined.[33]

If you don't look after the stones, if you don't water them, they weep. So every so often I take the stones out and I wash them. You know, with greenstone, if you bury it, it will go to water — it'll travel to the water.[34] These are weeping stones. They cry if we take them to the pā for any of the family who have died. We leave the stones at their feet, and the greenstones weep. You feel them — and they're moist.

You see these two mere? That shorter one is the fighting one. That is Mikaere. It's got a chip in it — see? It is Te Kooti's. The other one is also his. It is the one for peace. That's called Kapiti, Gabriel.[35] Maybe they were made for him, but I think he inherited them.

The other stones are also from Te Kooti. The little short one there is for teething. You give it to the children for them to chew on. The long one with the silver band is his ear-ring. It's been mended with that band. And the heart is from Te Kooti's sister [Makaretu], and it goes to the girls.

But that big greenstone block, Mum used to use for a doorstop! It was just lying around the house and I used to go and pick it up. Then a man came to see her and said that he would take it. And then my Dad told her they should be put away.

A sketch of Te Kooti wearing the ear-ring. The drawing was made by Henry Hill (a school inspector) when Te Kooti visited Kokohinau marae, a major centre for the Ringatu at Te Teko, in 1892. The two fingers on Te Kooti's left hand had been shot off at the fight at Te Porere on 4 October 1869. He is wearing a plaid suit and soft tweed hat, which Hill included with curious emphasis. *Misses D. and G. Hill collection, Alexander Turnbull Library*

That started us putting them away and then *she* was always saying that I should look after them.

The most important thing to me, at the moment, is the land Incorporation — the committee that I am in. There are seven of us in the committee. That's for Te Whakaari. It's at the back here, at Paparatu. It used to be called Mangapoike, but when it became an Incorporation[36] we had to give it a name. Because the Pakeha half now is Paparatu — or is known as Paparatu — and Mangapoike. So Turi Carroll,[37] he decided that we should give it a name and that's why it is called Te Whakaari: that is what Te Kooti has prophesied. Whatever he says; whatever he prophesies. He prophesied certain things that happen. Like the one I enjoyed most, was when he prophesied this insect coming through Te Kuiti. He sat there, and out of the blue he said, he can hear this insect coming. As it went past, he said, smoke is coming out of his head and it had a noise. And he tried to make a noise that sounded like a train! And not long after that the train started running right through Te Kuiti. I said, when I heard that, 'Oh, I can't believe that!' But it did happen. I mean, that's one of the things he prophesied would happen. This *black* object would be going through Te Kuiti, smoke will come out of his head, and it will break up Te Kuiti.[38] Old Turi Carroll used to talk about all those little prophecies to me.

The only land we have from Te Kooti is that block, Te Whakaari. It's what Te Kooti has visualized: this man who is coming back, who is going to come all round here.[39] I think that's what he meant with all the blocks around here. When the East Coast Commissioner had all these Maori lands, Paparatu was the only place that had a bit of money. He [J. S. Jessep] used the Paparatu, the Mangapoike money, to get all these other lands going.[40] He did wonders for the Maori people around here. And I think that's one of those things that Te Kooti said, that it'll be Mangapoike to help them — all the blocks here. Put them on their feet. That was his prophecy. Mangatu is on his feet. Whangara is in good nick. All the blocks in the Gisborne district, and in the Wairoa. They've all started to pick up — they *have*. Everywhere else — except Paparatu! It's still struggling. The last, but not the least, will be Paparatu itself. Next year [1985], they say, it should be well and truly on its feet. Well, let's hope so.

I am a shareholder in it from Te Kooti to my grandfather. It's where Te Kooti first went, after he landed, when they got back [from Wharekauri]. He went up to Paparatu. And when you get there, they can show you where he has been and how this white horse of his jumped from one hill to another when they were chasing him. You have got to be there on the spot to get it. They show it to you, and it's *there*. There's two cliffs, and you wonder how on earth can a horse jump from that one to this one — to get away. And of course, these people chasing him would see his horse on the other cliff, while they could never get there until two days afterwards![41] It was Captain Tucker who was hounding him, to seize the land.[42] They were hounding him because he was the leader who would oppose the confiscations. And Maoris, also, were against him. Everything that went wrong, they blamed Te Kooti! Because of the reputation that he had.

The other block I am involved in comes from my grandmother to me. That's the Papuni one, at Tahora. Back of Wairoa way. I am involved in that committee, too, just running the affairs of the station.[43] I am more or less looking after our interests in the blocks. Since Mum and Dad died, I had to do all that. I am the adviser for the family. As I said, it has come to me.

It involves a lot of things, really. Like if any of the family, say, is in trouble and they'd come and say, 'Oh, so and so wants to get married – will have to get married!' 'Cause our family has all girls. 'Oh, she is too young! I don't know whether she should!' Little things like that. We talk about it. And with our lands. Say, one would want to sell their shares and get a bit of money from the block and I'd tell them, well, try and raise a loan from somewhere, instead of selling your land. Hang on to it. And they come and say that such and such a thing is happening – to the block, to their little shares. 'What shall we do about it?' I say, 'Oh well, you are getting money for it.' But it is not much, no, it is not much. Of course, there are too many of us – we only get this little bit. We get this little rent every year. And I tell them, when they want to sell their shares and get a house, we have no money. The block can't buy you out. It can't pay you enough. It is up to me to see that they don't sell all of their shares to somebody else. We have got to think of our families and our grandchildren, now. If my sister, Lena, comes to me and says, 'Oh, I want to sell my shares', I have got to stop it, and I *have* stopped it. I can't let us do things like that. Then our grandchildren would be left without. I tell them that it is their responsibility to hold it. Not try and sell it for the sake of getting money. I say, 'It goes tomorrow and where are you? The land will still be there looking at you.' That's about all the advice I can give them.

I took that role from my mother. Before she died she was making me – pushing me. She was saying, 'You'd better go to so and so', even to a Twelfth. 'I can't go!' But, I get along and I go! Anybody come to pick *her* up, it's always me that's got to go. So, I just got into the habit. With my husband too. See, if he had been Maori and in the *same* land as I am, well, he will be my boss. Seeing he is a man. That made a difference, I think, his being a Pakeha. If he is a Maori and in the same land, he *will* be the boss. I don't think I would like that, though! Maori women are made to respect their men – I mean, they come first in everything they do. That man comes first. He sits down while you stand up – that sort of thing – and if you've got anything to eat, he eats while you go without. *He* comes first in everything. No, I wouldn't like that! Because I have come to accept the Pakeha ways, I mean, my grandsons have got to learn to respect their women folks. My grandson, he'd come in and normally I would say, 'Oh, being a Maori he gets the first preference, in everything we have got, or whatever is the best we have got. Jacqueline will have to go without, or just with a little bit, while he takes the most.' But I don't do that. I treat them all alike. Or, if it's a better looking fruit, I don't give it to him, not to a grandson. I make him give it to the girls. And I expect him to. And he does.

It is because of the family that I went to Te Kuiti for the hundred years – the centennial of Te Kooti's pardon.[44] They asked for a representative of the family and Charlotte has to have me before she'll go to anything like that. To them, the people that organized it, the Haahi o Te Kooti Rikirangi,[45] it was important to take the family so that, one day, the Haahi will be stronger. Because different sections are breaking away. And some didn't even come – that's not getting back together! But we didn't really get a chance to talk about it. Because so many things happened.

It was very exciting at first. As I said when I was interviewed at Te Kuiti,[46] before, it was humiliation more than anything else to hear people talk about Te Kooti. And my family didn't know anything about their tipuna. We weren't encouraged to talk about him – as I told you. I found it difficult to express my feelings. I used to hear some stories and say, 'Oh, what a bad man he was.' Then I come to Te Kuiti and I hear nothing but good about him. I said, 'I still want to

make up my mind.' But after that, with the deaths, we didn't get a chance to talk.

There were two deaths, one after the other, and both were brought to the pā. Everything got to be held back — with the first, but that was all right. But the day *he* was to be buried, the second one arrived. You see, when we got there they said, 'Oh, somebody had died, and they're bringing him to the pā. It won't disturb our —', what we were there for. That was all right. And they took us around to the different places and there was somebody to tell us — where Te Kooti's been and what he's done. But then they were coming, tangi all the time! They couldn't very well sit inside the meeting-house and talk with us and go out and talk to the people that come to the tangi. On the second day, they said, he's going to be buried that day. And the next minute, another one had died! That was three days! Then my sister, Lena, got sick. We got the doctor out to her there, in the meeting-house, and that's what he says, 'It's a stroke'. Oh, it was *terrible*. I said, 'Oh, she's *not* going to die.' Of course, she had to go to the hospital. Nobody wanted to stay, then. Not after that. So they all come home and I stayed there with Lena. There was not very much that Wi Tarei could do. He said, 'Well, these things happen'. But then again, he said, 'There must be something wrong. All these things coming in.' Ah yes.

But the Ringatu have got to go back. I know they have to go round for these Twelfths, round here, Wairoa, Gisborne. Before they go back to Te Kuiti. There must be three complete rounds. I heard at the time. Round this district and then round — wherever. And from Te Kuiti, from there, they've got to go to Wainui to complete their circle.[47] If they ask *me* to go back to Te Kuiti — if they ask for a representative of the family — yes, I suppose so. I might have to go. Yes — I'll go back. It has always been my role. For the family.

The centenary of Te Kooti's pardon, February 1983. Back: Rama Kahika, a tohunga from Whakatohea. Front: Tihei, with her mokopuna Kylie; Hariata (Mrs Wattie); Erina (Mrs Pohatu), planting a kōwhai tree as a 'maharatanga', remembrance, of Te Kooti. Photograph by Ans Westra.

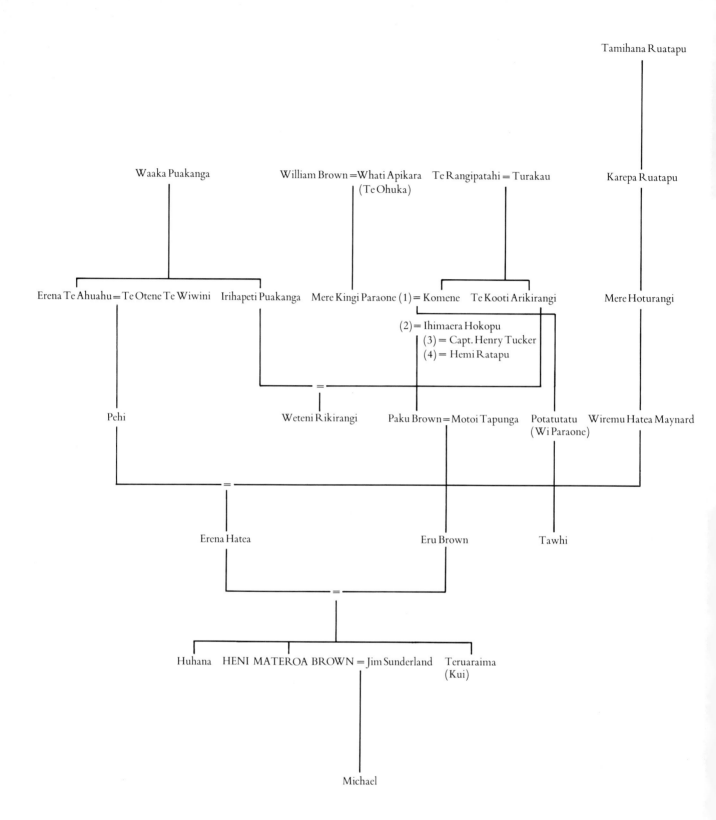

HENI SUNDERLAND

*H*eni Sunderland was born on 13 October 1916 at Manutuke in Poverty Bay. On her mother's side she is descended from the chiefs of Ngatimaru, Tamihana Ruatapu and his son Karepa, that is from the senior line in Te Kooti's own hapū. Old Tamihana Ruatapu was one of the leading figures in Poverty Bay in 1868, when the Exiles returned from Wharekauri. He opposed Te Kooti and distrusted his overtures to the Kawanatanga chiefs. While Paratene Turangi waited, deliberately unarmed, for Te Kooti at Oweta on 14 November, Tamihana urged his people to take refuge at Muriwai pā. However, despite his seniority and his considerable mana, he had few supporters in 1868. His younger brother was Anaru Matete, the chief of Ngatimaru who had committed himself and most of the hapū to Te Kooti.[1] His son Karepa had also become a supporter of Te Kooti and went with him from Poverty Bay. Later, he was too ill to fight at Ngatapa in January 1869 and made his way to Muriwai, where the Ngatimaru opponents of Te Kooti were sheltering. Finally he fought against Te Kooti.[2] Loyalties, as Heni stresses in her narrative, were far from simple. Families and tribes were divided, and those who know their history, as Heni does, learn to be immensely tolerant.

On her father's side, Heni's ancestral history is equally riven by these conflicts. Her grandfather Paku, who brought her up at Muriwai, was bundled away on his mother's shoulders when she was taken prisoner at Oweta in 1868. His father, Ihimaera Hokopu, who was partly instrumental in the capture and transportation of Te Kooti to Wharekauri, was one of the five chiefs Te Kooti executed, along with Paratene. But Paku's mother, Mere Kingi Paraone, had been previously married to Te Kooti's older brother Komene. Komene had been a Pai Marire believer and was sent to Wharekauri with Te Kooti in June 1866.[3] Komene and Mere's only son, Potatutatu, was later brought up by Te Kooti. The intertwining of these ancestral histories was to prove vital in preventing the continuation of the divisions of the wars. If Paratene's daughter, the high-born Mikaera Turangi, remained adamant in her refusal ever to permit Te Kooti to return to Poverty Bay, in the end these bitter memories have been largely healed through the interconnections between whakapapa.

Heni grew up at Muriwai, the settlement of Ngai Tamanuhiri, her grandmother Motoi's people, on the Wherowhero lagoon. She recalls more of tribal mythology than the others with whom we talked, because she is accustomed to being consulted as a kaumātua for both Ngai Tamanuhiri and Ngatimaru. She re-creates a world in which the transmission of traditional knowledge and ancestral identity – the very origins of the people and the names which they gave to the land – was an important part of the Maori child's inheritance. This is why Heni is deeply involved at Manutuke in the kōhanga reo. As she and others know, truly bilingual children will possess a confidence and a proud access to both worlds, Maori and Pakeha. Women of Heni's generation, native speakers of Maori, needed to acquire fluency in English. Those who succeeded, like Heni, move freely in two cultures. Her regret now is that she did not transmit her bilingualism to her son, Michael. As she commented, it was only when he said to her, 'Mum, I want you to do something for my daughter, something you never did for me,' that she realized that she had, as she says, brought him up as a Pakeha. 'I was shattered,' she said, particularly because they were both in England at the time. 'And I thought, "Oh, you fool of a woman! I've come a helluva long way to see you" – because I missed him so much – and this is what he said to me: "You never taught me Maori!" And I apologized to him.' Heni's involvement with the kōhanga reo derives from her belief in the need to give confidence to Maori families in their Maoritanga, so that we, Maori and Pakeha, can 'get back to where we were. Because there was that good fellow feeling.' The bitternesses derived from a deep sense of betrayal must be changed, she argues, if there is to be harmony.

previous page Heni Sunderland on the shore at Muriwai, December 1984. Photograph by Gillian Chaplin.

At Muriwai, Heni lived in a community that had lost control over most of its lands. The Pakowhai block had been mortgaged to the Bank of New Zealand in 1888, without the owners' knowledge or consent. It had been held in trust by Wi Pere's New Zealand Native Land Settlement Company, which was then in serious financial difficulties. The outcome, to prevent foreclosure and the alienation of vast areas of Maori land to the bank, was the creation of the East Coast Commission, which managed the lands until 1953, when they were returned as an Incorporation to the owners. Pakowhai is still, however, in debt and remains unsurveyed because of the great costs involved. The consequence of this tangled land history was that, by 1916, the people of Muriwai were left with only twenty-one acres which were recognized as freehold, and Heni grew up in a community of 'squatters', which lingered on by the shores of the lagoon. In 1913, a typhoid epidemic had broken up the original Maori settlement. The Muriwai community was then shifted by the Commission to its present location, inland from the lagoon, and only five or six families continued living on the lagoon 'outside the freehold'. Gradually the sea and the river encroached on Piiti Taone (Beach Town). The freshwater lake, which was the centre of their lives, has now gone. The sea has broken through its banks and drowned Heni's old home: 'I could never ever say where our house was.'

Heni attended the local school at Muriwai between 1926 and 1930. She left school and was immediately unemployed. For young Maori women in Poverty Bay there were simply no jobs, unless on a shearing gang, which as Heni indicates, were largely monopolized by the older women. She was living in a still predominantly Maori world: Muriwai, in 1936, was a community of 260 people, of whom 185 were Maori. She spent several years somewhat aimlessly, playing hockey and visiting Tihei's family at Manutuke, until she came under the influence of the Anglican Maori Mission there. Heni became one of their women workers, who were the backbone of the mission's efforts in the 1930s and 1940s. She was one of very few Maori workers. She married only relatively late in her life. Her husband, Jim Sunderland, was an Englishman, who had migrated to New Zealand. He became the secretary of the Kia Ora Co-operative Dairy Company in 1922. They married on 17 December 1955 and had one son, Michael, who for a time sought out his father's roots and lived and worked in England. Jim Sunderland died on 13 August 1970.

Since her retirement from working as a community officer for Maori Affairs in Gisborne, Heni's life has revolved around her many marae activities. The great house Te Mana o Turanga is her ancestral meeting-house. Some of its carvings originated from a wharenui which was planned by Tamihana Ruatapu for his pā at Oweta but never built because of the wars of the late 1860s. It was Karepa who undertook the construction of the present house at the Whakato mission, beside Oweta, as a record of the continuous history and traditions of the Rongowhakaata people. The house was completed in 1883.[4] The koruru on the gable is Rongowhakaata, the founder of the tribe to whom Heni's hapū, Ngatimaru, belong. It was here at Whakato, on 5 December 1984, that Heni invited us to the end-of-year party for the kōhanga reo children, a wonderful occasion for everyone involved. Papa Koko arrived, only a little bit late, and armed with sacks full of presents, each one named. The children had learnt the famous oriori, or lullaby sung to teach them their history, known as 'Te Pōpō'. It tells of their ancestress who brought the first kūmara to Poverty Bay:

> Ko Hakirirangi ka u kei uta
> Te kōwhai ka ngaora ka ringitia te kete
> Ko Manawaru . . .
>
> Hakirirangi it was who reached the shore,
> And, with the flowering kōwhai, emptied the kit
> At Manawaru . . .[5]

Fifty or sixty tiny children, dressed in their best clothes, sang this lullaby to their mothers. Heni was amongst them, helping and encouraging.

Another major commitment for Heni is to the new tribal council formed at Manutuke in 1985, Te Runanga o Turanganui a Kiwa. It is a council for the three major tribes of Poverty Bay: Rongowhakaata, Te Aitanga a Mahaki, and Ngai Tamanuhiri. Heni is one of its kaumātua. It is attempting to formulate a plan of tribal development for the region.[6] Because of the extensive and valuable land owned by the tribes, it could become an extremely powerful organization. Heni insists that the history of loss can be reversed.

We first visited Heni Sunderland in her home in Gisborne on 26 January 1983. On that occasion, we talked primarily about Te Kooti. We had been told of her knowledge. On two later visits we talked with her about her own life, which she describes with such strong imaginative energy. The first occasion was at her house on 11 May 1984. She was preparing some flax for weaving. Neat bundles were tied to dry on her clothes-line and when rain threatened we all had to stop talking and leap out to bring them in. The second occasion was on 5 December. After the kōhanga reo party we travelled to Muriwai and walked together in the rain beside the sea and looked across the brackish waters of the old lagoon to the tapu island Ahikaroa. The white cliffs of Young Nick's Head — Te Kuri a Pawa in Heni's narrative tradition — shone out across the bay. We called on Heni's younger sister Kui Emmerson, who lives nearby, and photographed the portrait of Motoi which she has hanging in her home. On both these occasions we tape-recorded our conversations. We have also drawn on the notes written at the time of our first visit to Heni.

I am going to tell you a little more about myself. My parents — probably their marriage would be the last true, traditional marriage by arrangement. Both grandparents — these two women — conceived about the same time. Prior to that, it was known within the family that my grandmother, Motoi, would have no issue. She was an only child; her father's sisters had no children, and it was said that the whānau, the family line, would die with her. Anyway, she conceived. And my mother's mother too. The people of that time got together, whose whānau she was. And to save the line — if your child is a girl and that other woman's child is a boy, these two children *must* marry.

Well, my mother was born on 9 January; my father was born on 23 February. They grew up knowing that one day they were to marry. This particular year from school, his father had a shearing contract out and Dad went shearing for that short time. Whilst he was there, word came back to Manutuke that he had got just a bit too friendly with one of the fleecers. So they sent my Dad's uncle up to the shed to see his elder brother, and ask him if it were true. He went from Manutuke, with a saddled horse, and when he gets up there, at Okahuatiu, this elder brother said, 'Oh, yes, I am getting worried about these young people.' The other brother said, 'I'll put this young lad on a horse; he comes back with me!' So they married!

Mum had a very large family; there is fifteen of us. The eldest child was a girl, and she was left with my mother. The next child, it was a boy, and he was taken by my Dad's parents. Then I came along. My great-grandmother, Mere Kingi, and my aunt, my Dad's sister at Manutuke, who was then not married, took me. Mum was to have children and not be worried with bringing them up. So within the family we were taken and became tamariki whāngai — but within the family. We grew up to know this.

Most of us were born at home. My Dad's aunt, Granny Tiakiwhare, was

Mum's midwife, until she thought that my mother was getting older and she was having her children so fast that she needed to come to a doctor. Up until then it was natural — my mother is going to have a baby — and when we saw everybody rushing around, and the fire going, and plenty of hot water, then we knew she was going to deliver her child very soon. As soon as that baby was born, and they had made Mum very comfortable, we're usually in there to have a look at this baby. We never saw the actual birth. Just this midwife. My father always made sure to have the hot water and all that, but he was never in there. You see, there were certain women who were midwives, who knew how to do it. My great-grandmother was a midwife; and this grandaunt. Granny Mata (Granny Mere Kingi) was my grandmother's midwife. I heard her say that because it was so very hard for Motoi to have babies — after the second one she had said no more, and no more it was! They quote different women, who would say to that person if the childbirth was too difficult, 'No more. That is your last child', and that it was! But just what they did with the afterbirth, I never had the sense to ask! That's how they controlled — something they do with the placenta. And they'd never bear children after that. When they quote those families, there it is — only two, two, two — or three.

Mere Kingi Paraone at Manutuke, in 1937. She was said then to be 103 years old, although she was probably born about 1841. *Auckland Weekly News, 9 June 1937*

It was also a ritual when the babies were born, how to massage the babies; different massage for baby girls, different massage for baby boys. You wouldn't believe it, but according to my Grannies I was born with crooked feet, club-feet, and I was the ugliest baby born! Granny Tiakiwhare said my head was long and my mouth was over there; I had no bridge to my nose, and she showed me what she did. She said, 'You are so soft, straight off.' She straightened my legs, my feet, there and then. Then she put my chin in her hand, and put her [other] hand behind my head and she demonstrated how she pushed, twisted, and shaped my nose, pushed my mouth back. She fashioned me from what I was, from the babe that was. When she herself told me that, I said to myself, if I did nothing else, if ever my Granny had to be cared for, I would help with that caring. From then on I have cared for all my family back home here, you know, when it comes to the end. She was the first one I did all that for.[7] It was quite natural because they used to die at home and you hear them talking or saying to the other one, you do this, you do that. For a long time Maoris didn't go into hospital; hospital was not a place that we liked. But whenever we are given the opportunity, when there is no more can be done, then we just asked, can we have them at home?

I had a very simple life — rich life — living with my grandparents at Muriwai. My grandfather, Paku, was a wonderful man. He was a farmer and a good agricultural man. He used to plough the fields for the other farmers and he would make the covering for their haystacks, a thatching of wīwī. He used to do our own bacon. It was nothing for him to kill a pig, and we used to have what they called miti tahu; this is how they preserved meat. He would have the fire going, because that's how they cleaned the pigs, just over the fire, and take all the hairs off. Singe them. He would sort out all the inner bits to eat and throw them on the fire so that we would have something to eat there and then, and my grandfather used to make the most beautiful blood pudding — he really did! And then he would make us miti tahu, cut up the pork and partly cook it, and then throw it into a camp oven of boiling, boiling fat. Then they put that into a container, usually a kerosene tin, and they would pour fat, and covered it with fat. Probably kept it airtight and the meat used to keep indefinitely. He used to corn meat — beef — he called it dry pickling, where you just rub salt on, then hang them up.

Motoi Tapunga. Photographed, by permission of Heni Sunderland, by Gillian Chaplin, 1984.

He was wonderful to us. He spoke beautiful English. But there were no books in the home. Their grandfather, William Brown, must have been a remarkable person, because we had an earth-floor kitchen – I was brought up in a kāuta – yet we had all the niceties of Pakehas. I didn't think they were, I just took it for granted it was the way that things were done. Not until I married, then I realized that these were really the niceties of English people. My grandfather always wore a hat; my father was like that; my brothers were brought up like that.

For the little that we had in those days, those were the kind of teachings. Our grandmother Motoi taught us all the legends. She was a reader. She would sing to us and she used to tell us a lot of European fairytales, all in Maori! She also had her uncle living with us and because we were all Maori-speaking it was so simple. He would tell us history. That old man, Hori Te Awarau, was an orator and he *knew* the history of Muriwai. We grew up knowing all these things; different stories about the different regions. We learnt about Hinehakirirangi, who planted the kūmara at Manawaru, where the old pā used to be. Manawaru means delighted, and for me that's the interpretation, because you know what a great delight when that kūmara sprouted. And I thought to myself, I know where that pā is, and I

Hinehakirangi, with her kit of kūmara seed, inside Te Mana o Turanga, Whakato. She appears above the doorway. (Compare this photograph with Plate 31 in Leo Fowler's history of the meeting-house, where the figure of Hinehakirangi, restored, carries a little suitcase!) On the left, above the right-hand corner of the window, is Pawa and his dog, Whakao. The date of this photograph is unknown, although the electricity box indicates that it is in this century. *Alexander Turnbull Library*

know how Hinehakirirangi would have walked along the beach until she came to the Karaua stream and followed it right round till she got to Manawaru. And she must have thought, this is a cosy spot, to get the first of the sun to the last of the sun, and planted the kūmara! That is our history, and that song we sing, 'Te Pōpō', is really the origin of the kūmara as a plant food.[8]

The hill Te Kuri a Pawa, that's the hill for the people of this little place, Muriwai. If you see the mist going from the bottom, way back, up to the top, and it goes along, you'll find the old people here say, if anybody is very sick, here, that's their time. They know that person's life is so short. But if the mist just leaves from the tip of the hill, it's from somewhere else. Someone is slipping away; we'll hear very soon, whoever. And it happens. We just take it for granted.

That hill is named for Pawa, he had a pet dog, Whakao. His image is in the meeting-house, Te Mana o Turanga at Whakato, with his dog. There's a place near here, too, where he lost his dog in the bush, Pipiwhakao. He called and called, and the dog whimpered! So he named that place after his dog's whimpering! They also say that, when the Horouta canoe got to Ohiwa and it was dashed up on the rocks and broken, they went overland — and this is what they tell us — when Pawa got to a certain place he had to do a mimi, and away he goes! And that's the Waipawa river! And the Motu river, from this one flow! Clever people! They make up a story as they go along![9]

We lived with that old man, Hori. It was his house. He was a great fisherman; we would help him take his flat-bottomed boat to the sea, and he would tell us where he was going, the fishing grounds, the days when to go and gather seafoods. He used to make all his own crayfish pots from supplejack, made all his own lures

Heni Materoa Carroll, with other Maori leaders from Gisborne, about 1908. Heni Materoa (Te Huinga) is in the centre, wearing a black hat with an elegant white plume of feathers. Seated in the same row, second from the left, is Wi Pere. *Alexander Turnbull Library*

out of pāua shells. So you grew up knowing that the Horouta canoe came into the Wherowhero lagoon, and that it rests somewhere here. We've got an island that we were never allowed to go on. They would just point out to us that is Ahikaroa, over there. The old people would never go to that island. We would go eeling with our grandmother, we'd skirt that island, but every time she would remind us, that is not for you. It was tapu and we were told that a sickness of the legs, waewae tatu, would result. They encouraged us to go and pick up duck eggs along the lagoon – there was a Pakeha there, he was a blacksmith and they were his. They'd say, 'Don't let Zenker see you (of course they'd tell us that), but never go across to the island, never, to pick up eggs.' My grandmother never went on to that island. So we didn't. We learnt by example, no other way.

They were very strict old people. Go to bed! Say your prayers! Never sat at the table without saying grace. They used to tell us ghosty stories – probably to frighten us! They used to say to us, at nights don't whistle if you are on the road by yourself. Because a kēhua might be walking beside you and it would whistle back! You can be eating inside and the ghost is outside, at night; you must pull the blinds down or the ghost is mimicking you! Every spoonful you have, the kēhua's having a spoonful!

You will find old people of *that* generation who are so special that they have their own kaitiakis. If you go and sit at the table with them, you will find they would drop food onto the floor before they themselves ever partake. They'll pick up something from that table and you think you didn't see them do it. My great-grandmother used to talk about this blue room that Lady Carroll had in her house and when I was a kid we used to come to her house.[10] One day, when I was working as Welfare Officer,[11] I had to go to this house to see a person who was living there then. I was just going up the staircase – and it was like somebody talking to you on the telephone – I heard this little voice say, 'You are going up to this blue room.' I stopped! I had goose-flesh! You see, there was this little room they called the blue room and they'd set a tray, and take it up to this room and they used to leave it there! For her kaitiaki! She really looked after it!

Those old people, when they are like that you know they are tapu people. You be careful, what you said to them! And we were told, if you are sleeping with them, don't you eat on them! They are too tapu. That's the kind of world they lived in, but they prepared us, should it ever happen to us — these are the things that you do. And these are what you don't do.

We grew up to know what our families' kaitiakis were. That family is special: their kaitiaki is an owl. Or that family, the eel is their kaitiaki. And our grandmother used to say, if you get bitter, unbeknown to you it can affect someone else. She meant, you be careful of their kaitiaki! And the old people would name the kaitiaki of that family if it affected you. And if they took ill, they'd yelp like a dog (if it was a dog), and then they'd have to exorcize the person possessed. My grandparents were devout Christians, but they would exorcize: they'd throw like a fit, froth at the mouth and they'd say strange things, and then when they finish exorcizing, the person possessed would flop, they'd give them something to eat, a cup of tea, put them to sleep, and they're all right. We've grown away from that and we don't know what to do. Now, they get depressed.

We had more than one kaitiaki. Granny Mere Kingi used to talk to a fantail, and *I* don't like a fantail coming into the house. And if an owl hoots, she used to say, 'Who is it come to say goodbye?' She would know it was someone recently died, one or two days before.

My grandfather was the son of Ihimaera Hokopu. Now, Ihimaera was killed at Oweta and it was said that, with those killings by Te Kooti that the prophecy of Toiroa, that had foretold his birth, had been fulfilled.[12] That there would be bloodshed. Oweta was seen as the fulfilment. But, you see, Granny Mere Kingi, she was married to Te Kooti's elder brother, Komene. By that union there was one son, Potatutatu, and that one child was brought up by Te Kooti. And Potatutatu's eldest girl, Tawhi, was also taken by Te Kooti. She was with him right throughout the time — she was with him when he died. They were all Ringatu. But when Komene died, then my great-grandmother married Ihimaera. And they had one son, Paku. At Oweta, Ihimaera took some of the people in a canoe across the river, so that they could escape. He put my grandfather — the baby — on her shoulders. And she begged him not to go back. But he did . . . Those people who were killed at Oweta, they were later gathered up and buried at Manutuke. Paratene Turangi's people changed their tribal name from Ngaitawhiri to Ngai Te Kete — 'gathered up in a kit' — because of Oweta. Yet, all we were ever told was that Ihimaera was killed at Oweta, and I know just where he is buried in the Manutuke cemetery. But that's it. Full stop. We were never ever brought up not to have anything to do with that part of your family. *I* never heard Granny Mere Kingi say dreadful things about Te Kooti — I didn't.[13]

When we went to Otewa, for the centenary of Te Kooti's pardon, it was the first time for us, as Rongowhakaata and the people of Te Kooti, and for his *own* great-grandchildren to have been there. I was very moved with his great-granddaughter, Tihei, when she spoke on that theme.[14] Within myself I wept for her, because, you see for her Te Kooti was a bad man. She has kept that all into herself; and you know she felt good, sitting in that house, Tokanganui a Noho, and to learn from those people that it was Te Kooti and his people who built that house and presented it to those people. For her, for the first time, she said, I could lift my head up. And Tihei is older than me. But for me, that was it, all these years she has carried that load and for the first time she was able to take it off, in the year of his pardon, exactly one hundred years. It was a privilege for me; they looked after us and that was no small thing to hear from those people — Waikato and Maniapoto — those things about Te Kooti that we did not know. I agree with Tihei; we never talked about it. The only things I knew, as I said, was when our

Grannies would talk about him, and how he was able to bring the people back from Wharekauri. Or you go to the Ringatu service and you listen to the service.

Perhaps the strength of my families was that they were of equal standing. Granny married Komene. Her second husband was killed by his brother. Now, firstly, Te Kooti is of Ngatimaru descent, and we are very strong Ngatimaru. We are of the one tribe. We are in line, tribally. Now, as to my mother – Te Kooti married Irihapeti and *her* sister, Erena Te Ahuahu, is my mother's grandmother. So one of these sisters married Te Kooti and the other is my mother's grandmother. So, you have that situation there; and this one on my father's side. They must have been very strong in themselves, as individuals, as whānau, and whānau groups. One was no stronger than the other.

I told you that my Mum and Dad, their marriage was by arrangement. When they were married, they had two wedding breakfasts. My mother's people said they are going to have the wedding breakfast. My Dad's people said, 'We are going to have the wedding breakfast!' My Dad's people are at Whakato; they've got a meeting-house. My mother's people are at Ohako; they have no meeting-house, no house whatsoever. Over here, they've got an earth-floor kitchen, to cook all their meals and they have got a grand carved house. And they are numerous. So they say, 'We are going to have the wedding!' But my mother's people said, '*We* are going to have the wedding.' And these ones, they look over at those ones and say to them, 'Where's your house?' And this old man said, 'I have a piece of ground, and Ohako is my marae. I have no house, but the heaven above is my house. If the ground here is God's footstool, and up there is . . .', and they put on *their* wedding breakfast, without a house. But when they did build a house, they named that house Te Kiko o Te Rangi, the Heavens. So that's why I think they were so strong. And they are very closely connected all the way down. And we are lucky enough to be in the middle, and to have been brought up with the strengths from over here and the strengths from over there.

At Whakato, as I grew up, the Ringatu had their services, their Tekaumaruas, there. And the Nannies went along, so we went along. When we went to the Twelfths, they did not let us go in to the services at night. Our Nannies didn't. They respected the Ringatu. They would make it their business to go there on the eleventh, but because they were local and they were not Ringatu, they could return to their homes and sleep at night. And when they did that, they would never go into that first evening service. They would just go and help and prepare meals, and they would go home. And that's all we were allowed to do, until we were quite a lot older. And it is something that I do respect. I would never go to a Ringatu service at our marae on the day of the actual Twelfth. I wouldn't, because we have always been told you go there on the eleventh and you stay there until the thirteenth. That's how it will always be for me.

The Ringatu had a great organization within their Church. Different ones were given different responsibilities. The nurses, they were the ones who tended to the sick, like Aunty Tawhi. That was their job at the Tekaumaruas. Tawhi knew all about whatever herbs they used. She could do harakeke, make that mixture from the roots of the flax. They used that a lot for different things. They used it as a laxative and if women went to her to ask her for that mixture, to boil up some flax for them, she'd ask them straight out, 'Are you pregnant?' and she won't make it. If women have a hard time having periods, she can cook that for that type of thing, too. She knew all the barks and the different things to use. They called them tākuta or nēhi – doctors or nurses – and they were always women.

The men are usually tohungas, that is the tohunga who has a gift. If it's healing, then he's the one who is able to say to them, this thing happened, that thing happened, this thing is *going* to happen. They're the ones who can read into the future. Within the Church there has been several men who have been tohungas, like Hori Gage, who was Hori Keeti to us. He was one who came up this way. I went to him with my husband. It was some years before Jim died.

Before we were married, he used to say to me, 'Can a Maori put a mākutu, a curse on you?' 'Oh', I said, 'that's for sure Maoris can't do that to Pakehas like you.' And I was quite sure of myself. I didn't think Maoris could have that kind of influence over anyone else but a Maori. But when we were married, he used to have terrible nightmares. And he would say to me, 'That woman!' And I would say to him, 'What woman?' And he would never say another word. Anyway, Hori Keeti came to the Tekaumarua at Waihirere. And Jim said to me he's going to that man. So I had a good talk with my husband. I said, 'You know what it is all about, to go, to seek help from a tohunga? And no way do you offer this man money. You have to take a flagon of salt water from the sea and a bottle of olive oil.'[15] 'Oh.' Before we left the house, which I do to this day, particularly when I am going to sick people, I always set aside a minute. I take time to commit myself into God's hands. So before we left to go and get all these things, I said to my husband, 'I don't know whether he's a good tohunga or a bad one. If they are good, and it is a gift from God, they would use it well. If they are not, they can use it against you, or against us. So we will ask for God's protection and God go with us.' Well, we get to Waihirere marae and I said, 'This doesn't ring right for me.' They told us we had to wait. I was not very confident. But I shan't forget that first meeting with this man. He was a handsome man, Hori Gage. He shook hands with us and he said to me, 'Your husband hasn't got a heart condition. He has he mate Maori.' And he said to my husband, 'A Maori woman came to you for money.' 'You know, that's what he's been telling *me* for a long time!' Jim was secretary for the Kia Ora Dairy Company and he had refused this woman money, because the woman's husband had said not to give it to her. And this is what she had said to him, 'You will get sick and no doctor will ever be able to tell you!' That woman had put a curse on him and I'd said rubbish!

This man took him to the tuarongo, the back part of the meeting-house. He was with Jim for quite a while. Took out a handkerchief, he would spread the handkerchief, and he would blow through the hanky, and worked all round his back until, I s'pose, he thought he's got rid of — whatever. You know, Jim never had nightmares after that.

A lot of people went to Hori Gage, a lot from the Bay of Plenty. And he was asked by the family to come to Rongopai, to lift the tapu on *that* house. He also had that Kotahitanga movement, though we didn't have anything to do with that. Yes, he was a matakite and a lot of people went to him.

. . . I would have been thirteen when my grandad died[16] and my parents came to live with us. It took me a long time to accept my own parents. We slept with our grandmother — we would still hop into her blankets though we were great big kids — and it was hard: I can remember resenting being ticked off by my mother. 'What business was it of that woman to hit us?' And we'd get another good slap up for that one! I can almost hear me saying to our grandmother, 'Tell those people to go back where they came from!' We had just seen them now and again. And our eldest sister, Huhana, we thought she was useless! Truly — she couldn't milk a cow! Not like us! We had the cows to milk, feed the pigs, and we had to get to school. We walked three miles to school. As I grew up, we never went to the pā. My grandad never stayed at the pā. Yet, whenever there was a tangi or anything concerning the community at the marae, he provided. There were six families living along Muriwai beach, and everybody had cows, and all those homes contributed. I can see now us running off with a kit of potatoes or a kit of kūmara, my grandfather killing a pig or it might be a sheep, and taking them down to the lane. Somebody's kōnaki, sledge, or someone would come along with a spring-cart and they'd pick all these things up and take them to the pā. Every house contributed in kind. But as to going to the pā, no we didn't, not until I was older. But the odd times that we did, we would be told just what to do. We knew never ever run across when people were speaking. As you go on, then you'd know the reasons why. During that time the marae becomes that sacred piece of ground and it is just not done to run across the marae while people are doing the speech-making.

When I grew up and was old enough to have a responsibility at the marae, we were given a crash course before we were allowed to help serve in the dining-room. We were quite privileged to be one of the waitresses in the dining-hall. The first time I was really privileged to go with our folk was when they opened Poho o Rawiri marae. That was in 1930.[17] As to looking after the meeting-house, that was a responsibility of chosen women. We didn't go into the meeting-house to lay the mats or to put out the mattresses, no, we didn't. I was quite old before ever I did it. On this particular occasion, I helped Mihikore, that's Mrs Turea, who was the chieftainess for us and women like her don't really do these things.[18] She'd asked us to come and help her prepare the pā for a tangi. It was for a woman who was a relative of ours, and who had helped quite a lot at the pā, but because she was married to a Pakeha her children wouldn't have any idea what to do. There was no one else with us. I didn't know that we had laid the mats wrong. I thought I was doing very nicely, until in the evening. Mum and I were in the meeting-house and Mrs Turea came in and said, 'You two going to sleep here?' My mother said, 'Yes'. 'Oh', she says, 'this is a ghostly pā. I'm not staying here. If you two are going to be silly and stay here, OK, you do that. I am going home.' She had gone home, and just my Mum and I, sitting on the mattress, and the immediate family (they were up on the stage), and in came this man, Apirana Crawford. He stood at the door, he looked at my mother, and he said, 'I was on my way home. I got as far as Tatapouri and I just couldn't go on.' He'd got troubled in his own mind. He said, 'You know, this house has not welcomed me from the moment I arrived. This house just says to me, be on your way, be on your way!' And my mother said to him, 'Why is this house saying that to you?' 'The mats, who put these mats down?' 'Oh, silly me', I said. 'I helped Mihi to put these mats down.' And my mother said to him, 'What is wrong with these mats?' See, my mother had never put mats down. And he said, 'The overlaps are all facing the door. That says you are not welcome.' Mum got up and helped me turn them all over.

That was my lesson for all time. We teach our young ones now. There is a way. You see I am going to make mats: you see all my flax here? When you start the mat, you use the butt end of your flax. The butt end is thicker, so when you finish your mat, you will finish with the fine end. You must put your fine end up against the wall and the thicker end has to be your overlap. It will also be weighty enough for the fine end, underneath. It is all sense, when you really look at these things. They didn't do things haphazardly; they really thought these things out.

We lived on the other side of the Wherowhero lagoon, near the sea. So we knew the phases of the moon. We fished by the moon and we planted by the moon.

Wherowhero was a freshwater lagoon then — it's all sea now, or almost, only the island is left — and we knew which nights were the nights for eeling. Gosh, if I were to go and gather worms, turn over the cow-dung and gather worms and string worms, the kids today at Poho o Rawiri would vomit! It would be so foreign to them. But it was just a way of life for us. Going out certain months, certain time of year for kahawai. That was the life we had.

At school at Muriwai, yes, we were punished for speaking Maori. It may sound terrible — now. It never affected *me* and I don't think it affected any of us of my age group who went to school and got the cane for speaking Maori in the playground, or in the classroom. It was so easy to forget and so much easier, because you were Maori-speaking, to break into Maori. It was only when the teacher heard you that you were ever called in. He never took notice of another child who reported we were speaking Maori. But if he heard us, then we would be taken in the classroom. We either got the cane — I preferred the cane to a hundred lines, I must not speak Maori, that's for sure! They didn't explain, but I didn't think there was anything wrong with it. I suppose, for us, true — my grandmother could read, my grandmother could write, my grandfather spoke beautiful English — but my grandfather could not write. Believe it or not, I was signing cheques for my grandfather, my brother and I, at eleven, before we left school. I can remember him putting his mark to his name; we would write Paku Brown, and he would put his mark. This is what they told us: you go to school to learn to read, to write, and speak English. Oh, I can hear him now, 'Don't be like me and put a cross to your name.' So, therefore, then, that was the rule of the school, no Maori; then it was for you to remember that! The teachers, our headmaster, all our teachers were really part of our community. Mr Quigley used to live at the hotel; so did Miss Francis, and they were very much accepted people.[19] They were our teachers right through. And all our fathers. You know, it has been a continuation of those particular families, those early settlers, and their children, and their children's children. They have cared for those people in the same way as their parents cared for my grandparents — oh, they got on anyway.

I was fourteen when I left school. There was no way for us to get to high school. If you got to Standard Six, you got your proficiency, or competency — that's all they were, eh?[20] Then it was home for you after that. So for that length of time, seven, eight years, I just stayed at home, milked cows, and you know when I come to think of it, we couldn't even get a job in the pub! That's all life was for us. You can go shearing, but only those of us who can get in the shearing shed and I didn't. There was only one gang and it was for a limited number. They had all these older women, who were all experts. They were the fleecers. My mother was out shearing when we were growing up. But we young things never got a look-in. We just milked our cows. But whenever I was at Manutuke — I used to go and play hockey, and stay with the Piki Smiths at the pā[21] — I would go to the mission house and I would always have a meal with the mission workers. I used to help them, these women, and I came under their influence a lot.

The mission at Manutuke was conducted by Bishop Bennett[22] and that's probably the reason why — he was so good — that I offered to be trained. It was four years. I went to Whakarewarewa and I was trained under Miss Bulstrode and Miss Emily Bulstrode. These two women, between them, had the Hukarere Anglican school for about thirty years.[23] But when I first went to Rotorua for my training, I very nearly came home!

The reason why, when I got to the mission house, they showed me my bedroom – it was a nice room, without a doubt – but outside the window they had this wire netting. I thought, that was a strange thing. I was nineteen when I went there but even at nineteen I was not really a worldly person. I soon found that it was the only window that had this wire netting, that's what really upset me. So I wrote to my vicar, Harawira. When he came to see me – I will never forget him – he just said to these two old ladies, 'I would like to see Heni's room.' So away we went! I told him, for me this was no place to be, they don't even give you a chance. All he said to me was, 'Don't ever give them that opportunity. They don't trust you; don't ever give them the opportunity that they were right.' But for all that – although that had happened – because of what they were – they taught me all the niceties. How to behave, how to sit at table properly. When I say all the niceties, for instance, I never knew before that you eat fish with a fish-knife and fish-fork! Ha! I thought. What next! But it is nice to know. If you are in that situation you can deal with it.

Then I was taken ill very suddenly and I was sent home. Actually, they were going to put me into hospital and I cried, because I had nobody in Rotorua and I had never been in hospital. So I asked if I could be sent home. And I get home – to Gisborne. I was actually on my way to hospital there and this woman in the street, this old lady – I had never seen her before – says it was a Maori sickness, mākutu. I can remember laughing at this old lady; I *can* remember that. Anyway, the next thing was my parents were in the car, and I was in the car, and my older sister was in the car, and then I was told that I wasn't being taken to hospital, I was being taken to Hairini, just past Tolaga Bay, where she lived then. Her name was Te Iwa, Mrs Morris. She was Anglican. But every so often, at a certain time of the year, she would have a meeting at her marae and it would be for healing. The Ringatus used to take part in the service. I had quite an argument with my father, then. I thought, here I was, I have been two years, three years, in the Maori mission, and of *my* choice. I said to him, 'NO! They can't do that to me, just couldn't! You can't take me to that kind of thing!' But, anyway, he won the day. Nevertheless, I must give credit where it is due. This woman described our little church – Te Arawa church in Whaka – she described the church, the pools, the people. It was quite extraordinary; she'd never been there. And she really did have a gift of second sight. She said I was never ever to go there and it is quite frightening when you are told, two things will happen to you – six foot down, or you finish up in a mad-house for the rest of your days. Clear cut like that!

My father went to see Archdeacon Hodgson, who was the vicar in Rotorua while I was there. He was in Gisborne, on holiday. He had a wonderful understanding of this, because he had been a mission worker in Melanesia for a number of years and this kind of thing was well known to him. My Dad also went through to see Bishop Bennett, so between them they agreed that I would be transferred. That's why I went to Tokomaru Bay. But I went back. You see, during that time I was in Tokomaru, my father was killed in a motor accident.[24] Then I got very sick again, and I was a suspect tuberculosis case, so I was sent home for six months. I was home during the period of Lent. I thought, well, because it is a very personal thing for me, I have to get on top of this tohunga, running off to a tohunga – my family was going to this woman for everything. I thought, 'Oh no, this just can't happen to us as a family, or else everything we will be blaming – it's all this black magic!' During this Lenten period, I used to say my prayers and one thing I really asked that I be given the answer to is this: Why I can't go back to Rotorua? I really wanted the answer to that, because I did not believe that I would go down with this Maori thing. I got the answer in a very extraordinary way.

Just before Lent was over, I was at Manutuke with my grandaunt; I was asleep and there was just breaking day. And I had a dream; I dreamt that I was lying in my grave — the whole length of me — and the earth was fresh, fresh, just like fresh soil just been turned over, and I had these three flowers, you know, those black-basin, glass-domed things — there was one just below my knees. I had a cross over here, on my chest, with red flowers, very like the poppies that we had, and another about the middle of my body. That was all my dream. But I was not lost; I was *not* covered [on my face]; that was the only part of me not buried in my own grave. And I woke up and it was just breaking day. I sat up in my bed and I asked God to interpret that dream for me, there and then, please. And the interpretation was, very like me being at the end of a telephone and somebody at the other end, and the message that I got was to go back to Rotorua.

So I made up my mind that is exactly what I was going to do. I didn't tell my mother, I didn't tell any one of my immediate family, but I packed all my clothes that would take me through for a while. I was going to a church convention in Hastings, so I nutted it out, oh yes, from when I go there I can get back to Rotorua. Then my conscience must have bothered me, because I went to a woman — this woman was a Ringatu; she was our neighbour. Shed all my worries with Nuki. I told her that I was going, but I never had the guts to tell my mother, because my father was dead. And do you know what she advised me? She said to me, you know, my dream, she goes along with what I have told her, and then she said, 'Are you like me, a Ringatu? When you leave the house to go visiting, or whatever you have got to do because of your work as a mission worker, do you ask God to look after you, protect you (this is all in Maori), and when you get back do you say thank you — thanksgiving — whakamoemiti — as the Ringatu?' I said, 'Oh no. When I say my prayers, I say my prayers in the morning, I say my prayers at night, and we always say grace at the table, and sometimes, when we are all there, we have a midday service and we pray for everybody else.' I will never forget Nuki — that's all she said to me — 'When you leave, ask God to go with you; when you get home say thank you God for looking after me.' And I said to her that I would do just that. That lived with me; and that does live with me.

I went back to Rotorua. One day I get a letter from my eldest sister. I wept over that letter. I was reprimanded for having gone off and doing it quite the way I did, but what really moved — what brought the big flow of tears — was the description of our mother. When our Dad died, our mother wore black for two years. She had come out of that, but my sister said, when they got the telegram that the Bishop had sent, my mother went back into black clothes. It was February when I went; and the Bishop himself brought me back, in May, to my mother. My sister came to the door and she called out, 'Oh, the prodigal daughter has returned!' I'll never forget that, because it had so much meaning — and I have gone on.

I was in the Maori mission for fourteen years. I worked at Tokomaru, at Rotorua, at Ruatoki, and at Manutuke; we actually did all the parish work wherever we were. All women; and they were all Pakeha women that I worked with. We were responsible for the parish work for the vicar and we also organized the church guilds and most of the fund-raising for the Church. And you only had a holiday once a year! Then, for six years, I looked after Public Health nurses in remote areas. It was from the Health Camp, here, that I went to the Waikato to do that. Later, in 1960, I joined Maori Affairs. It was easy going for me, as a community officer, with all that experience — having been a mission worker. It was one of the things that got through to me – during that period of time – what confidentiality is all about. People really took you into their confidence. What they talked about was only for your two ears. So you learnt to respect fellow men.

I was a community officer for twenty-one years. This is why I do say it was that kind of background that I had which was a lot of my own strength, that I was able to draw from. Quite a number of families, family situations, truly, I had no answer for! Because they were in such a muddle! I never, ever imagined people could let themselves and their families get into that kind of mix. Oh, I have actually got down on my knees with them. Now, in a Maori situation I could do this; if I was working with a Pakeha family I don't know if it would have worked. We had to get these strengths. We had to ask for some guidance. With a Maori, as long as you have got your facts, and you are sure, they'll tell you the rest. They just say to you, 'Yes', and they will tell you all about it.

There were some situations – some I can't – incest was one of the things I

Heni Sunderland, 1979. *Gisborne Museum*

found very hard. The first case I had was fairly close to home, too. It was an adopted child brought up from tiny as their own. I had to take myself quite apart: if you are very sure this is happening, then, what are we going to do about it? The mother and I decided we would take the girl back to its natural mother. I thought it was all finished with when this gentleman comes into the office, asking me what right did I have to take this girl? Well, that was enough for me! Ah, I let him have it! He is one of the very few men I have actually cursed in Maori.

Oh, there were bad moments! And lots and lots of good moments. I enjoyed being with Maori Affairs all those years. It is ever so much harder now than it was then. The movement of people into the cities took place in the early sixties. I was already with the department, and it certainly was policy that families were to be relocated and moved out into the cities. Because in the rural areas there was just no work. At first, the movement was of just individuals, getting off and trying to find a way for themselves. Peter Kaua, who was our District Community Officer in charge, he explained the policy to us, as community officers. He said, 'Each and every one of you — know your people.' He said, 'The policy was a very good one, because whole families are being moved, a house would be built in the city, a job would be found for Dad, and then the family moves. So it becomes a small move. But *know* your people. Those you know can't make it, leave them. Be very selective', that's what he told us, 'with the families you move off. If you are not, the breakdown is going to be for them; they won't have immediate families or people that know them to help them out.' Then he spoke to us, the ones who are living in the town as against the people living in the rural. He said, 'You know what it is living in town; you almost have to pay for fresh air. So when people move off, then you have got to explain to them; make sure that their work performance here is a good one. So that they already have the pattern; they don't have to be taught. So you shouldn't have any breakdowns.' He was a very wise person. That's how we were to do it; and that is exactly what we did.

But, you see, other people went in. That's how I see these kids that have gone into the city who became misfits, who are utterly dislocated. There was no connection for them. They belong to nowhere. A lot of our young people have got into gangs in the city and they do ask, 'Who am I? What am I doing here? I am just a "black" Maori, lost, and it's these damn Pakehas who did this!' There are a lot of people who back them up — verbally — just to suit themselves — just too many of them! My own personal view — I support kōhanga reo a hundred per cent plus. For the reason — for me — this upsurge, this feeling, with parents wanting to go back, wanting to learn, and for their children to learn Maori and things Maori — it's not just the language, it is the language and things Maori — it will give them confidence in themselves. They will never, ever question, 'Am I a Maori?' or, 'What kind of a Maori am I?' So these children of ours will not be disadvantaged, as I was when I went to school. Disadvantaged in this way, well, there was no paper, no pencils; I had to learn hard! But these kids of ours, we are of one mind in the kōhanga reo, that is, to give to these little ones every opportunity to learn the language and to know themselves. Also, because it is bilingual what we are doing, at Manutuke, we are preparing our kids for when they move from the kōhanga into the school. By that time, we should have given them all those things they need as a Maori child.

It is based on the marae, and they are going to move very freely — which they are already doing — and, for me, it *must* happen that way. They become a full person in themselves — from littlies. They have the opportunity to grow up in the best of two worlds. The two worlds, they need to go together. But to get the confidence, the reo is important, because that's what the young Mums have felt so bad about. They don't speak Maori. And my concern, today, is this Maori-Maoriness, saying – those Pakehas! this Pakeha thing! that Pakeha thinking! For me, we have to be looking very positively. The Maoriness emerging is going to give back to our kids confidence and pride. Those, for me, are the two things we have moved away from. That middle generation, they lost the language. Our parents said then, you go to school to learn this English language; that's the only thing that's going bring you your bread and butter. The Maori language – what does it buy you? Forget it, forget it! And that's what we have done. Now there is a bitterness and it bothers me very much, because there are some very strong attitudes. For me, it is a matter of having to believe that we are going to make it work. It's on our plate, and we've got to make it work.

Without a doubt, it is the women who have the strengths. Within the extended family and out on to the marae as a whānau as a whole, you will find it is we, the women, who are the ones who really motivate our men. They wouldn't like me saying that, but I do think that.

These are my observations with the marae. There's a word that is being used a lot now – 'kawa' – it's a word that I never heard until recently. There were certain things done at the marae, and they knew exactly what, but they never used to say, 'te kawa o te marae'. I never heard those old people use this word. Now, our world is such a small one; I know now that Tuhoe do differ from us. And in Te Arawa, for instance, I find that the men, the marae is very much the men's domain. And those men, they sit on a paepae. But here, the only time they used to speak of the paepae is when there is anyone lying on the veranda – when there is a tūpāpaku. They refer to that little bit, that front part of the meeting-house, as the paepae, and when anyone is dead then we know that that area is quite special, at that particular time. But now, these men, they are saying to us, 'Oh, this is just for men only, this paepae.' At home, on the Whakato marae, suddenly we were told they were going to put up this special seat for the men, and this is the paepae. I didn't think anything of it when our chairman said he was going to put a seat there, for whaikōrero. I was quite happy for that to happen; but he made it a permanent seat, and I just

The kōhanga reo Christmas party at Whakato, 1984. Papa Koko is giving out presents on the porch of the dining-hall; Heni can be seen in her usual role, that is, making sure that everything is going smoothly, around the back of the hall. Photograph by Gillian Chaplin.

couldn't accept it when we were told that was for men only, and no woman dare sit here. That puts a difference on it altogether. Because what they are saying to us — we are tapu men; we are so special that you women cannot come and sit here. That's never been part of us. The men, the orators — and they were orators in the true sense of the word, like old Te Kani Te Ua[25] — those men just used to sit around, for they knew who they were, and they knew when they were to stand up. They never made themselves special. And when they came up with this paepae for men only, I reacted badly, because I do know something of Te Arawa custom: there, *no* women! Now, I never ever saw it done to my Grannies, and I don't see why it should be done to me, and why it should be done to my children, because that was never *our* way.

We actually had a wānanga over this paepae. The theme of the wānanga was the protocol of the marae, so the paepae. One of our kuias was asked, what could she say about the paepae? And her answer to that was, 'I only know one paepae, that is the paepae hamuti'! The paepae hamuti is the latrine, but being who she was I was aware that she was actually putting them through the test to find out the depth of their knowledge of things Maori.[26] She pointed out that the older people, before her time (and she is in her eighties), they would use the word nohanga for where they sat. And, she said, they sat around and they never ever made it known to whoever their visitors might be, who was who. But *they* knew who they were. Then we had this man — this was all in this wānanga — he had a walking-stick, and he is dancing around there, on about this paepae, and he challenged us, as people of Rongowhakaata, to be very careful in what we do. He said to us, because if you don't do these things properly, things would happen to you people, not good things. As though that wasn't enough, he said that he would come and remove his tīpunas from our house! I looked at this one, I thought, 'Oh, my good gracious me! That one! His tīpunas are there, the pou tuarongo; I know who those figures, those tīpunas, are.' I thought to myself, 'He ought to know better. If he considers himself an orator, a tohunga, then he should know that the tuarongo of the house is our domain, and no one else! We are the tāngata whenua; we are the people who belong.' Anyway, we are sitting along there, and one Nanny says to me, 'What that man is saying is not good.' And I am saying to Nanny, 'And who is going to reply, Nan?' And I thought to myself, 'Well, you know, this is one time my tīpunas, you stand beside me, because there is nobody else!' And when I say my tīpunas stand beside me, I am very aware that we are very much a senior family; I am very aware of that, but I never ever use it — don't need to. But when you do have to, then you do something about it. And when he finished all his prancing around, and dancing around, and waving his walking-stick at us, he came across to shake hands with us. There and then I thought, 'What a cheek!' Auē! I jumped to my feet and I said, 'Nan,' in Maori I said to her, 'I will reply to that mokopuna!' I got up; I turned to this man: 'You stay where you are! When I finish, then you come and shake hands with us!' And I let him know! There are times you must take up the challenge, there and then! If you just let it — we would all have troubled minds. And my mind was not going to be troubled by those remarks! I do really believe this, that our tīpunas, spiritually, they are always with us. When the need arises they will help you. For me, at that particular time, all those tīpunas all around the house, up on top of the house, and Rongowhakaata himself! — and this man who said that he would come and take them away from us, from the house!

You know, for that house, when they decided to build the house, they placed all the tapu all around it. That's how that house was built. No women ever went near there. Only the men. And we have always been told with the first house, there was a tank and the water in this tank is for the washing of your body only; no water from this tank was to be drunk. And they told the reason: whilst the tapu had been placed, when they had the opening ceremony it was lifted and placed on its tāhū; the only restriction is waters off its roof are never drunk. So when they moved the house to its present site, when it came to putting its tāhū back, they decided (and my mother was one of those within the decision-making at that particular time) that the present generations were so Pakeha-fied they would never respect those things. So what do we do? So they said, 'No water goes into any tank, not even to be used for the toilets, or anything; the water off the roof goes into the ground.' So that's what they have done. I am very aware of that house, and, you know, as for the back wall, the tuarongo, that part belongs to us. And whatever the mauri is, it is there; I know that. That man who prances around, he did not know that; for him it is just those carvings. But it is far, far more than just those carvings. So, with confidence, I could tell him, no way can you do that. On behalf of us, or *because* of all of us. But you see he was gracious enough – he was very nice about it – and he said, for him, he was finding out what strengths, what Maori strengths, were still with us. And that was the way to bring it out. To test, and find. When I finished, my other Nanny, who brought this monkey up, she jumped up on her feet and she told him, 'How dare you!' She told him, 'Pack up; get out! Don't you dare do that to us ever again!' But after, when it was all over, she came up and threw her arms around him. Because they are also part of us. So you see, these are the kinds of situations we do get into now, because our men do do a few funny things to us.

It is also the absence of the men; we get so embarrassed at times. It is really a worry. It depends on who comes to your marae. For instance, if Tuhoe people came, I would never stand up and mihi; but if it is just local, us, well, if there is nobody else, rather than no one at all, we would stand up, us women. We have had to do it. But it is only when it is ourselves; not when we have anybody else. It is too important, much too important. The old people – they would just sit down and discuss whaikōrero, and practise among themselves, and give each other the confidence to be able to stand up and do these things, and play their role properly. Because we [women] can't play dual roles; not sometimes. And we certainly would never take their role. But you have to have so much confidence in yourself. You have to have all the background, you have to know yourself, you have to know your people, you have to know your history, and you have to know who your visitors are, their background, their history, how they connect up with you. And those links, which give you confidence, have been broken a lot of the time.

I never say that I am one of the kaumātua. I would like not to; but there are so few. So the role that I play there now, the role that I take, is, whenever there is anything on at the marae, I always go. For this reason: there's very few. My family, as far as the marae and Whakato is concerned, we have responsibilities. Responsibilities that were carried out by those old people, and those responsibilities somehow or other just twistle down to this immediate family. The actual person who was responsible for the building of the house that was Karepa Ruatapu, who was my great-great-grandfather. And he had a sister, and they also had a cousin, and it is their immediate families who have always been responsible for Whakato. We learnt by their example; no other way. They set the standards and they made it known to us that was to be our responsibility. And for me I do do that now. I will honour what has been asked of us.

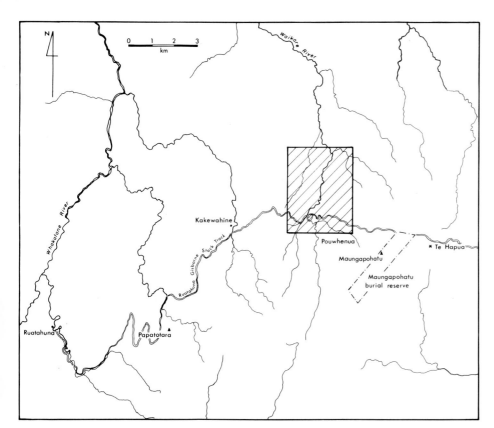

Fig. V: Maungapohatu and the Urewera country in the early 1920s. Details for Maungapohatu are derived from the survey maps of May 1923 and July 1924 (ML 13274, ML 13642, Department of Lands and Survey, Hamilton). ★ indicates approximate location.

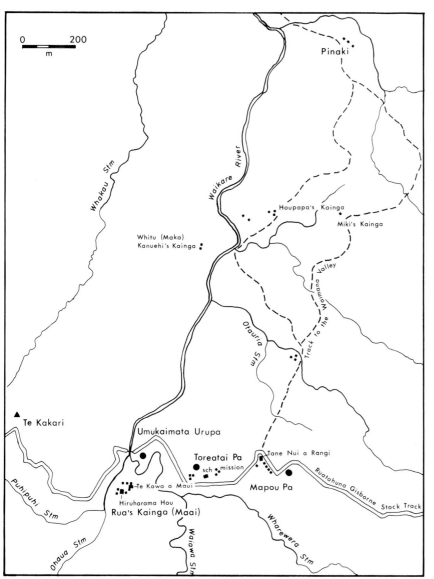

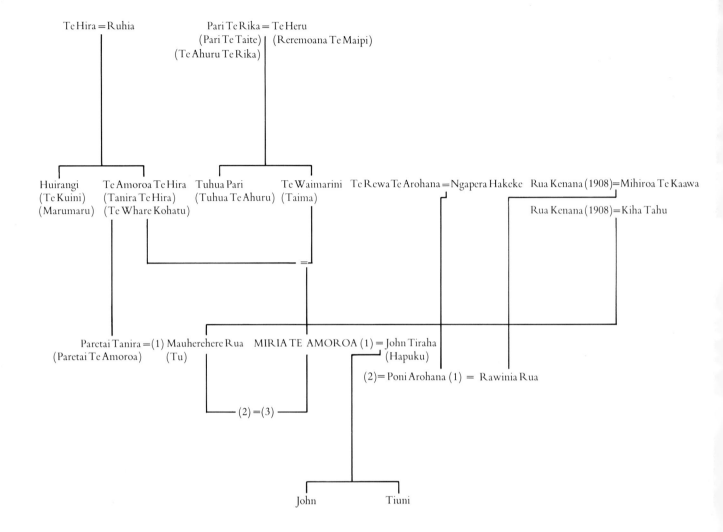

Te Hira ═ Ruhia   Pari Te Rika ═ Te Heru
                   (Pari Te Taite) (Reremoana Te Maipi)
                   (Te Ahuru Te Rika)

Huirangi   Te Amoroa Te Hira   Tuhua Pari   Te Waimarini   Te Rewa Te Arohana ═ Ngapera Hakeke   Rua Kenana (1908) ═ Mihiroa Te Kaawa
(Te Kuini) (Tanira Te Hira)   (Tuhua Te Ahuru) (Taima)
(Marumaru) (Te Whare Kohatu)   Rua Kenana (1908) ═ Kiha Tahu

                                                        ═

Paretai Tanira ═(1) Mauherehere Rua   MIRIA TE AMOROA (1) ═ John Tiraha
(Paretai Te Amoroa) (Tu)   (Hapuku)

                                                (2)═ Poni Arohana (1) ═ Rawinia Rua
              (2)═(3)

                          John   Tiuni

MIRIA RUA

*M*iria's story begins with her amusement that written records and European concerns for chronology can be misleading. Her birth date was ultimately registered, as the law from 1913 demanded of the Maori, but it is probably registered wrongly. She knows that she must have been born in 1924, a year earlier than the documents say. Her name means 'to be comforted' and it derives from her behaviour at the opening of the Matahi meeting-house on 1 January 1925. Miria is the daughter of Te Amoroa, one of Rua's Levites, the teachers of the faith of the Iharaira. She grew up at Maungapohatu during its second millennial phase, that is, its period of revitalization from 1927. She observed from her earliest days the veneration which the people gave to Rua. She explains the ways in which the teachers of the faith, men and women with different roles, went out to the surrounding communities conveying their beliefs in parable and song.

Miria's basic conviction is that there are old tapu powers in the Maori world, life-destroying powers, which can be overcome only by the faith of the Mihaia, Rua. She is, in fact, expressing a dualism inherent in the ancient Maori cosmology, in which there is a conflict between one intrinsic tapu and another. This tension between life-destroying and life-giving tapu is sometimes ritually stated in acts of eating, whereby one power is consumed, or absorbed, by another. Eating expresses 'the clash of tapu with tapu.'[1] This is precisely how Miria describes Rua's efforts to cleanse away, or devour, the powers of the old Maori atua to whom she attributes responsibility for much illness and suffering. Miria lost two of her three children as infants: an experience not uncommon among the Tuhoe, where the early death of children occurred with an appalling frequency. Consequently, wharengaro, or the destruction of the house, is feared more than almost anything else. Explanation is sought by a search through ancestral history in the belief that a curse must have been placed upon the family. It follows, therefore, that protection can finally only come through faith and ritual.

The high infant mortality was undoubtedly also the consequence of the poor living conditions endured by the Tuhoe. At Maungapohatu, during the time when Miria was growing up, twenty-five per cent of the children who were born died before they were four years old.[2] The causes of these deaths were, predominantly and predictably, respiratory diseases like influenza and pneumonia, and malnutrition. A noticeable number of the infants died not long after the birth of the next child in the family, suggesting that inappropriate and possibly indigestible food was being given to them after they were weaned. Miria's account also reveals that the traditional knowledge that had once been passed between women about childbirth was not being transmitted. One learnt simply by giving birth.

For Miria, one of the most important experiences in her life was the 'prediction in the flowers' which Rua gave her. Hillman Rua, Rua's adopted son, also remembered this occasion and the profound effect it seemed to have upon Miria. It was on Christmas Day, he recalled, probably in 1926, when Rua told each person to pick a flower and take it to him. He would then tell them what it meant for each one. Miria 'was just a kid'. Her father, teasing her, persuaded her to go and pick a purple thistle flower (as Hillman recollected it), knowing that 'she'll get prickles on her fingers. So this little kid went over and got that flower. Without hurting her fingers. She went up to take it to Rua. And when she got there, Rua told her, "Something going to shine up. In days to come." Well! We all start laughing about the old man telling his daughter to go over and get that — and she got it.' In Miria's account, she had a daffodil bulb, the promise of growth, clutched in her hand. Years later, in 1956, when the matakite Hori Gage came to the Waimana valley, and 'he start acting like Rua and Te Kooti, we all went there. I went in myself', said Hillman. Miria, he remembered, 'sort of lost her head when she was there. She was acting very funny things',

previous page Miria Rua at Tuapo, May 1984. Photograph by Gillian Chaplin.

as she herself describes, and for Hillman her behaviour seemed to be a rejection of Rua. Hori Gage, she said, was the Messiah. Hillman commented, 'I went straight back and think about that time' of the flowers. 'Be something funny going to come. Well, it is. All that time: 1926 to 1956.'[3]

But Miria's belief in Hori Gage, as being the predicted successor of Te Kooti and the one who was to complete the mission of God, lasted, she said, for only about two years. Nevertheless, Hori Gage's influence was strong among the Ringatu, as both Heni Sunderland's and Puti Onekawa's narratives indicate, and the support he gained shows the real need there was for a renewed spiritual leadership among the people. Hillman Rua described their dilemma, commenting on Rua's prediction that he would return to earth: 'He said, "I'll be dead now. I'll come back." That's what we're waiting for now. When it's going to happen. Well, he did tell us we might have a chance to see him come back. We might have not. I don't believe him. I don't believe he's ever going to come back. Well, it's a very hard thing to believe.'

Eva Rickard, an important figure in the revitalization of the modern Kotahitanga movement, has commented recently, when talking about Maori belief in prophecy and spiritual healing, 'Maori people believe in miracles. They believe in the unknown. There's nothing wrong with that. It's healthy. It only becomes dangerous when you use the wrong medium to try to convey it. . . . In Maori terms, tohunga use the healing powers of their atua to heal. And they seek the answers from inside the person not from outside.'[4] This is how Miria understands spiritual healing. The gift of foresight and the gift of healing are both seen to be divinely-bestowed powers. They may be used for good or for ill; that is their burden. They are also temporary powers, which may be withdrawn or lost through misuse. The testing of the leaders, therefore, to see whether the power, mana atua, is still with them, is always a part of the Maori tradition. As Heta Rua put it, 'Most of these people, like Te Kooti, they are all the same: there's always an ending to it. They must do one thing wrong somewhere. You're given one job, two jobs to do — but you can't do three, according to the law of God. You're not allowed to do that. The same thing with Rua. . . . They are all the same these people; they all go a little bit too far.'[5] Miria is never as direct or as critical as this. But she certainly believes in the gift of spiritual healing, handed down from God, a gift entrusted and to be used well.

Miria grew up in Maungapohatu, but when she left school, in 1938, she came to live in the Waimana valley (or Tauranga, as the Tuhoe know it). She had left a community which, according to the 1936 census, had a population of sixty-seven, of whom sixty-five were Maori, the other two being the schoolteachers. The government report on the Urewera and its people, which was compiled earlier in the same year, had recorded a somewhat larger Maori population.[6] People came and went, of course, but Maungapohatu was now slowly dying. Miria came to live in a river valley which was, and still is, primarily Tuhoe. The Waimana township itself is situated near the mouth of the valley, immediately south of the confiscation line of 1866. It had, in 1936, a population of 403 of whom 187 were Maori. Up the valley there was a string of marae and Maori homes. According to the census there were 291 people living in the vicinity of Waimana, of whom 189 were Maori. This population has steadily declined, as the families' means of earning has crumbled. In 1971 in the locality of Matahi, where Rua's family marae Tuapo, the Ngaitama marae, and the local school all are, there were then only 106 people, of whom fifty-nine were Maori.

In the 1920s a dray road was put in as far as Tawhana, then one of the centres of the Tuhoe population. Horo Tatu, one of Rua's followers, was living here and he ran a string of pack-horses through to Maungapohatu. Under Rua's guidance, the people planted maize all along the river flats of the Tauranga valley, and they had fruit trees, particularly cherries, scattered on the slopes. The dairy factories at Waimana and Opotiki also enabled *the people to develop small herds of cows. George Ihe, with whom Miria came to stay when she first left school, was one such farmer, running a milking herd of twelve. Rua himself, living at Tuapo in 1936, had seventeen. These years, particularly before the Depression, are still remembered as a time of relative plenty. The road remained passable to Tawhana, which they called the 'promised land' and had dedicated to Te Kooti. At Whakarae pa, where Miria now lives, there were, in 1936, a total of ten households earning their living by these various means. Today, there are only two. Dairy farming has largely collapsed. Hillman Rua used to drive the cream-truck up to Whakarae and Tawhana but by the early 1940s he could no longer even reach Whakarae as the road, neglected by the local councils, had deteriorated. Because the Maori families were not ratepayers, under the agreement made at the consolidation of the Urewera lands in 1921-2, the two county councils involved refused to maintain the road. The plight of the inland people was such that, in 1944, they petitioned the government to be able to exchange their family blocks for Crown land elsewhere in the Urewera. It was no use. The poverty of the Maori families of the Tauranga valley is due to their utter inability to raise capital or credit, and to the small size of their family holdings. These were created out of the consolidation of the lands, when the Crown determined which portions it had purchased since 1910, (345,000 acres) and divided the remainder (173,000 acres) among the families. In the Tauranga valley, thirty-one family blocks were brought into existence by this unprecedented division.[7] The pastures they own have largely been destroyed by noxious weeds, particularly ragwort. For most of the families today, the essential source of income is the pensions of the old people. The middle generations have left, gone to Wellington or Auckland. Only the very young, the mokopuna, live with their grandparents. If the valley is to be revitalized, the community urgently needs sustained and planned economic assistance.*

Though many of the people have left, others return. Iwi Hitaua, who joined us when we were talking with Miria on 7 May 1984, and who is present in this narrative, is one. Iwi is the second child of Meri Tukua, Rua and Pinepine's eldest daughter, and Tori Biddle. She was born probably in 1918, and was brought up by Whitu Kanuehi, or Whitu Tawa as he is also called, at Maungapohatu. Iwi and her husband, Tom, returned from Rotorua to Matahi, in 1984, to help look after Rua's tapu house. Tom Hitaua said to us later, 'I'm proud to be one of Rua's followers 'cause I've seen miracles he showed us. As you fellas are asking me, I have to tell you the truth. And I know if I tell you the truth, you fellas don't really believe it. What I'm telling you. . . . It's the thing that was given by God to him. Just the miracles to us. That's why I'm telling you, 'cause I've seen it with my own eyes.'[8] Tom and Iwi Hitaua returned because Tuapo is Iwi's family marae and their ancestral home. If it is only the old who return, the community will die, but in 1986 some younger families are seeking ways to live here again.

In her narrative, Miria touches upon the hahunga, or the occasion of the reburial of Rua's eldest son, Whatu, in 1940. This occasion was the last time ancestral bones were brought back to Maungapohatu. The hahunga, the ritual ceremony when the bones of the dead are exhumed, displayed, and mourned over before their final return to their ancestral land, was a tradition which the Tuhoe have maintained through most of this century. The various ceremonial sequences of the tangihanga are the major rites in Maori society, and Miria and Iwi are recounting two occasions when the spirits of the tīpuna were threatened by hara, errors or misdeeds, because the living had found it difficult to carry out properly these rites of passage. All those who took part in the disinterment of Whatu's body were tapu and, as Miria indicates, ceremonial food was eaten by them in order to lift the tapu at the end. This is another practice which had always been observed by the Tuhoe. Separate umu, ovens, were traditional for the priests.[9] Telling this tale brought back, for both Miria and Iwi, accounts they had heard from the time of the Flu, in November 1918, when rites for the dead could not be properly given. All these stories re-emphasize the heavy mortality which the eastern Bay of Plenty communities experienced, also underlined in Reremoana's recollections. For the very old people in the Tauranga valley, it is 'the Flu' which divides the recent past: events occur either before or after it. But in the heart of the Urewera country the people isolated themselves under Rua's instructions and thereby were able largely to escape its effects.[10]

The conversations we had with Miria took place at Tuapo. We talked together on the porch of Te Ao Hou, the meeting-house which Rua's children built after his death, when they turned his last home into a papakāinga for themselves. The meeting-house sits on a high bank, its back to the river. Just below, there is the pool where the guardian taniwha lives. It has given its name Tuapo to the marae.[11] Near to the meeting-house stands Rua's house, beside which he is buried in a sealed concrete tomb. The family marae is now the centre for the Iharaira faith. Brightly coloured flowers bloom beside the tapu house and the grass is always neatly mown. In January 1984, Rua's son Mau, Miria's husband, erected in front of the house a replica of the great gateway which had once stood at Maungapohatu. He had brought the photograph of it, taken in 1908 and reprinted in the book Mihaia, *to a welding firm in Whakatane to have the image recast for him in metal. The gate is emblazoned with Rua's signs for the New World that is to come. Its re-erection is Mau's statement of the continuing Iharaira belief that Rua is the Messiah.*

We talked with Miria on two occasions: 7 May 1984 and 8 December of the same year. Iwi joined us during the conversation in May. We have also drawn on an earlier recorded dialogue we had with Miria and Mau on 19 May 1978, when we were talking with them about Rua.

I was only a little girl when everybody went back to Maungapohatu. On my birth certificate it says that I was born in 1925, but my mother told me that when they opened the meeting-house at Matahi, Te Huinga o Te Kura, she got embarrassed with me because I cried a lot when they started having the service. My mother had to walk right through the meeting-house. He'd stopped — the tohunga — and she had to walk out with me because I wouldn't stop crying! It was Henare who named

The opening of Te Huinga o Te Kura, Matahi, 1 January 1925. This photograph was labelled 'a speech of welcome' by the missionary Grace Johnston, from whose album it comes. *Judith Binney*

me Miria after that.[12] They opened that house on 1 January 1925. Henare got shot in 1925, so I must have been born on 12 August 1924.[13] But they got the place right: Omahuru.

I must have been brought up on the road, because my parents were working on the road up through the valley. Then everyone went back in 1927. I used to hang around with the korouas; sleep inside the meeting-house with them! Every time we get visitors, I'll sleep in amongst the old people – Tioke, or Te Kaawa from Ruatahuna, and even old Ira Manihera.[14] He always came up there. I was a child that always goes up to whatever was going on. I used to see all these people go round with their hands pressed together, and bow in front of Rua, and I used to do that. I remember myself; whatever they do, I'd copy what they do! I'd see my father going down from the pā to Maai with Rua's men, and I used to go down with them. Real quizzy. I'd see my elders bow and I'd bow! He gives you a blessing. Of course, my father used to sit up in front of Hiruharama there. He's one of the Riwaiti, the Levites. He was a policeman for the services, but old Rua said there's a better place, going in with the Riwaiti. That was the last lot. So my father, Te Amoroa, became one of the teachers, with Teka, and Tatu, and Wharepapa, and Pita Te Taite. And when they had their karakias, their prayers, there used to be a male and a female for each district. My mother was one; she came in with Teka. Pita and his sister, Kumeroa, were the first, and then my mother was second, with Teka, and the rest of the women came after that. Each couple had their own waiata, and their hīmene and their pānui. And their parables. They would have a waiata that would be for the district – Waioeka, or Gisborne, or Opotiki. They'll take *their* song, a Maori song, and their hymn, and their pānui, and they'll take them to a certain district. Each one got a note for the waiata, and some of them are very hard notes! And they've got meaning in what they sing. When my father died, in 1944,[15] my mother, Taima, started going round with a man from Waikato and they all got wild. Because she was the second one and the old ones were afraid she might take all the waiata and the karakia away! But she never did go.

My father was the one who used to come down to Matahi a lot. He would ride down to see my uncle, Tuhua, and we'd go to my grandfather, Pari, who was living down past Nukuhou way. I was still small then – never been to school yet. We'd stay in the old home; my grandfather does scrub-cutting and fencing. But my father was always the one who brought the meat down for their Christmas

Te Amoroa Te Hira teaching at Maai, probably in early 1927. Te Amoroa is on the bench in the centre, holding a book. Rua is beside him, in the chair. Seated on the bench, left, is Pukepuke Kanara, a staunch follower of Rua's. In the foreground, left, is Wharepapa Hawiki, one of the Levites; right, Tawa Kanuehi, Puti Onekawa's grandfather. *Morris collection, Alexander Turnbull Library*

time at Matahi. When we come down we always bring something, meat and that. We don't come empty-handed!

My old man goes out hunting, and he might kill a tame one, tame pig. Or we might have got those — what the Tuhoe would call kai kiore.★ Or those little birds, pihipihis. Or pigeon in the fat. That's the only time, Christmas, when we'll go out and have a good time! My father's the main one to come down. He would go out in the bush and look if we've got some tame pigs, and he'll kill one of them. He's a great hunter and he kills just what he needs. Leaves the rest for next time. He'd go way out to Pinaki, 'cause most of them go bush anyway, and shoot one down, and preserve it until he comes out here. The pigeon, he goes out to shoot it — May, June, July.[16] They just skin them. They call it mākiri — take the skin off, just leave the bones. That's for the family. The family only gets the bones, and its insides! Oh, the first bird, the first shooting, they cook *that* bird whole. After that, they skin them. Hardly any for the family, just the guts and the bones. They put them in water. Wrap them up tight and put them in biscuit tins, and take them down to the river and put stones on them. Airtight too! Then in August they tahu. Not any time! They put them in the fat. Those tahu'd birds are not to go out of Maungapohatu; they have to leave them for Christmas. That Ruatoki crowd — they come up before, and old Rua chased them away: 'Those are my birds!'

When they put them in the fat, they put them in biscuit tins, you know those round-wines? Or they used to have those old calabashes, some of them. Of course, a forty's a hokorua. All depends what sort of shooter you are if you get them all! They are well kept for years. Wild pork, you tahu them in their own fat. They keep a long time. Not like today — it's different. The pork we get is different to the old. What pigs we get now, we try and tahu them, and they soon get the mould on them. The old people, they'd make the fat and they wouldn't use it just for nothing: they'd keep those fat, and tahu the meat. Nice too!

Those little birds, we'd tahu those, too. There's not very many that does that now; they can't even make the tune to get the birds coming out. The pihipihis — those little green waxeyes you call it — you hook them on a long stick. Mānuka is the best. Oh, the hardest job is plucking them. So small! But once you get them plucked, you put them on this long stick — still keep the guts inside, not like the pigeon — and put them over a big fire outside. You turn them, and when they are just about toasted, you put them in fat. Break off the beaks, and break off the toes. Because they are all burnt — singed off. You won't have to waste all the fat on them. Pack them in fat together; just pop them in while it's boiling.

Well, my father used to ride down with these for the 23rd. They still keep that day; the 23rd is Rua's day. It just stands for his birthday. It's a Scripture day. We have a church that day. After that, you can go out to anybody's pā for their Christmas.

When I lived at Maungapohatu with my parents, I remember when we had visitors and we'd have a big kai down at the marae. Out in the open so everybody can get on it! They used those muslin cloths — they'd get those big rolls and spread them straight on the grass. Later, oh well, all in the meeting-house, and then only the ope have a feed! When we're having special visitors, one man goes around with a bar of soap. In my time, Katiana [Tawa] used to do that. He'd go round with a big bar of Taniwha soap, and he'd cut a piece and he'd just say, 'Bake a plate of scones, so much, or a bread, about this size.' So many plates of rīwai for each

---

★bush rats preserved in fat

household. And meat. No matter how big the meeting, just about feed the whole lot, eh? But only in pots; they never had much hāngi in those days. You only had small pots and a steamer. And Katiana blows the horn; there's always three horns. Three calls. First one to wake you up in the morning. Second one, start cooking. Third one might be in front of the meeting-house — all go down and bring your kai. All he does is bring the sugar and butter. They had butter in those days! Bring them all in the meeting-house. Just the ope would eat; tāngata whenua not allowed, no! Rua doesn't like the idea of having dining-halls. If you were to step on the ope — 'cause you don't know which is the ope and which is the tāngata whenua! So only the ope would eat, on the floor. When the ope is finished, they'd call out another horn, blow another call, and everybody comes and gets their own. Each one has got to look round for their own plates, and crockery, and their own teapot. Then they take them back to their own place. When there's an ope up, they never take their meals with the ope. The visitors are really respected in those days. Not like today. You don't know which is the ope, which is the old people.

They also had a men's committee, and the women's committee. I have seen the women going round, every Friday — look around the wood-heap, and see if the place is clean. They would check around the fireplace in all the homes. Just imagine those homes up at those streets in Maungapohatu — going through every house, right to the wood-heap, right to the toilet! There was a threepence fine for dust, and the blue clay fireplaces had to be polished, too. And we had those rules about not running horses through the pā. Even dogs, we tied the dogs up, or we were fined for threepence. As soon as my father's back from hunting, I have to tie the dog up. When they go out hunting, there's always one man to go around, looking around to see who might kill their tame pigs. There's earmarks. You get fined if you get somebody else's pig. 'Look at that pig, eh! Earmarks!' Old Temata [Kiripa], he used to do that. He feeds the tame pigs, too. And there were quite a few on the women's committee. Tangiwaka was one, Pita Te Taite's wife.

Rua taught the people about rationing. He said there's a time coming, and he showed them how to ration everything. For each family. He taught them how to make the small supply of sugar go round, so that it would last you so many days. When the war came, my mother already knew about how to go about it and ration. For clothes, all we have up there is old clothes from the mission. We have a sale every Saturday. After the services, and say after lunch, the mission people sell

Tangiwaka Anania at Ruatahuna, 1961. She was said then to be 103 years old. Photograph by C. Lindsay. *National Museum*

Rua teaching from the veranda of his house, Hiruharama Hou (New Jerusalem), at Maai in January 1927. Photograph by E. T. Pleasants. *Judith Binney*

all the old clothes. Good clothes, too. Lena Te Heuheu used to go out early on the Saturday morning to catch the Road Service bus and bring the mail-bag back. The mission people paid her to bring the clothes through. She carted them, in bags, on horseback from Papatotara. Even old quilts. We had some lovely quilts. When we used to have a hui at Maungapohatu, those people don't have to bring their blankets. We had quilts at the bottom of each bed! We'd pay one-and-six for a good frock, or the quilts. They go up as high as a pound. But the only time we get a new pair of shoes is at Christmas, when we go out. Once a year!

I started school at Maungapohatu. Miss Paulger and Miss Shaw were our teachers.[17] I liked going to school. Although they were strict! We'd go down early in the morning. We have to form a line and march in, and we always have hymns first. Then do the school-work after that. We are not allowed to speak in Maori, even in the grounds. Miss Paulger can hear us from the schoolhouse! We get punished! We did all the school grounds through punishment. They were really sloping when we started! We have to go right down to the creek below there and get some rocks; or you have to take a wheelbarrow for a load of earth. We made the tennis court, pulled out ragwort, planted the pines, pulled up ferns! Some of the parents put up a fuss about it! Even if we lost our pens and pencils, we have to stay after school and do these things! Looking at it today, I think it helped us, it helped us a lot. Of course, we *have* to talk Maori back home. There was no other part. Miss Paulger did teach us to respect our elders. That came from the schooling. We respect Miss Paulger, too! But looking at the kids of today, they can hardly speak their own language. That feels bad. And they've got no discipline. That's why I say I think she helped us.

We did Scriptures at school. Of course, we'd go to our own service at Maai on Saturdays. Then there was the Presbyterian one after that. I think we all respected

Miria at Maungapohatu school, probably 1932. She is in the very front row, on the right, wearing shoes. Te Auhi Tori (Iwi Hitaua), is in the back row of girls, fifth from left, wearing a white blouse and scarf, her hair falling across her forehead. Ted (Te Hau) Rua, Rua's son, who appears in Te Akakura's story, is fifth from the left in the back row. Hakaraia Wharepapa, whom Puti Onekawa adopted, is seventh from the left in the same row. Te Au Hora Tori, whom Puti Onekawa also took as a whāngai, is the little girl who wears a dark coat, standing immediately behind Miria. The two teachers are Irene Paulger, on the left; Catherine Shaw (Mrs Ingram) on the right. *Catherine Ingram, Auckland*

both. On Sundays, the teachers take their own, at the schoolhouse. We had to go. They've got a little church-house by the school, and we had to go. Oh, well, we liked to go. There's nowhere else to go, eh? We'd learn our bit of text there and say it, and we'd get some good prizes. They didn't seem to be contradicting each other, they didn't. Of course, John Laughton always comes back and takes us on. We learn some Scripture with him, and he's almost a Maori, more of a Maori than some of the Maoris! He takes most of the Maori laws. He respects them. He was more of a Maori than his wife, Horiana![18]

When I left school, thinking myself grown up,[19] I stayed in Tauwharemanuka with the Ihes[20] and did a bit of milking because I liked the outdoor life. Milked for a couple of years, then got married to John. Don't know how old I was when I got married! It wasn't arranged — no, no. We just got married the Maori way. We just went together. And we came down here looking for work. In the first year we went up Gisborne way, a whole lot of us on old Hillman Rua's truck. We had a gang that goes up there to the shearing. It wasn't very good for the first life of being married. Then we looked for jobs around Matahi, digging posts, splitting battens, and that. It was a hard life. We were living right out at the back there, at the back of Miller's Road; I was living with my in-laws. That's when I had my first baby.

He was what you call a premature, just lived a week. I was riding horses, and that, not knowing how it goes. What to expect. The first one is hard. And not having my parents around, 'cos they were up at Maungapohatu. The second one I lost. He was born right here at Tuapo, on the porch of the meeting-house. I started having the pains, so we came back on the car or I'd have had it down in the road! They were all sleeping in here — it was early in the morning — I was calling out for old Whitu [Kanuehi]. I had John right over here, right on this corner! He was seven months old when he died — at Maungapohatu.[21] Then the old people had to go around, saying something about it, eh, losing your kids! They said, that's the wharengaro, losing your child. It goes in the family. A wharengaro is a family that doesn't conceive; what child they have, it dies.

So my family all got together. And that's why I got my third one, Tiuni. Old Tuhua was the eldest on my mother's side. He's the eldest of the Te Rikas. He is from Ruatahuna.[22] And there was another family, Nino Takao and Ngawini at Whakarae, they'd lost four, five, kids. Because it comes from our Te Rika family, Ngawini's family. Tuhua came down and talked about it. I had just had Tiuni when he came down. She was born on 10 January 1944. We always had the day, 20 February, in memory of the date of Rua's death — get together — and we call it Pepuere. He came down for that, the last one over here. It was Tuesday and these two families got together. You have got to be all of one mind, not one pulling one way, one pulling the other way. You have got to get together. And each one had to place a koha for their own family. He must have put a blessing on our children to survive. He looked through the line of the Te Rika family. It's always there. It's like a curse. And once you understand, then you get kids.

Other families went to Rua for that wharengaro. My second husband's parents went to him. Old Te Rewa and Ngapera, they were childless, and they went to Rua at Matahi to ask if they could have any children. And he agreed to it. He said, 'Yes, you can have them', and they had Poni. It all depends on what they're like, inside. In their hearts. Another couple, they asked the same thing and he said, 'I'll give you some children, but you'll get sick of it.' And they said, 'No. We won't.' They had a first child, when they were just about getting old, and after that, they got a second one. And they started talking about it, started saying, 'Oh, getting sick of it, washing nappies and that!' She was pregnant with her second child. She just haemorrhaged. She died — in childbirth. 'Cause they were the ones that he'd said, 'You'll get sick of it.'[23] It is in the nature of the man or the woman themselves. They might like a child now for a few minutes, and the next minute they won't. They shouldn't conceive. It all depends on your nature. They might be allowed to bring one up, but not to have one of their own.

There was a fellow here a couple of years ago, from somewhere round Taranaki, and he reckons his parents went to Rua, because they were a wharengaro. He came here with a group of school-kids; first time he'd been. He said he was looking around for his spiritual father. His old parents had come here and asked Rua for some children. So he called him his spiritual father. Quite a few went to Rua when he was at Taramaire. He used to stay there to take all the Maori kēhuas away. People came to him for a blessing. They might give an offering or something; or they might wait until they get the child to give an offering. He'll just talk to them; all depends what their nature is like. He might offer them what they want. He'll explain — there will be a reason.

I brought three into the world. I wasn't taught. I learnt by having them! The first birth was an easy birth; the only hard thing was that cord. Tried to do it my way. After that I knew how to do it. When Tiuni was born my half-sister was there, Paretai. I nearly had Tiuni on the horse, though! The well had run dry and I had to bring my clothes right down to another home, over the other side of the river. As soon as I sat down, the pain started coming. Oh, I hopped on the horse and I go home — my sister was there. So Paretai was my midwife! And I have been midwife the same way, just happened to be there! When a child comes out I get a towel and wrap it around — tie it up to keep the air away — see that everything is coming out, and cut that cord. You wash mostly after that, after the mother is finished. Then there's the afterbirth. I used to place a threepence in those days, a coin — we call it a koha — on the afterbirth. That's all we do; just put it on. Then the men take the afterbirth to the cemetery and bury it. The second one I was midwife for, I was with Hori Gage and I was still under the [baptism of] sea water.[24] So I put sea water on the afterbirth, but the woman didn't like it and she fainted. Because she wasn't under the sea water. But at Maungapohatu, they used the coin. Miss Paulger used to help. They'd send one of her adopted kids to her and ask if she has any threepence; she knows what it is for. She'll get one. And afterwards they bring the coins down to the house here, at Matahi. They still do that. 'Cause the window is still open. You just put it through the window.

Most of those women from Maungapohatu were skilled in birth. And sometimes there were very hard births. They used to have a karakia before the child comes out. They'd get a tohunga — one of those Riwaiti — and they'd do some karakia. But it all depends on what you do, when you are carrying your baby. Of course, women aren't allowed to take any food out of men's pockets while they are pregnant. You are not to take what's in a man's pocket. And not to swear. If you don't swear, you'll get an easy birth. Miss Paulger used to go around to help the women. Some might be having birth right out in the hills there at Maungapohatu, or at Pinaki, or right down the river. They might be out there feeding pigs. Sometimes, they do take that drink, that water, to make it easier. You put a coin, a threepence, in the water. Mau is still keeping the threepences for drinking water, and to bathe in, in the house here. Rua's house. The coins that have been blessed. These are the healing coins. You put a threepence in the water. You drink that water, so you get it inside you; or you can boil up some water for bathing. Hot water — you fill the tub and put the coin in. Don't use soap. You drink the water when you're not feeling too good, inside of you. It all depends if you have got the faith.

There is something very important in *my* life. It's what old Rua prophesied. That was that day when we brought in the flowers. Everyone — the women, or mainly the women — has to go and pluck a flower and present it to him. I got a bit of a daffodil, a bulb eh! I was one of the youngest; it was when I used to go with those old people. And he said, 'In days to come these shall bloom' — for me. Actually, I didn't know what he meant, then. There were quite a few of those flowers, but you take the same flower and you will find it has a different meaning for each person. You might just pick up a thistle. You see, the thistle is prickly, but for whoever is handing in that thistle he will foresee something totally different. It might be something good. It goes by your birth, and he foresaw what is going to happen. Sometimes, it's a warning. It's like your fortune. They wrote it all down in a book, what he said to each person. For me, it was in days to come I'll bloom. And the year I started coming out was in 1956. It was the meaning of those flowers.

It happened at Tataiahape. It was a First of July and we were all sitting in the meeting-house. That's when I saw Hori Gage. I started rising, walking towards him. It was like being struck by lightning. Just like being electricicated! That's how I felt about it and everybody that sat beside me, they all felt it. They got the shock, too. Old Hillman Rua had been talking and it went round the house and Hori Gage was the last speaker. I just stared at him and that thing seemed to come. I had a child on me but, when he took over, I started rising. Of course, Hori Gage used sea water. He puts it on you and blesses you with sea water. But he never did me. Just rubbed my legs, rubbed my feet. He never put the sea water on my head. I didn't get the sea water. And that must have been when I started acting, singing, calling out to people quite old names, whistling. What I say is strange. I might look at a person and I might act what he usually do. He might be a singer, and I'll be the singer! And I don't even know how to sing! I could even speak the Tongan language and I don't know what!

But I never went in under the sea water. Must be that I wasn't really in with him. It's up to you if you really want to go in under.[25] But when that thing came out I was acting what he used to do, what old Rua used to do. The other men were talking to Hori Gage and I was saying, 'It took you a long time to come out.' You see, it is the prophecies from Te Kooti: he said, 'There will be another one coming, after me, between Nga Kuri a Wharei and —' and I was saying, 'Why did you have to take this long?'

When Hori Gage first came here, it was a First of January. 1956. He was at Matahi, at the next pā. When he got there, he said he had been looking around for the atua, 'ko te atua'. He found him, in the bush, that's what he said. 'Cause he started quite a few years before 1956. That was when he got *here*. That was the first time I saw him. People were going to him for his blessing. Just his touch. He just rubs them — or he just touches you. It might be your back, or your arms. Some of them go just for that touch. I feel scared of him: he can see all my sins. That's what I used to say to myself, he can see how sinful I am. You see his face, pale, with all the people's sickness.

When he blesses them, he uses the salt water. Old Niwha Te Pou, from Tataiahape, was the doctor for him, and his wife was a nurse.[26] You get the water, cold sea water, and Niwha blesses it. He gets the water, in a bottle, and he just turns it up and down gently, three times. He tips it. You've got to say the Father, the Son, and the Holy Spirit. And they put it three times on your hand, getting out the mana, the Maori mana. And they always rub it down after that with the olive oil. Rub it down after with the oil. That's why Hori Gage had the nurses. He don't trust the men! The women had to do the women. After putting the cold water on and the oil, then they blow through a hanky. Even for that he uses the women. You might have two nurses, all depends how sick you are. If it's blowing through a hanky — your head is first — then that's where it all depends if you have got the faith. He blows your head first, through the hanky. You hold the hanky. It might be the top of your head, blow down on the top of your head; might be your eyes, through your eyes; and your mouth. The women have to do all those. Then you put the hanky where the pain is. Where the pain is, it blows out. Blows everything down. Blows out through you, blows through your toes. Sometimes you *sweat*. Perspire all right! Rubbing — and the blowing!

But I didn't go to him as a sick person. That first time I saw him, I didn't want to look, knowing how hard a job he is having with those sick people. And some of them are not sick, they just want his blessing, his touch. But that time at Tataiahape that thing came out of me and, now I think about it, I suppose it came out over there because that's Rua's land.

That place was given to Rua as a gift.[27] But he never took it in black and white. He said it was between him and God Almighty. He didn't want it on paper. That's why, when they started to take back the land there seems to be a curse on a generation of people. They get all sorts of sickness. Some of them went to Kapi Adams and he said, 'Yes, land troubles'. Kapi Adams was a healer, too, a matakite, but he always put Hori Gage above him as the one from the spiritual side. You see, Tataiahape was promised land; it was given to Rua. They can just leave the place as it is, but don't claim it back! 'Cause that place has been offered to him. That place is there for his people. It's promised land, whenua oat'.[28] He said my land belongs to God, 'mō Te Atua tēnei whenua'.

And that's where I got struck. I seemed to know all these things. I just couldn't help myself. But my mother, when she heard, she really didn't like it. And everybody started to say, 'Oh, she's pōrangi'. Pōrangi is pōrangi! The way I act! It lasted for about a month. Those fits. I know which is the right one, though, which is the true one. It was spiritual; the old Maoris coming back and talking to you! And I went out; they couldn't keep me; I had to go. I'd go out with the people, just to see Hori Gage. That was after my mother died.[29] She doesn't like this religion. This thing I had, she doesn't want me to show it out. I might do something funny; might say something out of place. But after she died, I came free. I used to go amongst strange people.

I followed Hori Gage to Mangatu; we had a Twelfth up there. We'd all go in busloads. Sometimes we had three buses. All sick people. Going up to see him. And we went up the coast there, to Reporua, Ruatoria, and Tikitiki. For their Twelfths. But after that I stopped going with them. I only followed Hori Gage for two years. But before that, he went up to Waitangi with all the crew — Poni went up and even my mother went then — and that's how the Kotahitanga started. I'd stopped home to milk the cows. I didn't want go with all the people and get excited. But we were in that Kotahitanga and we are still in it. Mau is one of the members from the eastern side, Waimana side. Hori Gage was trying to unite all Maoris underneath God Almighty and the Maori Queen. They've even got a flag. He did tell us the meaning; it's all on the flag, but I never caught up with the translations

Miria at Tuapo, when we were talking, May 1984. Photographs by Gillian Chaplin.

of everything! It's like self-government. But there's so many Kotahitangas! Some say Kauhanganui or something like that![30] And now with the younger people, the Te Rangatahi, going up there, trying to overstep the elders. They *are* overstepping the elders. You want to see some of the meetings they have! They're trying to go the Pakeha way! Some of them demonstrating — they wouldn't listen to the korouas, kaumātuas. Hori Gage passed the Kotahitanga over to Tom Te Maaro — he used to go round with Hori Gage — and then Tom Te Maaro gave it to Eva Rickard.[31] Some went off the track when Hori Gage left. But Rua's people here, they wouldn't follow up these sort of things. They're very stubborn!

Now, I am more close with Rua. I suppose it's being with my husband, Mau. We have to help one another. I started trying to help with my second husband, Poni. He used to take sermons and I wasn't very interested in karakias and that, then. I used to read the comic instead! I didn't listen much to him, anyway, until we had that flood. 1964. We were milking cows, living at Wairatu, across from Whakarae. We had a farm over there on the Waiiti. That's when we had the big flood, when Sam Biddle's house was smashed in the landslide, and our home was washed away.[32] I had to call out to Poni to say church for us! Had to listen to him, then! And I started helping him, 'cos he always takes the Twelfths, every month, down at Tataiahape. His father, Te Rewa, used to take them before. But we didn't have them at Tataiahape. Hori Gage brought the Twelfths back there. We never used to have them with Rua. To my way of thinking that flood was because they opened the timber road to Maungapohatu.[33] That was in January, and then they had that flood in March.

Rua had told his people not to start meddling with Maungapohatu. He said to them, 'Don't let the place go! You'll find you've got nothing.' But with the forestry and the road: they came round for signatures. And when they wrote their names on the paper to sell those timbers, they found Maungapohatu doesn't belong to the people that stayed there! The Maungapohatu people found they didn't own it; there was plenty of owners! All living all over the place![34] And that's what he said: 'You'll find you've got no part in it. Just more people living in every part of

New Zealand!' That's why my mother was always against it. She never did sign. And when the flood came, Joe Biddle was laughing at us. He told us what I told you: it was you fellows that went and takatakahi the place! Stamping all over the place! Spoiling everything up there! Hungry for money! Yet he was one of the worst ones!

After the flood, we had to sell the cows. There was no way to feed them all. Everywhere was sand, black sand. And even over here — the logs were down here, at Matahi. Even those little creeks, they started flooding. That was the worst flood ever. After that, we came over and stayed at Whakarae. Then Poni died, in 1969,[35] and I stayed on — with my mokopunas.

I had quite a few whāngai that I brought up as well. Too many whāngai! Waereti was the one we brought up from three days old. Her mother just brought the kid over and dumped it. Up to me! I had to bottle-feed *her*. One, I just went and got myself. She was about a year old. An old lady had her and she had too many to bring up. I just took her over. It's getting that love into you for kids. It took Poni a long time to get on with that child, but when he got used to it, most of the time he cares for her! And Poni's children, we brought them up. And mine, Tiuni.

I've been with Mau since 1972. I stayed at Whakarae and he was living there, on Paretai's — my older sister — the family's land. She had died in 1969 also,[36] so we got together. Now I help him. Since Meri Tukua died,[37] he's been looking after the house, Rua's tapu house. All we have to do is try and beautify outside. What we can do. It hurts me, when I come down here, to see the place with dogs running all over it. Knowing what he was like. He used to set the rules for cleanliness.

We have had that family reunion too. The book started it;[38] some didn't realize themselves who's who! So that's when they all came back. Mau and his son, Bishop, and Mei Rua were the organizers. That was on 7 January 1984. It took us a year and a half, getting all the funds and that. We had a big marquee over here. Maybe 400 people came. It was a lovely day. Mau put that gate up. It was his surprise for the people. Bishop had the idea for the cake. And no beer on the table! Most unusual for Tuapo! We had kinas, and pāuas, and mussels, from Wellington. The only thing was they never had any bread to go with the kinas! They only had cakes! The Auckland mob made their blue jerseys and one of Mau's daughters brought Mau's coat down for him, the one with the blue and white diamonds on

The replica of the entrance gate at Maungapohatu, which Mau Rua had reconstructed out of metal and erected before Rua's tapu house at Tuapo, for the reunion of January 1984. Photograph by Gillian Chaplin, 1984.

Cutting the cake at the reunion. It is a model of Hiona, Rua's council-building at Maungapohatu. Front: Noti Rua, younger sister of Te Akakura; Iraia Rua, Rua's son and the eldest living member of the family, holding the youngest, Lynn Ripia; Mau Rua, wearing a blue blazer — which was designed especially for the occasion — with an insignia of a club surrounded by two white diamonds, derived from Rua's emblems as King and Messiah. Photograph by Joe Te Maipi.

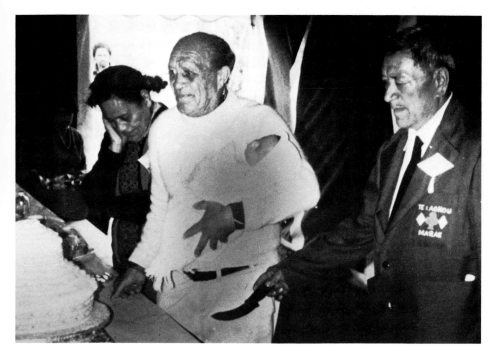

the pocket. We had it then so it would be all right for the working people. Not on the Pepuere.

Rua died here. He slept out in a tent when he was suffering; then, they had to put him on the porch of the house, and he died there. He said not to take his body to the cemetery. He get scared of the kēhuas! He didn't want to go back to Maungapohatu. He's had his time up there. That was why he had to spend the three months and then the nine months there, teaching karakia and that. After that, the people started coming out. He did not want to go back. He sold up everything. After he died, some of the people changed their names.[39] My father, Te Amoroa, is Te Whare Kohatu: that's the tomb they built at the back of Rua's house here. My mother's name was Te Waimarini; afterwards she was Taima, Time. Waiting for the time — the time he died — for six o'clock. That's the time he was to come back, after three days. Tio, that's Pinepine's youngest girl, was named Pera; that's his pillow. The old man's pillow. Huirangi, that's my father's sister, the one who looked after Pinepine when she was a tapu woman, she changed her name to Marumaru. That's his shade. He used to have a shade, just where the meeting-house is now. And he would sit under it. And Puti is called Karaehe, that's the glass he used to drink out of, when he was sick. Old Teka was Pororoa, for the long nights, the long nights awaiting. Wharepapa was Te Whare Kati, that's for the house: that's been closed.

Mau's name? Well, that was always for the time his father was taken to jail. It's really Mauherehere. His other name is Tu. Taotu really, that's for the wound, when Henare got shot. Just a few of them will call him Tu. Those new names, most of them stuck. Like Puhi. She was Materoa;[40] she wanted to be named Hinau, that's the berry you get from the bush at Maungapohatu, and then make into bread. But they called her Puhi, that's the name of Rua's car! The one that old Mac Onekawa used to drive around! Rua named the car; it was a pet car! And Iwi here, Meri Tukua's daughter —

Iwi: I *was* named Te Auhi, for that fighting at Maungapohatu, when the police came. It's like a lament. I was born just after that fighting, when my uncle Toko got killed. But when Rua died, I got another name and that's my name now. Iwi: his people. And they've forgotten all about my old name.

Miria: You know, when Rua came back to Maungapohatu after that

Building Rua's concrete tomb at his tangi. Heta Rua stands in the centre of the group of three men, looking towards the camera. *Whakatane Museum*

bloodshed, he started cleaning everywhere. Maai was named 'the very, very clean place', where the tapu had been lifted. He started again in the 1920s, with all his people. My mother was telling me, he went around *all* the places where the burnt coins were, the burnt offerings. One of the places was just below the old cemetery at Maungapohatu — there's some cabbage trees and some kopas over there. We all used to stay in the meeting-house at Maai, and some of those Levites would go round. We'll be staying there, waiting till they come back and everything is over. I remember that. Rua does most of it. I don't know what he does. Whether he stays and karakia at home, over at Hiruharama —. But they cleaned out all the places where the burnt coins were. He had to kai them. They couldn't just leave it like that, eh? All those kēhua places. He went all round, right as far as Waiotahe, I think. One of the worst ones was up at Te Kakari. Being old Maori homes, I suppose, in that clearing up the top there. If your shadow falls on it, you wouldn't last. As the sun strikes, if your shadow goes over it — then you won't last. Being cursed, I suppose. That's the only place left. You can feel it when you're there. He went round to all those places. He said, it's 'he kai, kai ngā tapu', eating the tapus. He had to eat the tapu, eh? And the places he didn't get to, you can feel it. But the places where he got to, they will be all right. He had to take all that mana Maori — Maori kēhua — away.

There was a man here, Ripia Tano; he is from Ngapuhi. He came to Rua to take away his kēhuas. He was staying at the pā at Maungapohatu.[41] And the old man said, 'No. I can't cure him. Those are to look after him.' Those things were placed on him from his ancestors, while he was staying away from them, at this pā. They were from his part of Ngapuhi. All Rua did was to warn the women not to give him cheek, because they used to pull funny faces at him. They made faces like his kaitiaki: the flounder. Pātiki. They'd pull their tongues, make a bit of a long lip, pull it forwards, teasing him. And they ended up like that! They stayed like that! Matatu was the worst one; her face was pulled right down on the side here. Deformed. He never cured that. He gave them a lesson. He knows quite well what's wrong with the women. And he won't take those Maori atuas away!

. . . I went back to Maungapohatu with my first husband, John. That was in 1940, the year I had my first child. We went back to my old people and we stayed there quite a while with them. We were cutting firewood and selling it. We would

Pit-sawing the timber for the school. Mangere Teka stands on top of the pit, called the waapu, the timber 'wharf'; the woman is probably Irene Paulger. *Whakatane Museum*

split the wood for the school, or for the old people. Get a cord. The hardest job was carting them down. Got to have a good horse and a sledge. We would get two pounds, or two pounds fifteen, for a cord. That was our living. It was a lot of work. And we used to work in the saw-pits. We had to stand on the bottom, too. Pit-sawing the timber for the school and the meeting-house with Mangere Teka. I was there when they renewed the meeting-house and when they brought Whatu back.[42]

I remember them coming. It was pretty late, dark, when they got in. Just about midnight. I heard them say, 'Who are you', and so on, calling them. One had to call, and the one that is carrying the body has to answer back. They have to bring them home, you see. They have to take them back to their resting place, to their own grounds. They brought Miki back from Te Whaiti at the same time. He had been buried there after that truck accident.[43] He was on his own there. And Whatu – Tane – was by himself, way up on top of the hill at Otane. Of course, I've seen them bring the bones back to their old homes, before. There were the ones that died in the Flu; they were just buried all along the road going up to Whakarae.

Iwi: I used to go with my father, Whitu – I always call him my father – picking up bones from different burial places. He was telling me people were just dying everywhere during that Flu.[44] That's why they had to bury them on the side of the road, just in fern. They were wrapped around with ferns. They reckon ferns keep the body intact.

Miria: Can't make any coffins. No time to make coffins.

Iwi: It all depended on my father. For that job. He brought Tane back. He brought his body strapped on his horse. If you are doing that kind of job you are not allowed to use your hands to pick your kai up. So I had to go wherever he goes and I had to feed him.

There was a pine tree that used to be next to my grandfather's house here – we chopped it down – and they brought all those bones from the time of the Flu, all wrapped up in white sheets, and they're hanging on this tree. Overnight. Before they were taken up to Matahi to the cemetery. Oh, myself, I *really* get scared! But Tane – and Te Akakura – they were taken back to Maungapohatu.

Miria: And Tane, well, he was still whole! Embalmed; he must have been well embalmed. They never opened the coffin when the body arrived from Gisborne; old Rua didn't like to open the coffin. They all knew it would be like that. And Whitu, making him sit up in front on the horse like that! Oh, crikey! Everybody getting scared! And then somebody has got to feed the ones that brought him. They don't want to touch the kai! Tangiwaka often used to feed them. Sometimes they

The hahunga for Whatu and Miki Te Wakaunua, July 1940. Whatu's coffin and Miki's bones (enclosed in a white bag) are displayed for mourning outside the meeting-house, Tane Nui a Rangi. The four flags are ceremonial marae flags and bear ancestral names, which indicate the lineage of the dead. *Meri Taka, Auckland*

open their mouths — and she takes the kai away! Whitu used his gloves and a fork: he was the one mostly handling the body. Mr Laughton was there that day, when they exhumed Tane at Otane, and he knew what he had to go through. He stayed with the tohungas; they had some preserved birds, hinu. No rīwai, no bread. They had to eat the whole thing up. When they are exhuming the bones, they have got to take all the fat, without anything else to eat. You *have* to eat it. They had it in that little wharepuni at Maungapohatu. Just the tohungas and Mr Laughton. With the big kai, after, they had it down at the marae. Out in the open. Lucky the days were fine! They had two long tables — those muslin cloths on the grass.

In those days — before — when they take the body back, there was always something to give away. There'd be real silk and that — material, mats — given away. Goes with the body. But not Tane's: just the body came back. Mau's mother, Kiha, she died in the Flu. They buried all her things with her, then. So when Mau took her bones back to Ruatoki, he found all kinds of scents and old perfumes inside the coffin. She had a lot of those. But now, just lately, they've started to keep the personal things away from the body.

Now I am with Mau, there's a lot of things that we do do. If it is a dead person, well, that family comes to Mau. Just to bring an offering. Bring it to the house, 'cos the window is still open. Just a matter of two dollars. That's for the spirit of the dead. To get through to where Rua is. The way will be cleared. Sometimes, when they give the koha to Mau, he'll hold onto their hand for a long time — he weeps, he weeps. Oh, there are times, too, when he's wild. Just like his father. With some sort of people, you've got to be wild. It might be a cure for you.

So, we look after the house — and I help Mau with his work. We have these sessions now and again. People come to us. Sometimes, I might meet somebody on their own. But I know myself. If it's all right for me to talk, it comes out. If it's not right — my lips — if I try and force it out, I can't do it. If they bring a koha, an offering, I say, 'Don't give it to me. I'm only a mouthpiece. Give it to him.' If it's someone really in trouble, well, if they want help, they will get help. They've got to give you an opening, though, a way for you to get in with them. To work together. We don't go over to them; we wait for them to come over. Otherwise they might just ignore us; don't want us. But a troubled person, or a sick person, if they give you an opening you can go in with them. I just talk. And just by talking you'll get to the right point. Sometimes, Mau sets them puzzles. That's what old Rua used to do. And *you* have to look around. They're riddles — you only come to understand them later. It all depends if you have got the faith. Sometimes, I don't think I can even help myself. But for others I can do it.

Those are the experiences that I have been through.

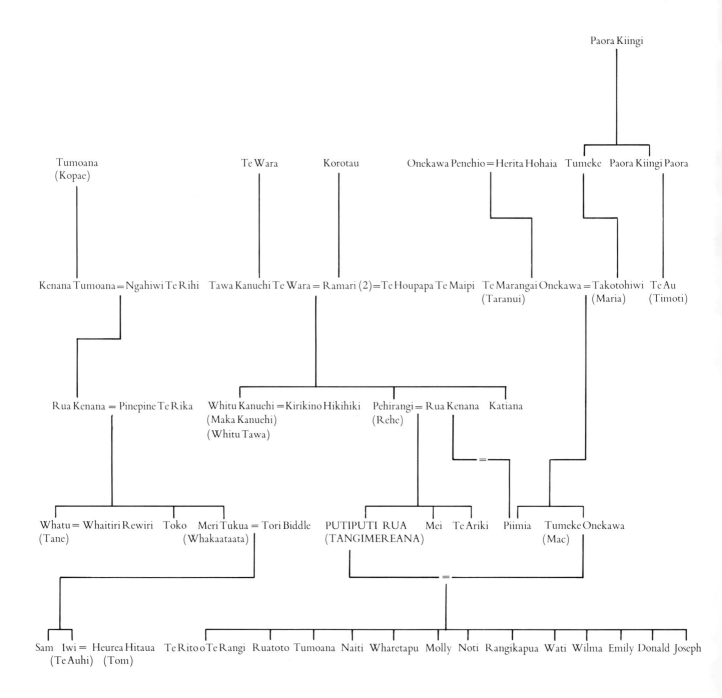

PUTIPUTI ONEKAWA

*P*utiputi Onekawa is the eldest child of Rua and his second wife, Pehirangi Kanuehi. She was born and grew up in Maungapohatu. She believes in her father as prophet and as Messiah. She is also a Presbyterian. Her husband, Tumeke — Mac — is one of Rua's strongest followers and has been since he was a young man, when Rua gave him back his health.

In her story, Puti recounts one of the seminal narratives about the transference of prophetic power from Te Kooti to her father. This is the tradition concerning Rua's journey to Gisborne in March 1906, when he entered the forbidden meeting-house, Rongopai (or Eriopeta). The mission was a task set by Te Kooti for his successor: to enter the house which had been built for him in 1887 for his return, but which the government's actions prevented him from ever seeing. Rongopai is one of the great sacred houses of the Ringatu. It was erected by Te Whanau a Kai hapū of the Te Aitanga a Mahaki tribe. Its interior bursts with colourful paintings of blossoms and vines, including the Tree of Life (described in the Book of Revelation), which bears on it twelve different fruits and twelve different leaves, all known for their healing properties. The brightly decorated house is truly the new garden of Eden. There are also many paintings of the people's ancestors. Hinehakirangi is here, wearing a European dress and carrying a red rose in her hand. On the rear wall stands a portrait of Wi Pere MHR. He is elegantly dressed in a dark suit and bears a detailed ancestral moko. Perched like a watching owl on his shoulder is his mother, Riria Te Mauaranui, from whom his mana flowed. Both had been taken prisoner by Te Kooti in November 1868, and although they escaped, they later gave covert support to him, for like many Rongowhakaata and Te Aitanga a Mahaki they were angered by the land confiscations being threatened by the government. It is said that the big Scotch thistle in flower at the back of the house (which was painted over in later years in an attempt to lift the tapu, but which is now restored) stands for Te Kooti himself. That prickly plant grows profusely around Rongopai. The house had remained tapu since its construction and none dared enter it on fear of death.

As Puti tells the story, Te Kooti himself rode ahead of Rua on this journey to Rongopai: it is 'the last story of Te Kooti'. The white horse Te Ia (the Crest of the Wave), which Rua rode, was Te Kooti's horse; it had been predicted that it would be ridden by his successor.[1] It was the white horse which unlocked the door for Rua into the tapu house, and allowed him to establish himself as the one predicted by Te Kooti who would complete his work. This task fulfilled, Rua travelled inland to Maungapohatu, where on the Twelfth of April, the Ringatu sacred day in the month, he announced his intention to return to Gisborne to meet the King. From Maungapohatu, Rua began a circuit of visits to the Tuhoe communities, including Wainui, the Church's marae built on Te Kooti's land, before he went on to Gisborne with all the chiefs of Tuhoe. Here, he revealed the meaning of his prophecy: he himself was the King who had united Tuhoe.

All these events occurred about three years before Puti was born. She was, initially, adopted by her oldest brother, Whatu, and his wife, Whaitiri, but shortly after Whaitiri died, Puti came back to live at Maungapohatu, where she was brought up by her parents. Her mother Pehirangi, of Te Hamua hapū from Ruatoki, was a favourite of Rua's, who stayed with him all her life. Puti talks about Rua's several wives and the ways in which they managed their households, particularly during the 1920s when they were all living at Maai, Rua's separate pā at Maungapohatu. Rua married twelve wives from Tuhoe, to reinforce the ties of all the hapū with him. Although all bore him children, not all the wives remained with him. The six who stayed, Pinepine, Pehirangi, Te Akakura, Te Aue, Mihiroa, and his last wife, Piimia, became close friends. Te Aue made all their clothes and they all worked together on their garden patches. But each wife maintained her separate

previous page Puti Onekawa on the road to Matahi, May 1984. Photograph by Gillian Chaplin.

kitchen for her whānau, and each dealt with the problems of rationing their basic food supplies, which Rua gave to them. Puti's story emphasizes the domestic aspects of an often harsh existence. She also talks about the importance, especially to the children, of the early Presbyterian missionaries at Maungapohatu, the Reverend John Laughton and his father, 'Daddy' Laughton. They worked there between 1918 and 1926, and both are still alive in the memories of the Maungapohatu people.

Puti went to school at both Maungapohatu and Matahi, where her parents also stayed, between 1921 and 1925. She was then sent away for a year to Turakina Maori Girls' College. She describes the pain of struggling with a language that was not her own and an utterly alien environment much more forcibly than the other women with whom we talked. Yet Puti is an outgoing person, with a capacity to share with others her own joyfulness and energy. The contrast between the woman and her memories of school becomes acute.

She was summoned home at the end of 1926. She was intended to be married to Piimia's younger brother Mac, who had been living with his sister in her household at Maai. Arranged marriages for women of rank, in order to reinforce specific family and kinship ties, were still a part of the Tuhoe world. Mac's descent is from the family of Paora Kiingi I of Te Waimana, whose powerful ōhāki, or dying speech, 'Kia tāwharautia a Mataatua' ('Let the people of Mataatua be sheltered'),[2] was interpreted as having being fulfilled by Rua in 1906. In taking all the chiefs of Tuhoe, that is the rangatira of the Mataatua canoe, on the journey to Gisborne, it was said that Rua had united Tuhoe under their shelter, their tāwharau.[3] But at first Puti would have nothing to do with her husband, even though he had been chosen for her by her father. She was not the only child of Rua's to struggle against his will in this respect. She ran away to the Presbyterian schoolteacher whom she knew from Maungapohatu, Ethel Roseveare. But, as she acknowledges, she was finally persuaded to marry Mac, and they have been together for fifty-seven years.

Puti and Mac had thirteen children. Their two eldest died as babies and the family seemed then to be threatened as a wharengaro. In her story, Puti tells how her father placed her under tapu restrictions during her third pregnancy. After her son Tumoana was born, on 24 January 1934, the tapu state was still preserved over both of them, but most completely over the boy, until he lifted it by his own actions. This divine protection, summoned by Rua, was considered to have been removed by the child when it was appropriate for him to enter fully the human world.

Puti and Mac brought up six of their own children. Two others died in childhood and three were brought up by different families. But they also brought up ten tamariki whāngai. The first was Zac, Hakaraia Wharepapa, whom Puti took in before she had borne any children of her own. Zac had been left at Maungapohatu by his father after his parents separated. Puti commented directly: 'Oh, a lot of kids — motherless, fatherless. Zac, he just wanders at the pā, at Maungapohatu. There's nobody to look after him. Every morning this boy used to come down to school with no clothes on, just an overcoat. I was staying at the mission. And I used to feel pity for him — I used to sneak a bit of bread from the mission and give it to him. It's just one day when he came back to school shivering, with no clothes on, and I ask Miss Roseveare. She said, "Oh yes". She sort out some of the clothings. And he stays with me all the time.' Her youngest whāngai, Moe, she took at birth to replace her own daughter Molly, who had died. Moe herself was the child of another of Puti's whāngai, Te Ao Hora. 'I delivered that one,' she said, referring to Moe, 'but the others they were just wandering kids from Maungapohatu.'

Puti evokes a world of hardship and poverty, which she has overcome by a vast vitality. Both she and her husband have worked hard all their lives. After they first left Maungapohatu, they went cutting fence-posts. Later, Mac was employed by the Opotiki and Waimana dairy factories; then he became a bus-driver for the Road Services and, finally, for the Education Department. They moved from one temporary home to another until they built their present house at Nukuhou, inland of Kutarere, on Mac's ancestral land.

Puti and her half-sister Te Akakura both reveal in their stories the serious conflicts of mana within the family which took place after Rua's death. These were associated with land and leadership. Akakura possessed the rank. Puti had the close bonds with their father. It was essentially the two sisters who decided to erect the family marae at Tuapo. Puti's mother Pehirangi had the papakainga legally defined in 1938.[4] Their meeting-house Te Ao Hou (The New World) was opened on 10 August 1941. However, it remains a matter of great sadness for Puti that they have not managed to establish a separate cemetery and, thus, their distinct ancestral identity within their tribal land.

The background to much of Puti's life is explained more fully in our study of Rua, Mihaia. We cannot recall how many times we've called at her home since we first met her in December 1977. On that occasion, we arrived out of the blue, with a bundle of old photographs of her father and the community at Maungapohatu, to ask if she could help us identify the people. We spent the day together looking at the faces and recalling them out of the dead past into living memory. It was the beginning of a friendship which has continued to grow. Puti's home for us is a place of warmth and welcome to which we always return. In Auckland we also came to know Akakura and, in January 1978, we brought her to visit Puti for the first time in many years. Together we went inland to Maungapohatu.

On the journey, we stopped early in the morning at Eripitana, the sacred house built by Tuhoe for Te Kooti in 1884 and whose name, uttered in glossolalia, stands for God's promise to him that he would save the 'remnant of mankind'.[5] At the rear of the meeting-house there had once also been a small building, considered to be extremely tapu, which Rua used as a 'House of God'. Inside its enclosure people left coins as an offering. As Akakura said then, 'Everywhere Te Kooti was, our father was.' We went on to Maungapohatu, where Puti and Akakura climbed the path together to the top pā and stood looking across the broad valley, to where the Ruatahuna track comes winding down the hillsides. Puti commented that you could see people on the path at certain points, and you would watch them in order to know how many there would be to feed — while the people coming into the valley in turn would fire their shots, or blasts of dynamite, to warn their hosts of their imminent arrival. We went down the steep road past the now derelict schoolhouse, dwarfed by the huge leaning macrocarpas, which were planted by the missionaries many years ago. The building still had inside it the twin desks, in four different sizes, carefully assembled by John Laughton. We scrambled across the Waiawa stream to Hiruharama Hou, Rua's old home where Puti and her mother used to live. For Puti, it was the first time she had returned since she and Mac had left in the early 1930s, and she found it a disturbing, ambivalent experience. But it contained particular happy memories: the community's string band, with its mandolin, violin and banjo, which played for the open-air Saturday night dances; the big black plums and cherries which used to grow on the hill slopes; the stick games the children played; and the little shop that she herself had run at Maai. Finally we left. On our journey back, we called in to visit Hikawera Te Kurapa, a Ringatu tohunga who lived near Ruatahuna and who had known Rua. He was a faith-healer and many people were waiting to see him. He said that he was different from the strict tohunga, the kaupapa of the registered Ringatu Church at Wainui. From Ruatahuna, we travelled the long route through Galatea, founded near the headquarters of the Urewera expeditions against Te Kooti, to the eastern Bay of Plenty, Te Kooti's last sanctuary and the centre of the Ringatu faith today. We had been on a journey which *brought the past into the present and which allowed us, the outsiders, to share in its significance.*

We talked with Puti about her father many times between 1977 and 1979. The conversations which we had about her own life took place on four separate days. We always visited her at her house, where like Pinepine, Rua's first wife, she has planted welcoming beds of bright flowers along the pathway to the door. She once said to us, 'That's how you always know it's a Maori home.' The first occasion which we recorded was on 30 January 1983; the second was on 8 May 1984; the third on 4 December of the same year and the last on 24 March 1985. We have also drawn on a recorded dialogue with both herself and Iwi Hitaua from 9 May 1984. As well, we have a recording of 28 December 1977, the notes made during our visit to Maungapohatu between 19 and 23 January 1978 and notes from various other visits to her home in 1978 and 1979.

My mother was Rua's second wife. Nobody knows how my mother, Pehirangi, came to him. It was just that feeling in his wives; they wanted to come and marry him. Sort of vision. She wasn't brought to marry him. No. She just came up from Ruatoki to Maungapohatu. All of them were like that, except Pinepine and Te Akakura. Pinepine was the first wife, and Te Akakura was the legal married wife, because of the fightings over her! *Her* tribe didn't want *her* to marry *my* father! Because he's got nothing! But my mother came to him. My mother, Te Akakura, and Te Aue were the three from the beginning, after Pinepine. Te Akakura used to go away back to Ruatoki — but the other three were always with him.[6]

I was born at Maungapohatu — in the tent! No hospital, no nothing! Just ordinary. It was a tent to sleep in. When my mother was in labour she went in there.[7] It's a tent to cover her, that's all. My grandmother, Ramari, was with her. They found my birth date when I was at Turakina school: 28 July 1908.[8] My own name is quite a long name, which I didn't know until I was a grown woman — Tangimeriana. That's Te Kooti's wife — I'm her namesake. I don't know anything about her.[9] My father chose that name for me. But my adopted mother, Whaitiri, that's Whatu, my brother's first wife, got this name for me, Putiputi. When I understand that Tangimeriana was my first name, I hate it. I cried. 'Don't call me that name. I don't want that name!' When Whaitiri was a dying woman — and I was a big, fat, fat bubba, my father said to her, 'Oh, Whaitiri, if you go, you're going to leave your baby behind. Who is going to look after it? If you go, you'd better take her with you! We can't look after your girl!' And she just managed to open her lips: 'I call her Putiputi. I'm not taking her. She can stay behind. All her life she'll be Putiputi.'[10] And when they told me about it, I thought to myself, no wonder I hate Tangimeriana. And though my name was changed when my father died,[11] I am still Putiputi.

When Whaitiri died they brought me from Waioeka to Matahi, for a few months, and then my mother and father came down from Maungapohatu and picked me up again. So my mother brought me up. I lived with her, at Maai, the pā down the bottom there. I was brought up by the old people, too — Ramari and Houpapa, that's her second husband. My grandfather, old Kanuehi, he stayed with us — with my mother, his daughter, all the time. He was very important to me. All he thinks of is my father — like as if he's his own son. Every money he earns he always brings it back to my father. Never say anything of any kind. Very quiet.

Whaitiri Rewiri with her husband, Whatu, on their wedding-day. Whatu wears his hair long, in the manner of the Iharaira. *Tane Nui a Rangi, Maungapohatu.* Photographed, by permission of the Tuhoe of Maungapohatu, by Gillian Chaplin, 1978.

Some of the women of Maungapohatu, about 1911. On the right is Pehirangi, Puti's mother. The others are (from the left): –; –; Whaitiri; Tangiwaka Anania; Meri Tukua.
Judith Ellmer collection, Whakatane Museum

And my mother is very shy. She never mixes up. She's shy and moody. She never gets around. She stays by herself and works outside, not inside. Ploughing, and doing all the men's stuff. Ride horses. All sorts! Yes, I did too. I love it! Because of the horses. She is really hopeless as a cook! There were seven kitchens where our home, Hiruharama, is. Each wife has her own kitchen. Each wife got their own family and they all come and stay. There were only three of us to our mother — me, Mei, and Te Ariki — but with the different nephews and nieces and whāngai to stay, there'd be ten children even without us, her ones! Te Aue had her kitchen; Mihiroa had hers; Te Akakura hers; and Piimia, the last wife, hers. And Kirikino, my uncle's wife. My father rationed the food. You know those biscuit tins, the little ones, those square tins? For round-wines? They put some sugar in there to feed you for a month. For the kitchen. You won't get any more till a month is up. Every kitchen has the same amount no matter how big the family. A sugar in there, and your bag of flour. A fifty of flour. And the half-pound of tea, to last you a month. With the fifty of flour you can bake any bread you want. But look after your sugar! That's why we loved Daddy Laughton, giving us jam and scones! We don't know about jam! Just scone, no butter — you open up the scone and put jam on it. Oh, it's lovely!

From 1919 we started rationing. When we came out here and sugar started rationing [in the Second World War], we knew what to do. Us, from Maungapohatu! My father prophesies everything — coming. Nobody believe it, till this rationing and we were told the famine is coming. We knew how to keep kai, then. It's no trouble with us, because we learnt the hard way. He set the rations. No matter how big the family, how little the family: the same. We were well taught.

You know Henare — Akakura's brother — and I: we're just like two sisters! Brought up in the same place. And we're really thieves! Our father has good water-melons — few patches of great, big water-melons — and nobody goes there. Nobody! Just one day we went up with Henare's pea rifle. You know what we did? We made stilts, to get over to the water-melons! We picked the water-melons! And early in the morning, the next day, our mother says to go over there, to look, because they cover those big water-melons. Whole lot is gone! Come to the next one: gone! And they tried to look for the footsteps — no, nothing! Our father knew straight away it was us. He says to Akakura, kuia Aka, 'Oh, I know who did that! E Puti and Henare! Those are the only cunning ones that goes over there. They had a poutoti.' We call those stilts, poutoti. 'They got their poutotis! Oh yes.' They went up again and they had a *good* look. There was these little holes![12]

We were always together, Henare and I. Everywhere our father goes, we go. Both of us. Until he got shot. That's where we're parted. I was with Henare then. He was cleaning out that pea rifle and it went off. He was shot from here — through the top of his leg. Oh, I ran back home to bring the word down that he's shot. They brought him in to the hospital, but when they tried to operate on it they couldn't find the bullet. That's why he died. Broke my father's heart though.[13]

My father was — he had this prophet gift from Te Kooti. This is the last story of Te Kooti — that I knew. My father went through to Te Rongopai, with that horse opening the door of Rongopai meeting-house. It's his horse, Te Ia. That's when my father was given — nominated as a prophet — by Te Kooti. It was given to him by Te Kooti. It was like this. He said it. Te Kooti was in front, telling everybody on his way up to Rongopai — every stop he made — he was telling all those people where he stayed, 'My word has it (this is in the Bible really) my son is coming. He is going to finish all — whatever has to be done. My son — not me.' He was in front, ahead of my father, and he was coming behind, just as a cheeky boy! That's when Te Kooti went through to Rongopai and back to Maungapohatu, and my father was right behind him. It's in 1906. I wasn't born then. But my brother Toko, he had a wife then, Taupaki, and they didn't go because they'd just had their baby. In 1906.

Te Kooti, he was just a plain man. Not like what they used to tell. He's just a plain man, just like any other man. But you wouldn't catch him; he's too smart! On that white horse. Te Ia. That's Te Kooti's horse, but my father got it. My father had two horses, a bay one and a white one. I don't know the name of the bay one.

Maai, about 1920. In the centre is Hiruharama Hou, Rua's new veranda-ed house. The meeting-house Te Kawa a Maui, which was opened in February 1919, is the lower of the two wharepuni seen on the left. The separate kitchens for Rua's wives are scattered in the foreground. *Grace Johnston collection, Judith Binney*

Rua going to Gisborne to meet the King, June 1906. This photograph was taken in Opotiki; Rua is walking, a dog at his heels, towards a policeman. Photograph by F. Braae. *Auckland Weekly News, 5 July 1906*

Portrait of Rua, about 1909.
Anthropology Department, University of Auckland

I didn't see him. The white one was the one that opened the house at Rongopai. Because the other people were against my father, and didn't give him the key. 'He's not a King!' They wouldn't give him the key: 'He's not *our* King.' He's got a cheek to ask for *their* key to Rongopai, that's a whare tapu! It was easy! Because my father, he was riding on Te Ia and the horse went in and opened the door for him — to go in. The people were watching: 'Who's going to open the door?' They were wondering, 'Who had the key?' They were laughing there: 'They can't open that door! I've got the key!' And when they got there, the horse came out; he got the door open. And Rua came after to talk to them, after the horse opened the door. The horse came out first and he came out after! They were all astonished. For the horse opening that house. How did *he* get in? As a horse! That was when my father went through to Maungapohatu; that's when he got tapu.[14]

My father was a prophet. He had these disciples, the Riwaiti. I can remember them still when they had their long hair. My father — and Ngakohu and Wharepapa, they were his two assistants that stay with him all the time.[15] My father, he never used to leave his hair like that, hanging down — always in plaits. Plaited, and then put a bun, over here, on both sides. And the other two plaits just tied around, tied in front [looped over the ears] and put a comb, over there. You know those ladies' combs with the sparkles in? They all had long hair, the whole lot of them. Lovely hair, well groomed. Always with a comb; each one with a comb. We used to give cheek to them! They're all going down to the creek, with a little wee mirror, and washing. We don't have bathrooms or basins. Just the creek — and the cold water. This Wharepapa was the worst, with really long hair, long, long, straight hair below his knees and he'd just leave it hanging down. Oh, it's beautiful — black, shiny hair. He's the worst ever with that mirror! When he combs his hair, he used to comb it the furthest he can, and pull it up, and finish it off, just to show you how long it is!

When they have a church on the Saturdays, sometimes my father would start it off, and then he'd pass the speech to the second minister, that's Ngakohu, from Waioeka. That's his first assistant, next to him. Ngakohu does all the talking about the Bible and all the churches. What's to come and what's to do. After him, Wharepapa takes over and finishes it off; he finishes all the karakias. The other Levites, they're asked to do something else, like healing sickness. They go out, all over the place. They scattered, like those disciples of Jesus, when he was risen from that tomb, they used to go out in twos and preach. That's what the rest used to do. But he's not a dead one, that's risen from the dead. They go out — in twos — and preach for him; to give out his words.[16] But Ngakohu and Wharepapa stay with him all the time. Anything he wants to talk over, they talk it out. He doesn't talk out himself: he passes it to that other one, Ngakohu. If he had enough talking, he passes it over to Wharepapa. That one could finish everything! But when Whaitiri died, all the Waioeka and Opotiki people came out. Those were the ones that left Maungapohatu. That's when Ngakohu left. Because my father didn't heal her.

Later, they all had their hairs cut, the whole lot of them, and then, after that, the tapu was lifted. Before that, they were full Ringatu and they all kept the tapu. There was a tin outside the gate to wash your hands before you came into the wāhi tapu. And your kitchen clothes would stay in the kitchen; your sleeping clothes would stay in the bedroom. Your good clothes you left inside the pā — there was a house to leave the clothes there, the good clothes, and you'd grab your old ones to go out. Only the little ones, under twelve years, they didn't observe the tapu — over twelve you did. That was the tapu that was lifted and the only one we kept was the Saturday church. On Friday, no kai after six o'clock. No, we had no Twelfths. The Iharaira don't have the Twelfths. That was the old Ringatu, the first Ringatu, Herora.[17] But on Saturdays those ones from the top pā comes down to our place and we sit under the fruit trees — there was an old apple tree and there was a grape-vine there, growing over the well — and my father and the Levites are on the veranda of his house, Hiruharama. One of the tohungas, the Levites, would take the karakia. And after that you would go back to your kitchen for your kai.

When there's visitors — we had no dining-hall, we never had tables: always laid out on the ground. We just put the cloth on the ground. There's one man that's always around on the marae telling you what to bring for each meal. Each kitchen brings out so many. Cups, teapots, how many teapots you're going to bring out. No trouble at all! You might have two butter saucers. Put it on the table. And, say, eggs, potatoes, meat, or anything. All depends how many people are on the marae. Maybe ten, twelve dishes of potatoes, or meat, each kitchen brings out so many. You put it on this table on the ground. Instead of having it all in the one hall. Each one has their own fire. We call it the pūtīa. That's the open fire, the cooking fire. And each one have their own hāngi. You hāngi meat. You cut it when you get all

Ngakohu Pera, one of the early Levites and chief of Whakatohea. Although he left Rua, he remained a strong Ringatu and died, at the age of ninety-three, on 10 January 1970. The young woman with him is Teratahi Matiu. *Whakatane Museum*

those kais out: how many lumps of meat you're going bring out. So and so – four. Whatever you got – chicken, pigeons, parrots – we call them kākā. Oh, pigeon's better.

I tell you the truth, my mother and my grandmother don't eat pigeon. Any birds. It's their own way. They've been taught not to eat – let the birds for the visitors. All they eat is the left-overs, like the legs. Anything that's left over on the bone. They will eat those. Not the whole pigeon. Leave it for the visitors. Only the first shoot of pigeons. The *women* eat those. And when it's time to close, the last shooting, then the men will have the pigeons. May, June, is when we get the pigeons. They catch them with the waka, the little canoe, with fresh water in it. Or by a freshwater pool, where the pigeons go to. You set the trap by their place. The waka kererū, with six or eight loops on the side of the waka. You trap them. The pigeon doesn't flutter. That's the only bird that doesn't. But the kākā we catch with a pet parrot. He calls the others down to rescue him – he's noosed by the canoe – and when they come down – pull the nooses and catch them![18] On the first shooting, the *men* eat the tūīs and the parrots. Not the women: they have the last shooting of the tūīs and the kākās. The men, they eat them better than the girls; clean it up. But the girls – some don't like the fat. Just break it off and leave it there! But, oh, it's nice.

One thing we eat is that fern root. Not any fern. There's a special [bracken] fern in the bush. Where's there's been no fire, where it's never been burnt.[19] It grows in the pumice. We are like pigs, digging away at this pumice! You can dig away and get long, long roots before it breaks. It's quite fat – about two inches thick, some may be bigger. If you strike a pumice, you're the lucky person! You can dig and dig and dig and get a lot. This fern root, it's all pure white in the middle. Not the black, hard thing in the middle – you've got nothing to eat there! I'm not a pig to eat those ones! The other one we eat, it's pure white and it's sweet, quite sweet. You can fry them. Or the best – put them in the ashes. Take it out and crush it down a bit and take pork fat with it.

There's this kuia – we used to pinch this kuia's fern root! She's tight as tight! Mean! Won't give any to anybody, only *her* mokopunas! So we used to pinch it. She used to have it hanging beside the chimney – oh, not where the smoke is. Just to dry. We sneak in, grab a bunch, away we go! She knows that some fern root is missing! I'm always in there! And the other thing is those dried pipis! We just dry them in the sun. And they're hanging on the string there, and we used to just pull the string, put it in our pocket, and take off! That's our PKs! They're really hard! But nice, very nice. We put it in our pocket and pull them off, one by one.

I had a little shop at Maai. I was still going to school and I used to keep this shop for my father. Everytime they come out here, they bring back all stuffs – smokes, and tobacco, and lollies. I never used to smoke, but everyone is coming down and buying smokes and I thought to myself, now is the chance! It must be nice. So what I used to do, I used to put it in my pocket and take it up to school. If we go back to Maungapohatu, I'll show you this hīnau tree. It's our smoking place! By the creek on the Pouwhenua side. I used to take this packet – it's a Capstan, those tailor-mades – put it in my pocket and when we have our lunch-break, we all dash over there. I don't know who told Mr Laughton about us! We hopped on this tree and he come trotting down, underneath the tree! And he saw me sitting up there with my smoke and he called out, 'Hei aha tāu e Puti?' In Maori. 'Heke, heke. Get down!' And we all got down. There was four of us with a tailor-made each! 'Now, don't you ever go there. Don't you bring those smokes!

I'll tell on you, ana, to the old man!' All right! Every now and then if we head that way, 'Hoki mai e Puti! Come back, come back here!'

You bought everything from that shop except tea, flour, and sugar. My father bought those — and we keep that ration. Everything else you bought from the shop. Biscuits, corned beef, tinned stuff, lollies. It was very cheap then, eh? When we stayed there by ourselves, when I was at school and I still had that shop, I stayed with my uncle Whitu, my mother's brother, and his wife, Kirikino. And we used to go and pinch. Starving. Once, three of us, all girls, we were going to get some cherries — way, way up in those hills, way beyond Maungapohatu — Orangi. At the bottom of that hill, there's a swimming pool. Before we got down to that pool, we saw some pigs, with their piglings. Just a weaner. You know what we did? We jam all the pigs, force them into that swimming pool! And we dive in! Trying to catch those little pigs. Round and round and round — to drown them. Ah, we caught one: kill it. Light the fire and singe it. But when we turn around to gutting it — we don't know how! But we hung this pig up — poor little thing. And we started it from the back — instead of the front! We open it at the back and we pulled the guts out from the back. And then open the front. Open straight up. When we got home, put our pig in the cupboard, and hid it there. Go to school. Auē! The next weekend, my brother, Whatu, went round to gather up all his pigs — that's his pig! And he found out there was some missing of the little piglets. And we went to church this Saturday and this news was going round, 'Anybody seen those little pigs?' We won't own up, no, no! Till one night, Kirikino went up to search our kitchen, looking round for any kai we've got. She found our meat! And took the whole lot! When we came back after school — no kai! You'd think she'd give us some! No way! So we live on apples. I said to Ripeka,[20] 'The only thing for us, I lock up the shop, and we go and stay with Mr Laughton. With the old koroua, eh?' Oh yes. He took us, and we stayed there with him. We got really fat, staying there with good kai. With Daddy Laughton. He was a real mother to us. Good kai, clean, and everything.

He gave us a rub down every night with olive oil. If we had a wash, he'd rub us all over with olive oil. And I stayed with him — because of the scones! When we go home, we used to tell our father, 'Oh, Daddy Laughton gave us a scone.' 'What's a scone?' 'Those little breads. Round ones. You put the jam in the middle.

Puti Onekawa at Maungapohatu school, 1920. Puti is second from the left of the girls standing. She wears a spotted pinafore. The teachers are John Currie and, in the centre, John Laughton. The schoolhouse is the original, circular whare kanikani, dance-hall, of the community.
Laughton Album, National Museum

And he gave it to us.' He was a good old fellow. But Horiana! My own colour! She didn't want us to call her Horiana. No. *Mrs Laughton*. And *Miss Rua*, always. Very strict! Very hard! You make a mistake: punish you, put you to bed, no kai! I used to try and run away from her! But we couldn't, because of him. He's so kind to us. And Mr Laughton.

One thing we used to do is go to this old koroua, Te Awahou. He had the moko, just over his face. We beg him to make us a marble. You know the stone? It's a special stone. He just goes down the river bed and finds this special stone. We call it he karā. It's a dark stone, and it's a very strong stone. You never crack it when you hit it. You just tap it round. He used to hit it, with a file or something like that – trim it – and put the colouring on. His won't break. It's a real strong marble. And you can start a fire with it, too. That's the flint. You use that stuff that's been all dried up, like a rubber, from the bush. Anūhē: that's that thing when it's all dried.[21] Course they've got no matches in those days. As soon as you get the spark, you just flip it on a woolly thing – make it fluffier – and up it comes, lit. As soon as you get fire, you just flick that on, and it gives you fire to burn. That's what my father uses when he was in jail. The guards won't give them any matches. My father used to tear their sheets; tear them up and make them fluffy. Because he had that thing. 'Where did you get your matches?' My father used to strike that – and they had their smoke!

I started school quite old. And I can't talk English. All we got to do is cry, because 'Don't talk Maori at school!' We can't talk English – so all we got to do is cry. Yes, for a long while. I can't talk English, no matter what. I try. But the only thing I know is 'stomach'! Yes, I know *that*! Oh yes, Sister Annie, Sister Dorothy, Sister Jessie; and Mr Laughton, and Mr Currie.[22] He's hard, very hard. No bloody humbug! A cousin of mine – we were all sitting on the floor, singing, and she was naughty. She did it on the floor. Because we don't know how to ask to go outside. All we do is go like that [putting your hand up] and point outside! And this girl, she didn't like to say anything. She was sitting on her slate. She had put her slate over it. We were just going to sing and I was going like that – pointing to her. Mr Currie gave me a good hiding, supplejack, eh, across my back. He was a murdering thing! And Mr Laughton didn't like it. He knew, because I don't know how to say 'outside'. It was awful. That was the first thing I had, that stick. Oh well, Mr Currie, he was quite a good man.

When I first went to Turakina I used to cry every day. Everything I did seemed to be wrong. I can't cook at home, because my place is outside with the boys. Couldn't wash my clothes; couldn't make my bed. Everywhere I go I always drop something for not knowing what those things are for. So I drop them. And I cry. They understand, though. But they are very strict. I can't do my spelling. You use slates, eh? I know how to pronounce the words, but putting them down to make a sentence out of it, no way! You know how long a chalk is? The teacher just grab the chalk and drew a line through it. Smudge it right down. Nothing to be ticked. No ticking there! Everyday.

But Nurse Doull told them,[23] she told Miss Kinross what I'm like. I'm a grown-up girl that doesn't know anything about English or anything like that. They excuse me for that. About five months I think, I was beginning to pick up a little bit. But whatever I seem to like to do is always wrong. I don't like beetroot because it's raw, and red, and bitter. Salad I won't eat because it's not cooked. Eating turnips – I don't see turnips at home. See, I never saw all those things. I just put my head down and cried. For giving me those raw stuffs. But after the five months

Turakina Maori Girls' College, 1919.
Denton collection, Alexander Turnbull Library

I begin to pick up. One of the teachers used to take me in her room and sleep with her — they all got jealous, all my mates! She used to try and teach me how to play the organ for Sunday schools. I picked up and I didn't want to come home. I was there one year. Just one year. Then I took off! Because I didn't want to come home and get married!

Because, when I was still there, Mac's grandfather, Temata Kiripa,[24] used to write to me a lot and tell me everything that's going on at home. Temata was living at the pā. This time he said, 'Oh well, when you come back — in Maori — we got a house ready for you and Mac.' I thought to myself, 'No way! I'm going to take off!' It was just near the school holidays and I wrote back to Maungapohatu to Miss Roseveare,[25] 'I'm not coming home. I'll meet you at Frankton, on the train. I'm coming back on the 18th! I'll be there at Frankton waiting for you!' She didn't know what I wanted to come with her for till we got to Papatoetoe and I told her, 'I don't want to get married. I want to go back to school.' So she gave me a good karakia, and we went down south, to her family in Dunedin.

I was away for a whole year in Dunedin. When Miss Roseveare came back to teach at Maungapohatu I stayed down, with her mother. I wouldn't come back![26] Then Akakura got her accident at Te Whaiti, that great big accident,[27] and my father told Miss Roseveare to send a cable down to tell me to come back to look after him. But he wasn't in the accident; it was Akakura that was! But my father said, 'She won't deny that. She'll come back.' So I came back. But I took off again! To Te Kaha. To the mission house there. I was running away and staying with the Presbyterians! I stayed with Tom Roseveare at Te Kaha. And I stayed at the mission at Matahi, with Timutimu Tioke as a minister. He got so very cheeky he wanted me for his wife! This is my own uncle! So I had to go back home. Mac's still there! I couldn't get any further from him then!

Temata Kiripa and his wife Kahu Te Awahou at Maungapohatu.
Whakatane Museum

But I stayed with my mother. He was with his sister, Piimia. One night my father came down — Mac was coming out here, back to his father. And my father said, 'Oh, Mac's going back tomorrow.' I said, 'So. What can I do?' He said, 'You tell him to stay.' 'NO!' I just went like that to my father. For the first time ever, I answered him back. He said to me, 'Why?' 'I don't know. I don't want to get married. Please, if you could send me back to school again for another year. Then I'll be happy. One year's not enough. Make me go back to school. I like it.' Oh no! So. I never said any more to him. But just for that I wouldn't have Mac. 'Cos I don't want him. Till my brother Whatu got really wild and came down to my place at

Irene Paulger and Ethel Roseveare.
Whakatane Museum

Maungapohatu, 1928. This photograph of the two main streets of the upper pā is a frame enlargement from Edwin Coubray's film, *Journey into Rua's Stronghold*, which has recently been rediscovered. *The New Zealand Film Archive, Wellington*

Maai. For two years Mac [had] never talked to me. Never say anything; we never slept together. All that two years. But I'm his wife, he reckoned, but he wouldn't come near. When Whatu knew, he came down one night and he said to me, 'You get your things ready. We're going over to Gisborne, shearing.' Oh yes, I'm ready. I had all my things ready.

But Mac's uncle, that's Timoti, Paora Kiingi's son,[28] was waiting on the road there, below the meeting-house. He asked me to come in to his place. Mac's there, waiting for me. I didn't want to go in. And I saw my brother coming down, with a stockwhip – as usual. He didn't want me to get married to Mac. He wanted to take me away altogether. It is wrong that, just pretending to be my husband and leaving me staying there by myself! Oh my good gracious! Before he got into the house, I hopped in where Mac was sitting, crying, and I hopped behind him. And he came in. He was just going to lift his stockwhip – for me, not for him, for calling in there! Tane – Whatu – he brought me up really. He was going to whip me. Timoti came over and tried to cool him off. And he said, 'Well, now it's broad daylight, if you are going to want her for your wife, I want you to go back home, to your home, as a man and wife. I want you to go down there, in this broad daylight, hand in hand. If you won't, you're not having my sister for your wife. I'm going to take her.'[29] So we came down to our place – to Maai. And that very night Piimia arrived from Matahi. See, my father knew there was trouble and she came up. And I cried. Still didn't want to. He knew all the time. That's why we got married. May 1928. We've been together for fifty-five years.[30]

We got *married* only when we had our daughter, Noti. We had this wedding at Te Huinga o Te Kura.[31] Mr Laughton and all my Pakehas were there, that loves me when I was running away! Every one of them. Uncle Tom, Miss Roseveare's brother, he came all the way down from Papatoetoe. It took Mac a while to get married! He wouldn't have it! He didn't like a wedding. Just to get together; just a Maori wedding. Miss Roseveare wanted us to have a real wedding. She had everything ready from Dunedin, which I didn't know anything about. But Mac wouldn't have it. Our veil was cut in half; I never used the veil! Half was for Aka, for her wedding, when the two girls, Aka and Okeroa, had a tapu wedding at Maungapohatu.[32]

Mac and I, we've been together all these years. But in a shack all our lives. Almost. When we first got married, we stayed at Maai. We had sheep. We had that farm for, say, about two years. We still had the farm when Te Rito was born. And when I had Ruatoto we came out. That's *when* we came out — left Maungapohatu.[33] Oh, it was really hard. They both died — at eighteen months. It seemed to be a wharengaro.[34] After those two died, my father reckoned it was because no boys had lived on Paora Kiingi's side. That's Mac's koroua: Paora Te Runga really.[35] Everything went wrong from the start from the old fellow, and to their descendants. Everything went wrong. Very active, nice old koroua; he's a kind old fellow, really. A great old warrior with Te Kooti; he got the sword of Te Kooti. It's a gorgeous sword. But because of that koroua, when I was carrying Tumoana I was kept away, tapu, for nine months. Only Mac goes in the kitchen. I was kept right away. One tohunga, our eldest, Tatu, was trying to keep that baby. After he was born I was supposed to stay in the tent for two years with Tu and Mac. One day, we came round the back of Nukuhou and Tu crawled into the kitchen, right into the oven, and he had taken the lid off the pot and he was in it! My father heard this cry. 'Hey, Putiputi, where's your baby?' 'Oh, in the tent.' I was free to go in the kitchen, but not the baby. But my father had laid on this little bed in the kitchen and he heard the cry three times. I looked. No baby in the tent! When I got near to this oven I heard it again and I looked down and listened carefully. I heard this crying inside, with the lid on top. I lift the lid — and he was trying to scramble out! I lift him and I took him over to my father. He was mumbling to that baby! Tatu arrived that very day; all Ruatahuna knew about him! No tapu anymore! He put himself in the kitchen and the tapu was off him. He was now free to go in to the kitchen, do what he like. Rua said to Tatu, 'Don't do any more to him.'[36] We had a hākari to finish it off. He was my first son to live.

When Ruatoto died, I got this baby from Te Whaiti. Poor little chap! His father's a full Maori from Rotorua; he went over to the war and he met up with a war-bride over there. They had six kids and she just took off and left him with all the kids. He came over to Te Whaiti and he give anybody — whoever wants one — a baby. 'If you want one you can have it!' Just like little pigs! We are having to go in to Te Whaiti to get some timbers. There was this baby boy. E ka! And my father said to me, 'Oh, we take that little baby for you!' I said, 'Na ia!* No. I'm still thinking about my dead one.' He said, 'Oh well, that's to take his place.' I thought it was a baby. So we got this little thing, put him on the cart, and we brought it home. We took it up to Tawhana. He got hungry and he was crying, and he said, 'Mum, mum, meikai!' I had a look at this little wee thing lying in his bed, calling out for meikai. You know what a meikai is? Maize. And we saw it. He's a grown-up baby. And yet he looks like a new-born! The way he was treated! At the time he was seven years old. And we all looked at him. He can talk, but not Maori. I brought Milton up since. He was twenty-eight years old when he left me, my whāngai.

We lived at Otane, the whole lot of us, the whole family, when we first came out. Then they push us away, somewhere else. The family come in and push us out.

Putiputi Onekawa. This portrait was brought home on her death in January 1987. Photographed by permission of her daughters by Gillian Chaplin.

*Him!

Everytime we have a hut of our own, there's always an argument – oh, I take off! I hate arguing. I always take off, anywhere – till I get shelter. But without my flowers – oh, no. Even in the bush I'll have a flower garden, all around, down my steps. Never lose my flowers. We had a tent at Omuriwaka there – from the road there's a climb up where we had just a stump of a dead tree. We hollowed it, and lined it, and live in it. With my five kids. That's Tu and my four adopted ones then, my whāngai. I built a step right up to this rimu log and planted flowers all the way up from the road. We lined the log with the tent inside. And you can always tell that's the camp up there – follow the flowers and the steps! Sister Miller wouldn't get over it![37] We were cutting timber for sale – in cords – and she used to come up there and stay all day!

Well, we worked our way down the valley till we came to the back of Nukuhou. I stayed there, and I had my first girl there. Molly. And I lost that one – at the age of eighteen months again. She drowned there.[38] It's just a little creek; just playing next to it. But it was a great whirlwind at the moment. We just got out of the bush; we've been cutting scrubs, cutting all the bush at the back, splitting posts and that. It was a fine day and I had a piano-case, box, and I had just cut the top off and put some wheels on it, like a cart, so I pull it around behind the house. And then this whirlwind just stayed there. So I ran out to pick that girl up – she might be covered with dust or whatever – and she wasn't there! I looked everywhere. And I saw her lying flat on – with all her clothes. It was quite cold that day, but it's fine, and that whirlwind came over. The little creek – not far from our kitchen. We were just eighteen months at Nukuhou when the baby drowned, and then we shift back to Matahi.

I had thirteen children: nine boys and four girls. We lost five. The first one is hard, because you don't know your pains. I didn't know anything about babies then. I didn't know anything about it, that one. I was unconscious. But my mother was there; my mother looked after me while the first two were being born. All the rest it's only Mac. Only the last two, Donald and Joseph, they were born in the Annexe.[39] The others were all born at home. We don't lie flat on the bed, like that. We just sit up, like this. And you hold onto a box, or a seat. Just lie on it. You lean on the floor and push it up, under you, put it up here [under the breast]. Just to keep it down [to press down]. And that's all.[40] The only time I want Mac is when the baby is born. I pick him up, and cut the cord, and everything. And wrap the baby in a towel and give it to Mac. I wrap it, instead of him handling the baby with nothing on, I wrap it in a towel. And tell him to put it upside down – for that nose. Oh, he knows. While I attend to myself for the afterbirth. Then, when that's done, that's finished, I bathe the baby after. Mac takes the afterbirth; wrap it up, take it away and bury it. Just him.

It was only Donald I had lying down, on my back. And that felt very funny. I don't know whether I'm going to get it or not! I had him as a breech baby; that's why I couldn't get it. That's why that one's called Donald, after my doctor. That's my first doctor, Dr Donald Meredith. He named that boy himself.

When he went away, I got this other doctor, Dr Simcock. I've been very, very shy and frightened to talk with my doctors. I got a haemorrhage with my last baby. And I wouldn't eat. I just couldn't eat. I live on lime juice; nothing else. Dr Simcock used to bring me soup and everything. Boil me fish-heads, anything at all. And I never eat it. For three weeks in the Annexe, no kai. Just lime juice. And he was worried. And he said to me, 'Will you tell me anything you want that I could get you to make you eat? Watercress, fish-head, tell me, and I'll get it for you.' No way.

Just one particular day, I was sitting there and I was leaning out, trying to throw my kai out the window, that's the only way to get rid of those kais! And all those sparrows, coming over, eating the bread. And he came in and he said, 'You tell me and I'll tell that cook to cook you anything — any Maori kai you want. Pūhā, watercress, mutton-bird, anything at all. You tell me.' And just that day I said to him, 'You know those little birds over there, poor little things? I want them! If I have some of those birds, I'll eat!'

So he had it in him, quite believing what I want, and he went over to Te Rere pā, to old Himiona Kahika, and he told this old koroua to get some of those birds. 'All right!' He knows. So he made his trap, put it on the lawn, get some bread, and he got six little birds. Poor things! Pluck them, gut them, and brought them back to the hospital. Dr Simcock came in and he said, 'I've got some little birds here for you! Now what do I do?' 'Oh, you give it to the cook and tell him to put it in the stove, but don't put it in fat. Just put it on the grill. No fat. Just turn it round and round till it gets brown.' Ah, start to get brown and the smell of it, oh lovely! And he came through: 'Oh, your little birds are ready, Mrs Mac.' And he came in to see me eating them. All he saw, lying on the dish, is the beaks and the little claws, and the bones from the chest! I can see him looking! They were so fat! And I ate the lot, those six little birds! I pick up, then. I started eating. They saved my life those little birds. They gave me the kaha to eat!

When Donald was born, we had no house. I brought him back to a tent. I never said anything to my doctor, Dr Simcock. We had no house, nothing. As long as I got my four-gallon tin to get my kids a bath. And a bit of blanket to cover it! 'Cause after we left Nukuhou we shift back to Matahi. My mother was still alive and she was at Matahi.[41] But then we went to live at the butter factory at Opotiki; and that's where I had the baby who was stillborn.[42] I used to walk from the factory at Opotiki right into town — walk. Just to get my pension, my family benefit. Well, I rest about six times. I was there about eight months, carrying that boy, and after I had that boy we went back to Matahi again. At Opotiki I wouldn't show my face to anyone out on the street — never. I never used to go and talk to anybody. The amount of kids I had. In Opotiki, at night when the moon's up, I used to go out and wash my clothes and hang them out in the moonlight. Then when I begin to get out of that hell, that shyness, I'd go down from Matahi and mix up with people down at the shop, at Waimana. It was nothing to do with colours. Nothing. Just my way then. I think the outside world is not my world, then. But it is different now.

We came to live at Waimana and Mac worked in the cheese factory there for quite a while. We lived right near the factory there. When they sold all the baches, we put tenders for our one, the one we'd been staying in, and we got ours. We brought it up behind Mrs Hodgson, opposite the butcher at Waimana, at the back. We put it up there and we were paying rates for the section. But we got booted out of there. When Mrs Hodgson, my landlady for the section, put her house in front, she said to me, 'You can stay there as long as you like, not paying. I don't want that piece. You're all right. Your family is all right. They're not mischief at all.' We didn't have to leave for two years. But when Henry Bell notice it,[43] that's when he came over and told me to pay up. I said, 'No, no. I'm not paying. Mrs Hodgson, she told me not to. I can stay here as long as I like.' But he reckoned that's their section. Hungry for money, eh? He said, 'I'm giving you twenty-four hours to get out of here.' So I pack all our things and came down here. No house. Nobody lives here. It's all bush, all scrubs. It's Mac's land. So we build the little bach up the top, here. That other one we bought from Waimana. That was Bella's house.[44] It was a condemned house, but we didn't know it was condemned.

I put a chimney on the tool-shed so we got somewhere to cook our kai. No window, just the door. With my little kids! And that's where I brought Donald, out from the Annexe, through winter. We lived in a tent for eighteen months, with my new baby. We put that one up – the bach – just for the boys to sleep in. And we got summoned! In court! And who saved us for that house being condemned? It was our district nurse. This nurse, Puti Eruera, said to me, 'How many kids have you, Puti?' She's a Puti and I'm a Puti! 'Oh, nine, oh eight and a half anyway!'[45] 'Well, you're all right. Only two to pay for your summons!' 'What for?' 'For that condemned house! Their family benefit will pay for it. Two of your kids will pay for it! Twelve pounds, that's the fine. You're safe enough! But put your house up. And get your family in it. You'll be summoned, but when they come to push you out, they've got to give you a house!' So we did.

We were here for about a week in that bach when we were called up to come to court at Whakatane. Then I said to her, 'Well, now?' – for she came up again, to put that bach up to a standard – 'Well? It's already a standard; it's taller than me!' 'Then put those big front windows in!'

But I want to put a house up. So when she next came up I said, 'I'm going to ask you something. I want a permit. I want to put a house for myself.' 'Get a garage, just the one big garage – with the big door!' So when the Health Inspector came, he gave me a permit for it, for a garage! So I shot in to Te Teko the same day, to the mill. I had Tu and Wharetapu with me; we had an old truck, chugalong, chugalong! We had all the measurements for the timbers – and we got the timbers, and everything. And when the Inspector came up, long after, it was up with the doors and everything. Not a garage! He couldn't do anything! I said, 'Oh well, you chase me out! But you put me a house up! You get me a house instead of this!'

Puti and Mac outside their home, May 1984. Photograph by Gillian Chaplin.

This house was about two years after that one. This is a Maori Affairs house. One of the county councillors, he came down from Waimana and he said, 'You've got to have a house.' He's been reading in the minutes all the time about this man who didn't have a house and being summoned! And all the time he's living on Mac's land! All the land we've got over there at Waimana, we didn't know anything about. He had it all the time! He was feeling guilty, 'cos he's living on Mac's land! That Pakeha fellow! So he said, 'Mac, you are going to have a house.' 'Oh? Who is going to pay for it?' 'Never mind. Don't you worry about that!' And when we got back from Auckland, one time, the shed was up for the power! The application was in to put a house up, and everything was lying here. And I said to Mac, 'Hey koe! This house is coming up! Look at all the metals over there! And that's the house for the power!' That's it! And the next four days afterwards, all the carpenters coming to put the foundation on.

We never put any deposit on it. They ask me if we've got kids. And I said, 'No. I haven't got any kids now! Why didn't you come before? I had tons! Tons before! Now it's all grown up. Only one left, but he's nearly sixteen. He is almost out of the pension! Here's my little mokopunas. Four of them!' This man said, 'Oh, you like your house?' I said, 'What house? I've got a house down there! I'm in a house. I don't want a house; I've got no money to pay for it. I've got no kids, no nothing.' And these little things come running up. He said to me, 'Who are those?' 'That's my mokopunas!' 'Oh, that will do!' He put all the mokopunas on it. And when I went down to get my pension — no pension! It's all gone! It's all gone to capitalize the house!⁴⁶

So my kids grew up, and up, and up — no pension! Then a few years after, they raise the family benefit. I said to my minister, a Maori minister in town, 'Can you do me a favour? The family benefit is coming up double.⁴⁷ I wonder if I could have that rise? The first benefit, they can have that one. That's in the agreement. This one is not in, yet. If you can do it for me?' And I had that one. I can use that one for them to go to school on. Before that we had just nothing. Nothing at all. We live from the garden. No meat — oh, buy a little bit. Mac has some coming in from his job, driving the bus, but it's not enough. It's very hard living if you don't look after yourself. We never had a car then, so we couldn't get pipis. Only if people bring us a few. At Maai, when we were living there, you could always get pikopikos or anything like that, and we had our own cows. But here — just bread and butter. Oh, they live anyway.

When we came out from Maungapohatu, we went from Otane to Matahi, to where that whare tapu is now. We were living down there with my mother and Te Aue, and all the wives. We had a six-roomed house; it looked like that Hiruharama Hou at Maai. But my father gave the whole of that land on lease to Bert Hughes, and then the old house we had got burnt. We were at Taramaire, round the back of Nukuhou. My father make up his mind to cancel that lease — buy it back. So we came back there and we put that whare tapu up. When he died, his last words were 'Keep that house holy.' His tapu house. Keep it holy. You deny it, you neglect it, you're frightened of what I say. You don't care about what God told you, what to do. Something like that. Because he's a prophet. He prophesies everything from long, long ahead of it. Well, that's his last word: to keep that house holy. So we have. And we put that meeting-house, Te Ao Hou, The New World, on that papakāinga.

It's a great, long story really — and it's a sad one. Because my family's great for jealousy since my father died. We wanted to put up this meeting-house for our

Te Ao Hou, with the club as the emblem for Rua as the coming King placed on the gable and the side posts of the meeting-house. Photograph by Gillian Chaplin, 1977.

family, for our mokopunas. Mac and I got the timbers and everything. But we got kicked out of it. So we never built it; the others did. We had a house there, just over the fence [from] where my father's tomb is. But we shift away. I was telling Mac, 'We better move out, better go on the road where nobody owns it, just the government! We can put a hut anywhere beside the road!'

It's my mother's land, and Aka's land, and Meri Tukua's land – it's all shares.[48] We wanted to put that meeting-house up for ourselves, because we didn't have a cemetery for the Iharaira. Just the Ngaitama cemetery at Matahi. There was a big row at Te Huinga o Te Kura: two of our kuias didn't want to take Meri Tukua's mokopuna when it died. They said to her, 'Take your mokopuna away. This is our cemetery. You got no marae.' That's when I said to my sister Meri, 'Just hang on. Just control yourself. Our father wasn't like that. Just carry on. Don't worry about what they say. Take it over to the cemetery; there's no other cemetery but that one.' So we did. We put that baby over there. And then I had my baby, the stillborn, and we brought it back, and took it up to that cemetery. Then I had a talk with Meri and I said, 'From now on we'll try and put a bit of a meeting-house.' 'How could you put it up? You haven't got any money!' 'I know I haven't got any money! Just my pigs – and my tangi.' But it was those kuias: it's in me to build up courage to put a meeting-house for our mokopunas. This one we started to plan, Mac and I. But I didn't put it up though. Mau and Timoti, Paora Kiingi's son, they were the ones. And we still don't have a cemetery. That marae's supposed to be four acres, but there's not enough.[49] We should have our own cemetery. But we don't. As I said, it's a sad story.

So, we take our dead to Matahi. But my father said, 'Don't take me to the cemetery.' He was scared of the kēhua. 'Just leave me here.' He said, '*This* is the place for the birds of the sky; this is where they'll all come, crying and weeping. Te huihui a ngā manu':† that's all the people. We have no cemetery of our own, as Iharaira. Before, the old ones they went back to Maungapohatu. That's where Akakura is, and Henare is, and Hiki is, and my boy, Ruatoto. That rimu tree's standing there, now, and you go straight over to that rimu tree. At Umukaimata. Aunty Aka died at Matahi, and Henare, and they took the bodies up and they are under that tree. And a cousin of Henare's – that's Hiki. You know, the funniest thing, you won't believe it, no matter what, but it's quite true. We had all this place prepared for them, all the pillows are in this bundle, bundle of bones on each pillow. And their kuias were looking after them. They'd fall off to sleep. Every time, this one, Henare, he used to grab *that* one – throw it out! Threw him off his pillow! All the kuias knew it was him! 'Henare, why you do that? A, ka aroha hoki a Hiki!'‡ And put him back again. And the next morning, we didn't believe it until we saw it with our own eyes, the bundle of bones way down here! And him still lying on his own pillow! And Hiki, half-way down our whare mate! Every morning! It was three nights there, eh? Every morning they found Hiki away, and him by himself up the top. We could hear these kuias mumbling away. But that boy, Henare, loves him. Hiki, he can't walk, can't talk, just can't say nothing. All he can do is wriggling away, with his hand. But he loved this sick boy. He is a big boy, the same age as him. And then when Hiki died, that's what he gets! 'Do you have to do that to Hiki, Henare?' All the kuias nodding their heads and talking to

†The gathering of the birds
‡Oh, poor old Hiki!

Carrying the coffin and the bones for their final reburial, Maungapohatu, 1940. *Meri Taka, Auckland*

him, to these bones. But when they buried them, they buried them together. Him in his own casket, and Hiki in his, but together.[50]

Whatu we took back. He died in Gisborne, shearing. They sit him on a horse, just like a living one, sitting behind my uncle, Whitu. They strapped him just round the hips to keep him on the horse with him, his legs just swinging away over there! We wouldn't go near the horse! Couldn't! We were all so scared of it! There's a dead man behind that horse! We went up and stayed overnight on the road — seven of us — put him down, with a great big fire beside it, for us to sleep around. His face was just — beautiful. Rosy cheeks! When we get to the marae, everybody is waiting. We had a tangi first. When he was still on the horse. Took him off the horse, put him in the tent, the whare mate. And Miki: while they were waiting for Tane — Whatu — to arrive, they hung his bones in a white cloth out the back of the meeting-house! You could see them through the window at night, they said! But they were the last ones we took back to Maungapohatu.[51]

We are all right. Our father left us his talk and his teaching. We have tried to follow our father's footstep. To be kind. He told us, 'Never keep any grudge. Look after any animal. It may be a bird, but look after it. It may be the Son of God. Talk to it. Don't ignore anything. Be kind, because you don't know who it is.' It could be him. And I say to my brother now, 'Leave me here. What I am. I'm going to stay here as I am, when my father left me. Us, the Iharairas.' We have our own karakia. If the Ruatahuna ones, or Waikaremoana, ask us to come to a Twelfth, oh well, we always go. But not here. Not a Twelfth. We have karakia on the Saturdays, here.

A lot of them from here went to Hori Gage. A lot from Matahi and Waimana. When we go up to Tataiahape, then, before we can get into the pā somebody is always at the gate to spray us with water to take our sins off us, before we can go into the pā. They really do that to the outsiders! It might affect them, or something. You've got — like a hoodoo — ah, you're trying to come in there and you might mākutu somebody! We didn't like it. You've got to be sprayed with water, salt water, that is. Sea water. That's their custom. Sea water and olive oil. It's well beyond our — well beyond! I mean, we have water, just to wash our hands, where there's a tapu place. Just to respect it; if you go in there, a tapu place, we reckon we keep that place. So we've got to clean our hands from the outside and then we go in. That's all. Not spraying and looking round for your faults and your mākutus. Hori Gage started having the Twelfths at Tataiahape; but when he died those karakia they've been having there, all the Twelfths, they're just fading off. Rangimarie, that's their name, beside Ringatu. That's their other name. For Hori Gage's Ringatu.[52] But I don't like it, going to Hori Gage. He was mucking up everything for us, the ones staying where we are. I am going to stay as I am. When my father left me, he told me from the start, 'Well, wherever the Presbyterians — you may go there. But apart from them —'. He said, 'Go with Mr Laughton.' I might as well say I'm still a Presbyterian. And an Iharaira.

I've got my old Maori Bible. We start from the Old Testament. Not the New one. And these are our hymns and inois and everything. It's all in here — all in my head. All the karakias. And I stand up between the congregation and say my part. And I know all those kupu whakaaris. I had a book — it's only a little book, but it had a special way of putting it. Like a code. You couldn't understand what it is for. You've got to know those letters: A or whatever. It's not open for anyone to know. It's a real staunch way of putting it in the Ringatu church. You give out that one letter. That's the kupu whakaari for Maketu, say. I used to hear my father saying it like that, at Maungapohatu, at the karakias. This is it. So I'm staying to the old one — *our* one.

When our father was alive, there was one time when he told us what was coming ahead, for each one of us. It was a Saturday at Maai, and each one brought their flower.[53] We were under the apple tree by the well. I had two flowers, and pikopiko behind. Forget-me-not and dianthus. He told me the flowers were so that I would be kind to everyone — loving everyone. And for the pikopiko, it was to bring the people back. He found a meaning in each one, for me.

For him, it's that sparrow-hawk. Kāeaea. That's his kaitiaki. It's always circling around where he is supposed to be — at Maai there. When he comes back here, it always circles over here. That sparrow-hawk. And the rainbow. He only has two. But that sparrow-hawk — you know, we stayed in Maungapohatu to look after the place when my father and the rest came out here. You know what happened to that sparrow-hawk? My husband shoot it, and pluck it, and cook it! Because he was annoyed at that thing, crying up in the air like that. I waited for a long time — and then, the same thing — only not the same bird — was circling on top of the houses at Maai. Just circling on top of the trees. Well, I had Muscovy ducks and everything, and they all had chickens. Every time he sees these chickens, he used to circle, circle, circle. Mac thought to himself, 'Here's that bird again! I'm going to shoot it!' Because it's a hawk, it'll kill those little ones. But not this one. Every time they run towards the road, he'll fly around and stand over there. To chase them back. Half-way up the paddocks there, he'll come in front and drop something. He will be flying up, and drop something down. I went down there to find out what that thing was; it came down from his mouth. He kiore! A mouse! I really loved him then. When I saw that was a mouse, giving it for my birds. He mea tapu!* I really love birds! I really love animals! And my father told us to look after any animal. Be kind. You don't know who it is. It could be him.

*A tapu thing!

Mac: He told us the world won't be at peace. Nothing, nothing, will keep the world quiet. Nothing at all. The famine will come at the end. Starvation. Money is no good, he said. 'You'll find out.' And the Maori lands — the Pakeha will take it! He would sit down at Maungapohatu and give these things out. He would tell you how, what was coming ahead.

Puti: Nothing will quieten the whole world till that time comes, the coming of the Messiah. We are all believing in our hope — to see it. It's very hard though. But that's what we are waiting for. The Mihāia. If we can get that.

Putiputi Onekawa died on 12 January 1987. The name given to her in remembrance of her father — Putikaraehe — is the name under which she is buried.

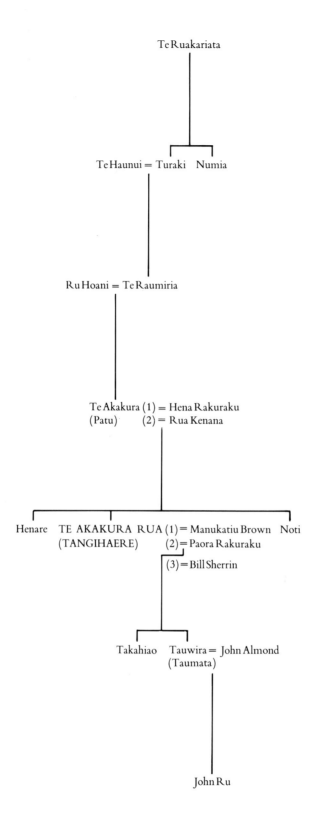

Te Ruakariata

Te Haunui = Turaki   Numia

Ru Hoani = Te Raumiria

Te Akakura (1) = Hena Rakuraku
(Patu)   (2) = Rua Kenana

Henare   TE AKAKURA RUA (1) = Manukatiu Brown   Noti
(TANGIHAERE)   (2) = Paora Rakuraku
(3) = Bill Sherrin

Takahiao   Tauwira = John Almond
(Taumata)

John Ru

TE AKAKURA RUA

In our end is our beginning. The origin of this book lies, in part, with Te Akakura. She was Rua's eldest daughter with his rangatira wife, Te Akakura Ru, who was also called Patu Ru. Their daughter Akakura died on 26 May 1980. Only a few months earlier we had taken the book about Rua, *Mihaia*, which we had dedicated to Akakura and her half-sister Puti, back to Te Ao Hou. That book completed, I had gone to England and there, in a bleak London flat, I learned of her death. Gillian phoned me and then wrote to tell me of the tangi. I found I could not stop crying.

Akakura was a woman of great strength and great passion. When we first went to visit her, in Auckland in December 1977, she commented that others had come before, seeking to know about her father, and she said, 'I wasn't going to tell you anything.' She came to trust us, and we to love her. Her feelings about her father, as she soon revealed, were very ambivalent. She was a woman who had fought for what she wanted, all her life, and her angry will had frequently brought her into conflict with the people of Maungapohatu and Matahi, as well as her father. But it was also her passion and vitality that we remembered. We spent many hours together over the next two years: talking, crying, laughing, and lingering — without any sense of time passing — over photographs of her people. From these bonds this book has grown.

We never talked with Akakura about her own life in the same way as we have with the others in this book, but from the conversations we had about her father and the community at Maungapohatu, we learnt something of her struggles. Two were tape-recorded, on 16 and 21 December 1977; the later conversations of 1978 and 1979 were recorded in note form. The present account is based on these sources.

Te Akakura, or Tangihaere as she was first named, was born at Tawhana, probably on 1 July 1914. Both the Maungapohatu school and Turakina College record this as her birth date, but when she died her birth date was given as 20 February. Her mother, Patu — as we will call her, so as to distinguish her from her daughter — was the daughter of the high-ranking chieftainess of Tauarau, Ruatoki: Te Raumiria Te Haunui. Te Raumiria's first husband, Ru Hoani, was from Ruatahuna and he became a devoted follower of Rua. But the people of Tauarau, and particularly their leader, Numia Te Ruakariata (or Numia Kereru, as he became known), who was Te Raumiria's uncle, were hostile to Rua's teachings. Akakura's mother and grandmother had been brought up as Anglican, not Ringatu, and, as she commented, her mother 'took me to the Ruatoki mission house. My mother didn't like me going back to Maungapohatu and Matahi. 'Cause she's a different person altogether. She didn't want — she really didn't want me to go back — oh, it's not nice of me to say this — to a backward place. Like tohunga ways and so forth.'

Rua's marriage to Patu was strongly opposed by the Tauarau leaders. She had been married — briefly — to Hena Rakuraku, who was from an Anglican family of rank from Ruatoki, but the young man had died. 'She was only a widow a very short time and my father went over to get her. He fought for her. He had already prophesied — he spoke about her. This is just what I heard.' 'There is the lament my father sang about my mother. He had to fight for her. There's an old, old woman from Ruatahuna, Te Uru, she sings it when she sees me.' Horo Tatu also sang such a lament for us, concerning Patu's influence over Rua. This is one which was composed by the women of Maungapohatu for Rua, when he was in Mt Eden gaol:

Patu, a portrait taken in 1908. The occasion may have been her marriage to Rua. As well as the sprig of flowers, she is wearing a huia feather in her hair, indicating her high rank. Photograph by James McDonald. *Alexander Turnbull Library*

Numia Kereru (right), chief of Ngatirongo at Ruatoki. The man on the left is Tutakangahau, chief of Maungapohatu at the turn of the century. *Alexander Turnbull Library*

previous page Te Akakura at Hiruharama Hou, Maai, January 1978. Photograph by Gillian Chaplin.

Matakai mai e Aka i Ruatoki
Aroaro ra i ai te rere mai a te manu
He mea ra tuki mai na Te Akakura!

From Ruatoki, Aka, you hold me in your gaze
Like the bird flying straight to me
Released for that purpose by Te Akakura![1]

Hena Rakuraku's death had been attributed to Rua. ' "Rua had put a taipō on Hena," said old Rakuraku. So the fight was between them.' It was a ceremonial taiaha fight. Puti Onekawa spoke of that day at Ruatoki: 'Kereru didn't like our father to marry Akakura. Kereru didn't. There was a big whaikōrero over at Ruatoki — with the taiaha and everything. Kereru doesn't like my father marrying Akakura — because she's really a princess to them. If she marry this fellow with all these wives, he'll make her a slave, or something. He'd like their princess to marry one husband, to keep that name as a princess. So there was a big whakano' there. At the finish, my father stood up and said, "Waiho. Kai ahau tēnā. That's up to me. And you've just got to wait. You find out for yourself. You might come over here and kneel under her feet one day to come. I'm still taking my wife." Whether they like it or not, he grab her, put her on the cart, and come back to Matahi! He just couldn't bother about those taiahas.'[2] And, consequently, as Akakura said, 'All these people at Maungapohatu upheld my mother. She was Queen itself to them. They did. Especially being pinched from someone else! They had to bow down to her.' Patu was herself a headstrong woman and maintained her independence. She often used to go back to Ruatoki for lengthy periods, and she kept control over her extensive land shares. She also had a profound influence over her husband all her life.

Hillman Rua, Rua's adopted son, told a story of 'how Akakura [Patu] did things': 'There's a woman up at Matahi — Te Ripo.[3] Well, this woman was very bad, sick. I happened to be at Maungapohatu and Patu said to Rua, "Rua, think about that woman." We'd got word that she was just dying. Te Ripo. And the old man said, "What good is that woman to us?" And Patu says, "Don't you remember our daughter — Te Akakura's sister[4] — old Te Ripo look after that baby, and she's a woman now." And the old man says, "Oh well, I'll see." And he went into his house and he came out: "All right." And he send me down, from Maungapohatu. He says, "You go down and have a word with this woman." The whole day I came

The Tuhoe elders gathered in splendour at Tauarau in 1904. (The occasion was the visit of the Governor, Lord Ranfurly). *National Museum*

from Maungapohatu. I got into Matahi. Some kids saw me and said to this woman it was me – that came from Maungapohatu. She sit up in her bed, just thinking about Rua. Try to help him eh? Put out her hand to me – where I came from. From Rua. Rua might have given me something for her. So I shook hands with her. She went out of her bed that very day. She was well. And there she was lying in bed to die! Ai. That's how Patu did things, eh? That's all I had to do – just shake hands, nothing else. I don't know what's on me, or what. That very day she got out of bed.'[5]

The mission house at Ruatoki, November 1951. Photograph by E. Woollett. *National Publicity Studios collection, Alexander Turnbull Library*

Patu's eldest daughter inherited her mother's strong will and her tempestuous contradictions. Akakura described her early years, when she herself used to run away from the Ruatoki Anglican mission, where she had been sent by Patu. 'I was most of the time at the Ruatoki mission. I lived with this old Pakeha woman – Miss Hare her name was. I really lived with her. See, my mother took me there to stay with them. But I didn't want to.'[6] She used to run away to where she had been brought up, by Tuwairua and his wife, Materangatira Te Whiu, at Piripari in the Tauranga valley. Mate Te Whiu was the daughter of Te Whiu Maraki, who had been a staunch fighter alongside Te Kooti and to whom he had entrusted the leadership of the valley. It is said that, when Te Kooti was dying, he gave Te Whiu the mauri whenua for 'the whole of the Waimana people'. In some versions, the mauri is a key. It was from Te Whiu, in turn, that the authority of prophetic leadership, of which he was the guardian or kaitiaki, was transferred to Rua.[7] Akakura said, 'I was brought up by this old couple. The Tuwairuas. But my mother didn't like me going back to them. These old people that brought me up – they had a son. Every time he comes over to Ruatoki to visit me, I'm missing from the mission! I run back to my grandmother, Mate. I wanted to come back to Waimana! I didn't like staying at Ruatoki. I *hated* the place! I didn't want that place! I wanted to come back to the people that brought me up; I always wanted to come back to them. No. My mother won't have it! They used to take me on their buggy – on the gig, eh! Their son, he used to take me up to the mission – and I'd watch him going back. I'd go to school and after school I'm missing from the mission. I'm hiding in the Waimana truck! Going back! It was Daisy – Teehi[8] – their Maori policeman, that got them to let me go back. They told my mother, "You can't keep her. She'll never live here." Daisy did. See, I bleed a lot, through my nose. That's through riding. I used to ride with my father. I would stand behind his back – on the horse – and the horse shies and I get thrown! All those hurts. See, here's another one. I used to be a rough rider. Every time I cry, it bleeds.' Akakura linked these early hurts with her serious illnesses in the last years of her life: 'Well, it has come out now: the sickness I have. They took me to the doctor's at Ruatoki. That's what the doctor told them: send me back.'

She returned to Waimana and the Tuwairuas in 1924. Akakura then went to live with her father the following year, just before her only full brother, Henare, was killed. From late 1926 she lived with her parents at Maungapohatu. She described her impressions of the services which she saw being held at Maai: 'Our father talked about Church and that. We used to have it three times a day. On Saturdays. *All* the people from the pā goes down. I used to wonder what they were doing. See, as I said to you, I was brought up by other people and I wondered what was going on. That's when my father took me. My mother didn't want me. I was about twelve and I knew what was going on, then. See, they'd all sit down in a group in front of Maai. We had a little dug-out there. And we all sit there. They do. Ted, that's Te Hau,[9] and me used to stand and watch them, thinking, "What

Patu, with her son Henare. *Sister Annie Henry collection, Alexander Turnbull Library*

are they doing?" We didn't know these sort of things. Well, after a while I understood what was going on. But being brought up by other people is a different thing! I didn't believe anything. And they knew. Ted and I didn't. But my father loved me. That's something I can say. I didn't like him — oh, I didn't like looking straight at him. I don't know why. Maybe I didn't like his ways — that would be it. Being brought up in a mission.'

But as she stressed: 'I *loved* Maungapohatu. I did. Still do. It was my father who took me there — he took me away from the mission — he fought for me really. And he was a good provider, our father was. He had everything. And he prepared the place before the famine — I might as well say famine — came. There *was* famine there.' Akakura was always most blunt about the harsh aspects of life at Maungapohatu, which finally drove the people away: 'That famine — about 1929. They all stayed there when that famine was on. All the men went out to work and come back. But they all broke up about 1931-2. People started to go back to their homes. There wasn't any living there. They couldn't get any jobs.' She added, again, in this context, 'But my father taught us well. Yes, he did. All sorts. Hard to forget, you know.'

She herself lived there only from the latter part of 1926 until 1928: 'only the two years I lived with them, that's when I went to school at Maungapohatu. I just knew my father two years. I knew him very well, then. I learnt a lot from him. The only thing that was hard was, well, he might be right and then again he mightn't. And what I heard I didn't like to believe it. So I just thought.'

At the beginning of 1928 Akakura was seriously injured in the accident at Te Whaiti, when the truck carrying the people of Maungapohatu away from a tangi came off the road, and two of the elders were killed.[10] Patu suffered serious back injuries and had to be carried home to Maungapohatu on a litter. Her death two years later (of spinal cancer) was possibly the result of these injuries, although it had been thought that she had recovered. Akakura herself bore scars on her thighs for the rest of her life. This accident was attributed to Patu's wilful disobedience of Rua. 'I was with her, the accident at Te Whaiti. I still limp with the accident I had there. See, I went through with my mother, without my father knowing, eh? And, course, he always vowed there would be trouble with her disobeying him. Well, it did. We went over to Te Whaiti and two people died, that's Miki and Houpapa. Those old people – all Ringatus.'

In 1929, her mother sent her away again, this time to Turakina College. Akakura commented it was because Patu didn't 'want me mixing around with these people. They were very backward, the Maungapohatu people. They went out to work – but in a lot of ways it was very backward. But I loved them. Yes I did. But my mother didn't. She wanted me to have an education. She did. She sent me away. I was in Standard Five I think.'

Indeed she was. She attended Turakina for two years and was fetched home in December 1930 because of Patu's death on the 17th. 'When I got back she was already dead. That was a hard knocking. She thought nothing but the best for me, but I didn't know that. I didn't really know her.' She had also returned to a community that was, as she said, starting to break up. However, on 8 May 1931 she married at Maungapohatu. This was an arranged marriage to Manukatiu Paraone, who was the son of Paraone Pukepuke from Ruatahuna. 'I was married in the meeting-house, Tane Nui a Rangi. John Laughton married me. It's like this: I was to marry him, he's the Ruatahuna chief. I'm the chieftainess of Maungapohatu, I suppose. Something like that. It went with our lands. At Ruatahuna, his lands joins onto mine. Oh, my mother – all her doing. She organized it – she did, and his mother did.[11] No choice. Not a choice. 'Cos my mother died – course *his* mother came up. At the time we were only young, very young. I was sixteen. And there was some big funeral out at Ruatahuna. I went through. Little did I know *he* was there! They brought him back from Kaiangaroa. He was working there. That's when this woman stood up in the meeting-house. Asked for my hand. There and then. My grandfather, Wharepapa[12] – he refused. Everybody trod on his neck: "Well, you don't know! You just keep out of it!" So. It was talked over, like this: I said, "Let me go back to Maungapohatu." They did. And they'll bring him through. Mr Laughton was there.' Thus Akakura was married, against her will and wearing half of Puti's veil. The marriage lasted exactly a week. She ran away and came out to Matahi, where her father was. Puti remembers that Rua 'came over to pick her up and take her back, but she wouldn't. He was angry about it. That boy was arranged for her. Just like my one. It's been arranged from the eldest, on both sides. But oh, no.'

Almost immediately afterwards Akakura went to live with Paora Rakuraku. They stayed at Paemahoe, on the Tauranga river flats near Matahi. Their first daughter, Takahiao, was born on 25 November 1932, but she died of pneumonia eight months later, on 31 July 1933. Their second daughter and last child, Tauwira, was born on 15 November 1933. 'My daughter was named after my father had all his wives. It wasn't me that named her – it was Piimia. See, I was very sickly. As I said to you, I was young, very young, when I had her. Skinny as a rake! That name – it was for my father, the things he did, and he prophesied. That's why they called her Tauwira – the things he did. Tauwira. I didn't know the name at all.' At her birth, the baby's name was actually registered as Taumata. This name conveys the notion of Rua's prophetic vision or foresight, mata, being completed, as the cycle

Rua at Whakatane, 29 November 1919. Photograph, *Ben Keys MSS Papers 407: 32, Alexander Turnbull Library*

comes round to fulfilment, tau. The name which she was known by, Tauwira, places the emphasis on his will — wira — being fulfilled. Both are expressions of the Iharaira belief in the ultimate completion of the visionary predictions of the prophet, as time revolves in its seasons towards fulfilment.

In these years, Akakura and Paora sometimes lived with her father. They stayed at different places, 'in the bush', up the Tauranga valley — at Otane, or Omahuru, or Matahi. 'Really happy times! Living around, driving through the bush. Then we'll camp there for the night, sometimes for a week. We have all these kapongas, homes, just on the road going through to Tawhana. Omahuru — where my father built his first home. I was just a girl at the time. He built a little village there, just for a couple of weeks. He cut all the scrub down and he built kapongas, shacks, around. All the young people living there, then. Well, after we left Maungapohatu, our father likes going out camping. So we used to go out. We were then at Otane. That was the other place where we lived. Homes there. A paling thing. That's where my brother was buried, above that. Tane — Te Whatu.

'When he was brought back from Gisborne, when they brought him out, it wasn't bones. He was still whole.[13] This is something — I couldn't sleep. 'Cause I keep seeing him. Five years he was in the coffin. You know what they do with them — they embalm them. He was still in one piece. Hasn't rotted away. They stood him up — exactly like a mummy! They had to break the coffin! His whole face, even the skin, was still there. Just his eyebrows fallen off. When they brought him up, the dank air got into my — seeing him brought out of the coffin! Well, we have tohungas. They had to take me; I was raving mad. They took me out. My sister Puti was there; the two of us. We could still see him. According to what they said, we'd keep calling out, "There he is! There he is!" So they took us away from the meeting-house. A lot of people was in the meeting-house. I don't know what they did. But we were better in about two days. We were better.

'When they put him on the horse, they had to bend him from the hips. Pity the man that is carrying him: Whitu Tawa.[14] They had to feed him. Then I used to run for my life! I had an ambling mare and it goes around with the horse he was riding. And this man used to call out for me to wait. He kept calling out, "Wait! Wait! Don't run!" I was scared stiff! Going round the corners of the road I could feel — oh, on my nose! And my sister, she had her own pony and it was lagging behind. And, somehow, I got left behind. She let her pony go — she jumped behind mine! She was so scared!

'Little did I know they had whisky and wine. They had it in my bag! I didn't know! That's why they'd kept calling out to me, "Wait! Wait!" Till they come up to my bag and started to sort the bottles out! They had all that! And her — screaming and calling out to me, "Wait, wait". Then jumping onto mine!

'We had three horses, working horses. They had to chain the horses. The dank air was getting on to them. You know what horses are like: they could feel it. They wanted mine, the ambling horse I had. I said, "No. No. Get one of the draught-horses!" Might have killed it! 'Cause it was very gentle.'

For Akakura, this was the last time that she returned to Maungapohatu until the opening of the timber road, in 1964. She had separated by then from Paora Rakuraku and was living in Auckland with Bill Sherrin, a Pakeha whom she had first met at Matahi. Her return to Maungapohatu was an occasion of painful memories. As the oldest child of her mother, who was the rangatira wife of Rua, she was asked by the Maungapohatu elders, including Paetawa Miki, the kaitiaki,[15] to open the road. A road to Maungapohatu had been, since 1907, at the

Te Akakura with her sister Puti at Hiruharama Hou, January 1978. Photograph by Gillian Chaplin.

Paetawa Miki, kaitiaki of Maungapohatu. Photograph by Gillian Chaplin, 1978.

centre of Rua's vision for the City of God on earth. It was the base of his hopes for the community's economic survival.[16] Akakura explained what her role should have been: 'It goes from her, my mother. She's the first. She didn't have any boys.[17] And I didn't. Te Akakura had me: I fell in line. I was supposed to open the road through to Maungapohatu. But I didn't. I refused. Anyhow, my daughter, Tauwira, opened the road. It has to go to my daughter. In line.' She went on, 'They appointed me. I shook my head. "No". I wouldn't be right. I just sat there and I couldn't say anything. Like for why. Being with a white man. Being married to a white man. This is the reason. See, my father didn't like white people: once. And I couldn't do that. I couldn't overstep my father. It's on account of him. I couldn't.' Her anguish became a nightmare, because Tauwira died not long after.[18] In the whaikōrero during her tangi, her death was attributed to Akakura's refusal. Tauwira had undertaken that which was not hers to do. 'It wasn't her place. I thought, "Oh. I didn't think that. I just didn't think *I* was right."'

Following her own father's death, Akakura, as the senior child, the mātāmua, was taken to the tapu places associated with Te Kooti and Rua. 'See, when I went back from college, the first year, they were all sitting there, in my mother's bedroom, at Matahi. And that's when he told them. I'll be the anointed child. This is true. 'Cause my mother was the legal wife. She was married to him. She made sure of it.[19] And he blessed me, then. In the Maori way. Well, I was beginning to know who he was, what he was. And every time he speaks to us, he calls the lot of us, the ones living then, and he talks about this child. And he always says, "what comes towards her belongs to her mother, not to me. What kingdom she has belongs to her, not my name." He talks to the children, to us. Tells us.'

But if Rua emphasized her lineage of authority from her mother, he also entrusted her with his 'kingdom' of faith. Teka Hekerangi, Wharepapa, and Tatu were the Levites who took Akakura on the circuit of the Ringatu meeting-houses in Poverty Bay and the Urewera. They visited, in particular, Eripitana, the Tuhoe house built specifically for Te Kooti, and Pakowhai, where Wi Pere's family meeting-house Te Poho o Hiraina stood, near Patutahi. There Rua had camped in 1906, when he came to Turanga to claim the kingship. He had at first been rejected by the chief Ruru Pataromu, but after the Waipawa river rose in flood and brought them all the food they needed upon its waters – potatoes, corn, kamokamo – the people had given Rua ten acres of land there. Akakura also went with Teka to remove the coins, gifts from the faithful and the healing coins, from the prophet's tapu houses at Maai and Matahi. As she herself commented, Maori have a saying, 'You can't use the money for sores', meaning the coins used in blessing the sick. Consequently, one source of the quarrels that followed was her use of some of the money from Matahi. A portion was taken by Puti and Meri Tukua to build Te Ao Hou. But Akakura took her share to educate her daughter at college. 'I stepped in. I took it. And they didn't like it. We fought over our father's money! And I used my share. Mine – well, my girl went through college. There was seven hundred pounds – but all in threepences! Yes, and sixpence – shillings. And old pound notes. And there was a fifty pound note. I took all those! They come talking round. I said, "You had your share. I'll have my share!" Paid for part of my house. Then the others wanted a share. Too late! Gone!' These quarrels over the land and the money divided the family after Rua's death. He had foreseen this possibility and had tried to forewarn them. Akakura's determination – 'I fight for myself' – was probably one cause of the rifts which developed. In turn, it was partly because of the conflicts that she finally left Matahi and came to live in Auckland in the mid-1940s.

She often commented on the tensions of living in the two worlds, Maori and Pakeha: 'My father brought me up well. And the mission did, too. In the Pakeha way. He, in the Maori way. It worked together. It did. 'Cos I judged it for myself. My husband knows what I'm like. I can be white — Pakeha way — and I can be a Maori. When I get in with my people, I'll always be a Maori. I told him that. I said, "No. I'm a Maori. And I'll be a Maori when I'm with them. When I'm with you, I might be a Pakeha." With a white man, eh, he's got very different ways. Once you're with him, well, you're *his* to keep! Different with us! I don't give in. I don't give in to him. Ha! On TV I was listening to an Island woman — Rarotonga — the same is happening to her. Her white husband doesn't like *her* ways — like keeping with her race. He doesn't like that. And she was asking, what should I do? It's very hard. Especially when you grew up with your own, with your own colour. It's *hard*. It took me a long time to give in to him. You see, we don't wash our clothes where you wash your dishes. I don't wash my head where you wash your plates and so forth. No. Well, I do now. See, what could I do? I see him washing his clothes in the sink. I used to fight him. It's no use. I had to take. I gave in to him on account of that. Well. At home, the men has their own tubs; the women has their own. When you haven't had your period it's all right: you can have a bath in the men's — in our father's. I do wash in my father's. Well, I was the only child that stayed in our father's house. At Maai. The front room is my mother's. And the other wives were there: Rehe, Te Aue, Mihiroa. Our father was right at the back. Opposite our father's, that's Piimia's, the young wife. Rehe's — Pehirangi — was next to Dad's. And I had a room. We used to do these pao, Maori paos. I knew how. Today I can't. Don't remember. And we used to have prayers in the meeting-house. *Everyone* has to stand up and say prayers. I could do it, once. If someone was to start it for me, I *would* know. Especially chanting; I can chant. I can't now. And Maori hakas. I feel sorry for myself. My husband always says, "Course you're not a Maori!" I said, "Yes. I might be. I mightn't be a Maori — *now*." It's hard. I can't — I feel so — I don't know —

'I think of myself just as somebody that was thrown out.

'I used to love going through to Maungapohatu. Going through the bush. Sometimes it's all boggy and you go down — the horse's hoof is in there and it sits down! Then it walks down again. I used to love that: going through the bog with

Piimia Onekawa, Rua's youngest wife, with Akakura. This photograph belonged to Te Akakura.

the packhorses at the back. It's hard to forget, you know. Now we are living here, it's very different. At times, I like going back there. I was thinking of going to Paetawa. Oh, they are always good to me! Being my father's child. Everytime I go back, I love to see him. I *talk* to them! His father-in-law, old Teka, was one of the Levites. Very nice man, very sensible. He doesn't leap – he just looks at you. Oh, something to do with my father. See, they almost worshipped me. You know, if I hadn't come out into the city –. I went out of Maungapohatu just to get away from that. See, I didn't like the way they were doing to me. I got out. When the opening of the road came, as I told you, I refused. They wanted me to do this, they wanted me to do that! I refused. I didn't like it.'

Our visits to Akakura probably deepened these divisions within her as we took her back into her past. She also travelled with us on many of our visits to the people of the Tauranga valley. In January 1978, Akakura and Puti came on the journey to Maungapohatu. Every one there brought with them their own memories and their own associations. Akakura had said earlier, in talking about her mother's grave at Maungapohatu, that she had once wanted to put up a headstone for her. 'But I was told not to. Well, I listened to them, the old people.[20] Oh, it's no use now, I suppose. Everybody's gone. Only Paetawa lives there, sometimes. Because he was brought up there – was *born* there. He wants to go back. They *do* go back.' And she, too, went back on this occasion. It was to be her last visit. It was full of pain, but it was also a time of great pleasure. It brought back the memories of the police assault of April 1916 – 'it's too cold for eels, really, at Maungapohatu. They are a sign of death, here. Te Aue saw one, at Hautapu, there, where the creeks join the river, just before the police came.' The kiekie, also, doesn't grow on Maungapohatu because of the cold and as we talked about the kiekie mat that is in the meeting-house, Akakura remembered another fine mat that was made from the one kiekie that was found on the mountain – and cut – by a group of women, including Matekoraha Miki, Paetawa's sister. 'Maungapohatu's hair', they called it. It was a tipua: the woman of the mountain. Some say it was Rangiwaitatao; others that it was Whaitiri herself, the divine ancestress of Tuhoe and Rua's 'sister'.[21] Because the women had cut the long, pure white strands, Rua told them that they must use them. Later, all the women died. Puti explained, 'He knew it was a tipua. He wanted to take that thing off. So it wouldn't hurt anybody that goes near it. It's been covered all those years since it's been there. It just happened that these women went over there. Seven of them. All those women – there's

The kiekie mat, which was made from 'Maungapohatu's hair'. This photograph was taken in May 1927 at Rua's house at Maai. Back: Te Urikore Tihi from Ruatoki; Te Aue; Patu; Hikihiki (Ngahiwi) from Ruatoki; Rehe, with her baby son Te Ariki; Piimia, with her daughter Winiati. Front: Harata Toko from Ruatoki, who was on the women's committee at Maungapohatu; Rua. *Alexander Turnbull Library*

nobody living today.'[22]

The kiekie mat which is in the meeting-house at Maungapohatu today is not this mat, although it was made about the same time by Matekoraha. It has two bands of butterflies worked carefully into it and the English words, taken from a popular song, 'Darling why do I get butterflies every time I'm kissing you'! Thus we travelled easily from the magical to the whimsical; from fear of 'old Maori things', as Miria put it when she herself mentioned the kiekie woman on Maungapohatu, to an infectious joy, as the people talked the night away in the meeting-house at Maungapohatu.

In the last seven years of her life, Akakura was a woman who lived with serious heart illness, and in the last two years, a tumour in the stomach. She dealt with these problems as she dealt with everything else: 'I fight them back!' Nor did she hide her doubts about her father's teachings and methods. She once said forthrightly, 'Rua had the brains and the people had the hands.' He organized all the work: the clearing, the planting, and the ploughing that made Matahi, like Maungapohatu before it, a flourishing valley during his lifetime. As she said, 'Our father's word was law.' But with his death, much of the energy which he had generated vanished. If he had manipulated and used his followers, his daughter knew that he had also served them well.

In 1979, when the book *Mihaia* was given its second launching, at Auckland, she met, for the first time, Tom Collins, who had been a constable with the party of police who had assaulted Maungapohatu in 1916. His account of that day had been central to our history and had helped to establish that there had been an 'orchestrated litany of lies', an organized police perjury initiated by senior officers at Rua's trial. Akakura was shy, curious, and powerfully affected by this encounter. She later said with great emphasis, 'He reminds me of my father.' She meant not so much that they were alike but that, as they talked together, Collins had brought back to her the memories of her father.

Akakura lived in full knowledge of her dual lineage and her inherited mana, which was the basis of her fierce independence. She always remembered that her father had said to her, as he lay dying, that although the others would be lost without him, she would survive: 'You are of your blood.' She also knew that she doubted that he was the Maori Christ. This essay is offered in remembrance — he ōhāki — of her courage and her complexities.

Tom Collins and Akakura, November 1979. Akakura is wearing her mother's greenstone brooch. Photograph by Gil Hanly.

NOTES

Full references are to be found in the alphabetical listing of all manuscripts and published books and articles, pp. 212-215. Standard abbreviations used are: MS and MSS (manuscript/s); AJHR *(Appendices to the Journals of the House of Representatives)*. Others are explained in context.

Introduction

1 Recorded in 'Te Maori', TVNZ documentary, 1985.

2 Thompson 1968: 13.

3 Chamberlain 1983: 2.

4 The Scriptural text from which the name is derived is Joel 2: 32:

> Na, te hunga katoa e karanga ana ki te ingoa o Ihowa, ka mawhiti: no te mea ka whai whakaoranga a Hiona, ka pera ano me ta Ihowa i ki ai, a Hiruharama ano hoki, me nga morehu ano e karangatia ana e Ihowa.
>
> And it shall come to pass, that whosoever shall call on the name of the Lord shall be delivered: for in mount Zion and in Jerusalem shall be deliverance, as the Lord hath said, and in the remnant whom the Lord shall call.

5 Conversation of 20 August 1984.

6 Waiata 1: Te Kooti 1766-1890.

7 Paora Delamere's text of this prediction reads, 'he iwi kino taua iwi hou'. The younger child was born of the elder brother, Te Rangipatahi, and the reverse order of the birth of their two children was the first indication of the ill omen. (Delamere n.d.: 59, 65-7.) This prediction is dated in some Ringatu sources as 1802 and Te Kooti is said to have been born in 1814. However, most Europeans who knew him in the 1860s considered him to have been born about 1830.

8 'Ko te teina ano e riro o enei tamariki.' Delamere n.d.: 60. Te Toiroa lived to see all these things come to pass. In September 1865, when he was still residing at Nukutaurua, he predicted the onset of war in Poverty Bay. (W. L. Williams, 6 September 1865, Diary II, 1865-6.) He is said to have died the following year.

9 See J. W. Harris to D. McLean, 7 April 1852, McLean Papers 32: 327. This is the earliest known reference to him, and indicates that he has been baptized by this date.

10 Hobsbawm 1972: [17].

11 '... nga po hehe o Turanga ka pau te muru nga Pakeha'. 9 March 1852, McLean Papers 32: 327.

12 *Gisborne Times*, 16 February 1916.

13 Harris to McLean, 7 August 1865, McLean Papers 32: 327.

14 Harris to McLean, 22 May 1865; meeting of the chiefs with Harris, 25 July 1865, in Harris to McLean, 7 August 1865, McLean Papers 32: 327.

15 Te Kooti attended a Pai Marire meeting held on 12 July to consider giving support to those fighting at Waiapu. W. L. Williams, 12 July 1865, Diary I, 1865.

16 As Mokena himself said, when he was offered a reward for his services in November,' "Mauria to moni, naku tonu taku riri ehara i a koe i te pakeha" ("Take your money away, the fight was mine, not the pakeha's").' Kohere 1949: 59.

17 Neal 1976: 41.

18 Oliver and Thomson 1971: 94.

19 Col. Thomas Porter's account, *Otago Daily Times*, 16 February 1914; also *Auckland Star*, 28 February 1914.

20 To McLean, 14 April 1866, HB 4: 7.

21 Cowan 1956, II: 223.

22 W. L. Williams, 17 February 1866, Diary II, 1865-6.

23 The settler was John Hervey, who had recently moved in amongst them and complained about their perpetual theft from his stores. To McLean, 3 March 1866, McLean Papers 32: 337.

24 To McLean, 4 June 1866, HB 4: 13.

25 'Notes on the Ringa-tu Religion', n.d.: 10.

26 Te Kooti was treated for chronic asthma, which he had all his life, and rendered him 'unfit for work' for lengthy periods. The time in which he recorded these early visions during his fevers is the same period as the medical reports refer to his recurring asthma attacks: particularly, February, March, April and May 1867. (Medical reports, AD 31: 15.) However, it is probable that he was also suffering from tuberculosis, with its recurrent fevers.

27 Te Kooti Arikirangi 1867-8: 1, 7-8. A contemporary transcript, with the translations used here, is in G. H. Davies, Maori Manuscripts III, n.d.

28 21 April: 'Ko tona kakahu kei te hukarere te ma ko tona mahunga kei nga whetu nui ko tona karauna kei te ra ko tona whitiki kei te torengitanga o te ra kei te rerenga ake hoki ko tona kowhiuwhiu kei te kopere ko tona tokotoko kahore ano i kitea i tenei ao. . . . Ka mea ia e kore koe e mahue i a au me toku iwi ano hoki. . . . Tuhituhia ki to ngakau no te mea e kore koe e mahue i a au a maku koe e whakaako.' Te Kooti Arikirangi 1867-8: 12-13, 15, 17.

29 R. Biggs to McLean, 17 July 1867, McLean Papers 32: 162.

30 1 July 1868, AD 31: 16.

31 Explanation of the covenants by Robert (Boy) Biddle, Greenwood 1980: 95.

32 Colenso 1871: 23.

33 The quotation is taken from the Kenyan novelist Ngugi Wa Thiong'o (1972: 89), who was writing of the Hebraic traditions adopted in precisely the same way by the Black West Indian resistance movements.

34 13 June 1867, AJHR 1868, A-15E: 19. That this advice was taken is confirmed by Biggs to McLean, 28 September 1868, McLean Papers 32: 162.

35 W. L. Williams, 20 July 1868, Diary 1868-9.

36 Paora Matuakore, Wi Pere, and others to 'Warana Pirihi' (possibly George Preece, interpreter for the Resident Magistrate at Wairoa and then in the Wairoa militia formed against Te Kooti, or more probably the interpreter James W. Preece, who was acting for Te Aitanga a Mahaki in the land confiscation negotiations at Poverty Bay), 22 August 1868, VF 993, Box 3.

37 F. Helyar to Commanding Officer of the Militia, Napier, 30 October 1868, AD 1: 71.

38 Morris (Morete) MS, n.d. Wi Pere had earlier been accused of being a Pai Marire supporter and of supplying them with both ammunition and information.

39 Morris MS, n.d. Also Wi Pere's account given to W. G. Mair, 7 December 1868, AJHR 1869, A-10: 30.

40 Nihoniho 1913: 36.

41 I am indebted to Dr James Belich for allowing me to read the draft chapters concerning Te Kooti from his forthcoming book on the New Zealand wars. Dr Belich analyses this planned raid and its purposes, as well as many other aspects of Te Kooti's military leadership, for which there is no place here.

42 Account given to J. H. St. John, 2 April 1870, AJHR 1870, A-8B: 26-7.

43 Wi Pere's account, 7 December 1868, AJHR 1869, A-10: 30. The original is to be found in W. G. Mair, MS 1868-9.

44 To McLean, 23 July 1869, AJHR 1869, A-10: 91.

45 Capt. A. Rich to Dr D. Pollen, 26 July 1869, AJHR 1869, A-10: 87.

46 AJHR 1870, A-8B: 28.

47 Gilbert Mair to Pollen, 30 December 1869, AJHR 1870, A-8A: 20.

48 Binney 1984: 365-6.

49 W. G. Mair, 14 January 1873, Mair MSS 1871-5.

50 R. Bush to McLean, 14 October 1873, AJHR 1874, G-2B: 4.

51 The house was not finally completed until 1882 and was opened on 2 January 1883.

52 'On the first day of the first month shalt thou set up the tabernacle of the tent of the congregation.'

53 '. . . In the seventh month, in the first day of the month, shall ye have a sabbath, a memorial of blowing of trumpets, an holy convocation.'

54 See Binney 1984: 363 for a fuller version of this narrative. Arihia, wife of Apirana Ngata, told her daughter Lena that Te Kooti wore the diamond in the little kit when he rode into Opotiki.

People had to hide their gaze from its bright light. In some traditions, the diamond came from the *Rifleman*.

55   *Rotorua Daily Post*, 15 May 1971.

56   Conversation with Heta Rua, 23 May 1982.

57   R. Bush, annual report, 30 April 1880, AJHR 1880, G-4: 8.

58   Bryce, 13 February 1883, AJHR 1883, A-8: 5. The date given was 1874, but a Maori text of the same speech makes it clear that Te Kooti said, 'This is the tenth year that has gone by since I ceased holding the sword, which I laid at the feet of the King.' The date 1873 is confirmed by Tawhiao's visit to Te Kooti and the latter's carving of the meeting-house, Tokanganui a Noho, which he began in September of that year.

59   From Te Horo, Ohiwa, 1893. Quoted, for example, in *Te Whetu Marama o Te Kotahitanga*, 5 September 1931.

60   'Nga kupu kei roto i enei takiwa ko nga tangata o Turanga kei te hanga whare mo Te Koti mo tona taenga mai ki konei kia matakitakiti[a] [te] hoki e te ao katoa tona ahua'. Contemporary translation. 27 October 1886, MA 23: 8(b).

61   The text is waiata 53: Te Kooti 1766-1890. The lineation and the translation is based upon a version generously prepared for the authors by Wiremu Parker, Ahorangi of Victoria University, Wellington, but to which we have made some alterations following a recorded sung version (in the Archive of Maori and Pacific Music, Anthropology Department, University of Auckland), together with other sources. The song is immensely complex, partly because it plays off and retains many references from the original Ngati Kahungunu oriori, two versions of which may be found in Ngata and Jones 1969, III: 54-61. In the original Ngati Kahungunu song, Turanga was also described as the seat of warfare, with its matāwha (bewitching spells), which had driven others into exile. A note in the Te Kooti manuscript explains 'nga pure tawhiti te kaunati hikahika' as 'te ahi tohu', the fire of divination, which in the original song is said to be generated by the fire-stick (kaunati) of the ancestor Tura, but here is attributed to David, King of Israel. The language of Te Kooti's threatened destruction after his escape from Wharekauri is also derived from the original. Korotimutimu (or Karotimutimu) was a tipua who devoured men at Napier and at Taurangakoau, a landing place for canoes on Cape Kidnappers. The reference here, therefore, is also to the fact that Ngati Kahungunu were then pursuing Te Kooti, to whom he was to be 'fed'. The Te Kooti manuscript text concludes with a note which states that those Maori and Pakeha opponents who were waiting for him at Turanga in hatred, in 1888, were hostile to him because of the death of their relatives in 1868, and in the bitter siege of Ngatapa on 5 January 1869.

62   See Ward 1980 for an account of Te Kooti's arrest and the consequent long drawn-out trials. We have not gone into this episode because it does not arise in any of the narratives told in this book and it has already been well documented.

63   To T. W. Lewis, Under-Secretary Native Department, 22 February 1884, AJHR 1884, G-4A: 5.

64   Conversation with Robert (Boy) Biddle, Ringatu tohunga from Kutarere, 17 February 1982.

65   Wilson, n.d.: 141.

66   'Prediction', n.d.: 76. 'Anatekere' is an example of 'writing in tongues', which Te Kooti adopted from the traditions told of the prophet Daniel, who alone could read the writing. See Daniel 5.

67   Private MS.

68   At Awanui a Rangi, Poroporo, 1889. 'Prediction', n.d.: 76.

69   Maungapohatu Notebook 1881-1916: 90-1.

70   Conversation with Te Puhi Tatu, daughter of one of the Riwaiti, Tatu Horopapera, 22 January 1978.

71   Te Puhi Tatu, 22 January 1978.

72   For a full account of the arrest and trial of Rua see Binney, Chaplin, and Wallace 1979: Chapter III; Webster 1979: Chapters VIII and IX.

73   Conversation, 25 January 1978.

74   Conversation with Harimate (Materoa) Roberts, of Tataiahape, 17 May 1978.

75   Ned Brown, 14 February 1982.

76   Green 1960: 67.

77   Private MS.

78   Leviticus 6: 30.

79 Revd Thomas Grace to the Church Missionary Society, 8 February 1878, CN/045.
80 Best, Maori Notes, n.d., I: 57. Taken from an unidentified MS of John White's, 2 August 1912.
81 Gudgeon 1907: 74.
82 Mitchell 1944: 90-1.
83 Gudgeon 1905: 179.
84 Conversation with Joe Te Maipi, her grandson, 10 May 1984.
85 Lesson visited New Zealand in 1824. Sharp 1971: 97, 99.
86 Best 1903: 24. Italics mine.
87 There are wide tribal variations today. Ngati Porou of the East Coast are known particularly for accepting leadership by senior women. Many of their hapū have taken women's names and strong women leaders were, and are, preferred to weak male leaders. Ability and primogeniture of birth are clearly favoured over gender in determining status in this tribe. Tuhoe also contain hapū whose names derive from women. Primogeniture is accepted as the base of leadership among Ngai Tahumatua of Ngati Kahungunu from Nukutaurua, where if the women are from the senior descent line, they undertake all aspects of leadership, including the formal speech-making. Generally in Eastern Polynesia, primogeniture rather than sex, was favoured for establishing seniority. A close look at early nineteenth-century Maori society from this point of view would be interesting. There are sufficient examples in the nineteenth century of women from various tribes possessing mana and tapu that it seems likely that the status of Maori women has been unduly depressed in the standard historical interpretation — partly because the recorders were often European men interpreting and observing the 'proper' behaviour for women through the prism of their cultural expectations. European attitudes towards women's roles may also have been gradually imbibed by nineteenth-century Maori males and women's roles made more prescribed by them. Margaret Orbell suggests, in her essay on the traditional Maori family, that the power of the woman's family and matrilocal residence declined greatly during the nineteenth century. Orbell 1978: 114.
88 Hanson 1982: 356; Shirres 1982: 44-5.
89 Hanson 1982: 375.
90 Locke 1981: 156.
91 Murchie 1984: 82.
92 Albert Wendt, opening address to the Pacific History Conference, Suva, Fiji, June 1985.
93 See Ong 1982: 31-85 concerning patterns of thought in oral societies.
94 Sissons 1984: 323.
95 Reneti and Roche 1982: 76-84; *Rotorua Daily Post*: 15, 22, 29 May; 5, 12, 19, 26 June 1971. A slightly abridged version of the latter also appeared in the *Whakatane Historical Review* 1972, 20: 19-27. A portrait of Moerangi Ratahi may also be found in King and Friedlander 1972: n.p.
96 Reneti and Roche 1982: 76.

Heni Brown

1   'Kihai koe i rongo he mana no Kuini'. Waiata 50: Te Kooti 1766-1890.
2   Ned Brown, welcome speech given in the house Te Ngawari, 6 June 1982.
3   Ibid.
4   In this story, Heni has confused Captain Thomas Porter with Captain Reginald Biggs, who was held responsible for sending the Pai Marire prisoners from Gisborne. The story is often told of how Te Kooti was ordered onto the boat, despite his protests of innocence. Paratene Turangi, the Rongowhakaata chief, was particularly brutal as he imitated the Pakeha, crying, 'Go ona the boat!' It is still recalled that the women fell and cried for mercy, as they gathered soil from their native land to take with them as they were kicked onto the ships. When he returned from exile in 1868, Te Kooti killed both Paratene and Biggs as utu. Porter himself was also deeply involved in the siege of Waerenga a Hika and the later pursuit of Te Kooti.
5   Hori Gage (Hori Keeti) was a Ringatu tohunga and a matakite (visionary) and faith-healer from Omaio, Bay of Plenty. See also Heni Sunderland's and Miria's narratives, pp. 119, 142.
6   There is the whakataukī, or saying, 'Ka mate te matua, waiho [te] iho ki tona uri ana mākutu': When the parent dies, his (or her) mākutu power is handed down to the offspring. (Recorded

in Grey NZMMSS 31:14, cited Shirres 1982: 40.) The line of descent from the ancestor is through the hair, iho.

7   Ngaitai were the people of Torere, to whom Meri Puru's mother, Wikitoria, belonged. They had had bitter conflicts with their neighbours, Whakatohea, and also Ngariki Kaiputahi, the people of Mangatu, where Meri Puru's father, Hori, lived.

8   Heni's mother Dawn — Te Atapo — died on 13 October 1961. She was the daughter of Wiremu Wharekino of Te Aitanga a Mahaki.

9   It would seem more likely that Te Kooti took the placenta, whenua, rather than the womb or uterus, but it is possible that Meri Puru had a prolapse of the uterus. This was rare and dangerous. There are also traditional accounts of rendering the womb barren. Huiarei, wife of the ancestor Toi, after she had given birth to a son, had her fruitful womb dried — tūpā — by a ritual ceremony called tūpātia, 'closed'. (Best 1975: 41-2.) Rituals involving drying the placenta to induce infertility were used: see Heni Sunderland's story, p. 113.

10   From the dialogue of 27 November 1983.

11   Julie was born on 28 February 1957.

12   That is, tonsilitis.

13   In this story the word puku is used in two different senses. It is the stomach or belly, but it is also the name given to the inflammation of the throat.

14   Richard Ngariki was born on 9 September 1958. He died of pneumonia on 30 December and was buried in the Mangatu cemetery on the headland above the pā.

15   Kapi Adams was a matakite, visionary, from Taumarunui. He died on 30 August 1984 at the age of eighty-two. Unlike Hori Gage, he was not a registered Ringatu tohunga.

16   Heni is here referring to the Mangatu Incorporation, which was set up in 1947. Today, there are about 3000 shareholders, mostly people of Te Aitanga a Mahaki tribe. But Ned claimed descent from the original owners, Ngariki Kaiputahi, and rejected the view that their land had been conquered and absorbed by Whakatohea and Te Aitanga a Mahaki.

17   From the narrative of 30 November 1983.

18   See Reremoana's story, pp. 58-9. The Fifth of August is the remembrance service for the drowning of the Omaio schoolchildren, in 1900, which is vividly recalled all along the coast of the eastern Bay of Plenty.

19   Rutene Irwin, Heni's younger brother.

20   Hori Puru was sent with the first batch of prisoners to Wharekauri, landing on 15 March 1866.

21   Ngariki Kaiputahi, and its old chief Pera Uetuku, felt that their claims, as the original owners, had not been properly upheld by the Native Land Court. (The court was established in 1865 to investigate and determine Maori land title, but in practice it mostly became an agent for dispossession.) In 1881, the ownership of the Mangatu Block No. 1 had been given to twelve individuals, itself an illegal decision. They were also mainly of Ngati Waahia and Te Aitanga a Mahaki tribes, or those who claimed to have conquered Ngariki. Pera Uetuku was, however, included among the twelve as the Ngariki chief, as was Hori Puru, as a Ngati Waahia elder. (See Heni's whakapapa.) Wi Pere was also included as a Ngati Waahia and Te Aitanga a Mahaki chief. In practice, the Wi Pere family gained control of the Mangatu lands. In the subsequent complex history of the Mangatu Block No. 1, the majority of the Maori owners were excluded from control over their lands through the domination of the Wi Pere family, despite the fact that the land title was changed in 1893 into an incorporation of all the shareholders. Deeply in debt, in 1917 this land was taken over by the East Coast Commissioner, a Crown-established administrator. It was not until 1947 that the Mangatu Incorporation was finally set up under Maori control. However, Ned Brown's primary claims, through his descent from Rawiri Tamanui and Pera Uetuku, chiefs of Ngariki, have not been recognized. Ned put it bitterly, 'True, intelligent people like Wi Pere, they deprived the original owners, and the land started to drift down the river. But Te Kooti has always predicted it.' This is a reference to the massive erosion and the recurrent flooding of the Mangatu river, the consequence of the bad, early land administration under Wi Pere, which has resulted in the destruction of the original Mangatu settlement. Te Kooti had predicted this loss: 'I see your land going into the river and going out to sea. This is the work of prominent men.'

22   From the dialogue of 27 November 1983.

23   Heni is referring to the comprehensive benefit system which was initiated under the Social Security Act of 1938. Family benefit was paid for all children under sixteen years of age to low-income families, from 1939. Higher unemployment and sickness benefits for married

men with dependent children came into effect and maternity payments were made. For these purposes Maori customary marriage was not recognized. A marriage in the presence of an officiating Ringatu minister, who was registered under the Marriage Act of 1908, would have been recognized. The Ringatu Church had been registering its ministers for such purposes from 1915. For many Maori families, dependent on farms which could not adequately support them, welfare payments, and particularly their expansion from 1946, made a real difference in mitigating the conditions of poverty in which they were living.

24 She died 11 July 1944. Her grandson, Heemi Kauta Wharekino, said then that she was 101.

25 Seniority is determined by birth, but in most Maori tribes, leadership over people descends to the male. However, among Ngati Porou of the East Coast, and to some extent among those tribes of the Bay of Plenty who trace their descent from the Mataatua canoe and the woman, Muriwai, who, in their tradition, rescued it — so giving the name Whakatane, 'to become a man', to the place where the event occurred — leadership can be exercised by women of seniority. See Maaka's story p. 88, where the rank of certain women is an important reason for their preparedness to be outspoken.

26 There is an expression, 'he iho makawe rau', 'a line of a hundred strands of hair', for the lines of descent from the ancestors onto the head. It emphasizes the lineage from the tīpuna — te iho, that is the line of descent and the strand of hair itself — and the sacredness that consequently resides in the hair and the head. The iho is also the umbilicus, attaching the child to its mother. Meri Puru possessed this tapu of seniority of descent, as well as the tapu bestowed upon her by Te Kooti. Tapu was not exclusive to males. Meri Puru's tapu was traditional in that it was the state of being under the influence of the atua. Hanson 1982: 344.

27 Reuben Brown was the son of Captain William Henry Tucker, an early settler in Poverty Bay, and Mere Kingi.

28 From the dialogue of 27 November 1983.

Reremoana Koopu

1 H. W. Brabant, Resident Magistrate at Opotiki, to Donald McLean, 3 June 1872, McLean Papers 32: 171.

2 Waiata 50(2): Te Kooti 1766-1890.

3 *New Zealand Times*, 7 October 1984; 9 June 1985.

4 Young to Secretary of Education, 12 September 1900, Omaio Native School File, E 44/4, III.

5 Omaio Maori Deaths Register 1918.

6 W. Coughlan to Elsdon Best, 28 October 1916. Best, Maori Notes, n.d., II: 143.

7 Revd Henry Young was appointed teacher at Omaio school at the beginning of 1900. His daughters, Lilian, Edith, Jennie, and Mabel all helped with the school, both formally and informally, until 1906 when the family left.

8 Reremoana describes how she went with the children from Omaio, walking to Maraenui after school on the Friday, when she was turned back from the journey that was to end in disaster. Sixteen children, and the two adults with them, were drowned crossing the Motu river in a canoe. Reremoana's sister Hariata, who was twelve years old, was among them. They had been returning from Maraenui to Omaio on Sunday morning.

9 Indeed, six immediate families lost two children each.

10 There are other traditions, too. One attributes the cause of the drownings to a land conflict between Whanau a Apanui and Ngaitai. Whanau a Apanui had been able to sustain their claims to the Tunapahore block against Ngaitai, in the Native Land Court hearing held in 1898. The loss of the children was brought about, it is said, by Whanau a Apanui's deliberate dispossession of Ngaitai. Subsequently, the block was partitioned between the two tribes. Another version attributes the drownings to the prediction of Te Kooti. He visited Maraenui and noticed that the meeting-house, Te Poho o Apanui, 'he whare tapu tēnei' ('this is a tapu house'), the people's house for worship, was deteriorating badly. Consequently, he foresaw 'te hinga a te wharenui' ('the fall of the house') meaning also that the faith would fail. Te Poho o Apanui indeed did fall and had to be demolished, shortly after the drownings. It had not been renewed by 1905, as Reremoana's story later indicates. In this explanation, among Te Whanau a Apanui, the drowning of the children is attributed to their neglect of the house and the faith. Consequently, later, the whare karakia was erected by Paul Delamere and he also made a

particular point of teaching the Ringatu beliefs to the Maraenui children. See, for example, the article sent by the schoolchildren to *Te Ao Hou* in 1957, 'Te Kooti Returns from the Dead'. See, too, Maaka's story concerning the transferring of 'the seed' of the faith from Maraenui, the old centre of power, to Whitianga, and her own grandfather's prediction of the disaster that would occur at Maraenui (pp. 75, 87).

11   See also Miria's story for when the people of Rua changed their names, p. 146.

12   Reremoana herself did not change her name, perhaps because it was already appropriate. It means tossed by the sea.

13   The family of Paora Ngamoki, the chief of Maraenui. Paora died on 1 August 1917. See also Maaka's story, p. 78.

14   A rāhui, or prohibition, was placed on fishing (and also the collecting of driftwood) for a great distance along the coast for five years. Only ten of the children were found, and the boatman, Pani Retimana. In one oral tradition, the people were so angry with Pani that, when they discovered his body they pushed it back into the water. They continued to search, but found no more children. Te Kohi Delamere, whose sister, Ani, was the woman drowned with the children, called a hui to discover what was wrong. When he learnt that Pani's body had been thrown back, he told them that they must pray to God for *all* to be found. After that, it is said, the children were found, one by one. But in revenge, Pani's body was buried, without Te Kohi's knowledge, not facing the east and the sun, but the west and the sea.

15   That is, the people from the Whakatane and Opotiki areas in the eastern Bay of Plenty.

16   Pani was not the regular boatman; he had been going to Omaio to get a horse that morning, so he was entrusted with the children. His own daughter was drowned.

17   The house Te Iwarau – which means '1900' – has above its door the date of its construction: 1905. The monument to the children, with all their names and ages listed, stands on the marae. It was unveiled at the hui of 20-22 March 1905. Within this story there is another story of destruction: that of Henry Young. In misguided zealousness, he erected his own monument to the children in the school grounds in 1901. It was far too premature; it was also inscribed in English; it had not been given by the community but by Pakeha well-wishers. From this time, Henry Young's relations with the community collapsed, because he had failed to listen to their objections. In 1901 and 1902, there were petitions from the parents to have him removed from the school. He finally left, destroyed by the 'season of bitterness', as he put it. None of this conflict, when the adult community closed ranks against the teacher in their anger, was recounted by Reremoana. But both Paora Ngamoki, the chief of Maraenui, and Koopu Erueti, the head of the Ringatu community, signed the first petition of 1901, and there were ninety-one signatures on the second, in March 1902. However, neither of Reremoana's parents appear to have signed, although two of her older sisters did.

18   Queen Victoria School for Maori Girls, an Anglican establishment, was opened in 1903 in Auckland. Reremoana attended in 1907-8. She gained her competency certificate at the end of 1907, when she was in Standard Five.

19   The policy of Queen Victoria School, then, was particularly to emphasize dress-making skills. The school also saw itself specifically as a 'continuation' of the 'native school', in that the staff did not wish to take younger girls. They were afraid that a young girl, taught from her earliest years there, would probably become 'so Europeanised as to be out of sympathy with her Maori friends'. (Inspection Report: 30 November 1907. Queen Victoria School File, E 44/6, I.) This awareness, and a commitment to the language, were among the strengths of the school.

20   Captain John Skinner, who owned and traded in many vessels along the East Coast. His schooner the *Kaeo* was the only boat that called at Omaio at that time.

21   This spectacular visit of the US Atlantic Fleet was in August 1908. It was a carnival occasion for Auckland: 100,000 people lined the shores of the harbour to see the entry of the white ships. As Reremoana clearly recalls, it was also an occasion for a display of outdoor electric lighting, the first the city had seen.

22   Reremoana was married on 20 April 1913 at Koopu Erueti's 'private dwelling' at Maraenui. Canon Hakaraia Pahewa was the vicar of Te Kaha from 1895-1940. He was also one of the very few Maori photographers. He took many fine pictures of Maori life on the East Coast in the early twentieth century, and, fortunately, sent examples to the *Auckland Weekly News*, where they have survived. See p. 83.

23   Toma August died on 29 November 1915.

24   The five Ringatu marae south of Te Kaha maintain this circuit for the Twelfths; Whitianga

does not have the Twelfths, only the Firsts of June and November, the celebration of the planting cycle. See Maaka's story, p. 80.

25 Koopu Erueti is registered as having died on 13 March 1937 aged seventy-eight. The monument erected to him at Maraenui gives a different age for him — seventy-four — and date of death — the 12th. This kind of discrepancy between local memory and written official record is common. The written record is only as good as the informant's knowledge and the recorder's comprehension of spoken Maori. It is not necessarily to be trusted. See also Maaka's story, p. 78.

26 The whare karakia was put up by Paul, a builder, helped by his cousin Te Aroha Toopi from Maraenui, and old Tuakana Poihipi, and all the Whitianga and Maraenui people. It was tapu. There was a special poti, box, or sometimes a jar, in a room at the rear for the burnt coins, the offerings, a practice which Paul Delamere later ceased. (See Maaka's story, pp.81-2.) On the sides of the main room there are four elevated and very narrow alcoves, inset into the walls. They are just wide enough to stand in, and are for the 'policemen', who being above the congregation can keep their eye on them. Paul devised this system instead of having the pirihimana walking up and down, disturbing the service. On one occasion, it is said, they tried to squeeze a vast policeman into one of the alcoves, but he fell out!

27 St. Stephen's School for Maori Boys, an Anglican boarding school in Auckland. Queen Victoria was founded as its counterpart, largely on the initiative of the Young Maori Party.

28 The Saxby station on the Motu river was one of the great East Coast sheep stations. It was leased from its Maori owners, overgrazed, and exhausted.

29 See also Tihei's story, pp. 101-2.

30 Huhana Moengaroa was born on 11 April 1912.

31 It is traditional Maori practice for the husband to be at the birth of the child.

32 The bridge across the Motu was opened on 25 November 1929, allowing cars to reach Omaio for the first time.

33 William Bird, Senior Inspector of Native Schools, 1904-18, and then Superintendent of Native Education, often nicknamed predictably, Te Manu.

34 The Black Flu was at its most severe among the Maori population, and, particularly, in the eastern Bay of Plenty. Reremoana's older sister, Mary (Kahurangi), and her brother, Te Owai, died in the pandemic. Tohi's sister, Kawhena (Susan), whom Reremoana goes on to talk about, died on 18 November 1918. She was fourteen years old. Tini August, Te Hurinui's son who was born shortly after the drownings and named for them, also died. Hori Gage, who was then farming at Maraenui, and Tuakana Poihipi lost their wives. The Flu affected every family in this tiny community. C. N. Vickridge, who broke in the Haparapara station nearby, as an old man also remembered the Flu as having been particularly devastating. He hauled the carcass of a bull on a sledge down to Omaio to make soup, which he brewed in an iron whaling pot on the beach. (*Opotiki News*, 2 February 1972.) See also Miria's story concerning the Flu, p. 148.

35 Tuberculosis was very common in the Maori rural communities. It was 'poverty's illness', and being highly infectious, spread readily through the population, partly because of their communal living style. Systematic diagnosis in the Maori population and, consequently, preventive measures were only begun in the 1950s, an indictment of the medical profession.

36 Tatana Koopu, Tohi's brother, died at Maraenui on 28 May 1930 of TB. He was thirty-four years of age.

37 Tohi Koopu died on 27 December 1959. He was seventy-five.

38 See Maaka's story, p. 84.

39 Horopapera Tatu was one of Rua's followers, from Tawhana, and was an important informant for the history of Rua, *Mihaia*. See Binney, Chaplin, and Wallace, 1979: 159.

40 The threatened ban on fishing at the mouth of the Motu, and particularly during the spawning season, 1 December-31 March is now involving the Maraenui community, and Arama, as a leader, in a struggle for their traditional fishing rights, which they claim under the Treaty of Waitangi. Such a ban, intended to protect the snapper, would also destroy the kahawai fishing, which occurs as they run up the Motu. Were this to happen, even Reremoana's spirit might falter.

Maaka Jones

1   Waiata 49: Te Kooti 1766-1890. The waiata is based on Meroiti's song, first published by Sir George Grey in *Nga Moteatea* in 1853: 27. Te Kooti adapted it for the occasion, and the references are to the journey he will take to Maketu, and on to the headland Kohi, the point at Whakatane, from where he will first see the Motu river. Maaka explained the last lines of the waiata as a request to Whanau a Apanui to take him to the water to wash away his sins, and the pain of not being able to come with them. 'Ki te wai wehe ai' refers to the rite of going to the water, and sprinkling oneself to confirm one's belief in the faith, and here specifically, the Biblically-inspired kupu whakaari. 'Aroha' is used in the sense of sorrow, or distress. The lineation adopted is derived from an article on the two waiata by Bob Pearson (where he compares the texts), to be published by the Maori Studies Department of the University of Canterbury. The translation is derived in part from Pearson, but changes have been made upon advice from Wiremu Parker and Mac Whakamoe, a Tuhoe elder, whom Mr Parker consulted.

2   Interview with Paul Delamere by Elsdon Craig, *New Zealand Herald*, 25 July 1970.

3   W. G. Mair to Dr Pollen, 7 December 1868, Letterbook 1868-9. Reprinted AJHR 1869, A-10: 31.

4   Ema is the youngest child of Paul and Hannah, born on 28 January 1930.

5   Ihimaera and Long 1982: 58-9; Wedde and McQueen 1985.

6   Delamere n.d.: 84.

7   Riki Gage is the son of Hori Gage.

8   The first woman who was registered as a tohunga, or officiating minister, was Mrs Airini Taoho in 1960. Mrs Ngoingoi Pewhairangi, from Tokomaru, was also registered in the same year as Maaka.

9   The waiata is dated Maraenui, 1 July 1887. This Rā Te Kooti did, in fact, attend. Maaka may be condensing this event and Te Kooti's later visit to the Bay of Plenty, in 1889, when he turned back at Omarumutu only to be arrested at Waiotahe, in order to prevent him from going through to his home, Gisborne. The road at that time turned inland from the coast at Omarumutu, south-west of Maraenui.

10   Te Kooti had been constantly watched by government agents but after his pardon of 1883 his movements had not been checked, until panic provoked his arrest in the Bay of Plenty.

11   The administrative headship of the Ringatu Church was formalized with the title of President when Koopu Erueti was chosen. Then, following his death, Paul Delamere was elected with the revived title, Poutikanga. See also Reremoana's story, p. 65.

12   Te Kohi died on 26 July 1932. The death certificate recorded his age as ninety.

13   Heremia had been killed in the First World War.

14   Sir Norman Perry, Moderator of the Presbyterian Church in 1964, and at present a consultant for the Whakatohea Trust Board, first came to the Coast in 1937 as a missionary with the United Maori Mission. Although Paul Delamere convinced him that he could not 'claim them', the two men became close friends, while Sir Norman's influence on the Ringatu faith and its teachings in the Bay of Plenty has been considerable.

15   Paul Delamere completed Standard Four at Omaio school, in 1901. Unable to get into Te Aute College he left and went to work in Opotiki. Subsequently he went to the South Island, where he worked for seven years at various jobs before returning to Whitianga.

16   Samuel Delamere was a French Canadian whaler who settled at the mouth of the Motu river in the 1840s. He lived with Irihapeti Te Ha, but when he returned to North America, she remarried. He later tried to reclaim his son, but the people of Maraenui forced him to give up the child to them.

17   From the French 'de la mer' (of the sea), or 'de la mère' (of the mother).

18   The Omaio schoolteacher's log book for 12 November 1934 has: 'There was great excitement this morning. A whale was sighted at 9.10 and the whole school went up on to the ridge by the gum trees and watched for twenty minutes. A boat went out to chase the whale.'

19   Paul Delamere became chairman of the school committee in 1935, two years after Maaka started school.

20   Sir Apirana Ngata, as Minister of Native Affairs between 1928 and 1934, supported the Native Schools' programme, which made English the language of instruction. He said, 'Maori parents

do not like their children being taught in Maori, even in the Maori schools, as they argue that the children are sent there to learn English and the ways of the English. The [Maori] language should be the language of the home.' He placed the burden of maintaining Maori as a living language on the family and particularly on Maori mothers: 'They have it in their power to inculcate bilingualism.' (Cited in Barrington and Beaglehole 1974: 206.) The kōhanga reo movement of the early 1980s is just such a response, but one which has come only when the survival of the language itself is threatened.

21 Turakina Maori Girls' College was opened in 1905, its founding purpose being to inculcate a strong Christian education, as well as a knowledge of hygiene and domestic skills. It became one of the famous Maori schools because, like Queen Victoria School, it upheld the language and the cultural identity of its pupils. Ethel Kinross was principal from 1920 to 1950.

22 Revd John Laughton had been the pioneer Presbyterian missionary at Maungapohatu and was then the Superintendent of the Maori Missions of the Presbyterian Church. He retained a close personal involvement with the Tuhoe and the Ringatu. See also Miria's story, p. 149.

23 As in Heni Brown's story, this is a reference to the sending of Te Kooti onto the boat, when the Rongowhakaata chief, Paratene Turangi, mimicked the Pakeha officers.

24 Project Employment Programme. This scheme was initiated by the government in 1980 to provide short-term work for the unemployed, its purpose being 'to assist in minimizing long duration unemployment'.

25 See Reremoana's story, p. 58.

26 Paul Delamere died on 19 December 1981. He was ninety-six.

27 Ngarori died on 14 October 1939. She was 105 years old.

Hei Ariki Algie

1 Capt. C. Westrup to D. McLean, 'Maories Murdered at Poverty Bay, Nov 10, 1868 and following days', McLean Papers 32: 21; W. L. Williams to McLean, 15 and 19 November 1868, McLean Papers 32: 22.

2 Cowan 1956, II: 450-1.

3 Obituary article on Putiputi Smith by Leo Fowler, cutting, n.s.: 7 April 1972, Whakatane Museum.

4 Weteni was described in the account of Te Kooti's capture of prisoners at Patutahi and Oweta written by Maraea Morete, whose own husband, Pera Taihuka, was shot on Te Kooti's orders. She said that the little boy, who was about four years old, was brought before his father by Natana, who was one of the chiefs from Oweta. Natana 'wished to make peace but Te Kooti took them all prisoners shut them up in a house & placed a guard over them'. Natana's life was at first saved by one of Te Kooti's wives, who kept him to look after the boy, 'who was away from his mother & very fretful', but he was shot the following day. Morris MS, n.d.

5 J. C. Richmond to Colonel T. Haultain, Defence Minister, 19 December 1868, AD 1: 75.

6 Putiputi was born on 31 June 1890, three years before Te Kooti's death. She died at Manutuke on 19 February 1972.

7 Tawhi Brown was the granddaughter of Meri Kingi Brown and Te Kooti's brother, Komene. She was brought up by Te Kooti as his adopted daughter and was regarded as a very knowledgeable old lady. She also (according to Ned Brown) played tricks on Leo Fowler, a local historian and author of a history of Te Mana o Turanga meeting-house, by making up stories about Te Kooti. She said, 'He is too inquisitive, he would like to know everything, so I give him the wrong stories!' See also Heni Sunderland's story and whakapapa, pp. 108, 117.

8 Hariata – Charlotte – was the elder of the two girls and as the daughter of Rangi Rikirangi was descended through the senior and male line. See Tihei's whakapapa.

9 Waioeka was steeped in Ringatu tradition. Granddaughter of Tamihana Teketeke, who had been taken prisoner at Waerenga a Hika in 1865, she married Mahaki Brown, a grandson of the whaler William Brown, one of the earliest settlers in Poverty Bay. (See Heni Sunderland's whakapapa.) She died on 13 November 1959 aged eighty-six. She had attended one of the last of the traditional schools of learning, the house Maraehinahina, at which Wi Pere MHR was also taught. There, pupils learnt by rote in the dark. (See Maaka's story concerning her father's methods of teaching his children, p. 75.) Waioeka told her son, George Brown, that at the end of the teachings they were each given a little piece of dried, hard, flesh to eat. She thought it

was human and found herself unable to eat more than a tiny portion. She kept some of it in her mouth and when she went out, spat it away. She said that she always wished she hadn't, because then her knowledge would have been better. This practice was, presumably, a variant form of whatu whakahoro, whereby pupils at the whare wānanga were expected to eat small fragments of stone to seal their learning. (See Heni Brown's story, in Binney 1984: 355, 387.) It is unusual that a woman attended a whare wānanga, but women of rank are known to have been, and still are, tohunga. See Maaka's story, p. 74.

10   Tihei got her certificate in 1928.

11   Rikirangi Hohepa was a nephew of Te Kooti, who was brought up by him at Te Kuiti. He is one of the four men who are said to have hidden the body of Te Kooti, after secretly excavating it from Te Horo, Ohiwa, where it had been buried. The last survivor of the four, Rikirangi died on 5 October 1944, apparently without revealing where Te Kooti's remains lie. It is a task of Te Kooti's predicted successor to discover them, which Rua failed to do.

12   Hoera Poaka is particularly remembered as the kaitiaki of the tapu meeting-house Rongopai during the 1920s.

13   See Miria's story for the similar manner in which the Maungapohatu people catered for their manuhiri, pp. 137-8.

14   That is, narrow lengths of carpet for hallways.

15   Charlotte was born on 7 July 1912; Queenie on 30 August 1915; Mary — Meretene Himoa — on 6 February 1913.

16   In 1878 Oriwia was escorted back from Te Kuiti, where she had been living with Te Kooti, to visit her family at Te Reinga. (Lambert 1925: 703-4.) Reihana (or Horotiu), the brother of Te Waru Tamatea, was her companion. Both men were strong followers of Te Kooti and were now also living in exile from their tribe — Ngati Kahungunu — at Waiotahe in the Bay of Plenty. Subsequently, Oriwia married Weteni, who was considerably younger than her. Their eldest child, Rangi Rikirangi, was born about 1886. Undoubtedly this union, which was disapproved of by the Ringatu and by Te Kooti himself, who is said to have cursed his son and all his issue, was a cause for Weteni's particular reticence with his grandchildren.

17   Dr Tutere Wi Repa was a graduate of Te Aute College and Otago Medical School. He was also knowledgeable on local Maori history and was an informant for J. A. Mackay in his account of Poverty Bay, Mackay 1966.

18   Harakeke. An infusion made from flax roots was commonly used as a laxative and it could also induce abortion. See also Heni Sunderland's story, p. 118.

19   See Heni Sunderland's story, p. 118.

20   Hori Rikirangi's death was attributed, by some, to the curse said to have been placed on the family.

21   Weteni died on 3 October 1928. He was said then to be sixty-eight years old. A birth date of about 1860 would make him a little older than Maraea Morete had estimated, in her description of him as a boy at Oweta in 1868.

22   Hukarere College was an Anglican school for Maori girls, founded by Bishop William Williams in Napier. Three of his daughters taught there until the early 1930s; Kate was the one particularly remembered. The Williams' daughters were known collectively as 'the Hukarere Aunts'. Miss Jane Bulstrode was principal of the school from 1899 to 1917; her sister, Emily, who taught there from 1901, succeeded her. See also Heni Sunderland's story, p. 121.

23   Tihei was ill during the school year in 1926.

24   John Clark leased Te Arai station and was one of the great runholders in Poverty Bay. See Mackay 1966: 319.

25   Percival Barker was another early settler, who became a great runholder in Poverty Bay and Whangara. His sons, Walter, Frank, Richard, and Percy (for whom Tihei also worked as a nurse for his children) broke in several famous stations, including Glenroy, near Whangara, and Rototahi. See Mackay 1966: 456.

26   The placing of the fine flax mat on Tihei was a ritual statement by her family that she was ready for the betrothal, or taumau.

27   The marriage would have been intended to reaffirm links with Tuhoe, with whom Te Kooti had entrusted the 'Godhead' and the 'Covenant' of his faith with the prediction, 'Te kupu whakaari a Te Kooti kia Tuhoe: Te Atua-tanga kei a koe, te Kawenata kei a koe.' Prediction n.d.: 76.

28   From the conversation of 26 November 1983.

29 On 25 January 1967.

30 George Rikirangi, Rongo's son, died at the age of eighteen months in 1930.

31 Tihei's only brother, Rangi, died of tuberculosis in 1941 at the age of twenty-one.

32 Oriwia died on 10 August 1931. She was said to be aged eighty-three.

33 The bringing together of the 'four quarters' – 'ngā koata e whā' – or the restoration of Maori unity, is a central preoccupation within Ringatu and Maori thought. It is, in part, derived from Biblical tradition. See Binney 1984: 374-5.

34 Greenstone needs water, or oil from constant human touch, to keep its life. Otherwise it very slowly dries out, darkens, and loses its light and life. For other accounts of sacred greenstones which move and allow themselves to be found, particularly in water, see Smith 1920: 150-8.

35 The mere are named after the Archangels, Michael and Gabriel. The angel Michael visited Te Kooti, it is said, on Wharekauri, and gave him the covenants of the faith. He is God's avenging angel of war. Gabriel is the angel of peace. See Binney 1984 for an account of the importance of the two Archangels in the Ringatu traditions.

36 Mangapoike was invested by its owners in the Wi Pere and James Carroll Trust in 1896. Encumbered with debt, and undeveloped, it subsequently became part of the East Coast Commission lands and only finally returned to Maori administration when the Commission was wound up in 1953.

37 Sir Turi Carroll, son of Sir James and Heni Materoa Carroll. He was born in 1890 and died on 11 November 1975. He was a well-known figure in East Coast Maori affairs and was President of the New Zealand Maori Council 1962-71.

38 This kupu whakaari, or prediction, is one of the more famous of Te Kooti's. The opening of the King Country for the railway was one of the main purposes of the government's negotiations with the King movement and Ngati Maniapoto in the 1880s. One of the terms set by Maniapoto was the pardon of Te Kooti. The train-tracks ran right through Te Kuiti and forced the removal of the meeting-house, Tokanganui a Noho, whose carvings and paintings had been supervised by Te Kooti and which was given by him to Maniapoto, in gratitude for their protection, on 1 January 1883.

39 A reference to Te Kooti's prediction of a successor, who will complete the tasks that are to be done.

40 J. S. Jessep, was appointed as the first full-time Commissioner by Apirana Ngata in 1934. One of Jessep's working principles was to use the more profitable stations to help clear the debts encumbered on other blocks under his vast administration. Despite Tihei's comments, this decision caused enormous friction between the Maori owners. Turi Carroll had, even before Jessep's appointment, petitioned Parliament for Maori block committees to make their own decisions and for each block to bear its own liabilities. However, in the long run, Jessep's decisions were sound, although he made them in an autocratic manner. Paparatu itself, in the Mangapoike block, was one of the best-founded hill country runs on the East Coast. When the blocks under the Commission were separated in 1953 and management committees of owners established, twenty-four new incorporations were set up. For a history of the East Coast Commission, see Ward 1958.

41 Paparatu was the first engagement between Te Kooti and the pursuing forces, where Te Kooti captured the horses and supplies of the militia. It was the first of a series of victories for Te Kooti in 1868. See Cowan 1956, II: 236.

42 Capt. William Henry Tucker was an early settler and land holder in Poverty Bay and fought actively against Te Kooti. He was also a mayor of Gisborne – and the father of Reuben Brown. See Heni Brown's story and whakapapa.

43 Papuni was another of the famous stations. It was developed early this century on the Tahora block, under the East Coast Commission. In 1902, when the block came under the Commission, it was heavily mortgaged to the Bank of New Zealand by the Wi Pere and James Carroll Trust. The setting up of the Commission (urged by the bank) was specifically to prevent mortgage sales, and thus the alienation of land blocks like Tahora from the actual owners.

44 12 February 1983. See also Heni Sunderland's story, p. 117.

45 The section of the faith which is now led by Wi Tarei of Te Teko, Bay of Plenty. It was formed as a separate Church at Poroporo on 12-13 September 1937, and its officiating ministers are listed separately, but it considers itself a part of the Ringatu faith.

46 On 16 February 1983, 'He Rerenga Kōrero', Radio New Zealand programme.

47   Initiating a circuit of visits for a purpose is traditional in Ringatu practice. At each place the nature of the mission to be fulfilled is explained, while three is a ritual number of fulfilment. The completion of the circuit at Wainui would be the closing of the cycle on the land given by the government to Te Kooti and now held by the Ringatu Church.

Heni Sunderland

1   Evidence given 6-7 September 1880, Maori Land Court, Gisborne Minute Book VI: 307, 309, 312.

2   William Williams to McLean, 17 February 1869, McLean Papers 32: 640; W. L. Williams Diary, 4-13 February 1869; J. W. Harris to McLean, 17 February, 18 August 1869, McLean Papers 32: 327; G. B. Worgan to McLean, 20 February 1869, McLean Papers 32: 23.

3   'Roll of prisoners landed at Chatham Island, June 10th. 1866', AD 31: 14.

4   Fowler 1974: 1-4.

5   Ngata 1961, II: 154-5.

6   *Gisborne Herald*, 18 June 1985.

7   Tiakiwhare Brown died on 2 December 1951 when she was seventy-four.

8   'Te Pōpō' was composed by the visionary Enoka Te Pakaru, of Te Aitanga a Mahaki. In this tradition, Hinehakirirangi came on the Horouta canoe. She lived at Papatewai on the Wherowhero lagoon at Muriwai, where the Horouta is said to have landed, and planted the first kūmara at Manawaru. Hinehakirirangi is carved in the meeting-house Te Mana o Turanga.

9   There are many tales of Pawa (or Paoa), his dog, and his mimi. See Fowler 1974: 23-4; Simmons 1976: 132-7, 142-5.

10   Heni Materoa Carroll, the wife of Sir James Carroll. She was the daughter of Mikaera Turangi and the granddaughter of Paratene Turangi. She was, therefore, a leading figure within Rongowhakaata and, through her mother, Riperata Kahutia, was the head of Ngaitawhiri hapū. She died 1 November 1930. A brief biography, together with a photograph of her elegant house in Kahutia Street, Gisborne, is in Macgregor 1973: 24-8.

11   For the Department of Maori Affairs. See later in Heni's story, p. 123.

12   Heni is here referring to the ominous song of the seer Te Toiroa of Nukutaurua on the Mahia peninsula. See Introduction, p. 4.

13   Mere Kingi Paraone died on 13 July 1942. She was said then to be 107 years old.

14   See Tihei's story, pp. 106-7.

15   See Miria's story, pp. 142-3.

16   Paku Hokopu Paraone died on 11 July 1930. He was said then to be fifty-eight years old, but this was an underestimation of his age.

17   The house was opened on 11 March 1930.

18   Mihikore was the daughter of Heta Te Kani a Takirau and was a leading figure within Rongowhakaata.

19   M. S. Quigley was the headmaster of Muriwai school from 1924 to 1928; Miss B. Francis was an assistant teacher.

20   From 1923 to 1925 Heni had attended school at Manutuke, where both her father and grandfather were said to be living. She then attended the Muriwai school and left, with her proficiency certificate, at the end of 1930.

21   See Tihei's story, p. 99.

22   Bishop Fredrick Bennett of the Te Arawa tribe was the first Bishop of the Maori diocese of Aotearoa. He was consecrated in 1928.

23   Miss Jane Bulstrode was the elder sister and had been principal of Hukarere Girls' College in Napier, and her sister Emily succeeded her until 1927. When they resigned, they each took up Maori mission work for the Anglican Church. See also Tihei's story, p. 99.

24   Eru Brown was killed on 5 February 1938.

25   Hetekia Te Kani Te Ua, a major chief of Turanga, who was one of Leo Fowler's main informants for his history of Te Mana o Turanga. Hetekia Te Kani died on 30 September 1966.

26   The paepae, a horizontal beam placed at the latrine, is specifically associated with a whakanoa, tapu-lifting, ritual. Sick people were taken to the paepae hamuti and told to 'bite the beam'; this act was believed to remove the cause of the illness, that is, a contamination from a violation

of tapu. The paepae was seen as the threshold between the world of darkness and death, which lay beyond it, and the world of light and life, which lay in front of it. See, Best 1977, I: 1137–41; Binney 1980: 18–19.

Miria Rua

1   Shirres 1982: 44.

2   Binney 1983: 384.

3   Conversation with Hillman Rua, 21 May 1978.

4   *Sunday News*, 25 August 1985. My emphasis.

5   Conversation of 23 May 1982.

6   Thirty-eight adults and seventy-two children. Inhabitants of Maungapohatu, MA 13: 92.

7   AJHR 1921–2, G–7: 4; Sissons 1984: 353–4.

8   Conversation with Tom Hitaua, son of Iraia Heurea, brother of Rua's wife Te Aue, 9 May 1984.

9   Best 1905: 211–8.

10   *Lyttelton Times*, 20 January 1919; conversation with Harimate Roberts (Materoa Roberts) of Tataiahape, 17 May 1978.

11   Te Akakura Rua commented that the name was misspelt as Tuapou on the Land Court records and that it should be Tuapo, that is, 'to act by midnight'. Conversation of 5 October 1979.

12   'To be soothed or comforted'.

13   Miria's birth was registered by her father finally in 1938 and as 12 August 1925. Henare Rua, Rua's son by Te Akakura, accidentally shot himself and he died on 20 October 1925, when he was fourteen years old. See Puti's story, p. 157.

14   Tioke Hakaipare was one of the teachers of Rua's faith; Te Kaawa was the father of Rua's wife, Mihiroa; Ira Manihera was a Ringatu tohunga from Waiohau.

15   Te Amoroa died on 26 April 1944. He was fifty-nine.

16   The shooting of native pigeon, generally illegal from 1921, was permitted for Tuhoe in the Urewera until 1938.

17   Irene Paulger taught at Maungapohatu from 1925 to 1947; Catherine Shaw from 1931 to 1934. Paulger was, by some strange stroke of fate, our first contact with Maungapohatu. Years before the authors ever considered its people's history, Judith Binney happened to be in an Auckland hospital bed next to Irene Paulger, when Paulger was dying. Her constant loving visitors were her adopted children — and their children.

18   John Laughton married Horiana Te Kauru, a missionary teacher, in 1921. He had been the first Presbyterian missionary to Maungapohatu from 1918.

19   Miria was at Maungapohatu school from 1931 to 1938. She ran away from Maungapohatu to Tauwharemanuka during the school holidays, after a 'hiding' from her father and refused to return to school, according to the school records. Irene Paulger wanted the department to write to Miria's father; of course, Paulger thought that Miria was only thirteen years old and, therefore, really should return to school.

20   Te Raihi (George) and Marewa Ihe.

21   John was born on 29 September 1942 and died of a hernia on 25 April 1943.

22   Tuhua Pari was one of Rua's Levites and was the elder brother of Miria's mother.

23   The woman of whom this story is told died of a miscarriage at the age of forty-five, in December 1945.

24   The matakite Hori Gage used sea water to bless his followers. Under his influence, Miria travelled out from the Tauranga valley almost for the first time in her life. The baptism of sea water is, perhaps, based on the Scriptural texts concerning the Israelites' 'covenant of salt' with the Lord (Numbers 18: 19) and adding salt to the waters (II Kings 2: 21).

25   There is an apparent contradiction in Miria's remarks here with her earlier statement about her baptism under sea water.

26   Hiwira Te Pou.

27   Ngatiraka chiefs, Te Pou and his brother Taura Papaka, gave Rua a hundred acres there, to found a settlement, in 1909. This land was reclaimed by Te Pou's son, Wi Kamaua, and Rua and his followers were driven out in 1912. See Binney, Chaplin, and Wallace, 1979: 78–9.

28   That is, 'whenua oati', sworn land. Tuhoe often drop the last vowel when speaking.

29   Te Waimarini died on 10 December 1960.

30   The Kauhanganui, or Great Council, was the separate parliament for the Maori King movement in the Waikato, formed in 1894. The Council assumed its authority and the Kingitanga, because it possessed this parliament, refused to join the Kotahitanga of the Treaty of Waitangi. This Kotahitanga developed in the mid-1890s into a demand for a Maori parliament. The Kotahitanga of the Treaty of Waitangi was revived in the late 1950s, particularly around the East Coast under the influence of Tom Te Maaro. It has sprung to life again in the 1980s. The 1984 peace march to Waitangi, Te Hikoi, was conducted under the flag of the Kotahitanga, redesigned and bearing the emblems of a mere and the Treaty crossed. This rebirth of the Kotahitanga of the Treaty of Waitangi, unlike the beginnings of the movement, has originated with the Kingitanga, whose goals have always been to win a dual sovereignty under the Crown.

31   Perhaps more correctly, Tom Te Maaro brought the Kotahitanga into Hori Gage's movement, although it became known as the Kotahitanga amongst the people. Based in Ruatoria, Tom Te Maaro was the secretary of the Kotahitanga. Hori Gage himself died on 3 June 1961 and by then the movement had become very divided. The revival of the Kotahitanga in the 1980s was largely initiated by Eva Rickard of Raglan and taken up by the Kingitanga elders.

32   A severe flood in the Bay of Plenty, accompanied by massive landslips and the destruction of the Matahi bridge, isolated the upper Tauranga valley on 11 March 1964. Sam Biddle, who was Iwi's elder brother, had to be rescued by helicopter from Matahi after he had been badly injured. The *New Zealand Herald,* 16 March 1964, has an account.

33   The opening of Bayten's private timber road into Maungapohatu was a major event for the Tuhoe of Maungapohatu. 1500 people came – in twelve busloads and 200 cars and trucks – according to one newspaper account: Urewera Scrapbook, clipping, n.d., Whakatane Museum. John Laughton, who attended as chairman of the Maungapohatu committee, had hoped that the milling would provide work so that the 'exiled children of the mountain' could return. (Laughton 1961: 28.) See also Te Akakura's story, pp. 181-2.

34   A reference to the multiplicity of shareholders, created by the Maori Land Court system, which recognizes descent but not residence as the basis of tribal ownership.

35   Poni Arohana died at the age of forty-seven on 30 August 1969.

36   Paretai Rua died on 12 October 1969.

37   Meri Tukua, or Whakaataata, Rua's eldest daughter, died on 1 January 1973. The dining-hall at Tuapo, erected in 1948, is now named after her: Nga Wai Whakaataata.

38   Miria is referring to the publication of *Mihaia*, which drew extensively on oral and photographic sources from the people of Matahi and nearby. Binney, Chaplin, and Wallace, 1979.

39   See Reremoana's story p. 59 for the occasion when her people all changed their names.

40   Materoa, daughter of Tatu, who married Rua's eldest son, Whatu. She was the central figure in Vincent Ward's evocative film, *In Spring One Plants Alone*, which was made in 1979-80. She was then believed to be eighty-two years old.

41   Ripia Tango (to use the northern form of his name) lived at Maungapohatu through the second millennial phase of the community, 1927-36. He died in 1939 at Te Waiiti.

42   Whatu, or Tane, Rua's eldest son, died after a shearing accident near Gisborne on 10 December 1933. He was, it seems, embalmed there by an undertaker, the consequence of which this story reveals.

43   Miki Te Wakaunua, the chief of Maungapohatu, was killed at Te Whaiti on 27 January 1928. This accident was attributed to Te Akakura's (Rua's wife) disobedience of her husband. See both Puti's and Te Akakura's stories, pp. 163, 180.

44   Maori mortality in the 1918 influenza pandemic was far worse than the European: probably 42-45 per thousand in comparison with 5 per thousand. One of the worst areas for Maori mortality was the eastern Bay of Plenty, where many Tuhoe lived and worked. See Rice 1983: 54-6 and also Reremoana's story, p. 67.

Putiputi Onekawa

1   See Winiata 1967: 75 for this tradition.

2   Best 1977, I: 494.

3   Conversation with Paetawa Miki, Maungapohatu elder, 25 January 1978.

4   Maori Land Court, Whakatane Minute Book XXVI: 27.

5   'Te toenga o te tangata'. See Binney 1984: 369-70.

6   Pehirangi Kanuehi was born in 1891 and attended the Ruatoki Native School between 1901 and 1905. By April 1908 she was living with Rua. Te Akakura Ru, who was fought for and won by Rua (see Akakura's story), was two years younger than Pehirangi. She, too, had attended the Ruatoki school, but only between 1902 and 1903. She was living with Rua by April 1908 and was recognized as his 'rangatira' wife. Te Aue, Rua's fourth wife, was from Ruatahuna and she, too, was with him by April 1908, when all were photographed at Maungapohatu by George Bourne. See p. 20.

7   All the women at Maungapohatu of this generation stayed apart in the whare kōhanga, or the birth tent, for seven days. This is the time it takes for the pito, the navel cord, to drop off.

8   The date recorded by Turakina school was actually 28 July 1909. On the Maungapohatu school registers, Puti's date of birth is recorded both as 28 July 1910 and 16 April 1911! Puti's birth is now formally registered according to the Turakina records, as 1909. These happy variations are not uncommon for older Maori people.

9   Tangimeriana was with Te Kooti on Wharekauri. She is included in his diary in a list of names he wrote of some of the women prisoners.

10 Putiputi: flower. From the English, pretty, pretty.

11 See Miria's story, p. 146.

12 This story is a modern version of a very ancient and favourite tale. Tamatekapua, the canoe ancestor of Te Arawa, was a famous thief of fruit, and is often depicted in carvings with his stilts, which he also used to this end.

13 Henare died on 20 October 1925 when he was fourteen years old. He went into the bush to go hunting on 11 October and accidentally shot himself. It is usually said that he was alone, and Puti may have, because of associations, remembered herself as being there. Placing oneself in the story is a common form in oral narrative traditions, even though the narrative may be about ancestors who lived and died long before one was born.

14 Having fulfilled this task set him as Te Kooti's 'son', that is, his successor, Rua then went inland to Maungapohatu. At the gathering on 12 April, he announced the visit of King Edward VII to Gisborne on 25 June in these words: 'Maungapohatu, Aperira 12th 1906. I tena ra ka whakaaturia; i [te] 25 o Hune haere au ki runga i te torona, ka tae mai a te kiingi ki Turanga.' ('Maungapohatu, April 12th 1906. On that day it was revealed; on 25 June I will ascend the throne; the king will arrive at Turanga [Gisborne].') (Transcript from the diary of Wi Kamaua Te Pou, then a follower of Rua, April 1906. By courtesy of Dr Jeffrey Sissons, University of Otago.) In this statement, Rua is implicitly the King who is to come. For an account of the tasks set by Te Kooti for his successor, see Binney 1984 and particularly p. 357.

15 Ngakohu Pera, chief of Waioeka, and one of the early Levites. Wharepapa Hawiki from Ruatoki was also one of the first Levites; he died on 23 October 1949, aged seventy-six. The Levites, and all of Rua's followers, wore their hair long between 1907 and 1915, as a statement of their 'separation . . . unto the Lord' (Numbers 6: 5). See Binney, Chaplin, and Wallace 1979: 77; Binney 1983: 357.

16 See also Miria's story, p. 136.

17 Herora, Herod's people, was the name given to the original Ringatu, who held to Te Kooti's directions. The Iharaira, the Israelites, were those who followed Rua. He abolished the Twelfths as part of the new teachings, and separated the Iharaira from the traditional Ringatu.

18 Catching kākā with a tame bird is the traditional way. Sometimes women did the snaring, as the name Kakewahine, the clearing above Maungapohatu, indicates. See Best 1942: 249-53, 294.

19 Where the bush cover has been burnt off, the soil becomes sour. Bracken fern was a staple wild source of starch.

20 Daughter of Mihiroa and Rua.

21 The dried woody fungus, puku tawai, was used as the punk to generate fire. Anūhē is the term

used here.

22   Sister Annie Henry, Sister Dorothy Keen, Sister Jessie Grieve, Revd John Laughton and John Currie, Presbyterian missionaries and teachers at Maungapohatu and Matahi in the early 1920s. Puti first attended the Maungapohatu school, in 1920, and then the Matahi school, when it was opened by the missionaries in the old meeting-house Pare Nui o Te Ra, in 1921. In 1922 she attended both schools and continued intermittently at both – 'I'm always up and down' – until 1926, when she was sent to Turakina, the Presbyterian girls' school.

23   Phem Doull, who began the school at Matahi in October 1921 and was in charge of the Matahi school and mission from 1925 to 1934.

24   Temata Kiripa, or Paapu, was the husband of Haromi Hohaia, whose older sister, Herita, had married Onekawa. Herita and Onekawa were the parents of Mac's father, Te Marangai Onekawa. (See Puti's whakapapa.) Puti is using the term grandfather in the Maori sense of consanguinity. Koroua is the term she is translating.

25   Ethel Roseveare, who taught at the Maungapohatu school from 1925 until 1931.

26   Puti apparently did return for a month in April 1927, according to the Maungapohatu school records. She then took off again in the May holidays.

27   Te Akakura, Rua's wife, was badly injured in the truck accident at Te Whaiti on 27 January 1928. See Akakura's story, p. 180.

28   Timoti, or Te Au, was the eldest son of Paora Kiingi Paora.

29   Brothers and uncles were the male relatives commonly approached for an arranged marriage and public acceptance of sleeping together is the statement of being married. Whatu's involvement, then, is as orthodox as his impatience at the situation which had developed!

30   From the conversation of 30 January 1983.

31   Puti and Mac were married by John Laughton on 20 March 1941 at Matahi. Noti had been born on 10 February.

32   Puti is using the word 'tapu' in the sense that a religious ceremony took place, celebrated by the Reverend John Laughton in the meeting-house at Maungapohatu. (See Te Akakura's story, p. 180.) In a traditional Maori marriage; religious ceremony did not play an important part – as Puti's account of her own marriage indicates. Te Okeroa Timi was married at the same time as Akakura.

33   Puti's first son Te Rito o Te Rangi was born prematurely at Maungapohatu on 1 May 1930. He died on 19 November 1931 at Matahi. Her second son, Ruatoto, was born on 7 November, at Matahi. He died of influenza at Otane on 18 November 1932.

34   See both Heni Brown's and Miria's stories, pp. 48, 140.

35   Puti is referring to Paora Kiingi Paora, who died on 8 February 1934 when he was eighty-seven years old.

36   There is an old karakia, used when the child was made noa, or free of tapu restrictions, which conveys precisely the significance of this event:

Ka aha te tama nei?
Ka huhu te tama nei.
Ka tuku rawa te tama nei, ki muri rawa te tama nei.
Ka kokiro te tama nei, ki muri rawa te tama nei.
Ka kokiro te tama nei.
Ka tuku rawa te tama nei.
Ka hōpara te tama nei, ki muri rawa te tama nei.
Hōpara, hōpara, hōpara ki te hōpara nui a Tū.

What is this child doing?
This child is stripping off.
This child may go just where he pleases, even to the cooking area, this child.
This child bathes himself in warm water, even to the cooking area, this child.
This child bathes himself in warm water.
This child may go just where he pleases.
This child steps out, even to the cooking area, this child.
Stepping out, stepping out, stepping out with the big steps of Tu.

This karakia is from the Grey collection in the Auckland Public Library (GNZMMSS 28: 137-8). A note in the manuscript indicated that the term 'kokiro' means to bathe in warm water, to lift the tapu restrictions. This karakia is partially cited in Shirres 1982: 39 and we are greatly indebted to Michael Shirres OP for the full text and this translation. The karakia was traditionally said at the completion of the hair-cutting rite for young boys.

37 Sister M. H. Miller, stationed at Waimana and Matahi between 1926 and 1952.

38 Molly — More — was accidentally drowned on 21 September 1939. Her birth had not been registered but she was said then to be fourteen months old.

39 That is, at the Opotiki Maternity Hospital. Donald was born on 17 July 1948; Joseph, the youngest, on 11 November 1949.

40 As in many cultures, Maori women squatted, or knelt on their hands, to give birth. Sometimes a post was used to hold onto, or the knees of the attendant, who would also be squatting, facing the woman who was giving birth. Pressure was sometimes applied by the husband (or the female relative attending) against the upper abdomen, in order to help the delivery of the foetus, as Puti describes — but she used a wooden box.

41 Pehirangi lived at Matahi until her death on 21 July 1956, at the age of seventy-five.

42 Rangikapua's birth was on 22 September 1942.

43 Henry Bell, son of Frank Bell, founder of the old Waimana family store, Bell and Hodgson. Mrs Robena Hodgson was Henry's sister.

44 Bella — Pera — the youngest daughter of Rua and Pinepine.

45 Joseph was yet to be born.

46 Capitalization of the family benefit up to a thousand pounds in advance, for housing needs, was introduced under the Family Benefits (Home Ownership) Act of 1958, coming into effect from April 1959. It allowed low-income families to build a State house. Maori families were able to acquire homes with the assistance of the Maori Affairs Department. Under the Act, this scheme was not supposed to cause hardship to the applicant.

47 In July 1972 the family benefit was doubled from $1.50 to $3.00 a week for each child.

48 In June 1938 a two-acre block was partitioned off for a papakāinga. It was a defined area ('Tuapou B 5') in which the owners of the whole block, 'Tuapou B', were proportionate shareholders. Pehirangi, Pinepine, Meri Wi Kamaua Te Pou, who was also Rua's wife, and Akakura (as a successor to her mother and to her grandmother) were thus shareholders.

49 A cemetery for the ancestors, who belong to the land, would complete the marae complex. But some of Rua's other children do not wish to separate their ancestors from the Matahi marae in this respect. Four acres would be required for the papakāinga in order to set apart land for a burial ground. But to be without a burial place, an urupā for Rua's family, in Puti's belief is wrong.

50 Bones fighting each other are the subject of many favourite Tuhoe stories. There is the Ngapuhi warrior, who is buried in the cave at the base of the northern pinnacle on Maungapohatu, Te Tara a Tutemaungaroa. It is said that every time you go past you'll find his bones on the path, thrown out by his companions, all of whom are Tuhoe! The pinnacle is very closely identified with the mana of the mountain and its people. Some say that is where the diamond lies, the mauri whenua of Maungapohatu, hidden by Te Kooti, but revealed to Rua.

51 The missionary John Currie described the occasion: the two rangatira were brought home at the same time that the meeting-house, Tane Nui a Rangi, was renewed. Tane's body arrived at night and was greeted with 'some 200 rounds of shot & dynamite explosions. . . . All next day was spent in argument as to where the bodies should be re-buried. Ancient Maori custom demands that when two bodies lie on the same mat they must be buried together. Here was a difficulty as one party wanted the Te Whaiti "tupapaku" buried in the cemetry. Whereas the widow of Rua's son, Tane, wanted him buried in front of her — (& *their* while he was alive —) house. . . . So the battle swayed all day & far into the night & remained unsettled.
    . . . That [next] night the argument in Maungapohatu was settled very quickly & in a surprised manner. A visiting party from Ruatoki "asked" for the widow for one of their men. Directly the "tono" was made the fire of Maungapohatu's wrath blazed forth. What! ask for the wife & the husband not yet buried — (or rather reburied). They were insulted & that deeply. Early morning saw the two remains re-committed to the earth in the same grave & thus the custom (ancient) was not broken. The offending parties were Taua-a-poke & were heavily fined by the "Tangata whenua".' Currie to Godber, 16 July 1940: Godber Papers 78: 13.

52 Rangimārie: 'to become peaceful'.

53 See Miria's story, p. 142.

Te Akakura Rua

1 Sung by Horo Tatu, 21 January 1978. Transcription by Rangi Motu.

2 Conversation with Puti, 4 December 1984. As will become evident, many of Akakura's and Puti's narratives overlap.

3 Te Ripo Horomona, wife of Hori Hiakita of Matahi.

4 Noti, Akakura's younger sister.

5 Conversation with Hillman Rua, 21 May 1978.

6 Irene Hare came to work at the Ruatoki Anglican mission house in 1918 and remained there until her death on 8 July 1925. She took in about seventeen or twenty children from the Ruatoki community, to whom she gave 'daily religious instruction'. In 1924, the Bishop of Waiapu, commenting upon her work, stated that there were few 'Christian Maoris' in Ruatoki, as the majority were Ringatu! He saw the mission house as 'a strong centre of Christian influence'. Waiapu Diocese Yearbook 1924: 36.

7 See both Heta Rua and Hillman Rua's accounts of the transference of the mauri from its guardian, Te Whiu Maraki, to Rua. Binney 1984: 377-8.

8 Teehi (or Te Ihi), brother of Wharepapa Hawiki. Wharepapa was one of Rua's Levites; Teehi was the Maori police constable at Ruatoki. Both were kin to Te Akakura through their mother, Te Pera, who was a half-sister to Te Ruakariata, Akakura's tipuna (see whakapapa). Teehi had been one who had originally opposed Patu's marriage to Rua.

9 Te Hau was the son of Meri Wi Kamaua Te Pou (who was a granddaughter of Te Whiu) and Rua. He had also been brought up at Ruatoki, but by George Melbourne of Rewarewa.

10 See both Miria's and Puti's stories, pp. 148, 163.

11 Kuini Te Morehu, from Ruatahuna.

12 Te Wharepapa Hawiki had brought up Patu and was, therefore, Akakura's grandfather. He was the son of Patu's great-grandfather's half-sister, Te Pera, who married Te Paerata Hawiki.

13 The return of Whatu to Maungapohatu was also vividly recalled by both Puti and Miria. One reason why this event horrified everyone involved was that embalming was profoundly offensive to Maori custom: the hahunga, or ritual exposure and reburial of the bones of the beloved dead person, could not occur properly.

14 That is Whitu Kanuehi.

15 Paetawa Miki is the son of Miki Te Wakaunua. After the death of his elder brother Te Heuheu, on 30 October 1961, he became the chief of Maungapohatu.

16 See Binney 1983: 363-6.

17 Henare, her son, had died. See Puti's story, p. 157.

18 Tauwira – Jean Almond – died on 14 May 1965, after the birth of her last child, John. Akakura brought John up.

19 We have been unable to find any registration of the marriage.

20 It has been explained to us that the Iharaira believe that headstones and concrete prevent the spirit, te wairua, from rising from the grave and travelling to the afterworld. The implication is that Patu's spirit was to be allowed to roam free, and we have been told that none of Rua's children are ever to be given headstones. Thus Akakura will have no 'unveiling'. Her father's heavy concrete tomb is set apart from all other graves. It holds his wairua for the time of his predicted return as the Messiah.

21 Te Rangiwaitatao was a Tuhoe woman of high rank, who was killed by Ngati Kahungunu in the early nineteenth century, when she travelled with the conveyors of a new faith called Te Noanoa or Te Wheawheau, because it was concerned with tapu-lifting rites. (Best 1977, I: 535-7.) She is also said to be a sister of Rua. Whaitiri is the ancestral goddess of Tuhoe and in Iharaira narratives she is called Rua's sister. As Maungapohatu itself is a maunga tipua, a mountain of power, so Whaitiri, who in the traditional Tuhoe narratives is the 'cause of thunder', is considered to be a tipua, a strange power. When she visited this world and conceived the tipuna of Tuhoe, she was recognizable by the bright light associated with her, and a particular perfume. (Best 1977, I: 908.) She appeared to Rua on Maungapohatu and revealed the diamond, the mauri whenua of Tuhoe, to him. Although she was hidden in a garb of rags, she was able to be identified by these signs: the bright light and her perfume. See Binney 1984: 360-1.

22   Conversation with Puti Onekawa, 10 December 1978. In some versions there were eight
      women. Matekoraha was the one Akakura particularly remembered as having found the
      kiekie root. The other women included Matekoraha's sister Hine, Te Hirata, Whitu's
      daughter, and Puhata Teka, who married Paetawa. This kiekie mat is being proudly displayed
      in the photograph of Rua, taken in 1927, p.184.

HE KUPU MĀORI
GLOSSARY OF MAORI WORDS

The meanings given are appropriate to the context. In the body of the text the long vowel is marked by the use of the macron in ordinary words, but not in place names or proper names. Quotations are cited exactly as in the original.

ahau I; me
ahi kā 'keeping the fire lit', maintaining occupation of the land
akoako learning together
Ākuhata August
Āmine Amen
ana! there!
anūhē dried fungus used as the tinder to generate fire
ao world; **Te Ao Mārama** the World of Light, or this world; **Te Ao Hōu** the New World which is to come
ārā so; and then
ariki great chief
aroha love; sorrow
atua supernatural being; deity; God
au I; me
auē! oh!
auhi sorrow; grief; distress
Haahi Church
haere come; go; **haere mai** come here
hahunga ceremonial display of the exhumed bones of the dead
haka dance of defiance, with chant; **haka pōwhiri** welcome haka on ceremonial occasions
hākari feast; love feast (Scriptural)
hāngi earth oven
hapū (n) tribe; (a) pregnant
hara error; violation of tapu; sin
harakeke NZ flax (*Phormium tenax*)
heihei hen
heke get down
Heperu Hebrew
Hepi Hebrew
Herora Herod
hīkoi walk; also specifically the peace walk to Waitangi in 1984
hīmene hymn
hīnau tree (*Elaeocarpus dentatus*), the kernels of its berries are used to make bread
hinga fall
hinu fat; birds preserved in their own fat
Hiona Zion
Hiruhārama Jerusalem
hōhā fed up; angry
hōia soldier
hoki return
hokorua forty; a calabash of forty birds
Hōri derogatory term for Maori (derived from Maori form of George)
horomoana drowned
horowai drowned
hōu new
huamata planting rites on 1 June
hui gathering; **huihui** gathering; assembly
huia bird (*Heteralocha acutirostris*), now extinct, whose tail feathers were worn by people of rank
Hūrae July

hurinui all turned over
Iharaira Israelites
iho strand of hair; umbilical cord; line of descent
Ihoa Jehovah
Ihowa Jehovah
inoi prayer; to pray in the Ringatu service
irihaere hung up
iwi people; large descent group; bone
kāeaea bush-hawk (*Falco novaeseelandiae*)
kaha strength
kahawai fish (*Arripis trutta*)
kai food; consume; eat
kaitiaki guardian; spirit guardian, often in the form of an animal or bird
kākā native parrot (*Nestor meridionalis*)
kākahu cloak; garment; clothing
kākano seed
kamokamo marrow; gourd
Kāpiti Gabriel
kaponga hut made of the trunks and fronds of tree fern (*Cyathea dealbata*)
karā basalt stone
karaehe glass
Karaiti Christ
karakia prayer
kāre he tapu without tapu restrictions
kāti that's enough
kati closed
Kauhanganui Parliament, or Great Council of the King movement
kaumātua elder (of the tribe)
kaupapa strict follower of Te Kooti
kauri tree (*Agathis australis*)
kāuta cooking-shed
kawa etiquette of the marae; protocol
Kāwanatanga government; supporters of the government
kawau shag (*Phalacrocorax*)
kawenata covenant
kēhua ghost; spirit
kererū native wood-pigeon (*Hemiphaga novaeseelandiae*)
kete woven flax bag; kit
ketewaro coal-basket
kiekie climbing plant (*Freycinetia banksii*), prized for weaving
kina sea-egg (*Evechinus*)
Kīngitanga King movement
kiore rat; also used for mouse
koha offering; gift
kōhanga reo 'language nest', Maori language kindergartens, started by Maori mothers in 1981 and still run mostly on a voluntary basis
kōhatu stone
kōhuru treacherous
koka leaves of NZ flax
kōkiri a party of men; section of a war party
kōnaki sledge (dialectical form of kōneke)
kōneke sledge
kopa earth oven
kōpere rainbow
kōrero talk
koroua old man
korowai cloak
koruru carved face on gable of meeting-house

kotahitanga unity; Unity movement under the Treaty of Waitangi
koti coat
kōtukutuku native fuchsia (*Fuchsia excorticata*)
kōwhai tree (*Sophora tetraptera* and *Sophora microphylla*)
kuia old woman
kūmara sweet potato
kūpapa neutral
kupu word; message; **kupu whakaari** revelation; prediction
maharatanga remembrance service
mahi Māori literally 'Maori work', meaning supernatural power; witchcraft
māhunga head
makawe hair
mākiri to bone pigeons, preparatory to preserving
mākutu curse; bewitch; power to bewitch
mana authority; rank; influence; **mana atua** spiritual power; **mana tangata** authority over
    people; **mana whakaora** power of faith-healing; **mana whenua** authority or trusteeship
    over land
manuhiri guest; visitor
mānuka 'tea-tree', shrub (*Leptospermum scoparium*)
Māoritanga essence of being Maori
māra garden
marae properly, the open ground for speeches and ceremony in front of the meeting-house, but
    often used to include the meeting-house and, in recent times, the dining-hall
maraekōhatu marae of stones
marumaru shade; shadow
mata prophetic song
matakite visionary; seer
mātāmua senior, the first born
mate (a) dead; (n) sickness; death; corpse; **mate Māori** 'Maori sickness', i.e. a spiritual malaise;
    matemoana drowned at sea
matua parent; **matua whāngai** adoptive parent
mauherehere imprisoned
maunga mountain
maungārongo lasting peace; the cessation of conflict
mauri the life principle; the talisman which guards the life principle; **mauri whenua** life principle
    of the land
mea thing
meikai maize
mere short flat club, made of greenstone
Mihāia Messiah
mihi greeting
Mikaere Michael
mimi make water; urine
miria to be soothed
miti tahu meat preserved in fat
moeawa die by the river
moengāroa 'long sleep', death
moko facial tattoo
mokopuna grandchild, descendant of a son or daughter, niece or nephew
mōrehu survivor
nēhi nurse
niu divinatory pole of the Pai Marire
noa not under tapu restrictions
nohanga seat; sitting place
ngārara lizard
ngāwari kind, gentle; generous
ngōiro young eel
ngongo pipe

ōhāki dying speech; that which serves in remembrance of a departed friend

ope party of visitors

oriori lullaby, sung to teach the child

pā fortified settlement; the site of a former pā

paeākau cast along the shore

paepae threshold; bench for speakers on the marae; **paepae hamuti** horizontal beam at the latrine

Pai Mārire Good and Peaceful, the name of the followers of Te Ua Haumene

Pākehā European resident in New Zealand

pakeke elder; knowledgeable adult; persistency; obstinacy

Pākerewhā Te Toiroa's name for Pakeha

panekoti petticoat

pānui Scriptural text in the Ringatu service

pao topical song

Papa Koko Father Christmas

papakāinga marae reserve

pare lintel over door or window

pātiki flounder (*Rhombosolea plebia*)

patu weapon

pāua shellfish (*Haliotis*)

pāuhua slip off; to lift life-destroying tapu; to free from evil forces

peihana basin

pēpi baby

Pepuere February

pera pillow

pihipihi 'waxeye', bird (*Zosterops lateralis*)

pikopiko young shoot of fern

pipi cockle

pirau rotten

pirihimana policeman, person in charge of behaviour at the Ringatu services

pito navel cord

piupiu skirt made of reeds

poi light ball, swung on string

pōkeka dance as a statement of unity

pōrangi mad; angry

porohiana wanting to go outside, or leave

poropiti prophet; prophecy

pororoa long farewell

poti box; boat

pou post; pillar (in the meeting-house); **pou tuarongō** post at the rear of the meeting-house supporting the ridge-pole

pounamu greenstone

Poutikanga Main Pillar, title of the head of the Haahi Ringatu

poutoti stilts

pūhā sowthistle (*Sonchus olerateus*), used as a vegetable

puhi betrothed woman

puku stomach; quinsy

purapura seed

pure traditional supplicatory and tapu-lifting rites; rites to lift tapu at the Ringatu harvest

putiputi flower

rā day; the Ringatu gathering on a particular day set aside for worship, such as the Twelfth of the month

rāhui prohibition

Rangatahi those who move quickly, young people

rangatira chief; leader

Rangimārie to become peaceful; also used for the gospel, the name of the movement led by Hori Gage

raupō bulrush (*Typha angustifolia*)

rautao platter made of leaves

rehita lunar rainbow

reo language; the Maori language

rimu tree (*Dacrydium cupressinum*)

Ringatū the Upraised Hand, adopted as the general name for the followers of Te Kooti's teachings

rīwai potato

Riwaiti Levites, teachers of Rua's faith

Rongopai the Gospel

rourou small woven basket for cooked food

taha side; used to express allegiance or commitment

tāhū ridge-pole

tahu cook in fat to preserve

Tai Rāwhiti the East Coast, where the sun rises

taiaha wooden weapon, about a metre and a half in length, used for hand-to-hand fighting and ceremonial challenges

tāima time

taipō goblin

takatakahi stamping around; trampling over

tākuta doctor

tamaiti child

tamariki children

tāne male

taniwha protective guardian force in the form of a water monster

tangata man; **tāngata whenua** local people, thus hosts

tangi funeral; lament; **tangihanga** the ceremonial occasion of the funeral

taonga anything which is valued or treasured

taotū wounded

tapu under the protection of divine forces; sacred; set aside

tariao the morning star; the religion founded by King Tawhiao in the mid-1870s

taua war party; **taua muru** war party seeking plunder

tāuhi sprinkle

taumata fulfilment of a prophetic vision

taupopoki a lid or cover, Te Toiroa's word to describe a hat

tāwharau shelter; **tāwharautia** to be sheltered

Tekaumārua the Twelfth of the month

tikanga the correct or proper way to do things

tini very many

tipua embodiment of a local spirit or supernatural force

tipuna ancestor (plural **tīpuna**)

tītari scatter

tohunga priest; expert

tokotoko staff or walking-stick, often used in speech-making for emphatic gestures

tono demand

tōpū sit together as a pair

torori home-grown tobacco

toto blood

tuarongo back part of the meeting-house

tūī bird (*Prosthemadera novaeseelandiae*)

tūpā dried up; barren

tūpāpaku body; corpse

tūramarama Te Toiroa's word for lighted tobacco

ture law, of this world, or Scriptural

umu earth oven

urupā burial-ground; cemetery

utu reprisal; requital; revenge

waapu wharf; pit for sawing timber

waewae tatu stumbling legs

wāhi place

wahine woman; **wahine tono** betrothed woman

wai water

waiata song

wairua spirit; soul

Wairua Tapu the Holy Ghost

waka canoe; small canoe holding water to catch pigeons

wānanga used as abbreviation for a school of learning (whare wānanga)

wira will

wīwī rushes (*Juncus maritimus* and *Juncus polyanthemos*)

whaikōrero formal speech-making on the marae

whaiwhaiā bewitch; bewitching

whakaari to reveal

whakahoro to lift tapu restrictions

whakakorenga to lift tapu restrictions

whakamana make effective, used in the sense of psychic power; **whakamanamana** to exult, or assert mana

whakamaroke to dry up

whakamoemiti to praise God; to give thanksgiving

whakano[ho] occasion held to give a woman in marriage

whakanoa to make noa, i.e. to lift tapu restrictions

whakapapa genealogy

whakapiri to bring together

whakararo to turn downwards

whakarau captives, sent to the Chatham Islands

whakataukī proverb; saying

whānau extended family; to be born; to give birth; **whānaungatanga** commitment to family; kinship ties

whāngai foster child

whare house; **te whare o aituā** 'the house of misfortune', the vagina; **whare kanikani** dance-hall; **whare kape** house where the sacred texts were kept; **whare karakia** house of prayer; **whare kōhanga** birth-shelter; **whare mate** shelter for the dead; **wharenui** meeting-house; **wharengaro** childless family or line; **wharepapa** slab house; wooden plank house; **wharepononga** prison; **wharepuni** communal sleeping-house; **wharetamariki** womb; placenta; **whare tapu** tapu house; **whare wānanga** school of learning

whāriki floor mat

whata shelter; **whata raupō** whata made of raupō

whatu whakahoro stone to lift tapu restrictions

whāwhā to feel or take in the hand

whenua land; placenta; **whenua oat[i]** land which has been promised; the Promised Land

wherowhero red

REFERENCES

I. UNPUBLISHED SOURCES

Army Department, Defence (AD). (i) Inward Letters, 1868. AD 1: 71, 75. (ii) Chatham Islands Prisoners 1866-8. AD 31: 14, 15, 16. National Archives, Wellington.

Best, Elsdon, n.d. Maori Notes I, II. National Museum, Wellington.

Currie, John. Letters to A. P. Godber, 1931-42. Godber MSS 78: 13. Alexander Turnbull Library, Wellington.

Davies, G. H., n.d. Maori Manuscripts III. Alexander Turnbull Library, Wellington.

Delamere, Paora, n.d. Manuscript notebook, compiled from 1931. Private collection, Monita Delamere, Opotiki.

Grace, Revd Thomas, 1878. Correspondence. Church Missionary Society microfilm, CN/045. University of Auckland Library.

Green, Pinky, 1960. A History of Northern Waiapu. A Collection of Material as a Research Project. Unpublished typescript. Alexander Turnbull Library, Wellington.

Hawke's Bay Provincial Government (HB), 1866. (i) Inwards Correspondence 1866, HB 4: 7. (ii) Inwards Correspondence Maori, 1866, HB 4: 13. National Archives, Wellington.

Te Kooti Arikirangi Te Turuki, 1766-1890. Manuscript book of waiata, written down by Hamiora Aparoa, one of Te Kooti's secretaries. University of Auckland Library.

————— 1867-8. Diary kept on Wharekauri. MS Alexander Turnbull Library, Wellington.

McLean, Donald. Papers MSS 32. (i) Superintendent, East Coast, 32: 21, 22, 23. (ii) Reginald Biggs, Private Letters, 32: 162. (iii) Herbert W. Brabant, Private Letters, 32: 171. (iv) John Harris, Private Letters, 32: 327. (v) John Hervey, Private Letters, 32: 337. (vi) Revd William Williams, Private Letters, 32: 640. Alexander Turnbull Library, Wellington.

Mair, William Gilbert, 1868-9. Press Copy Letter Book, MS 1077. Mitchell Library, Sydney.

————— 1871-5. Press Copy Telegrams Book. MSS University of Auckland Library.

Matuakore, Paora and Wi Pere and others, 1868. Letter dated 22 August. VF 993, Box 3, Gisborne Museum.

Maori Affairs Department (MA). (i) Maori Political and Tribal Matters: Te Kooti Papers 1873-91. MA 23: 8 (b). (ii) Shepherd-Galvin Report on the Urewera, 1936. MA 13: 92. National Archives, Wellington.

Maori Land Court. (i) Gisborne Minute Book VI, 1880. (ii) Whakatane Minute Book XXVI, 1938-41. Microfilm, University of Auckland Library.

Maungapohatu Notebook, 1881-1916. Manuscript notebook pertaining to Rua Kenana. University of Auckland Library.

Morris (Morete), Maria, n.d. Autobiography of a Maori Woman, MS 2296. Alexander Turnbull Library, Wellington.

Native School Files. (i) Maungapohatu School Register, 1922-5. (ii) Omaio School File E44/4, Part III. (iii) Omaio Teachers' Log Book 1933-42. (iv) Queen Victoria School File E44/6, Part I. Archives and Records Centre, Auckland.

Neal, Karen S., 1976. 'Maori Participation in the East Coast Wars 1865-72'. Unpublished MA thesis. University of Auckland.

Omaio Maori Deaths Register, 1914-29. Registrar General's Office, Lower Hutt.

'The Prediction of One to Follow', n.d. Typescript copy of original manuscript notebook of predictions uttered by Te Kooti and specifically associated with Wi Raepuku of Wanganui. Private collection, the late Frank Davis.

Sissons, Jeffrey, 1984. 'Te Mana o Te Waimana. Tuhoe History of the Tauranga Valley'. Unpublished Ph.D thesis. University of Auckland.

Urewera Scrapbook, n.d. Clippings book. Whakatane Museum.

Ward, Alan D., 1958. 'The History of the East Coast Maori Trust'. Unpublished MA thesis. Victoria University of Wellington.

Williams, William Leonard, 1865. Diary I. MS Alexander Turnbull Library, Wellington.
—————— 1865-6. Diary II. MS Alexander Turnbull Library, Wellington.
—————— 1868-9. Diary. Typescripts, corrected by J. A. Mackay, Gisborne, MSS 335. Auckland Museum Library.
—————— n.d. 'Notes on the Ringa-tu Religion'. Alexander Turnbull Library, Wellington.
Wilson, Tawehi, n.d. Manuscript texts concerning the Ringatu faith. Private collection, the late Ned Brown, Mangatu.

II. ARTICLES AND BOOKS

Appendices to the Journals of the House of Representatives (AJHR), 1868, A-15E; 1869, A-10; 1870, A-8A, A-8B; 1874, G-2B; 1880, G-4; 1883, A-8; 1884, G-4A; 1921-2, G-7.

Barrington, J. M. and T. H. Beaglehole, 1974. *Maori Schools in a Changing Society*. Wellington, New Zealand Council for Educational Research.

Best, Elsdon, 1903. 'Maori Marriage Customs'. *Transactions and Proceedings of the New Zealand Institute*, 36: 14-67.

—————— 1905. 'Maori Eschatology'. *Transactions and Proceedings of the New Zealand Institute*, 38: 148-239.

—————— 1942. *Forest Lore of the Maori*. Wellington, Polynesian Society in association with the Dominion Museum.

—————— 1975. *The Whare Kohanga and its Lore*. Wellington, Government Printer.

—————— 1977. *Tuhoe. The Children of the Mist*, Vol. I. (3rd edn.) Wellington, A. H. & A. W. Reed for the Polynesian Society.

Binney, Judith, 1980. 'The Lost Drawing of Nukutawhiti'. *The New Zealand Journal of History*, 14: 3-24.

—————— 1983. 'Maungapohatu Revisited: or, How the Government Underdeveloped a Maori Community'. *Journal of the Polynesian Society*, 92: 353-92.

—————— 1984. 'Myth and Explanation in the Ringatū Tradition. Some Aspects of the Leadership of Te Kooti Arikirangi Te Turuki and Rua Kēnana Hepetipa'. *Journal of the Polynesian Society*, 93: 345-98.

Binney, Judith, Gillian Chaplin, Craig Wallace, 1979. *Mihaia: The Prophet Rua Kenana and his Community at Maungapohatu*. Wellington, Oxford University Press.

Chamberlain, Mary, 1983. *Fenwomen. A Portrait of Women in an English Village*. London, Routledge & Kegan Paul.

Church of England in New Zealand, 1924. *Diocese of Waiapu Yearbook*. Napier.

Colenso, William, 1871. *Fiat Justitia*. Napier, Dinwiddie, Morrison, and Co.

Cowan, James, 1956. *The New Zealand Wars*, Vol. II. Wellington, Government Printer.

Fowler, Leo, 1974. *Te Mana o Turanga*. Auckland, New Zealand Historic Places Trust.

Greenwood, William, 1980. *The Upraised Hand, or the Spiritual Significance of the Rise of the Ringatu Faith*. (3rd edn.) Wellington, Polynesian Society.

Grey, Sir George, 1853. *Ko nga Moteatea, me nga Hakirara o nga Maori*. (2nd edn.) Wellington, Robert Stokes.

Gudgeon, W. E., 1905. 'Maori Religion'. *Journal of the Polynesian Society*, 14: 107-30.

—————— 1907. 'The Tohunga Maori'. *Journal of the Polynesian Society*, 16: 63-91.

Hanson, F. Allan, 1982. 'Female Pollution in Polynesia?' *Journal of the Polynesian Society*, 91: 335-81.

Hobsbawm, E. J., 1972. *Bandits*. Harmondsworth, Penguin Books.

Ihimaera, Witi and D. S. Long, 1982. *Into the World of Light. An Anthology of Maori Writing*. Auckland, Heinemann Publishers.

King, Michael and Marti Friedlander, 1972. *Moko. Maori Tattooing in the 20th Century*. Wellington, Alister Taylor.

Kohere, Reweti T., 1949. *The Story of a Maori Chief. Mokena Kohere and his Forbears*. Wellington, A. H. & A. W. Reed.

Lambert, Thomas, 1925. *The Story of Old Wairoa and the East Coast District, North Island New Zealand*. Dunedin, Coutts Somerville Wilkie.

Laughton, Revd J. G., 1961. *From Forest Trail to City Street. The Story of the Presbyterian Church among the Maori People*. Christchurch, Maori Synod of the Presbyterian Church.

Locke, Elsie, 1981. *Student at the Gates*. Christchurch, Whitcoulls.

Macgregor, Miriam, 1973. *Petticoat Pioneers. North Island Women of the Colonial Era*. Wellington, A. H. & A. W. Reed.

Mackay, Joseph Angus, 1966. *Historic Poverty Bay and the East Coast, N.I., N.Z.* (2nd edn.) Gisborne, J. G. Mackay.

Maraenui Maori School, 1957. 'Te Kooti Returns from the Dead'. *Te Ao Hou*, 20: 19-20.

Mitchell, J. H., 1944. *Takitimu*. Wellington, A. H. & A. W. Reed.

Moerangi Ratahi, 1972. 'Recollections of a Centenarian'. *Whakatane Historical Review*, 20: 19-27.

Murchie, Elizabeth, 1984. *Rapuora: Health and Maori Women*. Wellington, Maori Women's Welfare League.

Ngata, A. T., 1961. *Nga Moteatea*, Part II. Wellington, Polynesian Society.

Ngata, A. T. and Pei Te Hurinui Jones, 1969. *Nga Moteatea*, Part III. Wellington, Polynesian Society.

Ngugi Wa Thiong'o, 1972. *Homecoming*. London, Heinemann.

Nihoniho, Tuta, 1913. *Narrative of the Fighting on the East Coast, 1865-71*. Wellington, Government Printer.

Oliver, W. H. and Jane Thomson, 1971. *Challenge and Response. A Study of the Development of the East Coast Region*. Gisborne, East Coast Development Research Association.

Ong, Walter J., 1982. *Orality and Literacy: The Technologizing of the Word*. London, Methuen.

Orbell, Margaret, 1978. 'The Traditional Maori Family', in Peggy G. Koopman-Boyden (ed.), *Families in New Zealand Society*. Wellington, Methuen.

Reneti, Matarena and Stanley Roche, 1982. 'Of Love and Death: Matarena's Story', in Bridget Williams and Roy Parsons (eds.), *The Summer Book*. Wellington, Port Nicholson Press.

Rice, Geoffrey, 1983. 'Maori Mortality in the 1918 Influenza Epidemic'. *New Zealand Population Review*, 9: 44-61.

Sharp, Andrew, 1971. *Duperrey's Visit to New Zealand in 1824*. Wellington, Alexander Turnbull Library.

Shirres, Michael P., 1982. 'Tapu'. *Journal of the Polynesian Society*, 91: 29-51.

Simmons, D. R., 1976. *The Great New Zealand Myth. A Study of the Discovery and Origin Traditions of the Maori*. Wellington, A. H. & A. W. Reed.

Smith, S. Percy, 1920. 'Clairvoyance among the Maoris'. *Journal of the Polynesian Society*, 29: 149-63.

Thompson, E. P., 1968. *The Making of the English Working Class*. Harmondsworth, Penguin Books.

Ward, Alan, 1980. 'Documenting Maori History: The Arrest of Te Kooti Rikirangi Te Turuki, 1889'. *The New Zealand Journal of History*, 14: 25-44.

Webster, Peter, 1979. *Rua and the Maori Millennium*. Wellington, Price Milburn for Victoria University Press.

Wedde, Ian and Harvey McQueen (eds.), 1985. *The Penguin Book of New Zealand Verse*. Auckland, Penguin Books.

Winiata, Maharaia, 1967. *The Changing Role of the Leader in Maori Society*. Auckland, Blackwood and Janet Paul.

III. SOME RELEVANT BOOKS, ARTICLES AND THESES NOT CITED IN THE TEXT

Biggs, Bruce, 1960. *Maori Marriage*. Wellington, Polynesian Society.

Cowan, James, 1938. 'The Facts about Te Kooti'. *The New Zealand Railways Magazine*, 1 December: 17-21.

Fowler, Leo, 1957. 'A New Look at Te Kooti'. *Te Ao Hou*, 20: 17-19; 21: 18-22.

Heuer, Berys, 1972. *Maori Women*. Wellington, Polynesian Society with A. H. & A. W. Reed.

Hill, Akena A., 1982. 'The History of Midwifery [in New Zealand] from 1840 to 1979'. Unpublished MA thesis. University of Auckland.

Mahuika, Apirana Tuahae, n.d. 'Nga Wahine Kai-Hautu o Ngati Porou: The Female Leaders of Ngati Porou'. Unpublished MA thesis. University of Sydney.

————— 1975. 'Leadership: Inherited and Achieved', in Michael King (ed.), *Te Ao Hurihuri. The World Moves On*. Wellington, Hicks Smith & Sons.

Metge, Joan, 1957. 'Marriage in Modern Maori Society'. *Man*, 57: 166-70.

Misur, Gilda, Z., 1975. 'From Prophet Cult to Established Church: The Case of the Ringatu Church', in I. H. Kawharu (ed.), *Conflict and Compromise: Essays on the Maori since Colonisation*. Wellington, A. H. & A. W. Reed.

Oppenheim, R. S., 1973. *Maori Death Customs*. Wellington, A. H. & A. W. Reed.

Pearson, Bill, 1974. 'Under Pressure to Integrate', in *Fretful Sleepers & Other Essays*. Auckland, Heinemann Educational Books.

Pere, Rangimarie Rose, 1982. *Aku: Concepts and Learning in the Maori Tradition*. Working Paper No. 17, University of Waikato.

Ross, W. Hugh, 1966. *Te Kooti Rikirangi: General and Prophet*. Auckland, Collins. (The only full-length biography of Te Kooti but written in the style of the *Boys' Own Paper* and often unreliable.)

Salmond, Anne, and Amiria Manutahi Stirling, 1976. *Amiria: The Life Story of a Maori Woman*. Wellington, A. H. & A. W. Reed.

Tarei, Wi, 1978. 'A Church called Ringatu', in Michael King (ed.), *Tihe Mauri Ora. Aspects of Maoritanga*. New Zealand, Methuen.

Wilson, Ormond, 1961. *War in the Tussock: Te Kooti and the Battle at Te Porere*. Wellington, Government Printer. (Contains a sound brief biography of Te Kooti.)

INDEX

References to whakapapa (genealogies) are in **bold**; those to captions are in *italic*. References to end-notes are given in brackets.

Note on proper names: Early this century many Tuhoe and Te Whanau a Apanui families were still using a patrilineal system of naming, whereby children took their father's given name as their second name. Many individuals, therefore, are indexed here under their own given name, and not under their second, or patrilineal, name.

Proper names beginning with the definite article Te or Nga, and tribal names are indexed under the first element.

E ngā iwi o te ao, tēnā koutou.
E kui mā, e hine mā, tērā te haeata e tākiri ana
ko te wā tēnei o te puawaitanga.

People of the world, greetings.
Old women, young women, see the dawn glowing over the horizon
for this is the time of blossoming.

Miriama Evans, *Wahine Kaituhi*, 1985